SO-AAZ-128

FORBIDDEN FRUIT

ANNIE MURPHY
with Peter de Rosa

WARNER BOOKS

A Time Warner Company

WARNER BOOKS EDITION

Copyright © 1993 by Forthright, Ltd.
All rights reserved.

Cover design by Diane Luger
Photograph by Herman Estevez
Hand lettering by Carl Dellacroce

This Warner Books Edition is published by arrangement with Little, Brown & Company.

Warner Books, Inc.
1271 Avenue of the Americas
New York, NY 10020

W A Time Warner Company

Printed in the United States of America

First Warner Books Printing: August, 1994

10 9 8 7 6 5 4 3 2 1

Acknowledgments

I thank Fredrica Friedman, my editor at Little, Brown and Company; her enthusiasm for this project never wavered and her guidance throughout was invaluable. Thanks, too, to my attorney, Peter Albert McKay, for standing by me on some dark days; also to his colleagues, Alfred Hemlock and Bill Adler, for their generous support. Special thanks to Peter de Rosa, whose unique talent brought this work to light, and to his family for sharing with me a home full of good humor and compassion. Above all, I owe thanks to Arthur Pennell, who has been my support at so many critical moments, and to Peter, my son. Only he knows what this book has cost me; only he has made it worthwhile.

The Bishop was a jazzman.
As Annie stood beside him on the mountaintop,
he seemed to her to be playing
Dixieland jazz on a saxophone,
fingers fast moving,
body rhythmically swaying,
so she had the weird impression
that the music, his music,
was creating the world around them,
bringing to life sea, sky, stone,
misty islands,
and even the song of the birds.

Note

Though all the events in my story are true, in a few places I have changed names so as not to embarrass certain people where there is no need.

—A.M.

FORBIDDEN FRUIT

Chapter One

I FLEW from darkness into light. Never before had I been inside a plane that sped toward the sun. On the night flight from New York, sleepless in my window seat, I felt the black waters of the Atlantic receding beneath me. I was leaving behind so many dead things. A dead childhood, a dead marriage, dead dreams, a dead me.

Even before the sun rose I saw the miracle of morning, first a milky whiteness, then that whiteness turn to pink and gold before the entry of the dancing sun.

I was inside a shell. This was spring, after all, this was mid-April 1973. I tapped the side of the plane, a nearly twenty-five-year-old unhatched chick wanting to be let out, to be born. When did I last sense joy awaiting me? Maybe never.

My tall one-legged jazz-loving father told me before I boarded the plane that I would forget the bad things and find serenity in Ireland. His old friend and distant relative Eamonn Casey, the Bishop of Kerry, had promised him that.

"Ireland's the place," the Bishop had said. "I will take care of her personally." And peace was entering me already. Dear father with the sad, sad eyes, you, who guessed without being told all my former fears and my dread, were so right: I was headed for happiness.

The descent began. To the left were the Aran Islands and Galway, to the right Dingle and Tralee Bay. The very names were magic to me. As the plane's shadow traced the broad silver estuary of the Shannon, I could see snow-sprinkled mountains and quilts of tiny fields with white, thatched cottages from which blue smoke curled like ribbons. And everywhere green. I remember thinking, *So that is what* green *looks like*.

Touchdown. Everyone clapped, and I, who had not spoken a word during the flight, so full was I of wonder, clapped loudest of all. I had come home to a place where I had never been.

Eamonn, I had been told, would be waiting for me. I had met him once in New York when I was seven. Already a priest aged twenty-nine, he had come to Manhattan to take care of his widowed sister who had fallen on hard times. "Who are you?" I asked him, and, still looking out the window, he said, "Father Eamonn." Strange that I should remember only his big sad eyes. I, a little girl, sympathized with him. I had wanted to take him aside into a quiet room and tell him, "Eamonn, it's going to be all right. It's going to be all right."

There was a big crowd in the arrivals hall at Shannon. My fellow passengers pressed forward with the urgency of people who have not seen loved ones for a long time. Young couples with babies were enveloped by those waiting to see them. The middle-aged and silver-haired in the crowd rushed forward, grabbing and smothering with kisses their grandchildren seen for the first time. And in that flood of emotion, that avalanche of laughter and unmelancholy tears, who was waiting for *me*, who would greet *me*?

I picked him out at once in his black suit and clerical collar. His round happy face with his forehead—higher than I remembered it—was peering now through the trellis of people, now over their heads. He was in movement like a dancer, and his flashing eyes were not sad at all but creased with smiles.

It struck me that he was not merely open-faced and handsome but something else: elemental. He was full of light and energy, like the dancing sun.

He knew me instantly, though he had a puzzled look as if he had expected a child and met a woman. Or maybe he thought, as a result of my father's letter, he would be meeting someone gaunt and haggard. Instead, there was this relaxed slim young lady of 110 pounds in suede high heels and a flattering mauve dress with small polkadots. He glanced at my long blunt-cut golden brown hair and my face with a little blush on it, not too much lipstick because I didn't need it. I think he even noticed the title of the book under my arm, the only one I had brought with me, Thomas Wolfe's *You Can't Go Home Again*.

Squeezing my hand and kissing my cheek, so I smelled his Old Spice after-shave, he said in a kind of champagne fizz:

"Welcome to Ireland. Our little Annie's grown up."

"Little girls do," I said, the mischief in me responding instantly to the mischief in him.

His smile was enchanting, the feel of his hand warm and gentle. This was for me the strangest thing in an already strange existence. He, whom I had met only once and looked at with a child's eyes, had been known to me all my life.

What sort of chemicals were in the air? Not for one second had I anticipated liking any man, not after what some men had done to me, and here I was on Irish soil immediately being drawn to a *bishop?* Ever since I met one at my confirmation, bishops were not my favorite species.

Heavens, Annie Murphy, I thought, *settle yourself. Don't get carried away.*

He grabbed my two bags. As if he had already summed me up, he said, so breathlessly I could hardly hear, "Yes, little Annie's got blue eyes, thick curly hair and she's beautiful."

He certainly had charm!

He was off on twinkling toes, barging through the crowd. He was about five feet eight, a couple of inches taller than I, and there were threads of gray in his dark hair.

I ran after him on stiff legs out into the parking lot. I noticed that he was wearing scarlet socks and that his big black automatic Mercedes was taking up two parking spaces, probably because he had arrived in a hurry and just didn't care.

"How did you feel coming into Ireland?" he said, as he opened the car door for me on the left-hand side.

"Like I was coming into a fairyland."

"Good." With an exciting rippling laugh, he slammed the door on me, just missing my fingers.

As he jumped in beside me, making the car shake, I said, "Why're you wearing red socks?"

He paused for a moment to frown at me with fluid, penetrating eyes. "You *are* observant. I just like the color."

"You should be wearing purple. Red's for a cardinal. It must be a sign of your ambition."

"You'd call it ambition, I suppose, if my nose were to bleed red instead of purple."

His eyes sparked bright as he gunned the car and we shot off on what was like a ride on a bullet. I don't like fast driving unless I'm behind the wheel, but with him I felt safe. We tore through sleepy villages and towns. This man had a hurricane inside him.

Hanging on for dear life, I said to Eamonn, "You're driving at sixty-five miles an hour through a town full of people."

"Ah," he said, making things worse by lifting his hands off the wheel with a Lord-be-with-you motion, "there's nobody here. And if there were I'd give 'em a miss." With butterfly flutters of his gold-ringed hand he blessed the invisible people to right and left as if his benediction alone would keep them from all harm. "God bless you and you and you," ending with another rippling laugh.

I couldn't resist that. He was a fountain of laughter.

"You should be arrested," I said.

"Whatever for, Annie?"

I liked the way he spoke my name in his soft voice. No longer little Annie.

"If you hit someone, it'll be homicide."

"And won't I do them the honor of giving them the last rites of holy Mother Church? Imagine being sent to heaven courtesy of a bishop."

"You think you can get away with murder, Eamonn?"

I liked the sound of his name, too.

As he turned to me, I said, "Eye on the road, *please*. I'm not ready for heaven yet."

The car hit a bump, and my head touched the roof. He lifted both hands off the wheel again and laughed all the louder. He was theatrical without trying to be.

"Slow down," I gasped.

"I've never been killed yet, as far as I know."

I doubted it. I wondered if he were a wizard, like Merlin in the legends. Maybe Eamonn Casey was a warlock, a sorcerer. Maybe he had lived many lives, had many adventures, surprised his enemies, fought and died in many wars and been reborn as often as was necessary.

"I heard," I said, when I got my breath back, "you were supposed to drive on the left over here, not down the middle."

Not only were his hands now off the wheel, he was looking fixedly at me with eyes that flickered like distant lightning.

"You're a crowing hen, Annie Murphy, d'you realize that? You make fun of my socks, accuse me of being ambitious, and now I don't know how to drive."

"Look out," I yelled, to stop him from going straight into the back of an old Ford van.

He swerved just in time onto the grass verge and on again without a change of pace.

"Annie," he growled, "you are a positive menace on the road. For a split-second back there, I was close to growing grass instead of whiskers on my chest."

Heavens, I thought, *he blames me for his own mistakes.*

A few times after that he beeped his horn just for the fun of it. I smiled at him. We both liked fun. The signs were we had the same sense of humor.

Suddenly, coming toward us in the middle of the road was a big cow, ready for milking. We screeched to a halt, so the round-eyed long-lashed black-and-white creature found herself looking straight at us, not a little startled, through the windshield. A small bell around her neck rang tinnily.

"God Almighty," Eamonn said, honking. "Get away with you, moo-moo-moo, ye silly woman, before I excommunicate you."

Slowly, with swishing messy tail, the huge animal lurched by, brushing my door.

"Next time, mind where you're going, madam," Eamonn bawled after her, his head backward out the window, "otherwise I'll set a papal bull on you."

A mile farther on we passed the cow's owner, an old man with a lame sheepdog that hurled itself suicidally at the back wheels of our car just for the hell of it. Did everything around here like flirting with death?

Suddenly I yelled, "Look out for that bomb crater!"

"A modest pothole," he said, swerving wildly.

"*That* is a pothole?"

"The roads of Ireland are built around them. That one we just passed dates from 1123."

"I thought it might be earlier."

Eamonn was a great leg-puller. I liked that in a man.

After another wrenching bump, I said, "Why don't you fill these things in?"

"They have a preservation order on them. Local priests bless them twice a year with a bucket of holy whiskey."

There was a big crunch and a bang as we went in and out of a pothole he had not seen.

"Just testing my springs, Annie."

As he scooted along narrow, winding, potholed roads, I felt he was testing my willingness to put my life in his hands. He got a high from driving fast; I appreciated that because, deep in my soul, among the many bad things, I, too, was in love with danger. There was peril here and treachery for both of us amid the awesome beauty of the land.

His charm, his humor, his warmth made me feel happy. Fear and trust had merged in me; it felt so good to rely totally on another. Also, I had a strange sense that his crazy way of driving, his laughter in the face of death, was his way of flirting with me. He was, I admit this from the start, bishop or no bishop, a very sexy man.

I put this crazy thought out of my mind. Tried to.

Outside the bubble of magic I was moving in was a *Ryan's Daughter* of a land. I had seen the movie only three months before. The photography, color, music, had made me, a Murphy from New England, feel I had roots, and those roots were here, all around me. Something came up at me through the soles of my feet out of the earth, out of long-traveled roads and the dry bones of the dead. Through the open window I, lately a city girl used to concrete and gasoline fumes, saw fleshy green skin covering winter's wounds, smelled spring and growing things, the grass, furze, and cattle. And I, usually so irresolute, was ready for anything.

So this was County Kerry where my grandfather, old Pop Murphy, was born with a brogue not unlike Eamonn's and a couple of shillelaghs on the wall to prove it. Soon we reached the Dingle Peninsula and the coastal road that rose to Inch. Below and far away, the rocky din-filled gullies were snow white with the droppings of seabirds, which soared above or refuged in the heather-strewn cliffs. There were guillemots, kittiwakes, petrels, razorbills, even puffins, one of which flew by red-nosed and with a laughing sprat-filled mouth. Out there, beyond a harbor called Castlemaine, for as far as the eye could see was the sparkling ocean over which gulls and gannets flew, reflecting the sun's fire. Was there a more romantic place in the world? How could Pop, in spite of his rheumatism, have been crazy enough to leave it?

Eamonn said he was taking me to his country residence at Inch, which means "Island." Now a peninsula, it was probably an island once. He rarely stayed overnight at his Palace in Killarney. He preferred to finish each day in a seaside retreat, though he had to drive twenty-five miles to get there.

As we motored up the tendril-like road toward his house, I saw the four-mile-long seemingly inaccessible Inch strand. Before us to the west were tall mountains. Islands, dotted distantly here and there, were misted by the sea.

Eamonn was telling me I would be staying mostly at Inch but sometimes I would go with him to Killarney and even "abroad" to Dublin and other exotic faraway Irish places.

As we climbed, Eamonn gestured at the splendid features of the landscape, relating their history in his throbbing voice.

Soon we roared into his short sloping driveway. The high hedges on each side almost touched overhead, giving the impression that we were passing through a leafy tunnel into another world.

Once more I had moved from darkness to light, but this time he had carried me there. Here, in three acres of God's own country, was beauty within beauty, and mystery within a larger mystery.

Having braked sharply—how else?—he was on my side of the car and flinging my door open.

"Out with you, Annie. Out, out," as he beckoned me with bird-swift hand movements to stand next to him.

Then the most amazing thing: I looked into his eyes and there I was. It was so fleeting, I could not be sure if it had really happened or I had imagined it.

When I was on my feet, he gestured eloquently around us, breathing deeply and shaking his head; there, nestling on a rocky knoll, surrounded by exquisite flower gardens, was a single-storied slate-roofed Georgian house built of red sandstone, a beautiful aerie above the sea.

"My home, your home," he said, with an infectious grin.

Chapter Two

MARY O'RILEY, his thirty-year-old housekeeper, emerged from the front door and came down the steps to greet me. She had red hair and mint-green eyes and the sad furtive gaze of a countrywoman. She took charge of my bags while Eamonn led me into his home, my home. The pretty Georgian ceiling with fine old moldings reflected the rich red from the carpet.

"It matches your socks," I whispered, and he whispered back, "You are *wicked*," so that I felt flattered.

A corridor went the length of the house with fourteen Stations of the Cross around the walls. I had not seen their like since I gave up practicing the Catholic faith seven years before.

On the corridor there were small windows, like peepholes, onto the ocean. Almost opposite the front door was a small red-carpeted alcove with an altar where presumably Eamonn said Mass, and there were four bedrooms, two at each end.

"Hurry for lunch." Eamonn directed me to my room at the far end of the corridor. "You must be famished as a crow."

My room was a small rectangle, with light blue walls and its own bathroom. Built into the hillside and with hedges of yellow-flowering forsythia outside the windows, there was only the tiniest view of the sea, but I could hear it and smell it.

I barely had time to freshen up before Eamonn rapped on

my door and led me to the dining room. From the french windows there was a splendid sea vista. In the hearth was a fire that gave off a warm sweet earthy odor and a bluish flame.

He anticipated my question.

"Turf." His hand was shaking not from nerves but from the sheer vitality he put into every word. "Cut from the bogs around here."

In the center of the room was a gleaming mahogany table with solid silver cutlery and candelabra as well as silver vases bright with spring flowers.

Eamonn said grace, then Mary, who had learned to move at his pace, dashed a plate down in front of me. A furtive smile passed between them.

With my fork I probed the white sticky matter covered in a white sauce.

"Come on," he urged, his lips twitching. "Try it."

I put a minute amount in my mouth. It had an unusual texture. Was it sweetbread? No, surely the organ of some animal; and I hardly ever ate meat because most meats made me ill. I had a big problem chewing even this small bite. I began to apologize for being a fussy eater.

"Know what it is, Annie? Lamb's brains." And he laughed heartily.

I dropped my fork with a clatter on my plate.

Seeing my blanched face, his laughter ended abruptly.

"You don't like it?"

He was upset. He had wanted to introduce me to a local delicacy. But the result, though he could not possibly have known why, brought back a past I had come to Ireland to forget.

There was plenty of other food, potatoes, vegetables, salads, but I could not eat a thing.

"I am so sorry, Annie," he said, "I'll take you for a walk soon and restore you."

He busily finished his own lunch and, after I had brushed my hair and put on cherry-red lipstick and dangling Indian-style earrings, we went up the steep mountain path behind the house. I was nervy because I suffered from agoraphobia and there were no trees to hide behind.

He must have sensed my unease because as soon as we

were out of sight of the house he took my hand in his—
"Since there's no donkey's tail to hold on to." Moments
later, he stopped as if he had received an electric shock.

"That's odd, Annie." He peered closely at my hand and
echoed my thoughts: "I feel so comfortable with you. As if
I'd known you always." He looked at me, appealingly. "Do
you feel the same?"

I nodded. That touch had mysteriously bonded us.

We walked or, rather, ran up the mountain path hand-in-
hand like happy children.

"I am so honored," he said, "to have you as my guest."

Before I could say thank you, he started to tell me in his
excited way how much he loved this place though it had so
many inches of rain a year even angels couldn't count them.
Here he charged his batteries and sometimes it rained when
there wasn't a cloud in the sky.

"Really?" I said.

"Indeed, the good Lord has to keep His hand in." And
when I reacted, he added, "You really have the loveliest
smile."

We stopped on the heights and, though there was rain in
the strong tangy wind and I, lightly clad, was chilled, my
breath was taken away, not so much by the speed of the ascent
as by the beauty of the land.

Having checked that I was not too cold, with a huge intake
of salt- and heather-scented air, he said:

"Annie, when I . . . when I stand here, I feel I am holding
hands with the Almighty."

Feeling an inferior substitute for his normal climbing companion, I said a quiet yes.

He was the perfect showman. He loved surprising and
overwhelming people. Releasing my hand to enable him to
gesture to his heart's content, he exclaimed:

"I come here so I can be in a place that man can never
spoil. There it is, Annie. There are the clear waters, Annie,
and the silent mountains, Annie, and the air clean and fresh
as the Virgin's tears, Annie."

And each mention of my name seemed part of a litany that
went straight from our hushed mountain up to the throne of
God.

He was a jazzman like my father. There, on that mountain-top, he seemed to me to be playing Dixieland jazz on a saxophone, fingers fast moving, body rhythmically swaying, so I had the weird impression that the music, *his* music, was creating the world around us, bringing to life sea, sky, stone, misty islands, and even the song of the birds.

More mundanely: "See that hotel over there across the bay? That is Glenbeigh. I intend to take you to a meal there soon. And I'm hoping to give you"—a wide cruciform sweep of his arms—"a tour of the entire Dingle Peninsula. Then you really will feel reborn."

I was beginning to feel it already.

He clasped my hand again. He, doubtless, was praying. So was I in my own way. This was a timeless moment in a place beyond this world where I could become me. I glimpsed grazing sheep, their faces deep in spring. I heard, then saw, fluttering and trilling, a solitary lark below me, looking like a moth, singing like an angel.

All the guilt in my soul drained out of me. I had been hurt too much. I had a right to be happy. Never had I had the guts to do something for myself alone, but my hour had come. Proof of it was that I said:

"I have a headache, Eamonn. I'd like to go down and rest, if you don't mind."

This modest request was new to me. I had always let myself be led. I had such confidence in Eamonn I was prepared to ask for something for me.

"Poor, poor Annie," he said.

Hand in warm hand we slowly retraced our steps. I realized with a start that though my panic attacks from which I suffered might recur, my agoraphobia was gone. And forever. The wild open spaces were given back to me. One heart's disease had been emptied out of me into the sea or the clear mountain air. More likely, into Eamonn's magnanimous soul. How good he must be to be able to lift such a burden by the touch of his hand. I only hoped that in healing me he would not wound himself.

I was reluctant to say good-bye if only for a few hours. On that walk, I had felt his power enter me, power such as I had never felt in anyone else.

It was about three in the afternoon when I got to lie on my

bed, fully clothed, not having the energy to unpack. I slept as I had not slept in over three years.

I awoke at ten. It was dark and I was thirsty. I fumbled my way to the door. The lights in the hallway were dimmed, the way I like them. Hearing me move around, Mary came to tell me she had prepared tea and biscuits for me and the Bishop. She was off to bed.

Eamonn was already in the living room with the orange drapes pulled across all the windows except for one. He jumped up from his armchair and greeted me as if I had been away for months.

Who could fail to warm to a man who every time he sees you gives you a hundred thousand Irish welcomes?

Through the one window he had purposely left undraped we could see by starlight, so clear was the night air, across the bay.

I admired the heavy oriental rug, Waterford crystal, and gleaming black baby grand piano. Here, too, there was a turf fire in the hearth. In this romantic setting, I lay down in front of the fire for warmth. The room's colors, though earthy, were warm, including, I told him, his splendid socks of which I now had the best possible view.

At once, he began to question me about my life. My father must have written to him about my marriage. I sensed he knew I had wed a Jew in front of a rabbi in my husband's family home.

"Your marriage was far from happy, I can tell."

"I am over the worst of it."

He shook his head like a dog out of water. "It couldn't possibly be so; otherwise why did you come to Ireland?"

He seemed to speak with the whole of his body. Perhaps that is why he made so powerful an impression on me.

"I did have therapy before I came."

He tutted his disagreement. "There are many ways to healing. But therapy seldom works. The soul itself needs healing."

I said nothing. It was true I had reached a plateau in my life. I was not going anywhere.

I appreciated his concern but he was unwise, I felt, to dive into my soul as though it were a gentle lake when it was a deep and dangerous place. In my heart, I said, *Eamonn, beware, you do not know me yet.*

"How do you feel inside yourself?"

I waited a long while. I was thinking of the time eighteen months into my marriage when, late one night, I called my father. He himself had been brutally beaten by his mother as a child, which was why he had never laid a finger on me in anger. I was in Brooklyn and he was a half hour's drive away in New York around 23rd Street. Almost ready to fall apart, I had wanted to tell him I was being severely damaged by and suffering in my marriage. No, I didn't call him to say anything, I wanted just to feel his loving presence. And he said, hearing me sob, without me even speaking my name, "You don't have to tell me, Annie. I *know*."

Now as the minutes ticked by, misty-eyed, I had no answer for Eamonn but to shake my head.

"What is going on behind those pretty blue eyes?"

I managed to get out, "I suppose I do feel . . . damaged."

As I got up from the floor and sat in a chair next to his, he reached for my hand and stroked the back of it. He was so fearless and I so fearful, the attraction between us was enormous.

"Chicky Licky," he said, able to scowl and smile at the same time.

"You mean Chicken Licken."

He said, "That's what I said," and I realized he spoke it so fast it came out as Chicky Licky.

Therapy had taught me that we are responsible for our own actions. Eamonn had done me good already. But I could do him harm. It is hard to share pain without showing love. Harder still to accept another's pain without becoming vulnerable.

That was why I pulled back—I needed to be more sure of myself.

He did not readily accept my reluctance to open out. I would have to be patient for both of us.

He told me a long story about a beautiful young woman, Siobhan, married to and beaten by an alcoholic husband, Jim. She had had a nervous breakdown and attempted suicide.

He showed me her picture, and she was what I was not:

Beauty Queen material. Many men had told me I was beautiful but it was not of this competition-winning sort.

Siobhan was tall, with the slim and agile grace of a dancer.
She had yellow hair and blue eyes. She might have been a
Viking. I was far more of a colleen.

It took Eamonn two hours to tell me how he had overseen
Siobhan's therapy, found her a job as a governess abroad,
and recovered Jim from alcoholism. Finally, as though he
were a god, he had put the marriage together again. He must
have thought he could do the same for me.

"She also stayed in this house," he said.

The more he talked the closer we moved together. Eventually, he not only held my hand but gently stroked my hair. I
enjoyed the intimacy and thrilled in every pore. It was as if
the whole of my self, body and spirit, even parts of me I
never knew existed, came alive at his touch.

This was not sex but something far deeper for which I had
no name, something never before experienced. Part of what
I felt was his ability to give me a sense of the goodness of
myself till then denied me and, through my self-appreciation,
a sense of the worth of everything that exists.

Never till those precious hours had I felt that someone, a
friend, a fellow human being, was addressing *me*, my true
self, a self that even I had never known until he spoke to it
directly and it answered him. A new being, a new voice. It
was like being present, consciously and wonderingly, at my
own birth.

But as he told his story, through the swift blinking of his
eyes and the trembling of his sensitive hands, I got the distinct
impression that the beautiful Siobhan had aroused feelings in
him that he had not owned up to, even to himself.

What he may not have realized was that I was far more of
a danger to him. I was unattached and becoming ever more
attracted. Not unexpectedly in view of the life he led, he was,
I could tell, sexually very repressed. He was like a ripe tomato
on a vine; I had only to give a tiny tug and, pop, he would
be in my hand. I did not want that. Apart from anything else,
the woman in me wanted something that would last.

As the hours flew by me, he often got up to stoke the fire,
the poker sending sparks up the chimney. The jazzman could
even create the stars.

It was not until 1:30, with the fire burning low, that he walked me to my room past Stations of the Cross that now, for some reason, made me feel like a temptress.

"Good night, Chicky Licky, and God bless."

I was delighted. He already had a pet name for me.

I put on my nightdress and went to bed. Never had I known such a day. It had lasted a lifetime but was over in a flash. Every experience in it was new and at the same time older than I was. Time was so overturned I felt I had been handed a perfect and unfading flower plucked in a century yet to come.

I could not sleep for the tumult within me and the heavy hammer of my heart as I heard him walking up and down the corridor, reciting his breviary. I so wanted him to come in and talk with me, as my father used to do when I was a girl. Since I met Eamonn at the airport, even more so after we descended the mountain, I wanted him never to leave my side.

After forty-five minutes, he, too, went to bed, in the room next to mine. It could not have been better if it had been planned. Had it been? Surely not. He was expecting little Annie. Not planned, then, but providential?

To my surprise, once more I slept and would not have awakened but for someone calling me by name.

"Annie. Wake up, Annie."

I opened my eyes. I usually hated mornings. Not today, the anniversary of yesterday. For perched on the end of my bed, crooning my name, with a mischievous loving smile on his open face, was my newest, oldest, dearest friend, Eamonn.

Chapter Three

EIGHT O'CLOCK, sleepyhead. How'd you like to come with me to Killarney?"

"Oh, *yes*," I said.

I was usually rocky and half blind in the gum-eyed dawn, but as soon as Eamonn left I jumped out of bed.

Though I still showered in the dark, I was aware that I was a woman, that this smooth flesh of mine was made not to be abused but loved.

I soaped myself luxuriously, tracing the curves of legs and thighs and breasts with the flat of my hands.

I toweled, put on my face, finished dressing in a rush, and went to the dining room, where Mary brought me breakfast. The bread deliciously filled my mouth and the water from the well enabled me actually to taste tea for the first time in my life. All my senses were awakened, my fears gone.

Within minutes, Eamonn was ushering me out the front door.

"Come along now, Annie, it'll soon be night."

It was a glorious sunny day, full of budding and birdsong. I inhaled the fresh-from-the-oven smells of morning. Primroses and violets, azaleas and cowslips dotted the flower beds while ferns and dock leaves were green tongues unfolding in the sun. A butterfly, lovely as a peacock, clapped silently on a purple pansy. A wood pigeon called throatily from a poplar tree and I inhaled the fragrance of lilac and honeysuckle vine.

Not far from three nibbling rabbits was a ragged yellow-looking sheep come down from the hill to graze on the dew-rinsed lawn. As Eamonn shooed it away, the rabbits scampered off, ears pinned back, white tails showing. Yes, in a setting like this it was possible to wipe out reality.

He did not drive as madly as the day before. Maybe he wanted to talk and required, like God, complete attention. I sat quietly, a wren next to a falcon.

He spoke of his diocese, with its fifty-three parishes, 130 priests and 125,000 layfolk. He was especially proud of his work in the Cathedral at Killarney, which means "Church of the Sloe Tree." Designed by Pugin, the Cathedral had been consecrated in 1855. When Eamonn was made bishop, he moved to restore it. The Victorian plasterwork had been ruined by decades of damp. He had decided to strip it off entirely so as to reveal, through bare stone, Pugin's original design.

"I ran into mighty opposition for that, Annie. Pious people have the sharpest teeth. But you'll soon be telling me who was right."

We passed a field with newborn lambs in it. The friskiest of them ran like crazy, kicked its hind legs in the air, and ran back again to its ewe. I laughed aloud.

"What's the matter?"

"Oh," I said, "it reminded me of someone."

He cored me with a look and said, with mock severity, "I'm a shepherd not a sheep, I'd have you know."

I crossed my heart on the wrong side. "I'll remember."

"Guess how much the Cathedral cost to renovate?" He translated for my benefit into U.S. currency. "Well over half a million dollars."

"Who'll pay?"

"The good people."

"Whether they like it or not."

"They like it. If not, I make them like it."

And he was off on a story that typified Killarney, where we were headed.

"Only last week, Annie, I was standing in the street"—his left hand, off the wheel, was shaking in anticipation of what was to come—"when a horse-drawn cart stopped by me. And guess who was sitting in the backseat!"

"The Pope."

"Something even more surprising. A corpse." He roared with laughter. "Propped up like it was on an outing, with a hat on his head and a briar pipe in his mouth."

"Was the pipe alight?" I asked, lamely.

"He was a farmer, y'see, and before taking him to the funeral parlor to coffin him up, his sons were giving him a last tour of the town." Eamonn was alive electrically in his seat. "But I said to the boys, 'God Al*mighty*, the man is dead, have you no decency left that you treat him like a piece of furniture?' "

Without meaning to, I mimicked his voice exactly, "God Al*mighty*, the man is dead."

Eamonn stopped laughing. He recognized that I was so in tune with him I spoke with his voice.

"That's not bad at all."

For the moment, his face blanked out. Maybe he sensed danger.

"I'll give you a tour of the town first, Annie."

"Even though I'm not dead yet."

He said softly, "Even though you are very much alive."

Killarney was a meandering market town, small by American standards. Exotic colors clashed and not one building stood up straight. How unlike the tall, tiring symmetry of New York.

I was impressed by the 285-foot-high Cathedral spire. Inside, my first impression of St. Mary's was of soaring pillars, Gothic arches, and of white limestone, rough and bare as if the skin had been peeled off it. It was like seeing a clean white dawn spread over Lake Candlewood in the New England of my childhood.

For all its hush and beauty, something about the place alarmed me.

Eamonn genuflected toward the striking crucifix over a main altar that was lit by three tall lancet windows. Then he went on his knees in a pew at the back. As I knelt beside him, he blessed himself, bowed his head, and prayed with eyes so tightly closed they looked screwed down.

Which God was he praying to? Maybe a bishop has to have a special God. I suspected that on Day One of Creation, his God made not the heavens and the earth but the Rules.

Here was the source of my disquiet. This was Eamonn's

real world. He was a cleric before he was a man. Inside him was a sanctuary where he walked godward, blind and deaf. In this moment, he was speaking with the God who, in an ascending order of dignity, made him a Christian, priest, and bishop, and, if his socks proved predictive, a cardinal. I had no right to intrude where he was happy.

But was he? Buoyant, cheerful, dynamic, yes, but happy? It was my woman's intuition that he was not. But even if he were not, was it in the power of any woman to make him so? Was he praying for my soul or my happiness? Maybe he made no distinction. But I was a woman, irreligious by his standards, and I did. I wanted happiness.

So we knelt, he talking with his God who was nearer to him than my shoulder and I bemoaning the absence of Him whom I had worshiped in an uncomplicated way when I was a child.

Suddenly, as if God had dismissed him with a bang on the head, his prayers were over. He leaped to his feet.

"Come along, Annie," and he was off like a March hare.

As we toured the Cathedral, he kept receiving fawning bows and touching of the forelock from men, as well as little curtsies from women, and everyone murmured, "My Lord."

This set him apart from my world. But wasn't this massive building a testimony to what he was? On the journey he had spoken of "my" Cathedral. On the sanctuary was a chair that proved he was Eamonn, by the Grace of God and appointment of the Pope, Bishop of Kerry. This was his *cathedra,* or seat, with his coat of arms and a Latin inscription that he told me meant "I Am As One Who Serves."

"'Tis made of Tasmanian oak." His whisper could be heard in the back pew. To me the chair seemed hewn from the Rock of Ages. It spoke of loyalties that went back two thousand years to Jesus and Peter, James, and John.

I did not like to be in thrall to the past. Since coming to Ireland—was it really only twenty-four hours ago?—I wanted to live *now*.

He was pointing to the pulpit. He seemed to like its elevation. He enjoyed the pomp, pageantry, and theatrics of religion, which, frankly, I thought of as pagan.

Though he itemized the cost of repairs—to the roof, organ,

stonework, the big limestone baptismal bowl—I took little of it in. I was thinking, *How much will you pay to fix the tiny chapel of my soul, to clean the old stone to the bone?*

The spire of my being did not rise up into a supernatural heaven; it was thrust upside down, like a spear, into the rich dark earth. Down here I wanted happiness.

When I was eight years old, I took charge of my mother, Hannah, whom father called Wishie because she was always saying, "I wish this or that." Booze was her family, flag, creed, God. Dear Wishie, with the face of a rose garden and the mouth of rotten apple. How often I had to fish her out of the empty bath when she missed the can. I hauled her out by her arms which were limp as overcooked noodles. When she went completely crazy, I took a knife and cut a crisscross on the palm of my left hand and held it up to her, yelling, "Stop it, stop it!" The sight of blood, danger, was the only thing that could bring her, a mother, to her senses.

Could she drink! A thirsty camel at a water hole would have stopped to watch. It made your head spin just to breathe the air around her.

When Jack, my father, was at medical conferences, I slept beside her. Soon as she woke, she grabbed a bottle as if it were the alarm clock. She drank to cure hangovers.

I can see her standing, one hand on her hip for balance, the other with a bottle of Ballantine raised at the diagonal, "Shit on 'em"—this to no one in particular—before trumpeting a blast of Ballantine. Once she grabbed a bottle in each fist, and played two trumpets at once, maybe to prove how good she was. Often she cooked in a green sweater and nothing else, and I mean *nothing*. She was bottomless save for a blackthorn bush under her navel. In her tough, West Side, drinking Irish talk, "I'm okay, Annie, for Chrissake, leave me be, willya?" as she aborted another bottle.

My doctor father said I was born drunk. Instead of me, Mom should have given birth to a crate of Ballantine.

Whenever she boiled an egg I reached for the fire extinguisher. Get in our old Cadillac with her behind the wheel, I used to say, and don't kid yourself it isn't suicide. Is there no penalty for being drunk in charge of a child?

"Don't tell ya father, it'd only upset him." She made me

promise, as she sank the pint of vodka she had just bought to replace the pint she drank the day before. She could find a needle in a haystack if it had a lick of vodka on it.

So she wouldn't get too drunk, I used to dilute the vodka with water before she did, but Daddy saw the motes in it, till I learned to put the water through fine muslin first.

To save her, since I loved that nutty lady, I lied to her and I lied *for* her until lying was as easy as breathing. I enjoyed it. Like Mommy, I kept replacing the little sips taken from the bottle of truth with liquid from the faucet of my own imagining.

I also made a frightening discovery that most people—not my father—like being lied to; it makes life more comfortable. Nobody wanted to know the truth about Mommy any more than she did. Lying became for me a form of Christian charity.

What about you, Eamonn? Do you care for truth or do you, like the rest of us, demand that people tell you lies?

We left St. Mary's for his big stone Palace next door. The very word raised my hackles. Another barrier between him and me.

Did he intend to show me once and for all that he was a princeling of the Church? Inside the Palace, backs straightened like candles and "Morning, my Lord," "Yes, my Lord," "No, my Lord," all spoken by men and women, some of whom knelt to kiss his ring. Was this, I thought naughtily, the clerical version of kissing ass?

He introduced me to his lay secretary, Pat Gilbride, with, "This is my cousin, Annie Murphy, from America."

Pat was a big happy blonde in her late twenties with a Cheshire Cat smile and hooded eyes that looked right at you.

When Eamonn got me to shake hands with Justin, the odd-job man, he relaxed. He slipped easily into his one-syllabled man-of-the-people talk. Justin had patches on knees and elbows, and a brogue that completely foxed me. In his presence, Eamonn, almost dancing a jig, was funny and tender, paternal and exigent at the same time.

Afterward, Eamonn whispered, with twinkling eyes, "A grand Catholic is Justin. If he hanged himself he'd use a rosary."

He held up his own beads, with the crucifix on top, noosed his wrist and tugged upward in a vivid demonstration.

He liked Justin, I think, because Justin would never doubt that he was the greatest man alive after the Pope.

One person I liked immediately was Eamonn's priest-assistant. Tall, with a marvelously gentle sense of humor, Father John O'Keeffe was a blend of Jimmy Stewart and Sean Connery. He had heavy brows, soft eyes, and a fine ski nose. A laughing Kerryman, he was not in the least scared of Eamonn, who said to me, "Clever chap, he has three degrees."

In Eamonn's study, dominated by a portrait of Pope Paul VI, the phones never stopped ringing. As he took the calls he thumbed through a pile of mail. He could do several things at once—talk down the phone to an Irish priest in South America promising funds for a village well, read a Latin document from a Vatican official, and, muffling the phone, explain to me what we might do for the rest of the day.

Though this was routine for him, had he brought me there on my first morning to impress me with his power? Few women would object to that.

At lunch, the only other guest was a Scot named Ian Simpson from the Scottish Finance Office. Eamonn sprinted through grace whether his guests approved or not.

Mr. Simpson was a small, bald, soft-spoken man. "Come to Edinburgh, the Athens of the north, Miss Murphy." He promised to show me Princes Street and the Castle.

Even to be near Eamonn had its perks.

The best food and French wines were served by soft-shoed nuns with humble demeanor and downturned gaze. Did these women have eyes at all? How could Eamonn tolerate such servility?

The contrast between the two men was marked. Eamonn's face seemed made of pieces of brightly colored glass; Ian's was of a single grayish hue. Eamonn spoke in a rainbow stream of words, combined with broad heartfelt gestures; Ian's utterances were spare and dry as desert sand and came from no further than his lips.

Another thing: Whereas Eamonn addressed him as "Ian," the Scot never dared call Eamonn anything but "My Lord." No equality here. Ian was not descended from the Apostles.

They spoke of financial help to the deprived areas of Kerry. Tens of thousands of pounds sterling were mentioned. Eamonn guaranteed everything. Occasionally, with his right index finger, he banged on the fingers of his left hand one by one with the force of a hammer to make his points.

For a couple of hours after lunch I was left alone in his study. On his desk was a photograph album, surely for me to examine. It contained newspaper clippings and pictures of his ordination as a bishop in late 1969.

One picture showed Eamonn with the Primate, Cardinal Conway, President de Valera, Cardinal Heenan of Westminster, and the papal Nuncio. Eamonn, looking truly magnificent in his episcopal robes, was referred to as, at age forty-two, the youngest member of the Irish hierarchy.

Cardinal Heenan preached the sermon. "Bishop Eamonn is a friend and father of the poor, he sought shelter for the homeless." There were pictures of Eamonn's ring—a hundred years old—of Eamonn smiling under his tall miter, and standing on an open bus while waving to the crowds.

Was Eamonn challenging me? Was he saying, "Here is a mountain, Annie. Do you have the strength and stamina to climb it?" Or—far more likely—was this all in my imagination?

He liked the best, and how could I be described as good, let alone the best? Did I mistake a show of power for an invitation to love? To topple such a man would be like burning down a cathedral. I had no wish to do any such thing. Did I?

Memories stirred in me. I was twelve years old when my elder brother, John, came rushing into our house in Redding, Connecticut. He was white with anger and my father asked him what was the matter. John blurted out that he had just caught a visiting monsignor from Toronto in the garage with his secretary from Montreal. "Doing what, for heaven's sake?" my father asked. "He was . . . making love to her," John said. Mommy stepped forward and struck him across the face. "Can't you see Annie's here?" she roared. I was stunned, but my elder sister, Mary, went into hysterics at the thought of a holy priest having sex. Such things did not happen in Connecticut. "Who," she gasped, "is going to forgive him his sins?"

Next, I was a teenage waitress at the Avon Inn in New

Jersey. I often saw men who had checked in in priestly garb dressed as laymen and taking women out for the night—and taking them in. One priest in particular annoyed me because he was so preachy by day and so damned promiscuous by night. *Heavens*, I thought, *and these pious hypocrites give us poor mortals such a hard time of it.*

This was a major reason for my leaving the Church, that and the feeling that Catholics put a sin-tag on every thought, word, deed, and omission. I didn't want to reduce my Eamonn to the level of clerics who lead double lives. There was surely no danger of that since it was his strength not his frailty that overwhelmed me. With great generosity, his one thought was to resurrect a girl whom my father had told him was dead and buried.

It was this generosity that attracted me to him and made me want to get as close to him as I dared.

Chapter
Four

H E DROVE me home that afternoon in a quiet mood. He had a kind of puzzled look on his face as if he were grappling with a problem with which he could not cope.

I had seen enough to know that this masterful man hated to be led. He had so much more to lose than I: honor, prestige, power. What could I offer him in recompense?

Nothing, unless there was deep inside him a torrent of need still to be revealed. I could lead only by following. I could attract only by not attracting. On my part, there was no guilt or guile in this. It was instinctive. It expressed the intent of a woman who had come out of darkness for the first time in her life and felt she was owed happiness.

But how could Eamonn bestow happiness on me, and what form would that happiness take? I had no clear idea as yet. I only knew that I wanted to be worthy of someone so good and so considerate.

The second night, we edged ever closer as we sat and talked by the fire.

"I can do more for you, Annie," he said, neither humbly nor proudly, "than any psychiatrist."

I did not doubt it. If only I could find a way to open my heart to him. Yet if I succeeded, it might lead to his ultimate failure. So deep now was my respect for him I did not want him to fail. He was bigger than I was, bigger even than any possible love between us. How could I want to corrupt a man whom I loved because he was incorruptible?

His personality so overpowered me, maybe I believed that this wizard and this magical land could accomplish the impossible. I blocked my ears to the drums of doom.

He stretched out and stroked the back of my hand. "Care to tell me about your marriage?"

"It was a disaster."

"Your husband was a Catholic?"

My father had told him otherwise, but Steven's religion was not the reason why our marriage failed.

"He was a Jew. I was married in front of a rabbi."

"'Twasn't a real marriage, then." Eamonn said it with a certain amount of satisfaction. "The Church does not recognize the marriage of a Catholic in such circumstances."

"I had ceased to think of myself as a Catholic then."

He reflected for a moment. "That was your trouble, Annie."

I let it pass. I was still feeling the pain of a marriage that I had never been able to speak of to anyone.

Tears must have rainbowed in my eyes as I silently recalled all this, for Eamonn said, "Ready to talk?"

As I shook my head, a sharp chill came over me.

"You are free in the eyes of God, Annie," he said, stroking my hand fondly, "to marry again."

"No."

"To love again."

"To love." I omitted the word *again*. "Perhaps." The expressive motion of his hand on mine told me he liked both distinctions.

What is it about firelight that brings out deep things in the mind and heart? Especially this sort of fire made of peat, dug from the very land on which people walk and live and love. I had read that the great old Irish storytellers liked nothing more than to tell their stories by a big turf fire which, at the day's end, was never put out but simply covered over. Fires would thus go on for generations, until perhaps the house was demolished. A sign, this, that people's stories, like the land itself, its rivers, fields, and hills, would never end. Stories outlive mountains.

So we contented ourselves with telling stories—carving

the past in fabled stone—of our families, of mutual relatives, laughing and sobbing, and hardly knowing the difference.

He told me he was the sixth of "a pewful of children," ten in all. They lived in a yellow Georgian house at Adare in the County Limerick, with white and pink roses round the door.

John, his father, was manager of two dairies. He rose at 4:30 every morning and came home late at night but he always squeezed in Mass during the day.

His mother, Helena, dead now for over ten years, was a perfectionist. Good clothes for the children, finest food served at table with lace and silver, fresh flowers, and best china. She never complained, though her health was always bad. She was a brilliant pianist—Eamonn pointed to her piano by the wall. All the children took music and dancing lessons and Eamonn won many prizes in Irish dancing.

"I was a thin child, Annie, with stomach problems, bronchitis, fevers. I loved sport but was too sickly for it so I made do with music."

He told me of his seminary days—"I never broke a rule, not one"—and of his first years as a curate in Limerick. In those days, in some pool halls, youngsters aged fifteen to nineteen were abusing kids of nine years and up. It took courage to confront them. He knew he could not stop homosexuality. But he could stop child sex-abuse.

"I had a popcorn temper in those days, Annie, and got into a few fights. Twice I was hit with a billiard cue here"—I sighed as he touched the top of his head.

I liked the fact that he had no physical fear. He gained the small boys' confidence and together they unmasked the bullies to the authorities.

"I could not sleep at nights, Annie, for my anguish at this slaughter of God's little lambs." He smiled painfully. "One night, a twenty-year-old came at me with a cue. I grabbed it from him and snapped it in two. Then I twisted his arm behind him and put his head down the toilet bowl and flushed it."

His frankness encouraged me to tell him how, until I was about twelve, I used to break into houses with my friend Corey. I could pick any lock, get through any window. I chose people I didn't like and ate the food in their iceboxes.

Once, I broke into the house of Mr. Thompson, who used to abuse children.

"So," I told Eamonn, "I put the plug in his bath and turned the faucets on. When he got home hours later, the whole place was ruined."

Eamonn was shocked. "You are a terrible case for a Novena."

I was no less shocked. He saw no parallel between his attack on perversion and mine. He had nearly drowned a human being whereas I had only ruined a few floors and carpets.

I resolved to be more careful. Maybe Eamonn had double standards: one set for him and another for everyone else.

As the night lengthened, as the same fire warmed us and welded us into one, we returned once more to my marriage. I do not think Eamonn ever doubted his magnetic power to draw the badness out of me.

"Before we married . . ."

He came very close, stroking my hair, sensing that I was about to open my heart to him. "Yes, Annie?"

"He took precautions so we would not have a child."

"If you were not then married . . ."

He seemed to think I was speaking of morals but I wasn't.

"One night," I said, gulping, "Steven realized he was losing me. It had finally got to him that I feared something inside him that was wanting to corrode me."

"So?" Eamonn urged.

"He came to me without a condom so I would conceive."

"You mean, so you would be forced to marry him?"

I nodded, shaking all over at the memory of unimaginably bad things.

"Anyway, Annie, I'm pleased he failed."

"But he didn't."

He turned ashen. "You conceived?"

"Yes. We married three months later."

"So there was a child?" His jazz hand was quite still on my head. "I never knew."

I could almost read his thoughts through his musical hand's patting, resting on my hand and my hair.

"What became of—?"

"Because of me, it died."

He momentarily withdrew his hand in horror. Then the professional in him, I guess, made him put it back on my head.

"You mean, you had an abortion. Did . . . he"—I liked that he could not bring himself to use the word *husband*—"did he know about this?"

"It wasn't an abortion."

His blink was another small victory for me.

"No?"

I shook my head. "Women can get rid of babies without having an abortion."

He was mystified by this. It was new for him to be so out of his depth. It made me interesting, a challenge, and he, a competitive man who always got his way, liked a challenge.

"Was it a boy or a girl?"

"I don't know."

He was even more surprised. "How could you *not* know? Oh, I see. The baby was taken from you when it was born and adopted so you never knew whether it was—"

"It was not adopted."

"No, of course not," he said, soothingly, as if I were not quite sane. "You said you were somehow responsible for its dying. But surely"—this was the genuine plea of someone who cared—"you only mean that you gave him . . . Or her . . ." He shook his puzzled head. "But you said you did not give your baby for adoption."

He looked into the fire for a very long moment.

"Annie, you're not making any sense."

"Nothing in my life makes sense."

By now, I suspect, he did not know whether I was crazy, a monster, or a plain fantasist. Yet something told him I was telling the truth.

For the first time, *I* reached out and held *his* hand.

"In the fifth and a half month, Eamonn, the baby died."

"You said you didn't—"

"Didn't take poisons or use a metal coat hanger."

I could sense the relief of this good man who valued infant life flooding through him.

"So you didn't kill . . . the baby."

It had struck him that the sex of a baby at five and a half

months is plain and yet, for some reason, I had no idea whether my baby was a boy or a girl.

"I told you I *was* responsible for it not living."

"But . . ." He needed both hands now to express his utter bewilderment.

"Has it never occurred to you, Eamonn, that human beings die when they know they are not loved?"

"Die?"

"That's why I'm dead."

He held his warm hand close to my warm cheek and, with an almost frightened laugh, said, "You are very *much* alive."

"Not inside me, Eamonn. Not where it matters." I spoke the next words with as much passion as any woman ever mustered. "No one is alive who is not loved and I have *never* been loved."

"But—"

Once more he seemed to me to convey his thoughts through the touch of his hand: *But you are loved, Annie. I love you.*

If only I could be sure they were his thoughts.

"You said, Annie, that no one is alive who is not loved?"

I nodded, sensing that he was asking himself if God's love were enough for happiness. What if he, a bishop, was thinking the most terrible thought of all: *Could it be that I, Eamonn Casey, who believe myself to be so alive, am really dead, have always been dead, will remain dead forever and ever?*

For several minutes we peered together into the heart of the fire. Maybe the fire was telling us that we held the secret to one another's lives. Maybe it was not merely the focus but the creator of a story, a new story, our story, that would outlast the lakes and snowcapped mountains of Kerry. If I loved Eamonn and he loved me, two long-dead people, a lonely man and a lonely woman, might rise from the dead, hand in hand.

I suddenly launched into the story of my marriage.

I had hoped against hope for happiness, and Steven and I had a lot of fun together. But when I sensed danger, when I came head-on against the destructive part of him, I wanted out. He desired me only because I no longer desired him. That was when he grabbed me and took me violently. "I won't let you go," he said. "You'll never leave me."

That night I conceived.

Almost immediately I became ill. It was not the usual morning sickness. On a Brooklyn street, as I was almost fainting, women shoppers said, "Get this girl to a hospital, she's real bad." My doctor said, "Lots of pregnant women are this way." But I knew that something was wrong.

Now I was talking to Eamonn. My story was, so to speak, entering history, no, making history.

"Deep down, I *wanted* something to be wrong."

"Why?"

"Because *I* was all wrong, don't you see?"

He nodded, though whether he yet understood how wrong I was I could not tell. I continued:

"By the time I was five and a half months gone, I was sleeping all day and all night. No energy. Felt close to death. Then I started bleeding. I was taken to St. Vincent's Hospital, down in the city, you know, in the Village. Someone examined me and I was put on a drip. A nurse said it was to induce labor. But I was months away, my mind, my body, not ready. I didn't want that baby. Didn't want to see it. Let it stay in the dark, I thought, the dark in which I shower, the dark where it belongs forever. Then a doctor came.

"'You have to let that baby out,' the doctor said, and I said, 'Why?' 'Because it's dead and it's poisoning you.' I thought, 'Dead? Then we've poisoned each other.'"

"No, Annie, no," Eamonn said, reassuringly, his soothing hand pressed in a circling movement on my head.

"The doc said, 'If you don't let it out we'll have to cut you.' So I let go. It was still, my God, painful. Went on for hours, through the night and next day. And finally the baby came out and they . . ."

"Yes?"

"They put it in a bedpan."

"Oh, Annie, poor Annie."

"It was not a pretty sight. A big head, natural, I guess, for its stage of development. Then a beeper went. Emergency. The nurses rushed off, leaving me. And there was a dead kitten of a baby sitting in a bedpan next to my bed. And I said to this little stranger, over and over, 'I let you die, little one, oh, I wish I could be sorry, I really wish that.'"

"You did *not* let it die."

"I did," I responded heatedly, "I did, I *did*. It was so

fragile looking, with blood all over it. I could see how it was formed—muscles, bones, sinews, veins like in an autumn leaf—all this I saw through the transparent skin. And I was responsible for its dying because I hadn't loved it. Because I couldn't. Because babies should only come from love and this baby was my husband's doing and I hated *him* for making me so hate myself.''

Even as I took a big gulp, a gulp that pained me, I was theatrical, too. I mean I wanted to make an impression on Eamonn.

"So," I continued, "I *was* responsible, you see."

This time Eamonn wisely did not attempt to speak.

"I kept ringing the bell, Eamonn. Kept hollering, 'For God's sake, somebody come and take it away.' Everyone was too busy. I was left wishing desperately that somehow, somewhere, inside me I would find the love to love it.''

His hand stopped for a few seconds stroking my hair, then continued.

"I don't believe in God, only in the hell He created.''

"God loves you, Annie," he said, his eyes misting up.

"No, He's dead. Maybe He died because no one loved Him.''

Eamonn, dear Eamonn, let the blasphemy pass. I never told him that I became virtually a vegetarian, not from principle but necessity, the moment I saw that baby lying dead in the pan.

"I was a doctor's daughter. From age five I peeped into my father's medical books. I told myself that this covering"—I plucked at my cheek—"the skin, was not real; the real me was underneath, invisible. That's what I still feel. No one will ever see the real me.''

"No one?"

"No one," I repeated, challenging him. "The only real self I ever saw was my husband's baby, the baby in the bedpan, which ripped me apart. I saw into it, saw what it was made of.''

"Which was?"

"Death. I wanted it dead. That's why it died.''

"Annie, Annie, are you listening to me?" He pressed my hand vigorously. "Good. There was probably a simple explanation—"

"The doctor said later there was absolutely nothing wrong with it. It simply died. And I was responsible."

Eamonn, man of the world, one who had seen everything, knew everything, was stunned. "You looked at it for how long?"

"A half hour, maybe. I couldn't tell its sex because its little legs were crossed and I couldn't have got out of bed to look if I had wanted to."

"And you never asked? No."

By now, I felt as tired as the day of my miscarriage. The fire in me, like the one in the hearth, was low.

"Enough, Annie. It's past two o'clock." He drew me to my feet. "Time for you to hit the hay."

At my door, he said, looking pleased with me, with himself:

"Thank you for opening your heart to me. That took courage."

I went to bed, but my mind was racing so I could not sleep.

What was he thinking? He looked on himself as a great healer, and what healer could ever resist the temptation to raise the dead? I did so need his healing hand.

I heard him as before saying his breviary, walking up and down, past the Stations of the Cross. He reminded me of the tide ebbing and flowing.

Forty or so minutes later, he must have seen my light was still on—the lamp deliberately directed to the door—for he knocked gently, put his head inside, saw me sitting up in bed in my nightdress.

"Good night, Annie, and God bless you."

He said it so kindly, with such generosity, that the whole of me felt humbled and warmed.

Chapter Five

N EXT MORNING, I awoke late. I showered. A woman showered. I dressed. A woman alive for the first time to feelings of hope, dressed. I put on my face. To the mirror: Hello, stranger.

Mary heard me moving about my room. She had my breakfast prepared. The Bishop, she said, had gone off to Killarney as usual. Mary, it was plain, never spoke about the Bishop's private matters. She was completely loyal.

Or was she?

It struck me that Eamonn had not waked me because he did not want me around. He needed time and leisure to ponder what I had told him the night before. I hoped so.

Mary had set out my breakfast in the kitchen. Looking at the clock, she switched on an old radio. Out of it came nothing but the sound of many bongs. *Bong-bong-bong*. It was the Angelus. Mary made the sign of the cross and her lips moved in prayer.

I came from a country where there was a strict separation of Church and State, and here was a national radio network putting out the prayer of a particular religion. It made the job of men like Eamonn that much easier. No wonder they were so powerful.

After breakfast, Mary offered to take me with her to shop. She drove me in her tiny Volkswagen twenty miles to Killorglin. We first traveled east, past fields of golden gorse, with the Slieve Mish mountains on our left and Castlemaine Harbor on our right. Then we turned south on the Ring of Kerry, where giant rhododendron and fuchsia bushes were in bud.

First I had tasted strange air, tea, bread, and now a strange town. Killorglin, on the River Laune, was set on a hill so steep you needed a ski lift to get up it. Everything and all the people in it seemed wild.

They were so relaxed you got the impression they had nowhere of importance to go to. Even the postman, with a packed bag on his shoulder, gazed in every shop window as if he were out on a stroll to see his pals and had arrived two hours early. He stopped on the bridge to see if the trout were biting that day or were just up for air and wanting a chat.

We went into the butcher's shop. He was a big man with a red face and a bent knee of a nose with nostrils like a horse. All the time he was laughing and gesturing and wielding a bloody cleaver as though he were Oliver Cromwell.

He followed Mary out to the car and heaved in, off a bloodied shoulder, what looked like half a cow. He threw it in the backseat, without any wrapping, touched his forelock, laughed raucously again, and, brushing his meaty hands, went back to his shop. Used as I was to the neat expensive packaging of New York, this was quite an experience.

Killorglin, Mary told me, was a "pagan place." They held a three-day Puck Fair there every summer. The maidens of the town, and there were still some in Ireland in those days, competed for the affections of the Goat, a monstrous horned creature. The luckiest of them became his August bride.

In midafternoon Mary dropped me off on Inch strand, while she took the meat to the Palace in Killarney where she kept a couple of freezers full of food for when Eamonn entertained. The beach was deserted. It suited me to walk, squired by the sun, alone and not alone, along the frothy edge of the sea or to lie in the sand dunes.

When you are happy you don't mind being solitary. I was happy, though with what justification I could not be sure.

Eamonn came home earlier than Mary had predicted. I knew he would. This is why I had deliberately delayed so as not to be there when he arrived. Let Eamonn wait on me.

I finally walked the couple of miles or so up from the shore, past the Strand Hotel, along a stony and pitted path, to find him eagerly looking out for me at the door.

Did anyone ever welcome anyone as he welcomed me? My heart raced out to meet this man with the sunflower smile.

Taking both my hands in his, he said, "Yesterday, your face was a snowflake, Annie, and now your cheeks are red as votive lamps."

He pointed to where the spring sun, descending, was reddening the distant mountains. He noticed me shudder and those questioning eyes demanded to know what was wrong.

"It's just . . . it reminds me of blood on snow."

He sensitively did not ask why that unsettled me.

That night, by the hearth, I was reluctant to reveal myself further. After a long chat about friends and world events and Irish politics and even some Irish history, I clammed up. This was to be my Silent Night.

I was not consciously playing hard to get. I was simply not prepared to do what he wanted when he wanted it, as if all he had to do, so to speak, was ring the Angelus bell.

"Problems like yours, Annie," he said, "don't go away. Unless you talk them out, they'll follow you all your life. One day, when you're least expecting it, they pop up and"—he gestured eloquently to his own throat—"strangle you."

My continuing silence meant that from his point of view, it was a wasted day. But I felt it was good to reinforce the fact that I was a real person and not just an American cousin with a problem awaiting the touch of his healing hand.

Maybe he knew that already, but maybe not, and I was not prepared to take a chance. Not till I had lowered the odds.

That night, before he began his prayers up and down the corridor he came into my bedroom to say good night. He sat on the bed beside me and fondly pushed my hair out of my eyes.

"God bless you, Annie." As he said it, his eyes were shining, his hands and body trembling.

I felt I had only to touch him or stroke him and he would be in bed with me. I was ready for it, but he, in spite of his obvious sexual excitement, was not.

I kept to my plan. I felt for him this mysterious something that had no name but I was not sure if he felt the same toward me. If he did and if this feeling was to last, the first move would have to be his. I slipped further down under the covers to prove my good intentions.

Without looking back, he left my room.

Moments later I heard him walking up and down, praying. I would have given a lot to know what he was saying to his God—and what his God was saying to him.

Next day, I did not see him till he returned very late at night. My turn to know what waiting feels like. Maybe this was his way of getting even.

He had the problem, he said, of funding a parish in Africa. Irish missionary priests were keen to start a school for native children. He seemed much concerned for the poor, whom he called, Irish fashion, "green mouths," because, I guess, they had nothing to eat but grass and nettles.

By the fireside, after the usual talk about friends and family, he said, "Tell me more about yourself, Annie. For me."

I found that so touching, I could not hold back.

As he encouraged me by stroking the back of my hand, I explained that after the baby was stillborn, I kept getting terrible headaches and my stomach seemed ready to blow up. My doctor said this was quite normal after a late miscarriage.

Then, when my first period was due, I simply streamed with blood. It came flying out of me in great ugly clots. I felt I was dying. After all, how much blood can you lose?

"My husband," I told Eamonn, "took me to hospital. I was bleeding all over the place. It was winter and snowing, and as I walked, I dripped."

"Blood on snow."

I nodded.

"The hospital was Kings County, a terrible place. No sick person ought to be allowed in there. The two interns who examined me hissed, 'She's had an abortion. She murdered her baby.' They had a point. Perpetual mother, perpetual guilt, eh? But it was unfair of them to judge me. They didn't know."

Eamonn stroked my burning cheek. "You never hurt anyone, Annie, and you never would."

"They put me in a room with a man in the next bed. A nurse came in screaming, 'Get a tag for this guy's toe.' I thought they were talking about me. I wanted to tell them I was dying but I wasn't fucking dead yet."

I looked up and said, "Sorry." He patted my head for me

to continue. I gathered his own language was not always monastic.

"They wanted to put a tag on this corpse. As if without it no one would realize he was dead. He had fooled me because his eyes were open and he was looking straight at me."

Eamonn stroked my head strongly to intimate, I think, that I was not in the company of a corpse now.

"My husband came in then. Seeing him, I thought his baby I had let die was getting back at me. He tugged my boots off and my toes were all black."

"Frostbite?"

"No. I was losing a tremendous amount of blood prior to going into shock. I started to hyperventilate and had the first panic attack of my life. Everyone was running around, shouting and screaming, but nobody really cared."

"Oh, Annie," Eamonn said, sympathetically.

"A doctor was pressing down on my belly and great gouts of blood were spurting out. I wanted to run away. If I was going to die, I wanted out of that madhouse. I got up and ran for the exit. They grabbed me and ordered a big powerful nurse to wrestle me and stop me leaving."

I must have paused in my story, lost in memory, because I kind of came to with Eamonn asking, "What then, Annie, my poor, poor Annie?"

Hey, I thought, *stop that or I'll cry.*

"What then? The bleeding slowed down. Not much left, I guess." I said this with a wry smile. "I was transferred to Saint Vincent's. But I was never to be the person I was before. I was now an agitated, panicky, useless human being."

"Don't say that, Annie," the great healer insisted. "Never say that."

"I called my husband and told him I wanted to come home. 'Get yourself a cab,' he said."

"You had given birth to his child, you were sick in hospital, and he said that? How could he?"

"If you don't love, you can do anything, Eamonn. Anyway, I was devastated. That was when my agoraphobia started."

"Agoraphobia?"

"It stopped my first day here when I came down the mountain."

"Really?" He shook his head in disbelief. "But what caused it?"

"I had to go find a cab on my own."

"Animals," he muttered.

"There were no showers, no one offered me a towel, and I was covered in blood."

"But you were in a hospital."

"Correction. A New York hospital. No one cared a damn. After all, I was only a human being."

"Go on."

"I had only a handkerchief to clean myself with. There was blood all over me, on my face, even in my hair. The cab driver took one look at me and said, 'Christ, lady, you been in an accident?' I said, 'That's about it.' I climbed in and he took me home. After that, I never liked open spaces."

Eamonn seemed satisfied that my story was complete, though there were dark things in my marriage, in me, that maybe I could never tell him. He had his arms around my shoulder as if to enclose me and take away my fear forever.

For a long time, he stroked my hair and my hands, tender and silent, apart from an occasional long sigh. He seemed to be wrestling with some problem that I could not fathom.

When I glanced momentarily at him, I saw a sad, almost wistful expression on his face. He seemed to me then to be more vulnerable than either he or I had ever imagined.

That night, I was lying in bed when, immediately after he had said his prayers, he slipped into my room. This time, he approached my bed and lifted me into his arms and, after pussy-catting my cheek, he kissed me passionately.

This was a soul kiss. His tongue sharpened itself on my upper teeth before exploring the smooth warm cave of my mouth, as though he were desperate to find a refuge in me. Propped up on my pillow, I tried to move backward but he wouldn't let me.

What stunned me was the realization that he had done this before. No one could kiss like that without practice.

My God, I thought, *what if he isn't the incorruptible man I imagined but the horned Goat of Puck Fair?*

But he was a goddamn bishop; where had he learned all this?

I felt his whole body trembling and shuddering next to

mine, but I could not respond adequately because he pinned me so tight and my mind was in a whirl. After a minimum of two minutes, he let me come up for air.

In retrospect, my silence helped me. Saying yes or no would have put me in control by encouraging or denying him. My breathlessness told in my favor. He had no one to blame but himself. If he had broken a commandment, he had used his own hammer.

Then, abruptly, without a word, without an explanation or an apology, he was gone.

For a long time after, my mind was in turmoil. It struck me that my Eamonn found it hard to say sorry. I did not mind that, for he may have been suffering from embarrassment.

I was relieved that he was not after all a sun, glowing and pure all round, but, like me, a moon with a dark side. The moon has always fascinated me because it is two-faced. If I'm ever reincarnated, I'll come back as the moon.

My body ached to follow Eamonn into his room, to introduce the black side of me to the black side of him. In other words, I wanted, as was natural, to say, "Where do we go from here?"

But I didn't want to blow it. Play this cool, Annie Murphy. He is far too precious to lose.

I switched off my bedside lamp and both sides of me, black and white, went into a quiet, restful sleep.

Chapter Six

A FEW days passed. I said nothing, intimated nothing about what had happened. He may have been testing me to see if I could keep a secret.

I knew I could. As a doctor's daughter, I was often the first to know and the last to tell of his patients' ailments. But could Eamonn?

One morning, while Mary was out shopping, I saw him off on a three-day trip abroad. I dusted a pollen-like trace of dandruff from his shoulders, complimented him on looking so smart. He kissed me at the front door but not passionately. More like a man going to the office.

"Take care," I said, though he was already out of earshot and, with a cheery wave, he drove off in a cloud of dust.

The next few days I walked the white beach at Inch, watching the breakers and soaking up the May sunshine. I was more buoyant than I had ever been. Everything around me was precious. I could not bear to step on a crab or a sandfly for fear of hurting or killing it.

For days, I had caught myself looking with amazement at the stars, sunrise, the sea, a poplar tree, an ant, and felt what the author of Genesis must have felt when he said simply in God's name of everything freshly created, "It was good."

I had an awesome sensation that the relationship between Eamonn and me had been planned before time began. Is this what philosophers mean by eternity? Did this entrancing idea, more a feeling, originate in an overwhelming sense that something uniquely good in our lives was intended from the beginning? Yes, this communion between Eamonn and me was meant to be before the Creator said, "Let there be light."

Without searching for it and with the suddenness of forked lightning, I had a name for the nameless thing that had been slowly taking shape in me for days. It was a name so ordinary, so often used by me as well as by millions of others, I never realized I had not once appreciated it until I came to know Eamonn. It was love.

Recognition took all the strength out of my legs. I just made it to the grassy dunes where I collapsed and lay out of the wind under a blue sky. I was exhausted in body yet filled with boundless spiritual strength.

Love. So this, finally, was love. I laughed aloud at my long ignorance. Boyfriends, even my husband, from time to time had said to me, "I love you," and I had responded with "And I love you." I was now ashamed for having used this precious phrase so glibly, so mindlessly.

Love was pure and everlasting, and it surely happened only once if at all in any lifetime. In my gratitude at having found it, at having begun to understand it, I outflew the birds. So effortless the soaring sea-gulling of the heart in love.

But did Eamonn feel, as I did, that our meeting was part of a common destiny? And even if he did love me, would he ever feel free to express it?

I do not mean by kissing me passionately. That had to be a mistake on his part, never to be repeated, but at least it proved the strength of his feelings for me. Still less did I mean it sexually—he was committed to living a celibate life. What I had in mind was, rather, a lifelong sharing of intimate thoughts, hopes, dreams that neither time nor distance could obliterate. In his absence abroad, I had absolute confidence in a oneness of the spirit, his and mine, that would overcome all obstacles.

Calling to mind his sweet face, I realized that lately he had lost much of his former calm and self-assurance. Seeing him in a mirror when he thought I was not looking, I had caught him frowning uncharacteristically, as if he had a burden he would like to share. Often, while talking over the fire at night, this precise man had become entangled in a sentence that grew ever more complex until he had to stop and shake his head as if to clear it. He wanted to tell me something but either lacked the words or the courage to do so.

Was he, too, stumbling toward the discovery of a path that led to the magic and eternity of love?

I prayed that he would find some way of communicating with me, some way of opening his heart to me as I had begun to open myself to him. He would not find it easy, that was obvious. He knew more of charity than of love. He was expert at giving; receiving was far harder. He had schooled himself through years of service to offer sympathy, not to accept it. His vocation in life was to appear strong for the sake of others, not to show the weakness and need that accompany love among equals.

That day and the days that followed were the first test for my new existence. Eamonn never left my mind nor did distance separate us. I no longer had the slightest doubt that he was the one person with whom I could share everything and be completely me, if only he would allow it.

Something else was special about him. He was the one man whom I trusted physically. Others had abused me terribly. Eamonn never would. In this respect, his celibacy was a help, not a hindrance to our love.

I was in such a peaceful frame of mind I was totally unprepared for the manner of his homecoming.

Late in the evening, I heard his car on the drive, but so slow I realized something was wrong. I wanted to rush out of my room, fling open the front door, and embrace him, but it was Mary's job to greet him, not mine.

I sensed something terrible had happened. Maybe he had met up with a fellow bishop, made a confession of his sins and returned home determined to cast me out of his life forever.

In fact, he was ill. I could tell that by his slow tread as he went via the hallway into the living room. He was ill enough to have gone straight to bed; he had chosen to go instead to a public place where I could tend him.

I walked nonchalantly out of my room and ran into Mary.

"The Bishop's ill, Annie. I'm making him a cup of tea."

I went into the living room and, in spite of the loving appeal in his eyes, I was shocked at his appearance.

He held out his hand to me. I kissed it briefly and took his racing pulse. His pupils also told me something was badly wrong with him.

"Eamonn, I'm going to ask Mary to call a doctor."

He shook his head. He said he had caught amoebic dysentery on a trip to Africa the year before and it kept recurring in the form of colitis. He had just had a bad bout of it in Germany and been hospitalized. He only needed rest.

"No, no, no," I said.

With all that liquid gone from him and the loss of potassium salts, I feared he might go into shock. I raced to the kitchen and, while Mary called a doctor, I carried in the tray with the pot of tea. By the time the doctor arrived, Eamonn was in bed.

Mary told me afterward that he had been given an injection and further medication. The doctor said that in two or three days he should be as right as rain.

I thought of only him for forty-eight hours. I longed to go and sit by his bed. For two days, Mary said, he slept practically without waking. For a man who prided himself on making do with four or five hours a night, that was a new experience.

I was in bed when a storm blew up. The sea dashed against the rocks. The trees in the garden creaked and the bushes brushed eerily against my window. The wild wind made all the indoor shutters bang and rattle in their boxes. I tried to free my shutters and draw them across, but they were nailed down. Then came rain, hissing against the glass.

I switched on my bedside lamp and read a few pages from *You Can't Go Home Again*, but my mind refused to focus. I switched off the light and went to sleep about one o'clock. But only for a few minutes, because I woke with a start to what I thought was my door banging closed in the wind.

I turned over and tried to go back to sleep, but I was aware I was not alone in the room.

I switched the light on and there he was.

I was too shaken to utter a word.

His clericals were smart and new, always the crease in the pants and polished black leather shoes. But his nightclothes were old and worn. Over his pajamas he had on a frayed blue bathrobe. His unshaven face was flushed from a long sleep, and his eyes were narrowed owing to drugs.

His presence at once took away my fear of the storm. I expected him to sit beside me or at the foot of my bed, but he stood shaky and in a kind of daze in the middle of the floor.

Out of clerical garb, he was different, less in command.

"Eamonn," I squeezed out, "you shouldn't have got up."

His answer was to kick off his old brown flip-flop leather slippers, untie the cord round his robe, and slip it off his shoulders.

I pitied him from my heart, he was so vulnerable. I did not want things to be like this. He was fragile. His glassy eyes suggested he did not fully know what he was doing.

"You're ill, Eamonn," I whispered.

"I know what I'm doing," he muttered. "Know what I want. Know why I'm here."

"But the doctor—"

He took off his faded blue pajama top with the white piping and let it fall behind his back. With fumbling fingers, he dropped and stepped shakily out of his pajama pants.

There stood the Bishop, my love, without clerical collar or crucifix or ring, without covering of any kind. The great showman had unwrapped himself. Christmas of all Christmases.

This was for me more of a wonder than all the mountains, lark-song, and heather-scents of Ireland. He stood before me, his only uniform the common flesh of humanity. There were black hairs on his lower arms and in a band across his chest. His legs were sturdy but shapely; on and around his left knee was a big faint birthmark like a coffee stain.

He looked forlorn, almost like a child lost in a dark wood. I could see his love for me stirring, coming literally alive in that part of him till then unshown, the sacred part of him that could not lie about his feelings. I looked on mesmerized as he hardened below a black fringe of curls.

Since I still did not make a move, was too terrified to, he shuffled over and almost fell across my bed. He whipped my nightdress over my head, neither gentle nor rough. Then he opened the covers and heaved his overheated body in beside me.

Once he was lying down his thrashing matched the fierce disruptive rhythms of the storm.

I did not mind him sleeping in my bed, it was big enough. I wanted him as near as possible so I could give him solace, help him get well, but he had only one thing on his mind. What possessed me was my willingness to let him take from me whatever he needed.

I witnessed a great hunger. This was an Irish Famine of the flesh. Here was a man releasing energies and feelings pent up for over twenty-five adult years.

Panting heavily, his mouth and lips covered and then explored mine. He fondled and kissed my breasts, and ran hands, strong in spite of his fever, over every inch of me, hands that had spoken to me so eloquently of the wonders of Ireland, hands that could calm a runaway horse.

I still hoped that nothing would happen. It would break my heart if he acted under the influence of drugs. I felt like a man who has taken advantage of a woman.

Besides, he might regret it. He might even blame me as he blamed me when he nearly ran into the Ford van on the road. I did not want to be the cliff's edge for his flying feet.

I looked up and stroked him softly with both hands round his bristly cheeks. I murmured sweet words to him, enjoyed the sheer weight of him and his passionate caresses.

It struck me that, aside from his delight in the smells and smoothness of feminine skin, this all-knowing cleric and completely inexperienced man did not really have a language of sex. He might have kissed a woman, maybe many. But I was surely the first woman whose flesh had met the fullness of his naked flesh.

The more than twenty-year difference between us did not matter now. He was a novice lover. He did not begin to understand the geography of my body and in his hurry to discover it he came too early. I felt the sticky odorous wetness running down the inside of my thighs. So, while he was old enough to be my father, he seemed, in the end, young enough to be my son.

For a woman, there are many ways to explore a man and

express love. I did not need to have him climax inside me to know he was mine. I did not even want it.

In the past, I had kidded men, my husband included, that I had not taken precautions against pregnancy when I had. It was a ruse to make them withdraw from me without leaving their seed behind to blend with the juices inside me and leave an odor and a texture that I could not bear.

The reason for my dislike went back to when I was seventeen. I was in my last year at school. Don, my boyfriend, had a reputation for being sexy, but I thought it only meant he liked kissing girls. He was the first to arouse me; and when he kissed me I thought I was on fire.

One spring—mimosa, oleander, lantana in blossom—we were at school when a tornado struck a half mile away. Susan, my closest buddy, and I went under the desk for shelter. The noise was terrifying, I was shaking violently, convinced my last hour had come. Susan took out a metal hip flask and introduced me to rum. Rum and I were instant best friends. The tornado passed and, happy to be alive, we went out to celebrate.

One guy let me drink beer out of his ten-gallon hat and we danced on a picnic table. Don was jealous. He knocked my dance partner out with one punch to the jaw, grabbed me off the table, and, piling me into his black Pontiac sports car, drove me to the lake. There we scrambled, as usual, into the backseat. But he had a black glassy possessive look in his eye I had not seen before, and sweat pumped out of the pores of his nose.

He ripped my dress open, tore off my bra, and started biting me. I yelled at him to stop, but he wouldn't. I scratched his face so he recoiled, giving me just enough time to jump out of the car.

I ran screaming but he caught up with me, threw me to the ground, and bent over me, beating me.

"Please *don't*," I said. "I'm a virgin."

He stuck his fingers inside me. "My God," he said, "you *are*. Okay, get up."

I stood up and he carried me back to the car and threw me in the front seat. Sitting beside me, he grabbed my hair and pulled me toward him as if he were insane.

"Do something for me or I'll rape you, virgin or not."

I said, "Okay, name it."

He opened his pants and out popped this dun-colored snake, with rearing head and giant twitching mouth, swinging back and forth like a windshield wiper.

Never having seen anything this gross, I put my head in my hands and laughed hysterically. "What d'ya want me to do with *that?*"

"Jerk it, dope," he said, "jerk me off."

I tried, but my hand got stuck on that thing.

"Use some saliva," he said, but my mouth was too dry.

"Faster," he ordered, brutally elbowing my left side, "faster."

After what seemed forever, there was a kind of spitting and the inverted milking turned into a snow shower that went everywhere. It landed on my hand, my lips, my hair, and it clung so I couldn't get it off. The rancid smell of it in that confined space filled my lungs like a sewer. I begged him to take me home.

Once there, breathless, enraged, with, in my chest, a sense of impending doom, I scissored all my clothes into little bits and crouched in the corner of the shower like a spider, for the first time showering in the dark. I thought:

To some men, women are not people. They picnic on our bodies, on our feelings, and, sated, pass on. We women are but the litter of their so-called love.

Water, cold water ran all over me as I tried in vain—I'm still trying—to wash off me the stains and the godawful smells.

Next morning, Daddy loomed over my bed. "Get up, Annie."

He lifted my nightdress with the black cane he used after his leg was amputated.

That cane reminded me of the snake in the car.

I screamed, "What the hell, Daddy?"

Two crystal tears ran a close race down his cheeks.

"You're bruised all over. Someone rape you? Did they?"

"You crazy, we played touch football and I was tackled real heavy."

That was the first time I lied to save a man's skin. I did it as easy as breathing. Daddy gave me a couple of tablets, which brought oblivion. No gift more gratefully received in my entire life.

Next day, I told Susan. I was with our crowd including a newcomer named Jeff Fox, and when they saw my bruises, they went in search of Don and kicked his guts in and broke his arm. Jeff took me to hospital to have my ribs wrapped. He became my mentor and next boyfriend—that's another story with the usual picnic ending.

The shadow of that incident, the sour smell in my nostrils, followed me, maimed me, ruined many precious moments of my life.

No, I did not mind at all that Eamonn had not entered me. In my marriage, I had experienced the lust of my husband but not a love like this. Sex can be the most humiliating of all hurts.

Had Eamonn only realized the terrible things done to my body in the past, he would have known that what he did to me in his fumbling way was marvelous. He had loved me with his whole being, found me worthy, and I was content.

Unbarnacling, he dropped off to sleep without a word.

As he cat-purred, I had hours to think. For the first time I had the impression that a man loved me; and a man had loved me without reserve. If this was so, maybe one day I would be able to look closely at myself in the mirror again and shower in the light.

Of course, I could hear a voice telling me this love was doomed. But doomed or not, damned or not, this love, I sensed, would have a beauty in it that would endure.

My gentle, kindly, amusing Eamonn now lay quietly, trustingly, beside me, this man whose whole life was a restless sunlike dance.

But—moments later—had I truly won him? Did he love me, really love me, I mean, to the exclusion of all others and all other concerns unto death? Was this possible for one who had so much more to lose than I who was a nothing person? Would he, when he awoke, also abuse me in his own spiritual way?

The doubts persisted. I had so little regard for myself. Would he even remember the solace he had found in me?

Would he ask me when he awoke how I had tricked him into my bed?

Against the background roaring of wind and sea, I watched the rippling movements of his face. Even in sleep his mood had changed. He seemed now to be thinking, scheming, making deals, preparing for action. I wanted to stroke him all over, to soothe his disquiets, but I feared to wake him.

He awoke about three. He asked no questions. His smile seemed to say that he was in the right place with the right woman.

I whispered, "We did things earlier, Eamonn, you and I."

"I remember some of it. I'm so sorry."

"Oh my God," I said, "that makes me feel horrible."

Anticipating the question I most dearly wanted to ask, he said, "'Twasn't the drugs, Annie. 'Twas bound to happen because I feel for you as I know you feel for me."

Once more a kind of adolescent passion took control of him. His blind, twitching hands raced again all over the Braille of my body. His hands gripped me low from behind and drew me to him, twisting, grinding, while he whispered, "You are like silk and, oh, the heat of you."

I said nothing, content to be the fountain that quenched his desert thirst. A wrong word from me and he might lose concentration, maybe think badly of himself.

When he tried to consummate his love, again the fiery foreplay exhausted all the sexual capacities he then possessed.

No matter. I reveled in the feel on my equally desiring flesh of his magnificent hands and his moist expressive lips.

Afterward, he nestled up to me and tickled my face with his growth of beard; and I gazed into his hazel eyes that seemed to turn bright green. His were the only eyes I had ever been able to look right into. Yes, I was right from the start, I was in his eyes, I belonged there.

"Don't worry," he said. "This is between you and me. We'll keep it like that."

He went back to sleep again.

The storm had somewhat abated and, when the first hint of the sun pierced my burgundy velvet curtains, I reluctantly nudged him awake.

"What time is it, Annie?"

"Five o'clock."

"I suppose—"

"Yes, you'd better go back to your room," I said, smiling. "Don't want Mary to find you here when she gets up."

He wearily left the bed and got dressed. He blew me a kiss before quietly letting himself out.

I immediately got out of bed, threw back the bed covers, and raised both windows to lessen the musky smell.

I went into the small dark bathroom and turned on the shower at low pressure so no one else could hear it. Afterward, I partly dried myself with a towel before standing at the window to let the Atlantic breeze, scented by honeysuckle, complete the job.

In the tall wardrobe mirror that reflected the big white smile of the moon, I surveyed my body that Eamonn had delighted in. The tanned and radiant face and sparkling eyes, the young firm breasts, small waist, flared hips, long bronzed legs. I no longer wholly despised myself and the way I looked. Love was binding up my wounds.

The muscled, salt sea wind had freshened the room but I dabbed myself with cologne to drive away the last vestiges of the odors that so disturbed me. Then, getting back into my flowery nightgown, happier than I had ever been, I climbed into bed.

That was when the torment began.

Was this a one-night stand brought about by his illness and the drugs or the beginning of a long romance? Was he mine or wasn't he? Had I won his heart or lost him for good? What would the future bring to him, to me, to us? Did he already hate me for making him hate himself? Would he have such guilt that he would ask me to leave Ireland for the sake of his soul?

Strange, how after passionate lovemaking, I could not answer any of the big questions. Later that morning, he would dress as a bishop. Where would I stand then?

Apart from the fact that the inert sex-odor in the room still made me want to flee, there was only one thing that would put my mind at ease. I rose, slid out of my room, closing the door quietly behind me, and, after only a few paces, just as quietly opened Eamonn's door.

This was the first time I had seen his bedroom. It was far

bigger than mine, with two heavily draped french windows leading onto the patio, a whole wall with windows onto the sea. The noise of the sea was louder, more evocative here.

I took in the two double beds with Eamonn lying in the first of them under an exquisite laced eiderdown of apricot silk. I saw the raised yellow velvety wallpaper, the olive-gold drapes, a chaise longue, an old Turkish rug, black with reds and oranges and other warm colors threaded through it. And Eamonn's black uniform so redolent of death: the gold ring and pectoral cross on the antique mahogany dresser; the black stock, the shirt, surprisingly multicolored in reds, grays, and greens, the starched collar, the pants, folded neatly on a high-backed chair with his polished shoes beneath and a red sock of ambition inside each of them.

He heard me come in. Maybe he was expecting me. But the next few seconds were critical. This was his space. I had dared to cross his threshold. It must have been obvious to him that this was territorial. This was the bitch seeing if she had the same rights as the dog. What would he do?

Leaning on one elbow, his eyes completely clear, he said, "What on earth are you doing *there?*"

I felt I would die. I had made the most terrible mistake of my life by confusing love with the effect of drugs. Like Eamonn, I had climaxed too soon.

I tried to think of some excuse. I had come to say sorry or to check that he was feeling better.

Giving a typical scowly smile, he flipped the covers over. "Just come on in, Annie."

Lifting my nightdress over my head, I rushed across and jumped naked into bed with him and removed his pajamas. I had rights. I belonged here.

As my head hit the down pillow, I knew he loved not just my body but me, Annie Murphy. He could, as some men do, have rejected me because he had no immediate urge on him and needed sleep. But he didn't. He cared for me.

This was *our* room. I no longer hated or felt threatened by those clerical clothes. So much harness. My body fitted him much better. Womanly pink was his proper color, not black.

We lay together relaxed and possessive in one another's arms. His temperature was back to normal.

After a while, he began to stir and stormed my body again.

His lips brushed my nipples, which surprised him by the change of texture; he felt with wonder the wiriness of my pubic hair, my flesh smoother than a petal pressed between thumb and forefinger.

Once more, he disappointed himself for not being the perfect lover he had perhaps always been in his fantasies.

"I have a problem here," he sighed, expecting too much of himself. "I've mastered so many things but this has me beat."

"It's all right, Eamonn," I said. "It's going to be all right."

He kept apologizing, as he stroked my body. "It's not fair on you, Chicky Licky. You deserve better."

"It will come," I assured him, "don't try to force it," and I stroked him back to sleep like a young boy in my arms. We were one spirit if not yet one flesh. My cheeks, my breasts, my thighs smelled of him.

I, too, must have drifted off because I woke with a start. The storm was past. It was a morning of penetrating stillness; birds out-sang the sea. Through the thick closed drapes, the sun was flooding the room with blue-gold light.

Oh my God, what time was it? The bedside clock showed seven o'clock. Mary would be up within the hour to get his breakfast. I had to go, but he had given me the guarantee that there would be other nights.

Entwined in one another's arms like eels, we kissed for a long moment. Finally, with reluctance on both our parts, I dressed and returned, without a glance at the Stations of the Cross, to my room, where I slept dreamlessly.

Chapter Seven

H E WAS in my room at eleven, inviting me to spend the day with him in Killarney. Minutes after I said yes, Mary brought me tea and toast.

"These new drugs are marvelous," she said. "I never saw him looking so well after a bout of colitis."

I joined in praising the wonders of modern medicine.

"He ate two lamb chops for breakfast. Imagine that."

We set off at about midday. I was not in the least bit tired, and Eamonn seemed to have an additional bounce in his walk and a wide-eyed expression on his face.

His inability to bring me to orgasm had told in my favor. Sex, like mountain roads, challenged his abilities. He needed to find out how to drive my body so it thrilled to his touch.

"I knew it would happen the first moment I saw you. You, too, Annie?"

"I guess so."

"I had no idea," he admitted, "that I would find someone as beautiful and fresh as you."

"Fresh?"

"You started attacking me as soon as you saw me. My God, you were worse than Larry."

"Who's Larry?"

"You'll find out soon enough."

I touched his arm. "If you keep driving like this, one day you're going to run into someone and his face and yours are going to make one."

Maybe that image suggested the intermingling of bodies in the act of sex for, laughing, he proceeded to tell me how much our relationship fascinated him.

"It seems to me, Annie, that sex is far more complex than I thought."

He meditated aloud on it being multilayered.

"You teach me, Annie, and I have things to teach you."

I was more than willing.

After lunch in the Palace, I helped Pat in the office. Deadpan in expression, she knew how to get things done. I think she sensed the energy between Eamonn and me and it excited her because she wanted love in her life.

I took charge of her dog. Larry, a black French poodle, ruled the Palace with teeth of iron. Pat was crazy about him. He slept with her and loved her, hating the rest of the world.

It was some measure of Pat's usefulness that Eamonn put up with Larry. Between man and dog there was an undying enmity. They went for each other like an old-fashioned Catholic and Protestant. The first thing Eamonn did on entering the Palace was roll up a newspaper ready to swat the dog with it.

I whispered to Eamonn, "I remind you of *him?*"

"Ruff-ruff-ruff," he said.

I took Larry for a walk. He confirmed all my fears. Nothing in Killarney pleased him. I realized why Eamonn hated and admired him: the dog did not obey him and he liked a good fight. It was worth keeping in mind.

Back in the Palace, I took Larry into Eamonn's office. He was catnapping, but Larry immediately stirred him into life. It was instantly ruff-ruff-ruff from Larry and an even more vicious ruff-ruff-ruff from Eamonn. There they were, Bishop and poodle, eyeball to eyeball, trying to outbark each other.

Finally: "For God's sake, get him out of here, Annie."

Larry knew an enemy when he smelled one and, not liking Eamonn's tone, went for his foot.

Eamonn tried kicking him and when that failed, he put his feet up on the desk.

I said, "If you're not careful, he's going to bite your backside and how would Pat feel about that?"

I left the two of them to enjoy one another's company and went to chat with Justin. He was in the garden, which I loved because it had such neat rows of flowers and vegetables.

After that, I did some shopping, especially for eau de cologne, and explored Killarney. I liked its atmosphere, the sense that so much had happened there over the centuries.

That evening, Eamonn drank a large cocktail, and at dinner a bottle of Beaujolais, followed by a big Napoleon brandy. Not once did he mention our night together, not even when we sat for three hours by the fire in the living room. His policy was to give away as little as possible. Maybe he himself did not know what he would do. But a strange thing happened.

Without warning, he left the room and returned with a picture. He had been speaking of his mother and I assumed he wanted to show me what she looked like. It was, in fact, the photograph of a curly-haired boy about two to three years old. He merely let me glance at it as the prelude to telling me the child's story.

When working in London during the sixties, he had met a pregnant, unwed young woman.

"She wanted to keep her baby, Annie, and I warned her she could never cope. After six months, she realized it was better for Johnny—that's his name—if she had him adopted."

Instinctively, I said, "That must have hurt her a lot."

"Oh, it did. If only she had given Johnny up as soon as he was born."

"Did you advise that?"

"What else? 'Tis so much harder once the woman bonds with her baby. But she made the sacrifice for Johnny's sake. I had to help her over this difficult passage of her life." He gazed at the boy's picture. "Johnny was special, y'see, so much life and joy he had."

"What became of him?"

"I saw to it that the little feller was adopted by a wonderful family. He's very happy now."

It sounded as if he was still in touch with Johnny, who, by my reckoning, was now about ten. That pleased me.

I said, "Are you sure he's happier than he would have been with his natural mother?"

"Absolutely."

I disliked that kind of certainty. You could only be that sure by blinding yourself to most of the facts of life.

"What," I asked, "became of her?"

"His mother? She wanted to become a children's nurse."

I thought, *My God, she gives up her own child so she can take care of other people's.*

He was saying, God-like, "I provided the money. I presume she married. She probably now has a family of her own."

The indifference he showed to the mother's fate was in stark contrast to his interest in the little boy.

"May I see him, Eamonn?"

He handed me the picture. Staring out at me was what looked like a miniature replica of Eamonn. Even the bump in his top lip was the same.

"Well?" he demanded.

Was he confessing his sin or asserting his pride? Was he daring me or warning me? Did he want my criticism or approval?

Masking my desolate feelings, I handed the picture back with "A fine little boy."

He continued searching my eyes to find out what I was thinking, but I did not know that myself. I could not even be sure if my imagination had misled me.

I had taken it for granted that his fumblings of the night before were proof of sexual inexperience. What if they simply proved that he was not good at sex or that several years had passed since his last intimate relationship?

One thing had not varied: he liked to keep me guessing. With him, nothing could be taken for granted. Once again, I had the impression that only he was entitled to call the tune. And I could not guess the next note because this was jazz and he improvised.

When I retired for the night, he walked up and down the corridor, reciting his breviary. Those prayers scared me now and made me jealous. They also intimated that he had only the holiest intentions toward me and if bad things were to happen, he would not be the guilty party.

At about one o'clock, his bedroom door opened and closed.

My racing heart asked, What next? What did I want to happen? I had had enough surprises for one day.

Minutes later, I saw the doorknob of my room turning slowly. An exciting moment. How was he coming to me, as a priest or a lover? Would he be dressed in full pontificals, so to speak, and tell me, "Sorry, I made a mistake." Or was he coming to me naked in body and soul to confess his need?

The door edged open and he entered in stages. First his head with the keyhole eyes. A long-distance call perhaps? No, enter his sturdy torso in a dressing gown over pajamas with—no small detail—the cord of his gown tied so tight it almost cut him in half. He had a glass of brandy. Was this his shield, his comforter, or a painkiller for the big good-bye? If the last, what anesthetic had he brought me?

As he closed the door and came slipper-slapping toward me, he handwarmed the big glass globe. Watching the brown liquid going round and round, I felt drawn into a whirlpool. His body and mine entwined and eddied in the act of love. He and I were inside the glass, lovers' eyes hypnotized, mingling inextricably one with another.

He sipped the brandy. The first move had to be his.

"I had to say Mass today, Annie."

"Don't you always?"

He nodded. "But after what happened last night . . ."

Happened. He made it sound less like something we did than an act of God, say, a volcanic eruption.

He went on. "I felt I had to go to confession."

Ah, I thought, *so this* is *good-bye.* He couldn't live with a bad conscience. But why hadn't he said so by the fireside? And why get into pajamas and come into my room to say it? Was he wanting me to play the part of Eve so that he could enter my bed, enter me, and plead not guilty?

Sitting on my bed, he explained that he had told his confessor that he had had physical relations with a woman.

I hated that. A "woman." Wasn't Eve, mother of all trouble, called "Woman" in the Genesis story? And why the ambiguity of this phrase *physical relations?* This was plain, glorious, earthy sex. We weren't just wrestlers, for God's sake. It worried me that he used words to camouflage reality.

"My confessor told me to break it off, Annie."

Ah, his confessor had seen through the smoke screen. This *was* good-bye. It had been fine for the few hours it lasted.

"I told him, Annie, I didn't agree."

I gasped.

" 'I have an obligation to this woman,' I said. 'She is badly damaged in body and mind and can only be healed by a deep love.' "

He was speaking of me in the third person like a medical client. Was he to be my therapist or my lover? Was last night's wandering over my body with his hands a benediction, his priestly way of making me a good Catholic?

Eamonn was so like my father. Was that why I was so attracted to him? Daddy, too, had a split personality and enjoyed equally the good and bad in himself. His denial of the bad, like Eamonn's, was unconscious because it was necessary for his survival. He had been beaten by his German mother and his denial of the bad was his way of coping with the results.

In Eamonn's case, the abuse was spiritual. Mother Church had imposed unreal guilt and shame on him when he was a child, and this is the worst form of abuse there is.

Daddy was a gifted doctor, a devoted husband and father, a fighter for the downtrodden. At the same time, he drank so much he sometimes had to take a three-day break from his practice; and I know he whored around.

Eamonn was a marvelous, self-sacrificing pastor but he, too, drank too much and badly needed a woman.

Another similarity: Daddy and Eamonn were both jazzmen. Jazz entered deep into my psyche because Daddy had it in his bedroom, his car, he even had it piped into his bathroom so he would never be without it. Both he and Eamonn had a superb sense of rhythm. Most of all, they played life, they *made up* life as they went along. Eamonn was now jazzing around with me, inventing a music for me.

But he was right about one thing: I *was* wounded and far worse than he imagined. All the same, there was a massive denial on his part. He offered me love in the guise of medicine—"Take one twice a night." I accepted it because I needed it. The truth would out in the end. Either he loved me or he was just out for the kicks.

"Your confessor," I asked, "gave you the green light?"

"I think he saw my point of view."

One snicker from me would have torn apart his closely woven web of self-deceit. He and I had been brought up with the same moral code. We both knew there was no justification for what he was doing.

I had one advantage over him: guilt was not my enemy but my friend and accomplice. Being a bad Catholic is the best religion there is. Catholicism was my guide to happiness because by now I felt that it was unnatural. Turn its beliefs about behavior upside down and, behold, fulfillment.

However twisted men had made me, I was far more normal than Eamonn in one other respect: my fears, like my God, were real and not invented.

He never mentioned the confessor's name but I presumed it was Father O'Keeffe. In my brief meeting with him, I saw how he idolized Eamonn. Maybe, like me, Father O'Keeffe looked on him as a magician, as someone who was not bound by the usual rules.

"You mentioned your point of view. What is that?"

"Oh," he said, taking another sip of brandy, "that this is a passage in your life and someone must go with you and help you face its dangers."

The phrase *passage of life* brought me back to the mother of Johnny, Eamonn's spitting image. How had he helped her? Had he first messed up her life and torn her child from her before magnanimously helping her through a dark passage of life?

Moreover, did he intend to come into my bed so he could make me sound and chaste at the end? If he had sex often enough with me, might I end up like the Virgin Mary?

"Eamonn," I said, "I'm so grateful."

Another contented sip of brandy. "If God were here, He would approve of what I am doing."

I really didn't need this unorthodox foreplay. Only he needed convincing that sex was wholesome. That is why he had been forced to tamper with his God, making Him surprisingly tolerant toward a celibate bishop having "physical relations."

"Read the Gospels, Annie. The essence of Our Lord's message is love. I told my confessor, 'If love is what she needs, that is what I am obliged to give her.'"

I nodded understandingly.

"When Jesus let a street woman wash His feet, everyone was scandalized. Good men, they said, never let any woman touch them, let alone a whore."

Thanks, I thought.

"The same with Mary Magdalene, a prostitute. For all the snide comments of scribes and Pharisees, Jesus let her stay around so He could heal her."

Tears of laughter at the thought of Jesus taking Mary Magdalene into His bed sprang into my eyes, which, I think, he interpreted as gratitude.

"If Christ were in this room now, Annie, He would understand."

I could just see it: Jesus walking over to Eamonn while he burrowed away on top of me, tapping him on the shoulder and saying, "Well done, Bishop, keep it up."

In a quick mental somersault, it occurred to me that he really *was* doing a brave thing in loving me. What if from his point of view, it was a Christ-like sacrifice? What if we were driving along a road so perilous that not even his driving skills might be able to stop us going over the cliff? Into what? Not the sea, but the fires of hell. For me, heaven and hell were within but for Eamonn they were real places, and he was terrified of ending up forever in hell.

If these were his thoughts, thanks for your trouble, Eamonn, but I really don't want to be on the receiving end of episcopal sympathy. I didn't like Catholicism in a church; I certainly didn't want it in my bed.

"Love, Annie, covers a multitude of sins."

Because I really did love him, I spoke honestly.

"If you're only doing this for me, I'd rather go home. I don't need healing that badly."

"Believe me, Annie, you do."

I had had my say. The decision was his now.

Even talk of religion was sexy, in fact the sexiest thing of all because it stressed the forbidden. So the pump was already primed. Now we were both raring to go.

Chapter Eight

"IT IS QUITE chilly tonight, Annie."

"It's warm as toast in here."

"Would you mind if I—?"

"You want to sleep next to me?"

"Maybe."

After a minute or two's delay, he put his brandy glass on my bedside table, kicked his slippers off, and crept in beside me with his bathrobe on.

I said, laughing, "This is uncomfortable."

"Shush, girl, your giggle can be heard in Killarney."

I laughed even louder. "If you're concerned about modesty, why not wrap yourself in concrete?"

"Annie—"

"It's okay," I said. "If you really feel safe like that, leave the thing on."

I turned to the wall and pretended to snore.

I couldn't make him out. He had decided on my form of therapy; why delay implementing it?

He moved around restlessly while I, eyes open, still snoring, turned over again to play with the cord of his robe and tickle his face with the tassle.

"Don't do that," he begged. "You might leave a mark on my eye and how will I be able to explain it?"

Finally, I untied the cord.

"There, Eamonn," I said, coming awake, "more comfortable?"

"Indeed."

"Fine," and I started to play with the buttons on his pajama jacket, undoing the top three.

He hooted at this. "I am like a woman being stripped."

"No, Eamonn," I said, leaving his buttons alone, "you're a big boy and you can leave any time you want."

For answer, he put his hands under my nightgown and started to stroke my thighs and fondle my breasts. He was like a clothier testing the texture of his merchandise, the silkiness of the thighs, the bruise-like swelling of the breasts, the roughness of the nipples.

He removed my nightdress and threw it on the floor.

"Give it back," I cried.

For a moment, he thought I was resisting him.

"I might have a panic attack."

"You won't need that thing while I'm here."

"Don't count on it," I said. "I might run out of the house naked and you'd have to shoot me to preserve your honor."

He retrieved my nightdress and I rolled it up under my pillow. He then unclothed himself in a frenzy and the man took over from the priest.

Soon he was sating himself on me as before. And, though this time his erection lasted long enough for him to enter me, he ejaculated early, causing him to whimper, "God, not again."

I appreciated the fact that his distress was on my account, not his.

"No matter," I said, soothingly. "If you make that a big problem, it'll only get worse. Forget it."

"How can I?"

"Part of the trouble," I suggested, "is you drink too much. Guilt, shame, and drink are a pretty potent mix."

"But I'm thinking of you, Annie."

I waved his objection aside. If he knew more about me, he would worry less. For me, penetration was almost scary. What endeared him to me was that though he was starved of affection, he saw me as a human being and not an object.

"I really enjoy the womanly warmth of you, Annie," he enthused. "Inside you 'tis incredible."

He didn't just grunt and roll over. He verbalized the things he enjoyed.

He also encouraged me to say what I liked. I told him that when I was sexually aroused as now and failed to climax, I got a sharp headache, which was often the prelude to a panic attack. I reached for my nightdress just in case.

"How can I help you, Annie? Like this?"

"Yes, the nipples can be very sexy, but here below"— I took his hand—"is the most sensitive spot in my entire body."

He was anxious to do for me what I had done for him. He went on patiently, stroking my breast with one hand, searching for the sensitive spot in my vagina with the other.

The minutes went by and, "Still nothing?"

I smiled. "If you want a rest."

But he was a competitor. An hour passed. He varied his approach, going all over my body from head to toe, with his hands, lips, tongue, fingertips, kissing me and enjoying me while I told him stories about my life and my family.

In the long soothing silences, I had the courage to remember horrendous things.

My husband resented me. He was a prowler and very handsome, like a black-haired Steve McQueen. When we started going out together, he treated me so courteously I didn't realize what a stud he was. His ego hung on his ability to perform sexually. He was so attractive to beautiful women I often asked myself, "Why did he choose me?"

The answer when it came almost destroyed me.

One night of our courtship, we drove to a lonely beach. When I went to kiss him, he became enraged.

"Don't be a slut."

That was the first sign that we had problems.

"Are you crazy?" I said to him.

"Don't do *that*, you hear?" he yelled, brushing me aside.

I had simply kissed him without his permission. Must men always be in charge? He had the Madonna-Whore complex. I was meant to be unlike all other females: the one clean woman in his life.

That was not my idea of love. He was wanting to punish me for my own sexuality.

Eamonn interrupted my thoughts. "How are you feeling?"

This kind, considerate companion was wondering why women bothered to go to bed with men if sexual ecstasy was this hard. It had never occurred to his clerical mind that a woman's rhythms could be so different from a man's.

"Never felt better," I answered.

In the next hour, as I lay contentedly on my back and he stroked me all over, I felt safe to return to painful memories. I needed to bring them into consciousness to be healed of them.

I found out that Steven had run his father's candy store in Brooklyn from age nine. The store was full of girlie magazines. It wasn't Steven's fault, but this did him no good at all. I had to be the one pure snowy thing in his life to make up for the guilt he felt for all that smut. That was why if I showed the least sign of sensuousness, he raged at me.

He spent hours in the bathroom with glossy magazines, cutting up the women in them like a doctor doing surgery. Out of the prize pieces he created his perfect woman—flawless eyes, nose, breasts, legs, thighs . . .

I was unworthy because my skin was not silky enough, my nose not perfectly shaped, I had freckles. When I examined myself in the mirror, a pimple seemed bigger than my chin. This was another reason why I like dim soft lights and why I have to shower in the dark.

Why didn't I leave him? As well ask why a victim is transfixed by the rearing face of a cobra? The pious will never understand that evil is more fascinating than good, that some people sin in order to go to hell. And with the same single-minded fervor as the virtuous strive to get to heaven.

Often I thought murder was the holiest of deeds: my only defense against Steven would be to stab him in his sleep. But when he saw that I might leave him, he rekindled the old romance with passionate sex. Soon, of course, he was back to withdrawing, titillating while deliberately not fulfilling me. He was a torturer.

Eamonn, my dear kind Eamonn, was asking me whether I was any nearer to fulfillment, and to encourage him, I nodded yes. Was not this true fulfillment, to be loved and not tormented?

After Steven's baby was stillborn and I was suffering from panic attacks—I was down to eighty-nine pounds—he was once more very sweet. He could afford to be because I was broken. I would not disgrace him or rebel against him.

Why did I not pour out my heart to Daddy? Because I was ashamed of my husband's behavior. Because when you're exposed to such behavior you yourself become a special kind of victim; the high you get nearly blows your head off. And then the guilt, real guilt, not the sort that Catholics mumble in confession, made me cringe in the dark of my shower to try to get clean.

Thus was sex associated with wickedness. I was well prepared for such a connection by my Catholic childhood. The sisters did their best to convince me that I was evil, and that everything, especially the sexual, was a sin. This only made me fall head-over-heels in love with the bad.

When Steven saw I was beginning to enjoy myself, he was even more horrific.

I had to move out. The only question was when and how? The answer: At a time and in a way that hurt him most.

I must have smiled involuntarily at the thought of hurting Steven, for Eamonn said, "Is it working, Annie?" and I said, lying, but without malice, "Yes," and that made him happy, which, in turn, made me happy.

One day, Steven slapped my face five times. The shame of being beaten is more humiliating in some ways than anything. You feel more a thing, or, rather, a nothing. I knew that if I didn't leave then, I would die.

That night, having made myself look pretty to deceive, I said, "What would you like for breakfast tomorrow, darling?" Sitting on the end of the bed, he said, "I promise you I'll never hurt you again." I said, "That's good. Now about breakfast?" "I'll change, darling." I put my hand on his. "I know you'd like to, Steven." "I can, Annie. Without you I'd die," and I said, "I'm so pleased you feel like that. Breakfast will be a celebration of our reunion." He happily gave his order. Never have I enjoyed deceiving anyone so much. As soon as he went to sleep, I packed. I spent half the night packing. In the early hours, I called him a motherfucker for luck, laughed silently, and crept out of the house.

My sister Mary got me a job in Greenwich, in a boathouse by the sea. I looked after a darling kid called Joshua. I could just jump off our dock to swim. I had the use of a boat and a bike, so I got really fit. Mary lived nearby with her little boy, Bobby. We became really close, since she, like me, was in a busted marriage. I also went into therapy. It helped me choose never to marry again or have a child but to develop myself as a human being.

After nine months, Steven tracked me down through a private eye. By then I was booked for Ireland. One reason I fell in love with Eamonn straightaway was I hoped he would protect me from Steven if he appeared. Another was that I knew I could never marry him.

Now I was in bed, naked with my defender, the man who saved me from utter worthlessness.

Eamonn was finally sensing success and I could not believe it myself. He stroked the nipples and they were hardening. He saw the glazed look come into my eyes and the pool of perspiration in my navel. He felt the initial ripple of my belly and the shudder and the final huge fleshquake; and he heard my strangled consummation-cry and was overwhelmed with wonder. He derived more satisfaction from my pleasure than from his own. I had finally found, I thought gratefully, an unselfish lover.

When we had both recovered our breath, we nestled up to one another.

"When you started to react, Annie, I was scared that if you didn't climax, you would claw me to death."

"You are too valuable," I said.

"If I can do that with my hands," he said, in admiration of his own performance, "what'll it be like when I get my act together?"

We both looked forward to a fantastic future.

In his hours-long apprenticeship, he had grasped that a woman might be slower to have an orgasm than a man but when it came it was longer, of a greater intensity, and not so localized. A woman in love might prove to be a she-devil.

Exhausted, he dropped off to sleep in my arms about four while I was left with a puzzle. The men in my life who took sex lightly and thought it no sin had nearly destroyed me. Eamonn, who, in his heart, believed it to be a grievous sin, was, through his generosity, in the process of healing me.

In time, I, too, went to sleep and awoke through my inner alarm clock. If ever Mary found us together I would have to leave Inch. It was six o'clock.

I woke Eamonn and watched him search for his pajama

pants in the bottom of the bed. Bleary-eyed and dazed, he left me.

"Hey," I called after him, "you've forgotten something."

I put on my nightdress before gathering up the rest of his belongings. His pajama top was on the coverlet, his robe and slippers were on the floor.

I opened his door and threw them in, taking aim so his slippers hit him on the head.

"*Next time* be more careful," I said.

I was irritated that he was so irresponsible. He was, literally, leaving it to the woman to pick up the pieces. But for me, he would have stayed in my bed till eight o'clock before walking out of my room half naked to give Mary a heart attack. He would then have complained that she didn't have his breakfast ready. He was a selfish sex-sodden brute.

"It's fine for you," he said. "You can sleep on, I have to go to work."

"Good-*bye*," I said, resisting the temptation to slam his door. One of us had to be sensible.

I went back to my room and there, on my bedside table, was the brandy glass. My trophy.

I flung open the windows so I could breathe more easily and washed out the glass. After showering and putting on eau de cologne, I went back to bed.

What stage were we at?

The world was no more a stranger to me. I was kin to everything from pebble to star. I could die in an instant without one regret, without feeling anything unfulfilled in me. I was in love.

And he? Could what he felt for me be love when it was based so much on self-deception? Maybe not, but it was a beginning. Earlier, he had learned how good sex feels; tonight, he had tasted the inestimable joy of giving satisfaction to a woman. That, I told myself, is a form of power, bed-power, that his Lordship will not easily renounce.

In sum: was he mine now once and for all?

I had learned that my Eamonn of today was not the Eamonn of tomorrow. My jazzman seldom played the same tune twice.

But a woman in love can still hope, can't she?

Chapter Nine

WE ESTABLISHED a pattern for our nights.
After dinner, we chatted by the fire; he said the long prayers he was so fond of as a kind of aphrodisiac before coming to my room with his glass of brandy. We made love as part of my therapy. He had such a tender way of looking into my eyes, of embracing and fondling me, he made me feel valued as I had never felt before. He always left well before breakfast, never again forgetting his clothes.

One night, he said, "I'm not doing this just for carnal pleasure, Annie." He thought deeply before adding, "You're funny, you're playful and tempt me to do bad things, yet you can be very loving."

I proved it there and then until:

"Annie, a terrible thing is happening to me."

"Not a heart attack?"

"In a way. I think I'm falling in love with you."

By day, I often went to Killarney where I helped Pat Gilbride and spoke a lot with Father John O'Keeffe, whom I grew to admire more and more. Mostly, I stayed at Inch with Mary.

She loved cooking but hated domestic work. When I helped her clean the house, she was really grateful.

Mary, I learned, was a thorn in Eamonn's side but so good at entertaining he could not bring himself to dismiss her.

Once, she told me, she had disgraced him badly.

She had been to Castleisland, north of Killarney, to visit Eamonn's elderly cousin, Joan Browne, and got drunk. On leaving at 2:00 A.M., she crashed her Volkswagen through the gates of the police barracks, damaging the front door. The Guards rang the Bishop to ask him to fetch her home.

I told Mary she sounded as if she enjoyed the incident.

"Indeed I did. Himself had to pay for all the damages, including my new car, and it did his reputation no good." She winked at me. "He hates scandal, let me tell you."

"I know," I said, not sure if Mary was hinting or not.

"Oh," she laughed, "the expression on his face next morning when he brought me coffee! He said, 'You ought not to drink and drive,' and I said, 'You neither.' "

Dinner that night was something special. In view of Mary's story (I learned later that she was also on Valium, prescribed by her physician for a back problem—the combination was inflammable), Eamonn's rewarding her with a huge cocktail was surprising.

After his prayers, he came with a glass of hot milk fortified by brandy. To relax him, I ribbed him about Mary's escapade at the Guards station.

"Drunk she was, fluthered out of her mind."

"Drunk as a bishop," I said, realizing that Eamonn, who could not stand boredom, needed to be entertained.

"I had drunk quite a bit, true, but I wasn't legless."

He had been in bed that night. He ate something before he picked her up in case the Guards smelled liquor on his breath.

Propped up on a pillow, with his body swaying and his hands going up-up-up, he said:

"When I reached Castleisland, there was Mary with a bloodied head, stretched out and vomiting all over herself. Joan Browne and all my dear relatives were there to cheer me on, but really to gloat at my predicament."

He shook his head and ran nervy hands through his hair before swigging brandied milk to erase the memory.

"Anyway, Eamonn, it was good of you to bail her out."

"Bail *her* out. I only wanted it kept out of the papers. Had I not been a bishop I would have left her to her fate."

This worried me. He had an overriding need to safeguard his reputation even in this small matter. What lengths would he go to if he was really threatened?

That night, I began the lovemaking. But with a difference. To stop him wilting as soon as he was inside me, I smartly rolled him over on his back.

He looked really scared at this turn of events.

"God Al*mighty!*" he screeched. "Am I a log that you do this to me?"

I kept silent. Talk would help him relax so he could perform better, but I had to fix my mind on the sensuous.

Something in his eyes registered, *What am I doing upside down?* At first, I thought it was because he held that any but the missionary position was a sin. Certainly his dignity was compromised. A man, above all a bishop, had to be seen to be top dog, especially in bed. But unless he were underneath he would not have sufficient control to satisfy me.

From his unaccustomed position of inferiority he explained that his major concern was that I might get pregnant, especially as he was staying in me longer.

Being in the womanly position, he was thinking like a woman. It was almost as if he was asking himself, *What if I get pregnant?*

For the first time, he said, "This is a worry, Annie."

"Not for me."

"But if you conceive 'twould ruin your holiday."

"True," I said. "But I wouldn't mind having your child."

"Not right *now*, when we have only just begun."

I liked the promise in that remark.

"If you got pregnant, Annie, I'd die. I really don't want to make you sick and all that."

With me astride him, I wondered if what he really meant was, *I don't want to spoil my fun too soon.*

"You're a strange man," I said.

He looked up shortsightedly. "In what way?"

"Up to now, you've been upset because you couldn't enter me and now you're terrified because you can."

The expression on his face as he pondered this was so funny, I fell right off him and out of bed in convulsions and pulled the covers on top of me.

Eamonn was left lying naked on his back on a bare bed.

Moments later, two big swimming eyes peered over the edge.

"What in God's name," he yelped, "are you up to?"

I put my fingers to my lips and mouthed, "Mary."

"Why'd you think I gave her a special cocktail?"

With that, he tried to grab the bedclothes for fig leaves but I hung on to them so that he, too, fell out of bed on top of me. In doing so he banged his head on the wall.

I kissed his instantly bumpy cranium and we enfolded each other. Our whole bodies rocked with uncontrollable laughter. It made us more naked to one another than being without clothes. This was as one-making and sacred as sex. Twin selves were bonded by the greatest of all gifts: laughter.

"Oh, God," he gulped, his eyes disappearing in his mirth, "this is terrible. Sex is crazy." He clutched his chest. "I think I'm going to die."

"Don't try to kid me."

"Seriously, I've already had a slight heart attack."

"Sex is good for you," I said. "Without it, you might have a *big* heart attack."

"No, no, no," he said.

"It's not sex but the mad way you drive that'll make you ill."

He put the end of a sheet in his mouth to stifle his great guffaws. "Tomorrow . . . I . . . might . . . drive . . . faster."

"Why?"

"Thinking of all those fishes that just went into you."

"You've saved them up for forty-six years, can you imagine how potent they are?"

"Don't *say* that or I'll—"

"Wash my mouth out with soap and water?"

"How," he said, "did you know I was going to say that?"

"These fishes are more like bullfrogs."

"To kill 'em you'd need harpoons."

"At least."

"And there are millions of them," he gurgled.

"Maybe one of them will make a hit."

"Be serious, Annie," he said, with an owl-like hoot. "I've studied this a great deal. Stand up quick."

"Why?"

"Stand up, I say, and"—he demonstrated—"walk around."

"*I'm* not going to prance around naked."

"Sure I don't care what you're wearing or not wearing. I promise I won't look, just get those bullfrogs out of you."

Clutching the sheet more tightly round me, I asked, "What do you want me to do, gouge myself?"

"No, just walk around. These things swim. And they like warmth. Your egg is probably boiling after what we just did."

I couldn't get up because I was laughing too much. When he tugged on my sheet, I spun on the floor like a top.

"Please, Annie, you are in the worst possible position down there with your legs waving in the air. Keep them *still*."

"But you just told me to walk around."

"Waving your legs upside down is the worst thing. All the blood goes to your lower parts and these fishes love warm blood. *Get the blood out of there*."

We waited a couple of minutes for our gales of laughter to blow out before we got back into bed and pulled the covers around us. He felt more mine than ever.

As we nestled up to one another, he told me that his favorite niece, Helena, was coming to stay.

"You remember her from the old days?"

I reminded him that I had first seen his sad eyes when he came on a week's visit to the States in 1954 to see his sister Kitty, who was Helena's mother. I had wanted then to take him by the hand and tell him it was going to be all right.

"Remember, Eamonn?"

He shook his head. "Anyway, Helena is bringing her four children and her sister, Maureen."

"Is she okay now?"

Maureen, born premature, had weighed two and a half pounds and was given no chance to live.

"As far as she will ever be," Eamonn said.

When I was a girl, my mother visited Helena's mother. Kitty O'Hara, recently widowed, was living then in a run-down New York tenement. Kitty was so ill she couldn't care for her five children. My mother had the guts and good sense to tear the newborn Maureen out of Kitty's arms. The baby was starving and covered with lice. Also, mentally retarded.

My parents took the whole family to our home in Connecticut. Those kids were wild and they gave their lice to us. Everyone called us "dirty Irish." Even Daddy got lice and was unable to make his hospital visits for three days.

Daddy gave the O'Haras vitamins and Mommy fed them good food. In one month, they were all back to health.

Eamonn was saying, "I keep two double beds in my room to house families like Helena's."

He had a special interest in Helena. When she came back from America in the fifties, he had helped her overcome her fears. He had even taken her to London where he introduced her to her husband, Patrick.

Eamonn seemed to look on Helena as the reincarnation of another Helena, his saintly and prolific mother who had, besides ten kids, several miscarriages to help her on the road to heaven.

"If Helena takes over your room, where will you sleep?"

"In the spare bedroom."

This room was used for vesting when he said Mass at home.

I was not happy that his niece had rights over his room when mine were not yet firmly established. The forbidden deed was taking place in my territory. This, I think, helped Eamonn fool himself that sex was not sin but therapy.

"Remember Inafield, Eamonn?"

He smiled. "Didn't I spend a day there with your family? I met your parents, Peter and Johnny, and your sister, Mary."

"*And* me."

"Did I, now?" he said, teasingly.

Inafield, our home "in a field" of fifty acres, was a big old Victorian hunting lodge five blocks from the center of Redding, Connecticut.

I stored in memory almost every moment of that day. I heard crazy stuttering laughter coming from our pine-paneled bar and I, who could never resist laughter, wondered what sort of person could possibly make a noise like that.

It was Eamonn. I went into the bar and jumped up on the radiator because I wanted to hear it again.

That was the first time he met my father. He was always thankful to Daddy for helping Kitty. His gratitude was finally expressed in his offer to help me find serenity in Ireland.

He and my father got on famously. He made Daddy play all his Dixieland jazz. Eamonn tapped his feet and swayed from the hips and moved his hands as though music was coursing through his body like blood.

Sixteen or so years later, I found myself lying naked next to the jazzman, asking, "Hey, remember how I cursed you?"

"Wait, 'tis coming back into focus."

"You told me to stop and I said I would for fifty cents and you said, why should I pay you to stop cursing me? So I took you into my bedroom where I kept a big Indian head I used as a piggy bank. 'Put fifty cents in there,' I said, 'and no more curses from me.' You said 'Why pay you to stop being wicked?' So I called you a son-of-a-bitch and you ran after me threatening to wash my mouth out with soap and water and I yelled, 'Stop it, if Daddy hears about this he'll kill you.' And you said, 'I'll tell him you cursed,' and I said, 'I'll tell him I didn't,' and you said, 'Why would he believe you and not me?' and I said, 'Because I'm the best liar around.' "

"You were a liar even then, Annie."

"I've reformed," I lied.

"I can tell," he lied. "Didn't I chase you somewhere?"

It occurred to me that his chasing of me, like his famous laugh, had stayed in my mind through the years without my knowing it.

"You chased me into the garden where there were raspberry bushes and I hid inside them and laughed and cursed at you all the louder because I was getting scratches on my legs and you were laughing too but red-faced because your groping hands couldn't quite reach me and you said, 'Just you wait, little Annie, one day I'll catch up with you.' "

He stroked my breast fondly. "Didn't I keep my word?"

Sure, I thought. *But my curses did work, after all. Eamonn, you should've paid up your fifty cents.*

"When Helena comes," he said, "I will be spending quite a bit of time with her."

"Even nights?"

"Indeed. I settle down on the chaise longue and sometimes we talk into all hours. So don't be surprised if in the first couple of nights you don't see me at all."

"What'll *I* do?"

"Catch up on some sleep."

"You can surely pop in for a minute or two."

"God Almighty, Annie," he said, "you won't come to the door and whistle for me?"

I winked at him and purred like a kitten.

"If I'm hungry, I'm not sure what I'll do."

"I believe you," he said. "But remember, she's a woman with a woman's instincts."

"Then," I said, "don't use so much after-shave."

"Why not?"

"I smelled it on you the moment you kissed me at Shannon and we don't want Helena smelling it on both of us."

"True, and you use less perfume, then."

"And make sure you shave more closely."

He was puzzled by this.

I said, "My chin is getting red and flaky." I pointed. "How will Helena think I got this?"

"God Al*mighty*, 'tis as red as my socks. Even Mary'd notice it. And Pat would, certainly."

"It's okay, Eamonn, I've got some cucumber for it."

"Mary told me you are partial to cucumbers."

"Not for eating. I spit bits out into my table napkin. A slice of cucumber soaked in tea draws out the redness. Pancake makeup does the rest."

"Amazing," he said. "Maybe next time I should shave before I come to bed."

"Provided," I said, laughing, "you don't use an electric razor. Helena would stay awake all night wondering."

"And please, Annie, be sure not to scratch me above my collar, especially on my sensitive ears."

I giggled again. "Aren't I always careful to only scratch you where it doesn't show?"

"I don't mind love bites on my belly but not on my *nose*."

"What about your head?"

"That, too, is off limits."

When I roared at him like a tiger and showed my claws, he nearly fell backward out of bed.

"Life is very complicated sometimes," he mused. "But we have to be ultra-careful with Helena. She knows me well."

"Eamonn," I said, "I don't imagine anyone in the whole world knows you well."

Chapter Ten

I N MID-MAY, Mary took off for a few days to her farmhouse across Dingle Bay.

When Helena came from Dublin by train, we embraced
warmly. How different she was from the jumpy, blotchy-
faced girl I remembered. Her dark shiny hair was pulled back
in a bun. She was smartly dressed and serene, though she
looked tired from having four children in quick succession.
The last, John, was only a few months old.

For the next week, the character of the house changed. It
was noisy and full of fun.

I enjoyed Helena's company. She appreciated my help
and that of my family for her sister. Now aged seventeen,
Maureen's body sagged, especially her tremendous breasts.
She had bright red hair. Her eyes were slightly vacant under
long lashes. Being innocent, she said whatever came into her
head.

The bishop in Eamonn found this hard to take.

Maureen's job was to take care of the children. She proved
her common sense one afternoon when Helena was resting
on her bed and I walked with her up the mountain track.

I was pushing John in a red baby carriage when, high on
the hill, we came across a bull lying in an open field.

I was terrified. If anything happened to a child of Helena's,
Eamonn was old-fashioned enough to take it as a sign from
God that we should part.

The bull slowly heaved himself to his feet.

I laughed so hard, out of nerves, I fell on the ground while Maureen grabbed the handle of the carriage and tore downhill.

Alone, on the ground, with a bull moving inquisitively toward me, I cried out to no one in particular, "Save me."

When I dared to look, the bull had turned away.

I scrambled to my feet and walked slowly after Maureen. Once I turned a corner, I ran till I caught up to her.

When we reached the house, there was Eamonn.

"What happened to you?"

When I told him about the bull: "Sure 'twould have done you no harm."

My God, he was even an expert on bulls!

Eamonn had sent Maureen to a school to learn about hotel cooking and housekeeping. At dinner, she said:

"I like the dances."

"Oh, really," he said, suspiciously.

"I love it when they hold me tight."

"Who," he snapped, "holds you tight?"

"Boys. I love it when they kiss me."

The eyes of Eamonn, guardian of morals, were like saucers.

"*Kiss* you?"

He went very red, showing his long-standing horror of sex. Unless, as with Helena, it was inside marriage and fertile.

Later, at bedtime, we all hugged each other. It hurt me to see how Eamonn pulled away from Maureen. I gave her a long hug to try to compensate.

That night, he was able to come to me, after all, at around 1:30. We spoke and moved quietly in the bed. It was of horsehair and solid, but Helena was in the next room. The whispers, the proximity of danger made the sexuality all the more intense.

At first, we giggled over Maureen but he thought her wanting kisses was wrong while I felt he was interfering with nature, like belling a blackbird or painting a pheasant.

"But she *mustn't*," he said, hoarsely.

"*We* do."

"We are not handicapped."

"Anyway, if she gets pregnant you will be responsible."

"Me?" he shrieked. Then, more quietly: "Me?"

"You don't teach her about birth control."

"God Al*mighty*, Annie, you say such terrible things."

"More terrible than you suggesting she is not entitled to sex like us?"

"Nature," he sighed, "can be very cruel."

"If you pity her, why didn't you give her a proper hug?"

"Her big bosoms, Annie, are suffocating."

"Unlike mine."

"Yours are just right."

I flattened them against his chest as our fingers and toes interlaced.

"You have a lean, flat stomach, Annie. You're long legged and you have beautiful eyes."

He kissed and bit me and tickled me with his sensitive hands and probed my mouth with his tongue, then going below, he licked me along ribs and hips as a mare licks a newborn foal.

Next, I felt his body go into spasm and I thought, *He has climaxed already,* then, *No, he's laughing, but why?*

In fact, he was sneezing. Or, what is worse, trying desperately not to.

He came up heaving for air and gasping, "What have you dowsed yourself with down there? 'Tis worse than pepper."

I admitted to having poisoned his nosegay with perfume.

"God," he coughed, "something really bad's been done to you. Sex is beautiful. There is so much to heal in you."

I said, "You are like the bull in the pasture."

"Oh, so now 'tis like an unlicensed bull you make me out."

"You saved up pollywogs for years, millions of them. Keep having sex with me and you'll get rid of some of them."

After a stifled sneeze: "Going to exhaust me, are you?"

When his sneezing had eased, he entered his nest with, "Oh, how . . . I . . . like—"

He liked the feel of flesh on flesh but, best of all, he was caring of me. That was why I was able to respond to him and I came myself after not too long a struggle.

We were mellowing into love.

To add spice to the evening, I said, "Are you sure you don't want me to lock the door?"

"Not at all. Whoever tried it would know something was going on in here."

"Between Annie and Uncle Eamonn."

"With her brute strength, Maureen'd knock the door down."

I blinked and jerked my head back on purpose.

Out of bed in a flash, he scampered low and naked into the bathroom, closed the door, and whispered, "Turn the bathroom light out."

"Why? Who would dream you're in there naked?"

"Maureen might come in for a chat. You shouldn't have been so nice to her."

So that was why he had not given her a big hug earlier.

"If she comes," he hissed, "she'll probably want to use the bathroom. Sometimes she goes all night."

"Why didn't you tell me this before, Eamonn? Instead of kissing her, I might have hit her on the head."

"This is serious, Annie."

"Then what'll I do with your clothes?"

The bathroom door opened to let his head through.

"My pajamas, under the pillow, bathrobe, in the bed. No, Maureen might see the lumps. Bring 'em here."

"They're safer under my pillow."

"Do as you're *told*. Quick, it's cold in here."

"Shut the window."

"It won't budge."

"Only one solution. We'll shower together."

"Are you mad? It's so rickety, the hot pipes would fall off the wall, burn our private parts, and scald us both to death. Then the locals would take us both as we are, naked and copulating, to the funeral parlor."

"In an ambulance, I hope."

"Seated in the back of a jaunting car. Don't laugh, Annie, I know these people. That woman who owns the bull would put me naked in a car just to spite me."

If he were ever found out, I felt, he would run from the country out of fear of compatriots like that.

"But," he went on, "I'd crawl out of here if I were dead and dress myself in pontificals before the lying-in-state."

I sounded a note of caution. "If you turned stiff you wouldn't be able to dress yourself."

"My guardian angel'd help me. I've prayed to him enough."

I couldn't stop laughing or loving this man with his child-like imagination.

"Stop it, Annie. I'm never again sleeping with you without wearing at least my pajama bottoms."

"Why?"

"Because it'd be terrible for the Church if a bishop were to be caught dead with his pants down."

"What do you mean?"

"If I have a heart attack, my backside will be too heavy for you to put them on me."

"I'm not going to like you always wearing pants."

"I'll be naked at the appropriate moments."

"Thanks for that."

"Now, bring me my clothes."

A hand appeared round the bathroom door. As he scrambled into his pajamas, he gave me orders.

"Switch the light off. Wait three minutes and if no one comes, tap on this door."

I waited for at least ten minutes, giggling all the time, hearing him trying to stifle his own snorting laugh and muttering, "I never did like this fecking bathroom. One of these days I'm going to tear it apart."

Finally, there was a weak-voiced "Surely to God three minutes is up now."

"How would I know what time it is with the light out?"

"Then turn it on and have a see."

I switched on the light for a moment.

"Well?" he demanded.

"I don't know what time it was when I switched it off."

My bathroom door opened; footsteps approached the bed.

"Peep into the corridor, Annie, and check it's safe."

I prolonged the agony as long as I could but I eventually gave him the all-clear at about four. He went back to the spare room after noisily using the corridor bathroom.

Heavens, I thought, *he even tries to deceive people when he pees.*

Chapter
Eleven

I N BETWEEN domestic chores, Helena and I chatted for
hours at the breakfast table and over the fire in the living
room.

She kept getting flashbacks to her years in America and
these made her anxious. That was why Eamonn spent hours
of the night assuring her that everything would be well for
her and her children.

On the third morning, Eamonn said he intended joining our
beach party that day. At about eleven, he appeared in slacks
and an open-necked shirt. Surrounded by people who loved
him, he was in his element.

Maureen was in a thin cotton dress. Helena was in a black
one-piece swimsuit. I had not brought a bathing suit to Ireland
but the night before I had fished out a bikini top and a pair
of jeans, the legs of which I had scissored off to the thighs.
My husband had made such fun of my legs I was scared to
show them in public.

Eamonn whispered, "Why are you wearing *those?*" but I
did not want to talk about it.

As soon as we reached the near-deserted beach, he stripped
to his swimming trunks, white with blue stripes. Tearing at
his hair, he said, "I just have to get in there." He ran and
barreled his way into the sea as if he wanted to swallow it
up. After a dip and a few strokes, he stood with water stream-
ing off him and calling to us, in a thrilled voice:

"Come on in, 'tis won-der-ful."

I was toe-tickling the rills of spent waves on the sea's edge and telling Helena, "We can't go in, it's cold as melted snow," while Eamonn was all the while hello-ing us and yelling, "The only way is to run right in."

He stood there, his hair plastered to his head, his eyes wide open. When a big wave hit him, he merely laughed that loud velvety laugh of his.

Helena's daughter Jenny started to walk into the sea and was knocked over, which caused Eamonn to rush back and rescue her. Putting her on his shoulder, he walked out until the water was up to his chest. Finally, he restored her smiling to her mother.

Helena nudged me. "I don't know what sort of husband he would have made, but what a fantastic father."

Yes, there was Eamonn, no longer the great god directing people's destinies but the head of a family.

My mind went back to when my own family was on vacation at Rockaway Beach, New York. I was five or so. My mother was sober, tanned, and beautiful, and all four of us kids were playing on the sands. Till Daddy, with me on his shoulders, went marching into the sea on his stork-like legs. Waves crashed around us and over our heads. I spluttered, "Daddy, Daddy," and pulled on his circlet of hair and tugged on his ears. He reacted by stroking my leg. "It's okay, sweetheart." He swiveled me around on his shoulders so I could look into his eyes. "Nothing's going to happen to you." I felt safe in his arms, as safe as Jenny now felt in Eamonn's. As safe as *I* wanted to be in Eamonn's arms forever.

Helena's doubt about Eamonn's being a perfect husband challenged me. I looked out to sea and saw the sun transfiguring his lovely face and the waves foaming about his neck and shoulders. He was everything I ever wanted. He was the man with the helium-filled balloons that would help me fly.

All the things till now denied me could be given me through this man, *my* man. He was a wizard like my father.

As a kid I always looked on Daddy's surgical skills as a kind of magic. He cut into your flesh and poked around inside you; whereas anyone else would kill you, he healed you. He removed all the bad and sewed you up again so you were better than before. He healed minds, too. He healed them with his humor, sometimes caustic when he refused to let patients yield to the sickness of self-pity. Pain, he said, could be a healing force.

Used to the magic of life, I believed in the impossible.

Eamonn was a surgeon, too. He had taken on many sick people like Siobhan, Helena, and me and was presently challenging the mighty sea. Would he be able to break away from the stationary, immovable earth of his past and come away with me to dreamland? And if he would not do this for me, maybe he would for a child of his own? In my bed I had seen him as a man; on the beach I saw him for the first time as a father.

I had always loved children but I hated my husband so much that the only baby I had carried, his, I failed to love. But I could not fail to love Eamonn's. He would love and cherish our child and our child would love and respect him. And even if he rejected it as I rejected my first child, I would not. I'd still have a part of Eamonn to carry with me through life.

While the kids paddled in small pools and played with buckets and spades on the sand, I waved to Eamonn and shouted, "I'm coming in."

The sea, with rainbow colors shining on it, was our balloon, the element that buoyed us up and took us away from earth.

I swam right up to him and we went away together like a couple of fishes.

"You really can swim, Annie," he puffed, admiringly.

To prove it, I went under and pulled his trunks down.

He dragged me up to the surface, hissing, "Stop it. If I emerge from this water naked, I'll kill you."

"Take it easy," I said, laughing and making him laugh.

"I wish I'd never brought you out here. God Almighty, if I float on my back you'll nip the trunks off me. You said you were afraid of the water and you're not, you deceitful witch."

A big wave hit me, and crying, "Help, help," I sank. And he came searching for me and lifted me up.

As our heads rose out of the waters we saw it at the self-same moment. Reflected off diamonded water was the land, with yellow dunes, and children paddling and making sand castles. Sheep, lambs among them, and a single ram were grazing on the emerald green and corn-yellow slopes of the cliff, and above us was a motionless sky without a cloud.

And we, the only bathers, companions in peril, seemed to be apart from humankind, in our own magic bubble, our own watery birth sac, baptized with a real baptism into our own new world of being. And the cold cold sea had turned kind and warm in us and bonded us as sex and laughter had already done.

"The undertow can rip you, Annie. Don't get overconfident."

He was warning me not to get in over my head. He knew his limitations, but he was afraid that I did not.

"I might be able to save you, Annie, but drowning people sometimes beat the hell out of their rescuers."

He was back fearing what people would make of scratches and bruises above the line of the clerical collar. The spell was broken. But not entirely.

As soon as we were home, while Helena attended to her kids, Eamonn came into my room. I wore only panties as I dried my hair with a towel.

"Wasn't that invigorating?" he said, breathing deeply. "Before, I was very, very tired. And look at you, Annie. Radiant."

True. The anxiety that surrounded me seemed to have been rinsed out of me.

"I thought you'd be too scared to go in the sea, Annie."

I said, "I saw you delighting in it and I have shared so many things with you I wanted to share that, too."

He felt my breast. "*Touché.* I'm getting out of here now, so lock the door behind me." He winked. "So I'm not tempted to come back in."

All that day, he and Helena did the cooking. Dressed in black slacks and a bright, striped shirt, he was filling the kids' glasses with lemonade and ours with wine and cocktails as we sunbathed in the garden. He gave everybody an equal amount of time and attention.

Helena, now shiny with joy, confided in me that she had been hysterical when she knew she was carrying Jenny. She had wanted a rest from childbearing. When Jenny was a year and a half, she started having seizures, with a temperature of 104. Patrick, her husband, was away on business, the doctor couldn't come. Certain that Jenny was going to die, she put it down to her own reluctance to have her.

"It was only myself and God who saved her."

This explained why she was always edgy when Jenny disappeared for a few moments.

After Jenny recovered, Helena was ready to accept as many children as God sent her. Anything was preferable to the guilt of a dead child.

I understood only too well. Helena helped me realize that other women felt as I did.

She had obviously told this story to Eamonn and he had helped her see the spiritual dimension of it. As a result, he not only judged Helena to be the ideal Irish woman, he probably saw a parallel between her experience and mine.

Maybe he thought he would be able to heal me as he had healed her.

Chapter
Twelve

WHEN HELENA left, Mary came back and life at Inch returned to normal.

Tanned and full of energy, Mary looked around the house and called me a saint. She had expected to have to clean up after all the children but I had done it for her.

She made us lunch of spaghetti bolognese while I prepared a salad. We also drank sherry together. Only a sip, she insisted, time after time, winking.

That lunch was fun. She criticized the Bishop for being such a miser. Long-hosted spite came out of her for hours till the shadows lengthened and heavy rain started to fall.

"I see a tremendous closeness between you and the Bishop," she said. "Watch him."

Without a word, she staggered out of the kitchen into the living room. I found her on her knees at the liquor cupboard.

"When's he coming back, Annie?"

"About ten."

"Gives us plen'y of time."

She tugged out one expensive bottle after another.

I uncorked a decanter of Madeira and took a swig.

"Good for you, Annie Murphy," she said with a laugh. "I happen to know how he makes cocktails."

She mixed large measures of vermouth, gin, vodka, brandy, fruit juices, and crushed ice in a shaker.

"That," I said, "would kill a Shire horse."

As she poured the cocktail out into two nine-inch silver goblets, wind and rain gusted against the french windows.

She set the glasses on a low coffee table in front of a roaring fire. Having finished one drink, she helped herself to another. Soon she was wobbling.

We put on some Irish music. It was the signal for Mary to go back to the cupboard and draw out an unlabeled bottle.

"Gin?" I asked. "Vodka?"

She winked both eyes because she could not wink one on its own. "Ireland's own. Poteen." She uncorked the bottle and sniffed. "Oh God, dear God, the *smell* of it."

I grabbed the bottle and the licorice smell made my head rock back.

"'Tis the secret of everblasting life."

I giggled at her slip of the tongue.

She took a vase filled with flowers, tipped the contents into the fire with a smoky sizzle, half filled the vase with poteen, and drained it.

"Why'd you do that, Mary?"

"Never like mixing my drinks."

I was sober enough to realize that Mary was not just gone, she was beyond-the-Himalayas gone.

She squirted, out of the side of her mouth, "Bed."

She tried to get up and did a split.

I lugged her to her feet like a sack of coal.

"Thassright. Get poor Mary to beddy bed."

With that she fell to the floor. I grabbed her feet and dragged her out the room, across the corridor, and into her bed. Kneeling down briefly beside her, I begged her, "Don't die, Mary."

Recent events—Helena's visit, the swim in the sea—made me want to indulge an entirely new mood.

Good-bye, godly cleric, I thought. *Put all restraints behind you, Eamonn, and live.*

I put on an aggressive low-cut tie-blouse decorated with red roses and tight-fitting black velvet pants with a wide red belt. I brushed my hair so it stood up high and put on big jangling Indian earrings. Having applied makeup, I peered into the mirror and decided, pursing my lips to kiss my own image, good enough to wow the returning warrior.

I had enough of sleeping with him after he had insulted both me and his God by praying for nearly an hour. Tonight, no grace before meals. This was my show.

Back in the living room, swaying this way and that, I played very loud music. First, "Suspicion" by Elvis Presley. Then some Sinatra, beginning with "Bewitched, Bothered and Bewildered."

All the while I was jumping like a cat from the couch to the chair and growling.

Through the slanting rain beyond the windows, I saw the headlights of his car as it screamed up the drive and halted by the front door.

I turned the music up to maximum. Blaring away at the time was "Fly Me to the Moon." That was the sound that greeted Eamonn when he came through the front door. Nothing, though, could have prepared him for the sight of me, with glistening eyes and exploding hair as I lay barefoot and purring among the crystal on top of his glossy black piano.

He came into the living room dressed impeccably with his episcopal chain round his neck. After two steps, his chin fell as he surveyed the chaos, including his precious bottles scattered around.

"God Al*mighty*," he roared above the music, "you're *drunk*. Where's *Mary?*"

"Dead."

"All that liquor. Did you drink it?"

"Mary poisoned herself."

"She must have just passed out," he said. "But she may have vomited in her sleep and choked."

He ran out of the room and straight back in again.

"Annie"—he shook a wavy hand at me—"don't move on my piano till I get back. You might scratch it or break my best Waterford crystal."

He ran across the corridor to Mary's room and came back seconds later, saying, "She's gone, she *is* dead."

Though tipsy, I could see how excited he was. After a bare dark mountain road came this assault on all his senses: dimmed lamps and firelight on gleaming wood and crystal, thick-pile rugs, skin-tingling music, a young woman looking good with animal smells and movements, the sensuous, slightly orgiastic challenge to his own dull orthodox attire.

How would he react? A precious clue: his foot was tapping to the music. This was for him a much better prelude to lovemaking than walking up and down for ages past the Stations of the Cross.

He had only been to Mary's room to check that she would not wake in a hurry. The intoxicating music, the Puck-style paganism was new to him and he, taster of all life's wines, found it irresistible.

I congratulated myself on knowing my man so well.

"You have corrupted her, Annie."

"She got drunk before I came."

"Never before in this house."

He poured himself a brandy. Twirling the big globe, he came up to me and said, "Mind that glass. You could get splinters in your backside."

"You're worried about your mother's piano."

"That, too," he admitted. "Get down, now." He held out his hand. "Down."

When I refused he went to switch off the music.

"Don't do that," I warned him, "or else."

Seeing I wanted to control the scene, he came back to me and extended his hand. I took it and jumped into his arms. Taken by surprise, he fell back on the floor, spilling brandy all down him.

"My poor back," he yelled, "you snapped it in two."

I kept running around the room and jumping clean over the big high-backed cushiony couch. He lay down on the couch, maybe in the hope of getting me to lie next to him.

"C'mon, c'mon, c'mon," he urged.

I took no notice. I jumped on top of him from unexpected angles and before he could grab me I was off on another cat-like tour of the room, sniffing and miaowing.

Finally, I jumped on top of him and started to undo his clericals. I got his jacket off so I could work on the gold chain with the cross on it that always frightened me.

"'Tis very heavy." In holding up his hand to check me, he showed his ring with a big amethyst surrounded by diamonds. "You'll break my neck."

"I will if I'm careful."

I tried to pull his ring off but he clenched his fist as if to say, "Anything but that."

He feared that in my present mood I might fling it in the fire or over the cliff. He saw I wanted that ring not because it was worth a fortune but because it symbolized he was wedded to something other than me.

"I want to put it on, Eamonn. I do, I do."

"Don't be ridiculous, pet. You have tiny fingers and it would fall off you. Please, I love you, but stop."

I refused so he took refuge in another glass of brandy.

"Would you mind if I turned down the music a little bit?"

"Just . . . a . . . little . . . bit."

For the next few minutes I kept coming around the couch and growling at him.

Finally, in mock terror, he stood on a chair, which I tipped over, bringing him down on the floor.

"Don't scratch me above the collar," he pleaded. "Or I'll get the scissors out and cut your nails."

"I would stick you with them."

His gaze met mine without a waver.

"I'd do the same to you, Annie. You have met your match."

"Not when I'm drowning in a sea of alcohol, Eamonn. I have tre-*men*-dous strength."

When I finally cornered him, I started ripping more of his clothes off and scattering them. With each item of his removed, I removed one of mine—my blouse for his shirt, my velvet slacks for his pants—as though we were playing strip-poker. He himself chose to remove my bra.

"Does it unhook at the back or front? God, you need to be a magician to get rid of these things. Ah, it opens at the front and out they pop."

In the end, we danced naked before the flashing fire. It was rough but it was fun and very sexy.

Finally, we made love on the Afghan rug in front of the fire. Alcohol warmed us within and the peat fire without, and Frank Sinatra was serenading us and a compliant wind howled its approval from the sea.

He was more masterful than I, who was by then high as a kite. He went touring all the isles and inlets of me, verbalizing his pleasures in every place. That night, he was top dog and I felt he would not yield that right easily again.

After we were more than satisfied, we lay on our backs in silence, contemplating the still white sky of the ceiling.

"Now, Annie," he said, rolling over at last, "you must get some sleep. Your pulse is racing."

I *was* beginning to feel bad. He led me to my bed where I fell straight asleep with him next to me, so happy he broke his vow never to sleep again without wearing his pajama pants.

About four in the morning I sat up with an electric start. Owing to the alcohol I was having a panic attack. I felt that he/she/it/they were about to kill me.

I nudged him awake. It took a while.

"Eamonn," I gasped, "go to Mary's room."

"What? *What?*" Seeing me shaking: "What's the matter?"

"Panic attack. Valium. Mary keeps it in her bedroom."

"I can't go in *there.*"

"You must. I'm paralyzed with fear."

"What shall I do?"

"Just told you."

"But Valium after all that alcohol might kill you."

He got up and fell over before he managed to struggle into his pajama pants.

"Put something on, Annie, and come with me. I don't know where her tablets are."

"Bring me at least two or I'll kick your mother's damn piano to pieces with my bare toes. *Run.*"

He vanished in a totter down the corridor. I heard him in Mary's room rummaging around for minutes that took years off my life. I couldn't wait any longer.

Slinging on my knee-length nightdress, I ran into his bedroom for the nearest exit, flung open his french windows, almost breaking them, and crashed out onto the lawn. There I lay with racing heart and pumping lungs in the friendly dark, burying my head in my hands. I rolled around, feeling on my skin the cold wet grass and cold morning air.

Moments later, Eamonn was inside my room, calling out, "Annie? Where are you?" He must have heard his french window blowing in the wind because he came staggering blindly out of the house and changed to a frantic yell:

"For God's sake, don't play games with me. I'll die."

I was only a few feet from him but he couldn't see me—

why didn't he get himself glasses?—and I couldn't speak to let him know where I was. My tongue filled my mouth and my head was as noisy as a flour mill.

He called out pitiably, "Come back in, Annie. I've got the tablets. Take as many as you like."

I wanted them desperately but had to watch in silence as his silhouette went shuffling past me down the drive.

Was he going to walk in his flip-flops to Killarney?

I heard him fall heavily and get up, crying, "I might have gone over the cliff, Annie. Why are you doing this to me?"

Gradually, by meditating, by setting aside all distractions, I was getting my breath back.

"I'm dying, Annie, dying."

I really didn't care a damn at that moment. Rather, I knew he was the great survivor. My problem was staying alive myself.

He returned toward the house, moaning, "God help me, I am dying surely. I'm getting a heart attack. Or a brain hemorrhage. Yes, something's badly wrong in my poor head."

I wanted to say, *Shut your mouth and let me concentrate*.

"You goddamn bitch, Annie. Why don't you think of *me?*"

If I do, I thought, *that'll be two of us*.

I could see him with his hands held high in the air, one of them with a glass in it, praying dramatically to his God, who must have listened unsympathetically.

His gesture of supplication made me want to laugh. That terrified me. Laughter would lose me the last of my breath.

Westward, the scudding clouds momentarily parted, silvering the earth and allowing Eamonn, his head lifted in characteristic defiance, to bay at the big blind eyeball of the moon. Then he started to go back down the drive again. Now I really was scared that in his half-drunk state he might go over the cliff.

I finally managed to cry in a squeaky voice, "I'm here. I'm fucking *here*." Cursing gave me release. I shouted, "I'm fucking here, fucking here."

He came and stood over me like a shadow, really convinced he was about to die. Now *he* couldn't breathe or speak. He stood there in eloquent mime, pointing at me, pointing at his heart, pointing at the sky and the earth, holding both hands in front of his face in a gesture of bewilderment at the vagaries of life. Until he collapsed almost on top of me and we lay breathless side by side on our backs for the second time that night, only now in drenched grass.

Once more, we were locked in a strange and wonderful world of our own, gazing up at a gray rolling infinity.

Eventually: "Annie, I'm buck naked with sixteen thistles in my backside."

"There's plenty of room for them."

"And I'm beginning to hate you."

"Shut up," I said. "Where are my tablets? I want three."

"You'll get two. Ask for more and I'll shove them down your throat."

"Right, then this is good-bye." I rolled over on my side. "Send me roses."

He sat up and leaned over me. "Open, you bitch."

He shoved two Valium down me, nearly choking me, and offered me a glass that had in it only a few drops of water.

"I need three," I gulped.

"Three'll kill you. Maybe that's a good idea."

"Give me the bottle, then."

"No, no, no. You've got to pray, Annie."

Tonight, after he nearly met his Maker, it was prayers *after* sex.

"Who to, Eamonn? Pray to who?"

"Any God who's prepared to listen."

"What'll I say?"

"Merry Christmas, God bless You, anything."

"I'll give Her your regards."

He grabbed my hands and joined them for me.

"Your pulse is racing," he said. "Pray hard in case you meet God sooner than you think. I nearly did myself just now."

"By going over the cliff or through a heart attack?"

"My flip-flops—" He realized it was a rhetorical question. "I knew I could not expect sympathy from you."

"Ditto."

"Seriously. Suppose I'd gone over the cliff in my pajama pants and you had died half naked on the lawn. What would people have thought?"

"The mind boggles."

It never occurred to him that the worst anyone could imagine would not approximate the reality of what he did.

"Think, you bitch, of my obituary."

Instead, deeply grateful, this bitch was wondering why he, my jazzman-lover, still kept me by him when I did such unpredictable things. In all the night's mess a miracle had occurred. I had tested him to the limits and he had not rejected me. He was a brute and I was a bitch and I loved him more than ever.

"Pray, Annie, if only so you keep those tablets down."

With his hands tight over mine, I felt as secure as when my giant of a father carried me shoulder-high in the sea.

Beside me, I heard this strange, familiar man begin first to hum then softly sing an old Irish tune, "Down by the Salley Gardens." Another magic moment, for what could be more haunting than to hear a singer singing in the night, his bodily presence ghosted into song; and the song the only sound, my only light?

After ten minutes, I felt more relaxed. The clouds burst asunder diluting the dark, the sun was pink-rimming the east, birds were stirring and chorusing in the bushes and hopping around us on the soft stable-smelling lawn in search of worms.

We were both in at the birthing of day.

Even the past night's terrible experiences had bonded us further. Was there no end to human perversity?

Very gently: "Annie, did you pray?"

"Better than in my entire life."

"What did you say?"

"Over and over, 'Hail Mary, full of grace.' "

He leaned over and kissed me on the cheek.

"There's hope for you yet, Annie." He spoke the next words very softly. "One last thing I want you to know."

I turned so I could smile directly at him. "Yes?"

"I am fecking freezing."

"Is that all?"

"No, pet. I would like you to also know that this wind has no manners, 'tis not bothering to go round me."

I tried to stand up, but the Valium prevented me.

"God Al*mighty*, Annie, I am far too exhausted to carry you and—"

"I know, it'd give you your tenth heart attack of the night."

"After this," he said, hauling me to my feet, "I'll lock every door at night to keep you in."

As soon as we were inside his room, he tried to remove my wet nightdress.

"Don't you jostle me," I said, "or I'll have another panic attack."

He thrust me wet as I was in his bed, saying, "Mary will not wake up before midday," and switched on the electric blankets. He changed into a fresh pair of pajamas and went to get a brandy to still his chattering teeth.

"Lay one finger on my glass," he warned, as he settled in beside me, "and I'll cut your hands off. I'll see to it you never drink again."

The last thing I remember is being wrapped in his arms and him muttering, "I'll say this for you, Annie. Life with you around is never dull."

Chapter
Thirteen

A T NINE the next morning, I was dimly aware of Eamonn helping me to get out of his bed. Arm in arm we struggled to my bedroom and I slept on.

At some time, Mary came and lay down next to me.

"I'm dead, fecking dead."

I put my hands to my head.

"Shut up, Mary, and get me some Valium."

"They've disappeared," she groaned.

"The Bishop must've swallowed them."

"Liar," she said, "he never would. 'Tis you, you addict."

"What do you remember, Mary?"

"Spaghetti and a cocktail. God, was it himself put the liquor away?"

"No," I lied, "it was me."

Sighing gratefully, she left and came back with dry toast.

"And how about a glass of water, Annie?"

"That would act on me like champagne."

"Guess so. By the way, what did you do to the piano?"

"Danced on it."

"Don't let the Bishop see you do it or he'll kill you."

"Thanks for telling me."

"You're like a creature of the field, Annie, and he likes you more than anyone who ever came here but—"

Break the commandments and he doesn't give a damn, but scratch his piano and good-bye.

I picked up a piece of toast, but before I could get it into my mouth we both flaked out side by side. We woke up about three when she went back to her own bed.

Eamonn came home about eight. First, he went to Mary's room and I heard, "Good God, woman, get up."

Then he came to see me. "What are *you* doing?"

"Nothing. I'm staying here."

"You will *not*." He added softly, "I have been working all day and now have I to feed the pair of you?"

When I made no move, he ripped the covers off me but, very forgiving, he made a turf fire and prepared a dinner of lamb chops and boiled potatoes.

"Eat something, Annie," he urged.

Pointing to the wine, I said, in my mother's favorite phrase, "I prefer some of the hair of the dog that bit me."

"Not at my table."

He told us he would be away for the next two days and then we were having visitors. Jim Ross had been his solicitor and his wife, Dinah, had been his secretary, when he had worked in London.

Eamonn was a remarkable host. Jim had a special liking, he said, for Beaujolais and sirloin steaks, while Dinah preferred sweet sherry and gâteaux. Mary was also to stock up with French Camembert and water biscuits.

Summer came early, breathing on us its hot breath. The yellow was gone from the gorse but the grass was still green. On the Ring of Kerry, red fuchsia bells tolled silently and the rhododendron bushes were fleshed with swaying amethysts. Shaggy sheep grazed on hills above which broad-winged birds seemed pinned to the sky or floated in circles on hot air currents like leaves on a lake.

For the next few perfect days, while Mary did the shopping, I vacuumed and tidied the house and, in quiet moments, sunbathed in the garden.

The night Eamonn returned I greeted him at the door. He came late, after prayers, to my room with his glass more brown than usual with brandy. He moved toward my bed, sloshing it, a sign that our last session had left him far more uninhibited.

The break in London had improved his performance. He

sculpted my whole body. Without hesitation or guilt he went to his favorite oases, especially to my nipples, which he sucked with the relish of a newborn, and ran his hands through my hair as a miser would his gold. In seconds, he flew up from my toes to my neck, brushing with his lips every part in between, before plunging into me as though I were the sea.

We wrote another page of the diaries of our nights.

When, for different crazy reasons, we put on our night-clothes, we wrapped ourselves in one another's arms:

"I missed you, Annie."

I smiled to show it was mutual. "But?"

"No buts. Only ands. I missed talking with you, laughing with you. Even your devilment."

I whispered right into his ear, "You were only away a couple of days."

"That's the point. The days were easy enough but"—his fingers twinkled distantly—"long were the nights."

This brave strong man was expressing fear of the sharpest-toothed devil of all: loneliness.

"I never knew homesickness, Annie. Never knew there had been no one at the door till I missed you being there to greet me at the day's end."

His honesty touched my heart. He was as needy as I was. Healing me was no longer paramount. So I hoped.

"But, Annie, this physical thing is Samson strong."

"Isn't that why it's so good?"

"Samson pulled down the pillars upon himself," and, sitting up, he reached for his brandy glass.

"Time to talk, Eamonn?"

He took a big swig. "Jim Ross is a Scorpio, as sharp and deadly as anything you ever met in your life."

"I'm sharp, too."

"He's twenty times sharper and his stinger is up at all times. He was an only child, he's used to observing."

"X-ray vision?"

"One glance, one word, one gesture will give us away. If he suspects anything, he will entrap us and bring me down."

"Why?"

"Because he thinks my views on birth control are all wrong. That makes him suspicious toward me."

"Why invite them, then?"

"They come every year."

Testing him, I said, "Then I'll go away for a week."

"Impossible. Only, Annie, don't get all dressed up and look too pretty. And—" He touched my red chin.

"It looks," I said, "like being razor's edge all week."

Jim and Dinah, a handsome couple, arrived the next day. It was Sunday. Eamonn introduced me.

"You heard me talk about Dr. Jack Murphy from Connecticut and how good he was to Helena."

"I met him once," Jim said. "Unforgettable."

"This," Eamonn said, "is Annie, his youngest. She's staying for the summer."

The Rosses were given Eamonn's room.

Dinah was an Irish beauty with an hourglass figure, dark hair and dark eyes, and a freckled white skin.

Jim, about thirty, was blue-eyed with long lashes, a chiseled ski nose and fine chin. He was everything I had expected, all bright, nervous energy.

I disobeyed Eamonn and dressed my best. How could I not, in view of the opposition?

The Rosses' exquisite baby, Jim junior, never stopped screaming. The first night, no one slept. It can't have been the devil in him, for he saved a bishop from sinning.

At dinner the second night, the conversation turned to America, which Jim knew and liked, unlike Eamonn, who disapproved, in particular, of U.S. policy in Central America.

It wasn't long before we got onto birth control. Jim thought Eamonn had opted out on that one.

I agreed. I said, "Without contraception, the Third World will always be in a shambles and any aid will be only a Band-Aid."

Eamonn, plying everyone with drinks, said that the poor didn't like contraceptives and would never use them. He tried to close the conversation down abruptly.

I was ashamed of him, he was so reactionary.

"I'd blow the condoms up like balloons," I said, "and send them all over Africa."

"Condoms!" Eamonn spoke of them as if they were unexploded bombs. "What talk is this for a bishop's table?"

"Debate's good," said Jim, the lawyer.

I said, "Did you know, Jim, it's a crime to sell condoms in this country?"

Eamonn had to admit there was a 1946 law banning papers that advocated condoms. A Censorship Board enforced the act.

"See," I said, "Ireland's proud that it takes fifty years longer than any other country to accept the obvious."

Dinah sat all the while laughing and putting in the occasional word to stop the debate from turning into an argument.

Eamonn came in to me that night with the utmost caution, the doorknob turning with the speed of a clock's minute hand. A few fingers appeared down the side of the door followed by one bare foot resting on its toes, then his left hand with his watch on.

I was ready to burst. He outclassed Charlie Chaplin.

Finally, his torso appeared, pajamas but no robe, and the whole entry went into reverse. A hare would not have heard him. For the first time, he locked the door.

In his hand was a glass filled to the brim with brandy.

"Is this wise?" I whispered, to stoke up his fire.

"Did you not see how much wine and liqueurs I foisted on them? I'd have laced the baby's milk if I could."

He tiptoed to the bed.

"Will you do me a favor, Annie?"

"Why else are you here?"

"If you're going to have an orgasm, be sure and give me advance warning."

That night, sex was silent and secretive, and for that reason more intense. More barriers came down because I was able to snake all over him without his being able to stop me.

The usual irrepressible mischief came over me. I opened my mouth as if to let out a scream of delight.

In a split second, his big hand was covering my lips.

"No, no, no, Annie, please no. Enjoy yourself quietly."

As my body began to shake: "I don't think I can."

"Then I'm going to die."

"Again?" I squeaked through his fingers, my body shuddering against him.

"Easy now, Annie," he hissed. "Do not get carried away."

He pressed his hand more firmly against my mouth so I had to bite his fingers to be able to tell him, "Stop that or I'll have a panic attack and have to run out through Jim's french windows."

"Oh, *no,*" he sighed, sucking his sore hand.

He got out of bed and knelt down.

After a minute or two, I said, "It's okay. You can come back in. The panic's past, I think. But don't ever try suffocating me again."

Laughing with noiseless hysteria, he slowly and broadly signed himself and clambered back into bed.

"Women's orgasms are not that easy to control," I said, as our bodies pressed against each other.

We laughed and laughed, and the sheer silence and furtiveness of the laughter formed another bond between us.

At four, he whispered, "I have to go now."

"Good luck," I whispered back.

"Tomorrow I can't leave at four."

This puzzled me. "Explain, please."

"We mustn't adopt a pattern. In a couple of days, Jim'd be looking through his keyhole at around four."

Now I knew why Foxy-Loxy was wearing his watch.

I said, "Will you give me a timetable tomorrow?"

He put on his pajama jacket and, as he kissed me good-bye: "That walk down the corridor is going to be frightening."

I volunteered to hold his hand for him.

"No, no, no. Jim would really delight to find me out."

"If he finds you naked in my bed, I'm sure you have your explanation ready. He'd end up apologizing for thinking bad of you."

"Jim would like nothing better than to betray me."

"Why would he want to betray you?"

He suddenly looked at me. "Why do *you* want to?"

"Me?" He really shook me.

"You love me but you delight in treachery."

"What's the *matter* with you?" I said. "Are you sleeping with treachery and is treachery behind Jim's door? What are *you,* then?"

"I am what I am because I am."

I blinked because I recognized the words as being from the Bible, in which they are put in the mouth of God.

"You mean you are the only innocent?"

"Completely."

He meant it. His self-deception was total. I was back to being his patient.

I said, "Innocent? You? After what you just did?"

"I really am. I am only here as a passage in your life."

The magician had changed himself from sinner into savior.

When Helena and her family rejoined us from Donegal on the Friday night, I had to vacate my room and sleep on the floor in Mary's room.

Eamonn had arranged a special Saturday dinner at the Glenbeigh, the hotel he had pointed out to me from the hill on my first afternoon in Inch.

"This," he told me, "will be an unforgettable experience."

But even he, with his powerful imagination, could not have foreseen what was going to happen.

Chapter Fourteen

I WENT to the hotel with Jim, Dinah, Helena, and Mary, while Eamonn came on direct from Killarney.

In our party of about twenty were Eamonn's cousins Joan Browne, a widow, and Paddy Joe Brosnan, both from Castleisland. The rest were his friends, colleagues, and acquaintances, among them Pat Gilbride, her sister, and Father O'Keeffe.

Paddy Joe was a small man. He said little but heard everything and conveyed it by the blink of an eye.

Joan Browne, my mother's favorite cousin, was the exact opposite. A blustery warm-eyed Kerrywoman in her sixties, she was a rebel like me. You felt she was made of velvet. Her curses sounded better than many a benediction.

"I have heard so much about you, Annie."

Her eyes took in my tan, my thick hair, the subtly applied makeup and shocking pink lipstick, the big hooped earrings.

"Aren't you a gypsy of all gypsies?"

Now she was viewing my peasant blouse with its intricate patterns made up of unusual beads running through it.

"And those black velvet pants, Annie," she said, with a smooth laugh, "why, they would tempt a bishop. Especially when you are so very pretty."

As a waiter passed with a tray of drinks, she grabbed a sherry before putting an arm around my shoulder. "And how is my cousin, the big bad Bishop, behaving these days."

"He's very kind," I said.

She pursed her lips and pushed them forward, hooded her eyes, and shook her head as if to say, "We all know what that means." Though, really, no one knew.

In the restaurant, I sat next to Joan at a magnificently prepared table in an alcove with a view of the bay.

The food was excellent, the wines were vintage French. A band played a medley devised by Eamonn himself.

I was relaxed until I saw Mary O'Riley, a few places higher up the table, getting steadily drunk.

Joan passed a message to her brother, Paddy Joe, and he kept pushing the wine away from Mary but she simply stretched across the table for more.

After dinner, there were liqueurs. By which time, Mary's head was on her shoulder.

Eamonn at the top of the table caught my eye and went "Oh, God, God, *God*." But he had to be careful in case Jim Ross was watching out for any sign of complicity between us.

Now began Irish dancing in which I joined, though I knew nothing about it. There were hornpipes, jigs, four-handed reels, and a country dance, a kind of old quadrille.

A Russian in folk costume took over the floor and gave a dazzling display of dancing.

Then Eamonn stood up and did, solo, a few fast rigid steps of Irish dance, hopping and twirling. The applause that greeted him was deafening. Perspiring, smiling broadly, he took a bow. But he wasn't finished yet.

He nodded to the leader and the band struck up "The Rose of Tralee," which he rendered in a fine tenor voice.

He had no sooner finished than I noticed Mary lurching toward the ladies' room.

Joan and I caught up with her just as she was doing the splits. We lifted her by her arms and carried her to her destination. Where she threw up, partly over me.

A couple of women washing their hands were scandalized until I called over Mary's shoulders, "Please, *please*, this lady is handicapped."

Joan helped me clean Mary up and bathed her face with cold water while I dried my shoes and stockings.

Another lady came in and said, pointing to Mary, "Isn't

she with Bishop Casey's party? You can't take her out there, she'll disgrace him.''

"Who cares?" Joan said. "We have to get her out to the car and the only way is through the front entrance.''

Right outside the ladies' room was the Bishop.

As we marched Mary past him, she lurched out of our grasp and sprawled at his feet.

He took his pipe out of his mouth to say, "God Al*mighty*, she will not be coming again.''

We marched her through the dining room and out into the parking lot where we put her into the back of Eamonn's Mercedes.

When Eamonn had settled the account, it was past midnight. He told Jim, who had Dinah and Helena with him, to lead the way while we brought up the rear of the convoy.

I wanted to jump in the back to tend to Mary but he made me sit next to him in the passenger seat.

He had had too much to drink and Mary was groaning horribly. I did not relish the prospect of the trip home. To make matters worse, he put his hand down my blouse.

"Mary," I said.

"Completely gone, Annie. Open up your pants.''

Now I realized why he worked it so we were the last car. He did not want Jim Ross coming from behind and overtaking us.

Mary began to throw up again.

"Oh, *no*," he said, "not *that*," as he puffed more furiously than ever on his pipe.

I felt suddenly sick myself.

"Careful how you drive," I warned.

"Are you telling me again I don't know how to drive a car?''

"Think, Eamonn. If you have an accident, you'll reek of liquor, there's a drunk in the back of your car, and a young woman next to you with her blouse undone and her panties half off. Think of your obituary.''

"Let *me* think of that," he said, laughing a deep laugh.

All this time, he was driving with the right hand, which certainly knew what his left hand was doing.

He got a kick out of the fact that directly ahead of us were

Pat and her sister. The more unthinkable the deed, the more he had an urge to do it.

He nuzzled me. "C'mon, Annie, feel me, too."

"Give me a break," I pleaded. "I'm not feeling well."

"There may be no chance when we get back, not with Jim peeping round the door. This is great *craic* [fun], now."

To me it was lechery. But it was his night.

Ahead of us, Pat stopped for gas at a one-pump garage that was completely blacked out. Eamonn said he might as well fill up himself.

"Make yourself decent," and he zipped up his own fly.

He and Pat must have frequented this garage because they had no compunction about waking the owner up. Pat banged on the door, yelling, "The Bishop needs petrol."

A minute later, a tousle-haired youth switched on a small outside light as he stuffed his shirt in his pants. He stopped to light his cigarette, probably his first reaction when he woke up in the morning.

The young hand filled up Pat's car first, then carried the nozzle to the Mercedes without turning off the fuel ejection lever. In his confusion, he dropped his cigarette, causing the gas to ignite and fuse instantly in two directions.

Pat had already driven out of the danger zone.

Eamonn, jumping out of the car, whipped open my door and grabbed me by the hand.

"Annie, out, quick."

I needed no second invitation.

We went some distance to a hedge while the young hand went for a bucket of sand and a fire extinguisher.

Eamonn whispered, "I have been for a hundred thousand fill-ups and the first time you are with me, the petrol catches fire."

"Wait," I said. "Mary's still in the car."

Eamonn held me by the shoulder. "Leave her, Annie."

"*No,* I'm getting her out before the car explodes."

"She is a dead weight," he said, "and with puke all over her. There's no danger."

"Then what are we doing *here?*"

"I have no idea how to put out fires."

"That's the first confession of ignorance I've ever heard from you and a most convenient one."

As I made to return to the car he pulled me roughly to him. *"Stay where you are."*

This was our first row.

With his pipe still alight in tight lips, he said, "She has caused enough damage for one night."

"To your car?"

"Correct."

"To your reputation?"

"Indeed."

"Is that why you're prepared to let her burn to death?"

"She will not and if she does won't she go straight to heaven?"

I punched a tattoo on his arm. "Anything's better than Inch, you mean, even heaven."

"God, Chicky Licky, with you, the heavens are always falling in. Look, the fire is out already."

We got back in the car and, to my horror, he no sooner started the engine than he behaved exactly as before.

That was the moment when I knew without a shadow of a doubt that I had no hand in Eamonn's fall; he was bad before we met.

It made no difference to us. I loved him not for his virtues, though they were many, nor in spite of his vices, which were many, too. I loved him because I loved him.

But my man was no saint, and I felt an indescribable relief. Because neither was I.

However much he fooled himself that he was a holy man, he was worse than me; and unless it were so, there could have been no fellowship between us. How else could he, pledged not to love women, be the best lover I ever had? Yet, bad as I am, I could never have left Mary to fry in the car.

I realized anew that Eamonn was feeling me, fondling me, sleeping with me because he needed me. My need of a companion of passage was as unreal as Mary's supposed preference for heaven. Eamonn simply used religion to get his own way.

This meant, of course, that I could never wholly trust him. One day, should I, for instance, be a threat to his position, he was bad enough to set fire to me and everything I held dear—and call it God's will.

Our life appeared to be more than ever doomed. From

then on, I resolved to remember everything—words, smells, birdsong, feelings, facial expressions, the fall of petals, shadows on a wall—because in time I would be left with nothing else. I might even end up remembering things I preferred to forget.

As the holy man leaned over to lift the edge of my frilly panties and intimately finger me, I gave him a fierce love-hate-bite on the back of the neck only a fraction below his collar. My way of telling him that we were now on the margin of acceptable behavior. My way of saying that beneath the clerical regalia and sanctimonious talk, he was out for himself.

"Stop it," he said, digging his left hand into my softest part and driving around a treacherous bend on two wheels. "Do you want to kill me?"

Maybe I did.

Back at Inch, Helena and I washed Mary and put her to bed.

When Jim's back was turned, Eamonn signaled to me to come to his room when the house had settled down for the night.

For the first time I was reluctant to meet with him, but he greeted me very tenderly.

"What about Jim?" I said.

"He's gone completely. Dinah had to drive him home."

"He may be pretending."

He stroked my arm.

"You're sore at me, Annie. If only you knew what Mary has put me through over the years."

"What if the pain was mutual?"

He pondered that. "Maybe so. I have always tried to include her in my dinners when most priests wouldn't."

There *was*, I knew, a special kind of magnanimity in Eamonn.

In spite of my anger, I let him have sex with me—to punish him. I had not suffered the unspeakable agonies of childhood confession for nothing.

Next morning, Eamonn would have to say Sunday Mass in the house without a chance to confess. He had condemned Mary to heaven. Why not give him a taste of hell?

He was so besotted with me that he did not heed the consequences till the deed was done. I thought more like a bishop than he did. Or maybe drink had confused him so he forgot which day of the week it was.

He no sooner came out of me than: "My God, tomorrow I have to—"

In my head, I was saying, *Maybe it's good for you also to die a little.* I actually said:

"Why not forgive yourself?"

"Even the Pope cannot do that."

"Your real sin was to risk letting Mary die."

"Stop it, Annie, what we just did was a mortal sin."

"Speak for yourself."

It struck me that there was something kinky in his attitude. How could this completely innocent man repeatedly commit grave sin and just as often ask forgiveness for it in confession while fully intending to do the same again? Where was his purpose of amendment? The little nun who instructed me when I was seven would have called that telling lies to the Holy Ghost.

"Eamonn, *I'll* hear your confession, if you like."

"Pet, pet, things are bad enough already."

To prove they could get worse, I knelt at his feet, signed myself and said, "Bless me, Father, for I have sinned. A week since my last confession. Since then, I screwed Annie Murphy at least ten times."

He grabbed me by the shoulder and whipped me to my feet. "Can't you see this is serious?"

I suddenly could, and my heart hurt for him. Letting Mary die was not serious but his conscience, wounded out of love for me, was in agony. He hungered for a fellow priest to speak absolution over his unrepentant head.

Catholics, I told myself, can be such sad twisted people. Real wrongs are imaginary, imaginary wrongs are real.

That night, I slept on the couch in the living room. Fitfully, because I hopped up any number of times to check that Mary was still breathing.

Next morning, I attended Mass at the back of the small congregation. This was the most sacred moment in Eamonn's day. For this he became a priest in the first place.

The Mass was the bluntest challenge to our love. He either

danced in finery at the altar or he danced naked in bed on me. If ever he came away and shared his life with me, he would have to give this up.

Sometime, somehow, he would have to face up to his hypocrisy of the double-dance and say a final yes or no to me.

Being a gambler, I gambled.

As he consumed the large Host at communion, the rest of the household knelt and bowed their heads. I stayed upright, looking fixedly at him, suggesting, "This is a game, Eamonn. I know what these others don't."

In the melee after Mass I brushed past Eamonn as he was unvesting.

He glared at me as if I had trespassed on holy ground, which I knew I had.

He said, "Jim could have seen you leering at me."

"Maybe he did."

"He has eyes in the back of his head."

"Then he certainly did."

"That," he snorted, poltergeists playing under his facial skin, "was the wickedest thing done to me in my life."

"Wickeder than your sleeping with me?"

"Much."

With his homemade rules of right and wrong, he had no idea of what real wickedness was.

"I'm beginning to think," I said, "you're a bad hat."

"If so, you are a black bowler to match."

I joined Helena in the kitchen, aware that things at Inch were turning treacherous.

Chapter Fifteen

THE GUESTS departed, leaving just the three of us in the house.

One morning, Eamonn set off very early. He drove off faster than ever before, returning late and utterly exhausted.

"Why'd you leave so early?" I asked.

He indulged in magpie chatter before saying, "Today, I had the first of my annual confirmations."

"I didn't know kids scared you."

"Well," he retorted, "they damn well do." After a pause: "I had to make doubly sure I went to confession first."

The children's innocence was bringing him face to face with the contradictions in his own life.

In the living room after dinner—no fire, for it was June— he asked me, "Were you ever confirmed?"

I nodded. "It did me no good."

I was twelve. For weeks, the sisters had said nothing but "The Bishop is coming," as if he were an archangel at least.

"So you looked forward to it, Annie."

"The hell I did." The day itself was hot and sweltering. The Bishop turned out to be a huge, fat, ugly old man.

Eamonn chipped in with, "Not at all like me."

"Wrinkly skin dripped off him and he was dressed like a Hollywood actress fifty years past her prime. Our spiritual leader looked as if he had done nothing all his life except be chauffeured from one meal to the next."

When it came to it, he pressed his hands down so hard he demolished my headdress with lilies of the valley.

"I hope *you* aren't that rough," I said.

Eamonn held up his hands. "Gentle."

I acknowledged it with a smile.

"Could it be, Annie, the reason you dislike religion is that you've always been lawless?"

Wasn't *he?* But he may have thought that he at least acknowledged laws existed, even if he broke one of them nightly, whereas I didn't even know what sin was.

From my point of view, what we did was not a sin but the most natural thing in the world. I was the best judge of that because of the unnatural things that other men had done to me.

He read my thoughts.

"If you were to tell me everything that men did to you, I'd pass out."

He collapsed onto the floor and lay prone as if I had told him everything. I fainted on top of him. Seconds later, we were quaking with laughter in one another's arms.

But, as we got up, I realized that a serious point had been made. His great heart had got him to a place from which his head would have excluded him. For his head still believed that his love for me was a sin because of who he was. That is why he kept needing to beat his breast at the most splendid thing in his whole life.

"Tell me, Annie, why did you give up your religion?"

I stayed silent. The truth would have wounded him too much. At the age of seventeen, I did things the Church forbade, saying nothing about them in confession and then receiving communion in what priests, not I, called sin.

"All right, Annie, what about *after* you gave up religion?"

"You'd only collapse again on the carpet."

He closed his eyes and took a deep breath. "Fire away."

I shook my head. But I remembered.

We were living in Texas at the time, land of guns, snakes, and tornadoes, because my father was employed there in a veterans hospital. Mom was always saying, "No one ever gets out of Texas except in a Cadillac or an electric chair."

My boyfriend, Jeff Fox, who had replaced Don who tried to rape me, was a Baptist. He was my first sexual partner.

Jeff was always poking fun at Catholic rules. He only did this so he could lay me without me feeling guilty. I didn't mind because I, too, thought rules, made by guys like that overfed Bishop, were crazy. So we had a good time.

He used to say, in the usual imitation of John Wayne, "I know what you're thinking, Annie bunch. Your dirty-minded God's followin' us every inch of the way so He can hit you with a bolt of lightnin' before you have a coupla seconds to repent."

The landscape of the lake where he took me once scared me. Trees leafless as skeletons against a red Texas sky. From everywhere came a threatening locust-throb and there was oil-still water around. I knew there were rattlesnakes in the vicinity and water moccasins whose poisonous saliva was thick as a ball of cotton and tarantulas at twilight and red scorpions that roamed the bare rocks with their tails poised to strike.

We parked the car deep in the tall green reeds circling the lake and made love. Love in a car. Teenage stuff. Great. Pleasure began at the base of my spine and lightning-flashed to every part of me.

Satisfied, I opened my window to let in a light breeze. Time stopped while I sat there, unthinking, uncaring.

Without warning, something landed on my bare back, its suckers extended over several inches. I buried my head in Jeff's perspiring chest.

"What is it?" I screamed.

"What d'you think, honey, the devil in the shape of a moccasin snake come to bite you 'cause you just did somethin' dirty?"

He guessed right.

"What is it?" I demanded.

"Just a big old grasshopper."

I refused to make love there again that night.

Jeff was disgusted with me. "Don't forget to tell what we just did to Father Brannigan, in confession."

In spite of the gibes, I loved Jeff and trusted him.

As memories of those days came back, I began to cry.

"Don't, Annie," Eamonn said gently, rubbing his hand over my hair. "I'll help you rebuild your faith."

I was crying not because of my lost faith but because, in

the end, Jeff betrayed me. And in the worst way a man can betray the woman he loves.

It was a night of raw 107-degree heat and we were driving at sixty miles per hour with the top of the convertible down, toward a mad painter's sunset: impossible pinks, reds, oranges, blues. Jeff had booked us into the Ramada Inn. On the way, I fortified myself with gin and tonic.

Inside our air-conditioned motel room, he stocked a makeshift bar from his cooler and played Sinatra from his tape deck. By my second or third drink—who was counting?—we danced and stripped to the Big Bands sound, before making passionate love. My whole body thrilled to his touch. Afterward, another drink.

I lay relaxed for a while on my back in bed in an ocean of pleasure.

He stood over me. "You really turn me on, baby. This next time is for me, right?"

I smiled at him as he turned me over on my belly and, lifting me up from behind, put his arms under me while his hands weighed and caressed my dangling breasts.

This was security, bliss, the fulfillment of all I had ever hoped for in a man. Then he entered me cruelly just below my spine. The violence and unexpectedness of his approach in the rear passage made me shudder and scream with pain.

Like an unbroken horse, I tried to throw him off, but he was too strong for me. The sense of betrayal hurt but even more painful was the sense that I had brought this on myself by being so wicked.

Held in an iron vise, I could only listen to his wild cowboy yells of pleasure. I would never hear their like again. The flower of me, the world that was me, withered with the withering of his flesh.

"You are mine forever now," he cried, "body and soul," while I felt I belonged not to him, to God, to the world, or even to myself. I, Annie Murphy that was, had died in those moments of cruel penetration and frenzied orgasm.

Impervious to the physical pain, I got up and, late or soon, I found myself in the parking lot.

In the car, Jeff tried to tell me it was the gin that made him do it. I believed him because I had to believe in something.

Back home, having torn my dress off, I sat crouched in the corner of the shower in the dark, with cold water running over me for a whole hour. Mom came into the bathroom and switched on the light. "Switch it off," I screamed. She did, though she sat down outside the shower door.

"If Jeff hurt you—"

"He didn't."

"Your new pink dress is all torn."

"I caught it on some brambles."

After a long pause: "I'm scared, Annie."

"I'm *okay*, I tell you."

"For *him*, Annie. You fought with me since you were a kid. If he oversteps the mark, you'll kill him."

I nearly did, too. For, in spite of his promise, he did the same accursed thing to me again.

Afterward, I pointed his gun at his sleeping head. He awoke to find the barrel right up to his open mouth. What saved him? I wasn't worth the expense of the state sending me to the electric chair. I fled from Texas, driving faster than Eamonn himself ever drove even when, as this morning, the devil perched on his shoulder.

I joined my sister, Mary, in New Jersey by the sea. There I had a dream. I was seven years old and dressed for Mass— white gloves, prayer book in my hand. Suddenly, the bright morning darkened. Through the window I saw a stranger with a huge head. When he opened his eyes, they were blood red and he had a fierce tongue. This snake tried to smash the window to get at me. It was as high as the house and it curled and filled the entire landscape of Inafield. Up and down it went, smashing the house to bits. I ran away, but the space kept getting less and less.

That dream still haunts me.

While I was remembering, Eamonn looked into my eyes and saw something of my appalling anguish. That was why he, my White Knight, found it necessary to enter into my world and save me.

Dear God, I prayed, *if you are out there somewhere, thank you for sending me the one man who would never betray me.*

Without realizing it, I had been weeping for some time. Eamonn had his broad protective arm around my shoulder.

"I'll look after you, Annie," he was saying. "I'll bring you back into the fold."

That night, poor Eamonn was himself in for a shock. Even in my sad mood, I could not resist playing a little joke on him. After prayers, he came into my bed, only to find me unwilling to make love.

"Whatever's the matter, Annie?"

"I'm busy."

"Busy?"

His hand went wandering down me, only to come to a shuddering halt. He snorted like a water hose starting up.

"God Al*mighty,* is it a brick you have between your legs?"

He peeped below the covers.

"A *red* brick," I said. "Be grateful."

"Grateful to a brick?"

"Bow down to it. Without it, you'd drop dead."

"'Tis true, 'tis very true."

He had finally seen the proof that I was not pregnant.

"I really would expire, Annie, if that sort of monthly blood-letting happened to me."

"You're learning what we women go through to produce men like you."

"So," he said, "red is the green light, so to speak."

"If you're Irish you might put it like that."

His restless mind was already at work on a new problem.

"Why, Annie, don't you use those internal things?"

"You'd prefer them?"

"Wait, now, this is very, very serious." He was squirming with roguish delight. "I might enter you in a rush and push one of them things right up to your navel."

"Knowing you, you might."

"Promise me one thing. Don't leave them lying around."

"Okay. What're you going to do now, leave the bed?"

Wistfully like a dog: "I won't stay as long."

Why not? I wondered. Didn't I need healing when I had a period?

"Please yourself," I said.

"You don't seem as concerned as Helena about such things."

"That's because Irish women plan their lives around their periods, which is sad."

"But you are free from all that." Then that thought started to scare him. "Maybe you ought *not* to be so free."

"Maybe *you* ought not to be so free," I said, seeing that his only worry was that I was not worried.

At least he was able to administer confirmations for a few days without first having to race to Killarney to confess.

Chapter
Sixteen

ONE SUMMER'S evening around eight, Eamonn took me to see his relatives at Castleisland.

Joan Browne owned a bottling company, so I expected a distinguished house. Instead, as I passed through the open front door, I was too late in making a grab for Eamonn's arm as I fell down crooked stairs onto a crooked floor.

"I feel drunk," I said.

"You will be before you leave," he promised. "Eat plenty of cheese and crackers. Leave anything cooked by herself alone."

Joan came to meet us with her brother, Paddy Joe. Their welcome was overwhelming.

"After our charming evening at the Glenbeigh," Joan said, enveloping me in her arms, "I couldn't wait to see you again. Finally, the greedy *Bishop* has consented to bring you."

"Are you talking about anyone I know?" Eamonn said.

In the living room, after pouring us each a big glass of sherry, she said:

"You were brilliant at the dinner, Annie, turning Mary O'Riley's disgrace into a medical emergency. Eamonn could not have been more cunning himself."

"Cunning?" Eamonn echoed, helplessly.

"Why haven't you brought your housekeeper tonight?"

Eamonn said, "She is in Killarney, preparing for my clergy dinner tomorrow evening."

Joan put on some music and, as a crowd gathered, there was dancing. Pushing her dark glasses onto the forehead, she opened wide her big brown eyes, and said, "Why don't you leave, Eamonn?"

"I have only just come."

"Leave the priesthood, I mean."

Eamonn and I looked at each other and laughed.

"Leave and marry Annie," she went on, in her lilting voice. "A blind man can see you are mad for her."

"In the name of God . . ." He almost choked on his drink. "You know I am vowed to celibacy."

"I also know," Joan returned, "that the present Pope has dispensed thousands of priests to allow them to marry."

I was out of touch. Since I was a girl I had taken it for granted that the Church never allowed priests to marry.

"But I'm not an ordinary priest, I'm a bishop."

"You mean it's too nice being a bishop to give it up."

"I mean I don't want to give *anything* up when I've given my solemn word."

Joan rolled her eyes operatically. "Really. When Annie's around, I could pick up splinters by the light in your eyes."

"For God's sake, Joan, you're daft."

Paddy Joe chipped in with "One thing she isn't."

Joan said, "I read in the *Kerryman* you inherited three and a half million pounds from a parishioner. Sure you could leave"—she snapped her fingers—"any time."

"What *are* you talking about?"

Joan said, "That dinner and the band the other night must have cost you eight hundred pounds. Anyway, your name is Casey, is it not?"

He banged his palm with his fist. "Did the name have 'Bishop' in front of it?"

I said, "He has to deny it, Joan, whether he inherited the money or not."

"But I didn't," and he slammed three drinks down his throat in irritation.

Afterward, Joan said to me privately, "Why did you defend him?"

"I didn't want to spoil a great time."

Joan looked at me slyly. "I *like* you. You are a fellow conspirator."

Eamonn's mother, she told me, had been a real saint. His father, on the other hand, was obsessively religious. He put Eamonn in the care of the parish priest, who encouraged him to enter the seminary.

"With the father always working," Joan said, "it was young Eamonn who had to sort out family problems. Too much responsibility on young shoulders."

She went on to say how much Eamonn loved England. When he worked there soon after ordination, he had a motorbike and freedom and he started housing projects for young people.

Eamonn enjoyed being among his relatives. He danced with everyone. Later, the youngsters went on dancing and trying to eat Joan's food while the rest of us chatted in the living room. We had had far too much to drink when Joan took Eamonn in one arm and me in the other as if to introduce us.

"My God," she exclaimed, "it has just struck me."

"What, Joan?" Eamonn tittered, rocky on his feet. "What has just struck you and where?"

"What if Annie gets pregnant?"

Paddy Joe fell off his chair, clutching his heart and saying, "I am going to die. I am. I am."

"I always knew you would break your vows," Joan said. "Annie's an excellent choice."

"Joan Browne," Eamonn said, "you are murdering your brother with the wicked things you say."

Junior, Joan's eldest son, married to a Rose of Tralee, came over to hear his mother say, "If Annie gets pregnant, you will have to dip into your millions then."

She could say anything to Eamonn. Mischief was irresistible to him, even when he was on the receiving end of it.

Really high now, he grabbed me for a dance and even cuddled me in a corner with Joan looking on, smiling and nodding her wise old head.

She mouthed to me over his shoulder, "Sure, himself is gone on you, completely *gone*."

The drive home was scary because, for the first time, Eamonn was really plastered.

"Slow down," I said. "Think of the cops."

"Three and a half millions," he said, in a slurred voice, his left hand busy under my dress. "How would I get anyone *pregnant?*"

We were within a mile or so of Inch when, trapped in the headlights of the car right in the middle of the road, there was a lamb. There was a loud crunchy bang and a flight of wool.

"Why didn't you swerve?" I screamed.

"We would have gone over the cliffs ourselves."

"Stop, Eamonn, it might not be dead."

"'Course 'tis dead."

"You don't *know* that."

"I do, Annie. I have hit them before. 'Tis a lamb, only a lamb."

Slaughterer of lambs. Eamonn, supposedly a shepherd— "Behold the Lamb of God"—did this regularly and still drove like a madman with one hand poking me under my panties. My man was a ruthless man.

That lamb, spring-born, innocent, was suddenly a symbol of everything that stood between us. How could he hit it and not even bother to stop?

I started to open my door with us careering up the narrow mountain road at about fifty miles an hour.

"No, Chicky Licky, you will kill us both."

Seconds later, we halted with a screech and shudder at the front of the house.

He opened my door and saw I was almost in tears.

"Why didn't you stop, Eamonn?"

He touched my shoulder gently.

"I didn't want you to see a poor bloodied little lamb spread on the rocks. I'll drive back, it can't be more than a mile, and check 'tis dead."

I nodded and made to accompany him.

"No, Annie." He spoke protectively. "Your baby covered with blood still haunts you."

"I guess you're right."

He took the flashlight and drove away. That made me even more apprehensive. I was sending him back down a mountain road high on drink. If he crashed, I'd never forgive myself.

Fifteen minutes later, I met him at the door.

"I was right, Annie. 'Twas dead."

He was still puzzled. "What am I to make of you?" he said. "You have guilt about a dead lamb but no sense of sin. There's a tough part of you and another that is fragile, which I'm determined to mend."

Yes, we were both full of contradictions.

The frightening drive back and the search for the dead lamb in the dark had made him very amorous. He was no sooner inside the door than he was tugging off his clothes.

He led me into the living room, where, seeing I was shaky and cold, he put a match to the fire, which was already laid, and offered me a short brandy. "Thank you," he murmured, "for defending me over that inheritance."

"I knew you're such a liar we'd never get to the bottom of it, anyway."

We never made it to the bedroom. We ended up making love on our favorite rug by the hearth. He was not at his most proficient, but he was still amusing. Once or twice, he catnapped. That, too, was consoling; proof we were a couple.

There was nothing to stop us sleeping in his bed. The whole house was ours. Or so we thought.

We were about to retire when we heard noises. He put his fingers to his lips, switched off the living room lights, and we held hands like Adam and Eve after they ate the apple.

"Mary must've come back," I said.

"No. Her car is not here. Besides, I called her from Castleisland. She is in Killarney making ready for the meal."

Heavens, I thought, *he takes no chances.*

Who, then, had broken in? Had a dog, a sheep, or a fox come through an open door? A burglar? There was another blood-curdling bang from somewhere in the heart of the house.

"God Al*mighty,*" he said, "my clothes are strewn everywhere, beginning at the front door."

"What'll we do?" I said, enjoying every minute of this.

"Get your things, Annie, and hide under the piano. No, behind the curtains. Flatten yourself against the wall."

I had difficulty rounding up my clothes with the only light coming from the embers of the fire and him moaning his usual "I am going to have a heart attack, I am."

Behind the drapes I managed to slip on my panties, my dress, which I did not button up, and my shoes.

The rattling noise went on. He came across to me, whispering, "What'll I hit the bastard with, Annie? My silver candlestick or a decanter?"

I laughed aloud at the hard choice before him. He pressed the drape in the direction of my mouth to make me shut up. I made a quick curtain call to stop myself having a panic attack. There he was with his hair sticking out in all directions, with one hand stuffing his shirt into his pants while wielding a solid silver candlestick in the other.

"It's the wind," I said, zipping up his pants for him.

"You think so?" Pulling me away from the window, he pushed me ahead of him while he brandished his weapon in the rear. "Open the door and look see."

The corridor was empty save for his jacket, stock, and clerical collar by the front door.

"All clear," I whispered.

"Get me my clothes, then, quick."

I went to grab them when a frightening shape materialized out of nowhere and came soaring within inches of my head. I hurtled backward into the living room.

He looked really scared.

"What was it?"

I didn't answer. I grabbed a coverlet, a kind of shawl, from the top of the sofa and wound it round my head.

"Have you gone bonkers, Annie?"

"It's a bat," I squealed. "I hate them."

He snatched the shawl from my head and wound it around his.

"So do I," he said.

"You stinking coward," I yelled. "Give it back."

"I will not. You have lots of hair."

"That's why I need the shawl so it doesn't nest in here."

"I need protection so I don't get rabies on my unprotected head."

The strange thing was, because I suffered from panic attacks, I liked to see him panicking. Coward speaketh unto coward. His weakness was my strength; I depended on it. His lack of shame endeared him to me. We never in our heart of hearts *condemned* one another.

Not that I showed my fondness for him at that moment.

"Oh, you chivalrous gentleman," I cried. "Oh, my knight in shining armor!"

"I don't have to show chivalry, dammit, I'm a bishop."

"If I get rabies, Bishop, I'll need ten shots around my navel. If that happens, I swear to God I'll tell everything."

"Tell who what?"

"I'll tell whoever wants to hear the things you've done to me, every single sexual act. I'll go to Rome and tell the Pope."

Even that threat failed to make him part with the shawl. "Pet," he whined, "that bat could scratch my head."

"Don't 'pet' me."

"And I have a huge clergy dinner tomorrow evening."

"So?"

"If I appeared with a scratch on my head, which of them would believe a bat did it?"

"You always think of yourself first." I fought him for that shawl as if my life depended on it. "You just don't want to go to hospital and miss your damn dinner."

"Don't I suffer enough already from my colitis?" he asked, in a Chaucerian lament. "For hours I sit on the toilet until I am almost down the sewer and you want me to risk getting ten needles in my poor belly. I'd explode."

"You shouldn't drink so much."

"It's not the drink, it's the gas. When I get like that, I could drive my car across the mountains to Killarney without switching on the engine. Could propel you across this room like on a magic carpet from twenty feet away."

I giggled, mollified by his way with words.

"Searching for a dead lamb in the dark, Annie, and being threatened with burglars and now this bat coming does not help my colitis."

"Something's got to be done about this affliction."

"Now you know why I smoke a pipe with hickory in it."

"Not nearly drastic enough."

"When I'm really bad I smoke a cigar."

"The rabies needles will do the trick. They'll let the gas out of you."

"The bat," he suddenly screeched, "is the devil himself."

That cry got to me. Believing nothing, I feared everything. I felt Satan would give me rabies personally and carry me off to hell.

"How," I said, sobbing, "will *I* get to the bedroom?"

"Go down on your hands and knees and crawl."

"Wait a *minute*. Crawl yourself."

"I have a very bad knee, you know that."

"The first I've heard of it."

Well turbaned, he scampered without warning out into the corridor. I went on all fours after him, with the bat twice overflying me, terrified it would bite my backside. How unnerving the beating of wings within walls.

It hurt, too, crawling on those hard tiles, and, the ultimate insult, his door was shut in my face.

I flung it open and made a jump for him.

"I'm going to claw your eyes out," I said.

"Shut that fecking door, Annie."

I slammed it so the whole house shook.

"I'm going to bang your head till it bleeds."

"Now, Annie, don't do *that*," while I'm kicking him in the legs and stamping on his bare toes and shouting, "You rotten stinking bastard."

"'Tis late, Annie, please get into bed."

"I prefer to sleep on the floor."

"No, please, the danger's over. It got in through my french window. 'Tis closed now."

I crawled between the cool linen sheets, saying grittily, "You are a selfish skunk."

"Enough, Annie," he said, getting undressed. "I never knew so many disasters in one night."

"Are you saying *I* attract them or *we* do?"

"*You* do," he snapped. "Because you have turned your back on God."

"Don't you preach at me, you hypocrite."

When he tried to get into bed, I kicked him out so he hit his head on the corner of the bedside table.

"You believe in Providence," I said, leaning over to kiss the wounded part, "well, God has sent you a scratch for luck, after all."

He got up to examine himself tenderly in the mirror.

"If I have a bruise on my head, I will kill you."

"Two lambs in one night?"

"You are dangerous. I intend to sleep on the floor."

"Suits me."

With that, I turned over to go to sleep.

Minutes later, I felt him crawl in next to me, his back next to mine. Feeling the other shake with mirth, each of us burst out laughing at the same moment and, speaking for myself, I was still laughing when I dropped off to sleep.

Nothing is as wonderful as waking up in the morning next to the person you love. This was the first time one of us did not have to leave furtively before the house awoke.

Some people look ready to die in the morning, but Eamonn had an almost newborn face on him. He woke up rubbing both sides of his face madly and making a noise like ruff-ruff-ruff.

"God," I said, "there's a dog in my bed."

To prove me right, he bit my breasts and my belly, woofing constantly. The noise was multiphonic. It seemed to come out of his ears, his nose, his throat. To escape being eaten alive, I jumped out of bed and made to draw the drapes to let in the light.

"Stop," he commanded.

"I need some air."

"Get away from those curtains." Very slowly and dramatically: "Someone is probably out there." He put his fingers to his lips. "Get on all fours."

"I refuse to walk like that again for anyone."

"Disobey me and I will send you *home*."

Heavens, I thought, *what sort of standards does he have? We can go on having sex, no bother, but if I once open up his drapes he'll send me back to America.*

I said a frigid good-bye and made my way to my own room like a hunchback. Hardly the most romantic end to a romantic night. Especially as he soon came to me on all fours, crying in a trembly voice:

"Never do that again, you hear me?"

What terrible new sin had I committed now?

"Do *what* again, Eamonn?"

"Scratch me like that."

"Like *what?*"

He held up two fingers from which dangled an earring.

"You left it in my bed. What would Mary think if she found it there?"

Chapter Seventeen

A FTER WE had showered, dressed and had a bite to eat, Eamonn said, "I'd be grateful if you'd come with me to Killarney and help Mary polish the silver."

"Nothing I hate more," I confessed.

"I do like to have a nice table for my priest friends."

Apart from diocesan priests, he had also invited a couple of bishops to his dinner that night.

That morning, his driving aroused me to a fever pitch of sexual excitement. He handled the car as though he were fondling my naked body. Careering faster and faster around every bend, he kept taking his eye off the road to give me a sly lovemaking look, followed by a torrid laugh.

A heady mix of love and death resulted in a blizzard of butterflies in my stomach so that, without his even touching me, I threw my head back and gushed with a noisy orgasm.

"That was *wild*," he said, stepping harder on the gas. "It proves you can do *anything* you like."

"That was dangerous," I said.

"Dangerous?" He raised both hands off the wheel. "Fun. I just showed you how the mind can dominate the body."

At the Palace, Mary led me instantly to the large antiquated kitchen. She was in total command. She seated me at a long deal table in front of a pile of silver. It took me over two hours to polish it. If I left one smudge, she yelled at me to do the whole piece again.

We set the three-leaved table in the dining room for nearly twenty guests. Overhead was an antique brass chandelier. The chairs were tall and hand-carved with blue velvet seats. The cutlery was of silver, as were the teapots and coffeepots on the dark mirrored sideboard; the glassware was Waterford crystal. The flowers must have cost a fortune. Every color of rose, fan-like ferns, lilies of the valley rayed outward from vases of fluted silver. Each guest had a printed menu and his name printed in Gothic script on his placecard.

Exhausted by hours of work, I decided to take a nap. At the head of the stairs was a quiet shrouded room with nothing in it but a big mahogany table with a felt top. I lay down on it and curled up on my side with a damask pillow under my head.

I don't know how long I had been sleeping when Eamonn prodded me awake. I knew he would. He needed to know where I was so he could touch me or kiss me or make sure I was not disgracing him by having a panic attack. Preparing that table for the clergy made me aware of the competition, and I was determined to give them a run for their money.

"I've been looking for you everywhere," he spluttered.

Winking: "I was waiting for *you*."

"Here? Now? Get off there."

"Give me your hand, then."

As he helped me down I pulled him to me.

"Annie, this is nasty."

"It'll get even nastier if you don't—"

He gave me a long but uninspired kiss. He jerked away from me as the front doorbell rang.

"Cripes. Have to go."

I released him with "Until tonight?"

"You are *dangerous*," he hissed.

"All a question of mind over matter."

Seconds after he left the room, I heard him call with exaggerated calmness over the balustrade:

"Liam, Barney, how good to see you."

His guests had begun to arrive.

I was apprehensive as I saw the dining room filling with boisterous clerics already flavored with drink and nicotine. Eamonn was in his smartest, with his bishop's chain on. He tinkled his glass and everyone stood in silence as he blessed the food with his gold-ringed hand and said a brief grace in Latin as though he were presiding over an exclusive gentlemen's club. After signing themselves, the clergy sat down in an explosion of camaraderie.

Mary and I, in flowery pinafores, served grapefruit, prawn cocktails, and oysters. There were medallions of lamb and salmon and gamebird with special fruit stuffing. The French wines were never-ending.

Over and over in the next couple of hours I heard Eamonn complimented for the splendid turnout. Sometimes, he placed his hands, the fingers joined, under his chin as he listened intently. Occasionally, to express disagreement, he put his knife and fork down, spread his hands on either side of his plate and banged the sides of them down together while he surveyed everyone with whippy eyes.

"I *don't* believe that'll work."

Then he picked up his right hand, held it aloft with the index finger raised, then higher and higher, while, with great variations of voice, he made point after point. His guests seemed impressed by his certainties.

After the meal, they withdrew to Eamonn's study. The downstairs part of the evening began for me and Mary in earnest. Without a dishwasher, the cleaning of the dishes took forever.

"Mary," I said, "I don't know how you put up with this."

"Why do you think I'm so uptight?"

The only reason Eamonn kept her on was because she excelled at functions like this and, thank God, not one hitch. Not yet. The night, she said, was young.

She piled the trunk of Eamonn's car with shrimps and hors d'oeuvres before driving me back to Inch in a Volkswagen crammed with drinks and sandwiches to prepare for an invasion.

Ten of his special friends arrived soon after we did. These were the non-ring-kissers; they could pull Eamonn's leg and tell him that rarest of things: the truth.

They settled in the living room before a lighted fire. Lights were dimmed, drapes half drawn, and the furniture, piano included, was pushed back to the walls. This was Ireland writ large. It was entirely a man's world.

Women, in the persons of Mary and me, attended to their needs as they smoked, told jokes, some of them smutty in an adolescent way, swore alarmingly at each other, and played loud poker for money. God's name came up only in expletives.

The visiting Bishop was as mad as a hatter; he kept getting up and doing a song-and-dance without a talent for either, and they adored him for it. Eamonn was adding to the fog by smoking a huge Havana cigar.

He was permanently disruptive. He interrupted a hand of cards to yelp like a dog or tell a story or discourse upon the way the rest were playing their hands. Once he banged his head in disbelief at something said, jumped out of his chair, and had to be coaxed back before the game could continue.

Meanwhile, he had peeked at the others' hands so everybody yelled, "Dammit, Casey, will you stop?" "The gobshite's up checking your cards, Pat." Father O'Keeffe angrily said, "Sit down, you blackguard."

Every time Eamonn cheated they became rowdier. They tore off their jackets, pretending to want a scrap. When they broke up for a breather, two strikingly handsome priest brothers, Liam and Barney, came to the kitchen for a chat. I sensed they both knew that Eamonn was involved with me. Maybe they had picked up vibrations from Father O'Keeffe with whom it was always "Annie, darling, if you could spare me another cup of coffee."

Meeting him at Inch for the first time, I realized that if Eamonn was living a double life, so was his confessor. Under the kindness and banter lurked a bitter knowledge that threatened the peace of mind of two longtime allies, John and Eamonn. I felt responsible for that.

Barney, about thirty-five, made a beeline for me. I was a foreigner and an American at that. He could relax with me. Barney was an athlete, a hurler, and a smooth talker with a poacher's eyes. Eamonn must have known something about him, for he followed him suspiciously and gave me a look that said, "Careful, don't give him an inch."

My response, of course, was to edge still closer to Barney so I could listen enthralled. Out of the edge of my eye, I saw Eamonn getting more and more neutered looking and—oh, marvelous—green-eyed with jealousy.

Barney had a special way of flirting with me. He told me stories about Eamonn. He and his brother always went with him on vacation, invariably to exotic places. When they had been in India, they came across a snake that reared up in their faces. He and Liam had been terrified while Eamonn talked to it and laughed at it, allowing the others to creep to safety.

Their last trip had been to Africa. Eamonn was driving their jeep in the Serengeti when Barney said, "Do they have earthquakes in this area?" and Eamonn said, "Don't even say such a thing." But he increased speed, all the same.

Liam said, "Eamonn, have you taken leave of your senses?"

"Not to worry," Eamonn said, running his hand through his hair, the infallible sign of his worrying.

"Level with us, Eamonn," Barney said.

Then the earth shuddered, deafening sounds were all around them, and a dust cloud was coming in their wake with the speed of a whirlwind.

"Fecking elephants," Liam cried.

Eamonn's response was to yelp like a dog. "'Tis nothing. Pray. Keep praying."

Liam collapsed in his seat. "We're done for," he said, while Barney cried, "Hail Mary . . . pray for us sinners, now and at the hour of our death."

"The amazing thing, Annie," Barney told me, "was that Eamonn was enjoying himself. With a handkerchief over his face to keep the dust out, he hooted his horn and banged his head while he drove in and out of the herd as if he could see in the dark and laughed and laughed."

Barney paused to get his breath back and to recover from the insanity of the incident.

"His maneuvering among those elephants was a miracle."

Kerry roads must have been tame in comparison.

"Annie," Barney said, looking me straight in the eyes. "That man attracts disaster. And do you know why?"

"Why?"

"Because he likes to laugh."

Eamonn and I both belonged to a dangerous breed. Maybe we laughed so much together because we found one another so threatening.

An unhappy Eamonn clapped his hands to summon his friends back to the safety of poker. Safety for him, that is, because a lot of money passed over the table that night, mostly in his direction.

When I next offered them sandwiches at a break in the game, he said, "Go to bed, Annie. Clean up in the morning."

"I'm fine," I said loudly and, as I offered him something, I whispered, "Barney has such fascinating tales."

"He doesn't mean it, Annie, but he likes to flirt."

"Don't we all?" I said.

"But it's not good for him."

"Nor for *you*."

"Exactly," said Eamonn with a rare word of honesty.

"A good job he wasn't the one who met me at Shannon. He might have done something disgraceful."

"He might."

"Yes," I said. "He doesn't have your spirit of discipline and self-sacrifice."

He sighed deeply, miserably.

"Has it occurred to you, Eamonn, that I might help him?"

"What do you *mean*?"

"He's so obviously in need of healing."

"How do you propose to—" He slapped his head, unwittingly attracting attention. "Don't tell me."

"Well, I know *you* will never leave the priesthood."

I said this with complete sincerity. Hour after hour, I had witnessed the close cursing friendship of men who had studied and worked together for years. I saw how this tight-knit brotherhood honored Eamonn and looked up to him as a chief of their tribe. They would tolerate any of his sins except that of quitting.

I felt sad for Eamonn and for me. How could he face the shame of betraying their expectations when they loved him so much they even let him cheat at poker?

"Thank you," he said, ungratefully.

"But young Barney, now"—this was said only to provoke—"who knows?"

The very word *young* pointed to a major advantage Barney had over his Bishop.

"Temptress," he spat out.

"I'm sure the Pope would give us his blessing."

He turned from me in disgust, saying to his clerical friends, "Poker's about to recommence."

That evening, he showed me the fullness of his life, the sheer strength of the ecclesiastical system he served. I went to sleep full of foreboding.

Chapter
Eighteen

NEXT MORNING, Mary brought me a cup of tea in bed. The Bishop, she said, had gone to work. He was annoyed that the clergy had left tire marks all over the lawn in the early hours. He intended sending Justin to roll it out.

"Why not a local man?" I wanted to know.

Mary said local people might have guessed that the damage had been done by the clergy in a drunken orgy.

"He is very suspicious, you know, Annie."

We spent the day cleaning up. Jokingly, I put the vacuum cleaner to her hair and made it stand out. Then I put it on her breasts.

"Leave 'em alone, Annie," she screamed, "not even a man has touched those."

"More fool you."

"You are a good match for the Bishop," she said; "you're both crazy."

"Thanks."

"There's something going on here," she said. "One of the reasons I'm getting headaches. But"—a wild fling of the arms—"I don't want to talk about it."

A couple of days later, Eamonn asked me to attend a ceremony in Killarney Cathedral. He was ordaining a priest.

I could not make him out. I resented his being a priest and here he was wanting me to watch him make another.

I had promised to help Pat Gilbride that day but if the spirit moved me, I said, I would attend part of the ceremony.

The morning was rainy, so I wore a blue poncho-type raincoat. On the way, he told me it was a simple and beautiful ceremony. He had been through it twenty years before. "I really would appreciate it if you got to know this part of my life a bit better."

I could not deny I had some responsibility in this regard.

"It'll give you a glimpse, Annie, of the power and majesty of the Church and the sacrifices it demands of us priests."

During the ceremony, I did slip into the Cathedral. I walked up a side aisle and hid from the congregation behind a pillar. Eamonn, in full regalia, was seated on the sanctuary in front of a young man in a white alb who was stretched out on the ground like a fallen leaf.

His eyes met mine as I peeked out of my blue hood. To me, the whole thing was pagan and immoral. He was encouraging a youngster who knew nothing of life to renounce all its joys when he himself had failed in so many ways. I wanted to pull the ordinand to his feet and yell, "Don't be so stupid."

As Eamonn stood up, he tripped on his long robes and almost fell. I walked out before I disgraced myself by laughing aloud.

After the ceremony, when the new priest and his family were having their pictures taken with the Bishop, I returned to the Cathedral. I slipped into Eamonn's private vesting room and hid behind a curtain. When he came back to remove his vestments, I jumped out on him, saying, "I did not like that one little bit."

He whispered back, red-faced, "*That* was obvious."

The amazing thing was that my readiness to attack him only endeared me to him. He was fascinated by opposition.

"If anyone comes in," he said, "I'll pretend I'm hearing your confession."

"Can't you ever talk with a woman without wanting to improve her or forgive her her sins?"

"During that ordination, Annie, the hate in you—"

"I don't hate *you*. It's the system. Jesus would not have wanted that."

"How," he asked, his eyes blazing, "do *you* know?"

I pointed to all his finery. "Can you imagine Him wearing *that?*"

"Stop it, Annie, please!"

"And that nice young man gives his whole life to the Church when he knows nothing about anything."

"Maybe he doesn't need to. He's been chosen by—"

"*God?* No, the likes of you whispered into the ear of some guilt-ridden Irish mother who whispered into her son's ear from the time he was five that this is what God wanted him to do."

He stepped a few paces away to consider me. "What's got into you?"

I was not sure myself. I was taking a huge risk by attacking him in the place most sacred to him.

"Can't you see," I pleaded, "that that young man will end up like you?"

"Which is?"

"Corrupt," I snapped.

He looked as if I had slapped him on the face.

"I don't think I'm corrupt."

After a long pause, I said, "I do."

He went on unvesting, saying calmly, "You're having a tantrum."

"That ceremony, Eamonn, reminded me of what the Church made me suffer when I was a kid, all the guilt and the shame. Stupid rules made up by a bunch of old hoodlums in drag who want to take revenge on the human race for their own barren lives."

Eamonn ran his hands through his hair in exasperation. "Oh, no," he moaned. "O-o-oh, *no.*"

"Oh, yes," I said. "You wanted to brainwash me. Instead, that ordination only brought home to me that it was the Church that almost killed my mother before her time."

"Drink did that."

I was remembering how I, an eight-year-old parent-minder, had to tug my drunken ton-weight mother through the house. "Why the hell do you think she drank?"

"You tell me."

I said, "You shouldn't ask women to give up their hearts, minds, bodies, souls, to serve the likes of you."

He sat down heavily, sighed, and shook his head.

"Yes, Eamonn. You make them live in permanent fear of having children so you can control them and their husbands through them. Why do you think Irish men spend most of their lives in pubs? Because you have made a secret war between them and their women."

"Keep your voice *down*, Annie."

That ceremony had made me realize that the Catholic Church had stolen my childhood from me. It had set me on the path of accepting bad things from the men in my life. Why did I allow myself to be more or less raped, to be sodomized, to enter a marriage in which I was subject to degrading sex? Because the Church had groomed me to play the part of the victim *of* men and *for* men.

Tears sprang to my eyes. I was speaking from bitter experience. Its roots went back to the virtually unendurable marriage of my parents. It flowered in my marrying a Jew whom I did not love because that was the best way I could express my rebellion against my Catholic upbringing.

Heavens, I wondered, was my love for Eamonn just another form of my revenge against men and, in particular, against the Catholic Church?

No, no, no, surely, no. I really loved him but how could I love someone who embodied everything that I hated in the system that had ruined my life? There was no better proof of the power and mystery of my love.

Eamonn fondly took my arm, saying, "Tell me."

I told him how my father said the rosary over and over and often went to Mass. He believed God is within us, guiding us. He was never a blindly obedient Catholic. If your marriage is destructive, he used to say, get a divorce.

His chief argument with the Church was over contraceptives. That was why he refused to contribute to Church funds. According to him, everyone had a right to use them to plan their lives. Some couples wanted one child, some ten. The decision should be theirs and theirs alone.

He instructed his children in the methods of birth control. The pill, he told us girls, we were to take only under medical supervision.

One day, he caught my brother Peter fornicating. He raised his eyes to heaven and said, "Please don't bring me home babies.'' From that day on, Johnny and Peter were given money for condoms.

Once, when I was five, he tore into them because they got drunk and left condoms in the toilet bowl. I fished them out with a stick and wanted to know what they were.

Mom said, ''It's your fault, Jack, you encouraged them.''

When she was a girl, she was going to be a nun. Birth control terrified her. Daddy told her she had to use it after she nearly died from a miscarriage. She gave up her diaphragm so she could return to communion. The result was Mary and me. We were the price she paid for a quiet conscience.

Imagine, a religion that demands women have babies to get peace of mind. In Mommy's case, it didn't last. After me, Daddy couldn't afford any more kids. Now the only way Mom could cope with having to use a diaphragm was by drinking. Catholic guilt must make some of the worst alcoholics.

When Mommy got Catholicly drunk, she yelled out that she was in hell already. She was red and insane looking, and I could feel the heat of her. I stood on a chair and threw water over her to cool her down, a jug at a time.

After I gave Eamonn a brief but bitter résumé of all this, he took my hand and kissed it. Then, in a very soft voice: ''I do understand, pet. But you must understand me, too. You may think me all-powerful, but I am nothing.''

''None of us is nothing.''

''If I deviate once in the slightest from the Catholic position, I will have to leave the priesthood.''

I gasped with incredulity. Surely a bishop, a leader, was at least entitled to a point of view?

''The Church will forgive me, Annie, whatever sins I commit: murder, theft, adultery. But one careless phrase and all the good work I'm doing would come to an end.''

He could sleep around and stay a priest, but if he gave one honest opinion he would have to leave?

''Eamonn,'' I said, ''you couldn't do a finer thing for the Church and for Ireland than to leave.'' He looked puzzled. ''Any institution that treats people like that is a form of Nazism.''

He giggled. ''The Pope is no Hitler.''

"Speak for yourself. Your false loyalty corrupted you long before I came along. You're mixed up not only in your sexuality but in your thoughts."

"*Me* mixed up?"

"Far worse than I ever was. You're kind, but you can't confront the real issues. You hear the cries of the people but your so-called loyalty has stopped you from facing up to all the misery you cause."

He looked at me forgivingly for saying such a cruel thing.

"I really do try and ease the pain of thousands, Annie."

"You ease the pain of thousands so you are guilt free to hammer millions."

"But I do really believe, Annie, that contraceptives make couples behave selfishly and put sex before love."

"Tell that to the woman with a string of kids and a cruel drunk for a husband."

"Won't you consider the Church's position?"

"If I accepted it, I'd have to stop loving you." That shook him. I don't think it had entered his head that if he converted me it was farewell to our love. My lack of conversion was the only justification for our relationship.

I went to the door. "I apologize," I said. "I'm becoming a bully like you. It's not for me to tell you what stand you should be making."

"Come back to me," he said.

"I can hear you from here."

"I just want you to appreciate the way I feel."

"I do," I conceded. I went over to him, hugged and kissed him. "I'd love you whatever you thought or did."

"And I love you in spite of an awful lot that's wrong with you, too."

I went to the door again. "I know," I said. "It's not every Catholic who would go on loving a woman who sleeps every night with a bishop."

Chapter Nineteen

I SPENT the rest of that day in Killarney. Wanting to get closer to Pat, I took her snarly black poodle for a walk. It was funny seeing the apprehension on everybody's face when this little dog appeared on the streets.

That afternoon, Eamonn had a titled visitor from England. He invited me into his study to meet Sir Gerald. For fun, I let Larry in and he went straight as an arrow for the visitor's leg.

Forgetting himself, Eamonn cried out, "Let go, you bastard," and tried to grab Larry's hindquarters.

Sir Gerald hardly opened his mouth except to say politely, "Be a good dog, old chap. You will get down? Please."

I almost expected him to say, "Sherry, Larry?"

Eamonn was so angry I thought he might bite the dog.

Hearing the commotion, Pat ran in only to see her pet release the Englishman and make a jump at his old enemy.

"Oh, no, you don't," Eamonn cried, kicking out with all his might and scrambling up onto a chair next to the one on which now stood his somewhat less distinguished visitor.

"What are you doing to my darling?" Pat said, and all Eamonn could do was point to the blood on the floor.

"It's perfectly all right," the Englishman said, as if this happened to him at least once a week.

Mary came to fetch me because Eamonn had a business meeting.

He came home late after drinking heavily. He came into my room, twirling the brown liquor round and round in his brandy glass. "I don't want to lose Pat," he said, getting into bed, "but what am I going to do with that damned dog?"

"Arrange a party," I said. "Give Pat a glass of poteen and I'll give Larry a special cocktail of milk with Valium in it."

"You're mad, Annie."

"It'd be a crib death. He sleeps next to Pat. Even a man could die sleeping next to someone with a forty-D bust."

Eamonn gurgled on about Larry dying in comfort when I suddenly said, "Emergency."

I was laughing so much, I was in danger of disgracing myself, and being on the wall side I was trapped.

"I've *got to get to the bathroom* or else Inch'll become Tinkletown." I tried to clamber over him but my feet snagged in the sheets. As he jerked to free me I fell over backward into the gap between bed and wall, and the flood came.

I hated this humiliation. I raised my head to give him a piece of my mind but the bed was empty. Slowly, his head appeared opposite mine and we laughed loudly together.

It was some minutes before he recovered his breath sufficiently to say, "My life was once so disciplined."

"Stop blaming *me*."

I fetched a bottle of Dettol disinfectant and began to clean the carpet. Lying on the bed, he said, "You have ruined the mood altogether."

He went to his own bedroom and returned in a temper forty-five minutes later.

"My God, she is still scrubbing the floor."

"When I've finished," I said, "we'll go to your room."

"Mary'd smell the Dettol in both our rooms and put two and two together."

When I ripped the sheets off the bed, he bundled them up, saying, "I'm hiding them from Mary."

"Where?"

"In the boot of my car."

"At two in the morning?"

"'Tis safest so. I might forget them when I go to work."

"Are you going to throw them over the cliff?"

"No, take them to Killarney and mix them with the Palace

laundry. The nuns will presume they were from visitors' beds.''

Knowing his distrust of nuns, I said, mischievously, ''They're so clever they might trace them back to . . . *us*.''

After giving me a sour glance, he went for a duffel bag. He stuffed the sheets inside and crept out the front door. I heard his trunk quietly open and close. He returned with two sheets from the closet. As we remade the bed, his mind was still racing.

''If Mary sees that wet patch, she will ask herself why you couldn't get out of bed in time.''

''It's okay,'' I said. ''The truth is unimaginable.''

''No, she will know I was blocking your exit.''

I opened the windows for air and he got a thick towel from the bathroom to soak up the excess water on the carpet.

''What a way for a bishop to spend a night after a hard day's work,'' he said, oozing with self-pity. ''But now we are free for us.''

''After,'' I said, ''I've taken a shower.''

''But—''.

''You said I can't come into your room smelling of Dettol.''

''True,'' he conceded.

Later, in his warm room, he became instantly erotic.

''Please,'' I said. ''Spare me this.''

''But I've waited for over two wretched hours.''

''I'm exhausted.'' I rolled over. ''Good night.''

He rolled me gently back and touched my cheek.

''You have that little curl of mischief at the left corner of your mouth.''

''Eamonn. It's late. What are you—? My God, you are *worse* than Larry. Do you have to—?''

He had to.

Before I left his room at seven, he told me he was staying home that day to prepare for an early departure for Dublin the next day. If I went with him, we would have to spend tonight in the Palace.

In midmorning, I packed my bags. I was really excited to be going on my first trip with the man I loved. Pat and Father O'Keeffe were also coming, but I liked them very much.

Eamonn came to say, "You might like to dress up a bit."

"These jeans not good enough for you?"

"With your slim figure, you look grand in anything but you will be eating with me in a hotel."

He pulled the hair off my face.

"That's better. Clip it up like that with combs. Do not wear those jangly earrings which bit my bum in bed." I had to look the secretary type like Pat.

All that day, one thought buzzed in my head. What had happened the night before was so like the breaking of the birth sac it made me feel that one day I would be a mother.

Eamonn was compiling reports. When he was working, he looked amazingly capable and handsome.

On the way to Killarney that evening, he talked a lot about the European Economic Community (EEC). He was proud to have attracted so much financial aid to the West of Ireland.

He also told me of a four-year-old Kerry girl who was lost in the woods near Kenmare. Everyone was afraid she would freeze to death or drown in a lake. Yet all the officials did was to send out search parties in cars or on foot. He made them call up a helicopter. If they didn't and the child died, he warned them, he would tell the whole world. A chopper appeared as if by magic. Within hours, the girl was found safe and well. "I cut through the red tape," he said. "Oh, I cannot stand the pettiness of officialdom."

He explained that the reason he traveled a lot was because though he loved Ireland, he loathed its "backwardness."

"You," I said, "are backward yourself."

"I knew I should have put glue on my lips. I am *not* discussing contraception, again."

He could not see that he, too, was part of the Irish scene. The Pope himself was a Kerryman. They both bound themselves to rigid rules in the face of terrible crises.

In one respect at least Eamonn had disregarded the rules. I was a girl lost in a dangerous forest and he would feel guilty if he did not take extreme measures to rescue me.

To save my soul, he was willing, even in the Bishop's Palace in Killarney, to cut through the red tape of the Ten Commandments.

Chapter Twenty

I N THE palace, Pat and I prepared a modest evening meal for ourselves, Eamonn, and John O'Keeffe. We ate in the kitchen.

Eamonn was in high spirits, telling jokes and stories about his parishioners, of whom he was evidently very fond. Much of it centered on the trickery of Irish farmers and their lust for livestock and land. There was about the people, besides the gaiety, he said, a morbidness and an abiding sense of guilt. This is why he liked to sit in the confessional and forgive them their sins, which were often not sins at all.

"Above all," he emphasized, "the Kerry folk love taking the mickey out of people."

"Even a bishop?" I asked.

"*Especially* a bishop."

In a switch of mood, he told of a local scandal involving one of his aides, a woman with two children. In a pub, her lazy husband had passed his hat around for money to send her to England for an abortion. This got back to Eamonn just before his aide came to him asking for a four-week advance on salary for her vacation.

He told her he knew what the money was for. She said either she had an abortion or her marriage would fold. If she had to give up her job, her husband would go to England to look for work and never come back. Eamonn promised to help her financially and emotionally. He would see to it she was separated from her husband for a while so they both could be counseled. He would also leave her job open for her until she was able to return.

I said, "You doing your big magician's act."

"I gave her no money," he said coldly. "I refused to share in a murder."

"You told her she was a murderer?"

Eamonn nodded. "If she went ahead, yes."

"Must have done wonders for her morale."

The woman, he went on, found the money somehow and went ahead with the abortion. He felt he had to get rid of her.

I did not know the lady in question so I was in no position to judge her but I said: "Why'd you fire her?"

"I had no choice."

"Only cowards say that. We always have a choice."

"Not someone in my position."

"Does someone in your position have to be a coward?"

"I am not a coward if I do what I think is right."

"But, Eamonn, she was already down—did you have to kick her?"

Eamonn looked at Pat and Father O'Keeffe for support but they shrugged as if to say this was his scrap.

I went on, "Didn't Jesus put up with disapproval when he kept fallen women in his company?"

"They had repented."

"Did you ask this lady afterward if she had repented?"

"You don't seem to understand, Annie," he said. "I have to put my personal feelings aside."

"What feelings?"

He ignored the insult. "As a representative, I have to think of the whole community. This was an open scandal."

I wondered if he would feel compelled to fire a priest or, come to that, a bishop, if he were known to have cheated on his vows? I settled for saying: "If Justin was imprisoned for stealing would you have to fire him? Why victimize a desperate woman?"

"If I hadn't fired her, Annie, what sort of message would have gone out to my diocese?"

"Maybe that you were a Christian."

"You think I am not?"

"A Catholic first, a Christian second."

He eyed me sharply. "Explain."

"Catholics look first to the Pope, Christians look only to Jesus."

Eamonn sighed heavily, "Oh, dear God."

"You could have said to her, 'What you did was wrong but it would be an added wrong for me to fire you when you have problems enough.' Irish people would have understood that."

Once again, it struck me how concerned Eamonn was with his reputation. In his view, in spite of Jesus' treatment of Mary Magdalene, some things were unforgivable. "I know I'm an ignorant American," I said, "but I would have gone further and given her the money."

Eamonn covered his face with his hands, muttering, "Oh God, oh God," before turning—significantly—to Father O'Keeffe as if to say, "You see the problem I have on my hands?"

I said, "I'd have told her to follow her own conscience."

"Follow her own conscience," he repeated, with an almost pitying sigh that made me see red.

"Yes, hers and not yours. You'd have given her everything she asked if she had followed yours."

" 'Tis not *my* conscience, you fool," he responded heatedly.

"Oh, I beg your pardon," I said. "You are God's spokesman. I nearly forgot."

"God Almighty, Annie, I'm fond of the woman, I really am, but what she did was wicked."

"*She* didn't think so. Besides, bishops may be exceptions, but the rest of us poor mortals all do wicked things from time to time."

After the meal, we all had drinks and played poker.

"Hold your hand up," Eamonn kept saying to me, "you have no guile, girl."

"Stop looking over my shoulder," I said, angrily.

Having someone look at your cards was unnerving. It was like someone looking inside your brain. After poker, the three of them took turns at playing the piano and singing. They were talented and trusting of each other.

We retired just before midnight. Pat went home and Father O'Keeffe had a room on the ground floor. Eamonn and I virtually had the upstairs to ourselves. In that quiet old house, we climbed the majestic sweeping staircase with landings decorated with chandeliers and old pastoral prints. When he showed me my bedroom, it took my breath away.

"A shame," he said, "you are not sleeping here."

"Where, then?"

He winked and gestured me to follow him. His bedroom, two doors along, had a high-beamed ceiling, tall windows with burgundy drapes, and thick-pile blue carpets edged by polished pine. The big bed was of heavy brass. The eiderdown was a feminine salmon pink with exquisite Belgian lace and matching feather pillows.

The bed was high, reminding me of the beds in Inafield when I was young. As soon as I undressed, I jumped on it and trampolined, it was so bouncy. "If we have sex in this bed," I said, "we'll suffocate."

As soon as he was stripped, he jumped in beside me and dipped his head under the covers. I immediately squeezed his neck between my legs. "You're strangling me," he gasped. "You have terrible strong legs, Annie, skinny as they are."

I marveled at his gift for making me laugh at myself. How could I thank him enough for taking away my shame? Laughter was more cleansing than confession, more calming than Valium.

After I released him, he came up onto the pillow, puffing and blowing, just in time to see me leap naked out of bed. I was so exhilarated by the evening's company, the sense of being in a fairytale room, that I became a free spirit. I wanted to dance.

Leaning on one arm, he followed me with his eyes. "Is it the bad in you coming out?"

I did not answer. I was in a kind of trance, weaving along the walls, high-kicking, twisting, bowing, writhing from the hips, my hair cascading first down in front, then down my back.

After I had given a Salome-like performance, he beckoned me to join him in bed. Once I was there, his own sense of mischief took over. The night was memorable. A bishop's bed in the Bishop's own Palace certainly beat the backseat of a car. I was overwhelmed by his great tenderness.

It was my turn to be like an eel. As I went down under the

covers to kiss him, I seemed to sink in the feather mattress. Then it happened. I couldn't breathe. In a muffled voice, I screamed, "Get me out of here."

He didn't take me seriously and started to laugh even louder. That made me panic all the more. Tiny feathers went into my mouth, throat, eyes, up my nostrils. He finally hauled me up like a drowning cat.

When I had sneezed a few times and recovered my breath, I said, "In a mushy bed like this, there's only one position for me. On top."

"If that is what you want."

I climbed aboard and no sooner was he in me than I said solemnly: "I would like to have your child."

His eyes ballooned to their limits. "You would *what?*"

Gazing at him from close range, so that the whole of me, body, mind, spirit, seemed to be inside the whole of him, I said, "I want you to live forever."

I could not think of a better place to declare my deepest longings for him. I was challenging the system that he represented. I needed to tell him that I had no fears for the future.

"Eamonn," I whispered, "I have never met anyone like you before and I never will again. Whatever happens to us, I would like you to live on in our child."

"But that would be a—"

I stopped the sin on his lips with a kiss. Then: "I will not lie to you about this."

Though this frightened him, he clasped me even tighter. "Don't you see," he said, "how terrible that would be?"

"No, I do not."

When, after he had climaxed, I finally released him, he had a worried look on his face. He got into his pajamas and the expensive dressing gown with *EC* embroidered on it, which had been hanging on the back of the door.

"Where're you going, Eamonn?" He left without answering and I heard him walking down the stairs. He returned in a couple of minutes with a glass of brandy.

As he sat propped up in bed on the pillows, I got up and started to open up the curtains.

"What," he asked dramatically, "are you doing? The convent is across the way."

"I'm just going to wave to them."

"Don't, Annie, they will see you naked and me in bed behind you."

He trusted no one. I said, "Will they be spying on you at two in the morning?"

"Annie," he hissed, "they know I am here. They will have their binoculars trained on this room." I could not believe my ears. These sisters wouldn't dare look at him during the day and they were spying on him during the night?

"I have been there. They keep binoculars by the window. They'd watch this room for hours till their legs turn blue."

"You make them sound like a lynch mob."

"Get . . . away . . . from . . . the . . . window."

"If they've been up all night, they're entitled to a little entertainment."

"I am going to have a heart attack."

That did it. I slipped behind the curtains and waved to the non-existent prurient nuns.

Next thing, a rough hand was tearing me out and shoving me across the room toward the bed. His nails dug into my arms. "Don't," he said, "ever do that again."

Rubbing my sore arms, I said, "And don't *you* ever do that again to *me*."

He threw me in the bed roughly, which I liked because it was good to experience all his emotions. He tossed my nightgown after me.

"Put it *on*. Those nuns may have taken your picture."

"In the dark?"

"They might have a special camera."

He peered behind the curtains for a few seconds. "I think we might have been lucky."

Heavens, I thought, *I have never met a more suspicious man. And I want to have his child? I must be mad.* Then I looked at him, at his beautiful friendly face, and everything changed.

"This is bound to bring on my colitis," he moaned, "and all day tomorrow I have important meetings in Dublin."

I stroked his forehead. "I do apologize."

"I am never bringing you to sleep here again."

I snuggled up to him, started to kiss him, but he pushed

me away. "I am beginning to sympathize with that husband of yours. I never felt so much boiling rage in my life."

"It was spicy, Eamonn, admit it."

"All right, if you say so, I admit it. We'll all go to hell together."

On that comradely note, we settled down to sleep.

Chapter
Twenty-One

I AWOKE in the morning with an allergic reaction to the feathers in the bed. Choking was often the trigger to a panic attack. I was in my room dressing when I heard Pat come in the front door. I stumbled downstairs and explained my problem.

She went to the pharmacist's for some liquid medicine. She also brought me a Valium tablet from the room Mary used when she stayed at the Palace. "Drink plenty of tea, Annie," she said. "And I'll make a Thermos for the trip to Dublin."

Eamonn drove fast on straight but narrow roads while dictating to Pat. The faster he dictated, the faster he drove. I was in the back with Father O'Keeffe, nervous and coughing, and he was patting my hand to comfort me. From time to time, he poured me tea from the Thermos and gave me cough drops for the tickle in my throat.

Eamonn showed no sympathy. "It sounds, John," he said, "as if you have an old consumptive back there."

I tugged his hair in retaliation. "Stop it, please, you are making me worse."

He turned to Pat. "Did you bring her any Valium? No? Annie used to take ten a day, didn't you, Annie?"

When my marriage had been at its worst, I had been on Valium. But Eamonn only said this for Father O'Keeffe's benefit. If he had had doubts about my needing a cure, my present looks would have dispelled them. Eamonn, the great healer, was dealing, in however unorthodox a way, with a sick young lady.

"She was a Valium addict, John, like Siobhan."

Father O'Keeffe obviously knew what had been done for Siobhan, and Eamonn was intimating that I, too, was on the path to recovery. He may even have been pleased that Dubliners would assume that I was an American girl with a health problem and not a source of temptation to a middle-aged bishop.

"You are doing over a hundred, Eamonn," Father O'Keeffe called out. "Slow down, you are making Annie worse."

I had somewhat improved by the time we reached the Burlington Hotel on the southern edge of Dublin. Eamonn was well known there but he did not make a big thing of it. He carried his own bags upstairs. Our double-bedded rooms were together. Eamonn's and mine were next to one another, while I had Pat on my other side and he had Father O'Keeffe.

I spent a while in Pat's room because she wanted to make sure I was better. Then we all went down to the lounge where Eamonn was given a quiet table in the back. We had drinks and a bar lunch of soup and sandwiches.

Afterward, while the men went off on business, Pat and I took a cab to Stephen's Green, a kind of oasis in the middle of town. There we fed the ducks for an hour or so. Pat, a country girl from Sligo, guessed, rightly, that this would calm me. It was blustery for a July day but the trees were fully leafed and the grass shiny green.

From the Green we walked north, past the ancient university of Trinity College, turned west, and crossed the disappointingly narrow River Liffey by the Halfpenny Bridge. We took a cab to the key tourist sights of Dublin, including O'Connell Street with Daniel O'Connell's big black statue. Also the General Post Office, which, Pat said, was the chief stronghold of the Irish during the Easter Rising of 1916. After an hour, we taxied back to north O'Connell Street, where, in the Gresham Hotel, we had old-style tea.

Finally, we took a cab to Grafton Street, the most fashionable shopping center. I bought a blouse and Pat bought a dress. I had my hair cut and while Pat was having hers done, I went into Switzers store pretending to look at duvets. In fact, I bought something which I carefully rolled up and put at the bottom of my bag.

We met the two men for dinner around 9:00. They mostly talked business and we retired at 11:30.

Pat said, "If you get nervous, Annie, call me."

I had no idea if Eamonn wanted us to get together, especially as he had told me to be on my best behavior in Dublin. After midnight, he put his head round my door. "Come and see me in twenty minutes?"

We were within earshot of Eamonn's two closest aides. What if either of them found us in bed together? Knowing how Eamonn had treated the lady who had an abortion, they would have been obliged to quit and I did not want that.

I waited until Pat's room fell completely silent. Then I lazily showered and dried my hair, put on makeup, perfume, and pearl earrings. Finally, I slipped on my new purchases from Switzers: a pale nightdress with slits up the sides, covered with a bathrobe of pale pink with roses.

I had ordered a sherry from room service for my sore throat. From time to time, I eyed the femme fatale in the mirror and we winked at each other. Behind the play-acting, I wanted Eamonn to see what life would be like with me not in the quiet of Inch but in the busy world. He had connections at the highest levels in Germany, France, and Britain. Maybe he could get a job in the European Community. We both liked travel. He had choices.

It was a whole hour before I joined him. Never had I seen him so impatient, as he twirled his brandy. There was very little talk between us, apart from a huskily whispered "That's the sexiest thing I've seen you in. Where'd you get it?"

"In the States. I wasn't going to waste it on just any night."

"You're lying, as usual. But 'tis wonderful, Annie. Take the outside bit off. Fine. Why, in that negligee, you're more alluring than when you're naked."

He made me walk around in it. For a few seconds. His undressing of me was a work of art.

That was an exciting night. We were in a hotel together, like man and wife. The international setting, the lateness of the hour, a capital city full of bustle, noise, and winking lights, it all seemed to make this man, who loved danger, even more tempestuous.

We stood beside a full-length mirror. I was naked and he had his shirt open; and I saw him looking at us in one another's embrace. He was a voyeur of his own sexuality, which he had denied himself for so long. He saw himself kiss me all over and he delighted in his own expertise. He saw himself bring me to orgasm, filming everything in his head, as it were, for the years to come.

Throughout that night, all the psychological barriers that prevented us from expressing our deepest desires dissolved. It was no longer Bishop Casey and Annie Murphy. We were one animal, one being. Our individual selves had ceased to exist. We were not even playing anymore, nor wanting to talk anymore. There was no guilt, no recrimination. This was our right. This was self-ceasing, self-forgetting. This was pure woman and pure man. It was real, and forever.

I returned to my room about five in the morning and rose late. All through our relationship, in spite of the torrid nights, I was sleeping better in his arms than I had done in years because I no longer feared to see monsters in my sleep or when I awoke. He made sleep sweet to me as it had not been since I was a child.

Pat must have looked in on me because she left a message saying we had to vacate the rooms at midday. Having showered and dressed, I went out for lunch all by myself. It was nice to be on my own among so many people. To be alone when you are not lonely is the greatest luxury.

I met up with Pat at about three and we shopped before going to Jury's Hotel. We all four had a bite to eat before we set off for Kerry at around nine. Halfway home, I started coughing violently. My breathing became so labored, the others were worried.

Eamonn stopped the car. He told Father O'Keeffe I was having something like an asthma attack and asked him to drive. Eamonn joined me in the back, but none of the medicines worked. He took advantage of the dwindling light and my condition to hold me tight.

"You're crazy," I whispered.

We spent the last hour of that journey locked together like a couple of teenagers. He kept kissing me even though Father O'Keeffe, from time to time, glanced at us in his rearview mirror when Eamonn was unmistakably making out with me.

My mind was in a whirl. When we slept together in the Palace, he was so concerned not to give the least hint of our relationship to the nuns, yet here he was revealing his hand to his closest aides. This was suicide. Did he want to tell them without telling them?

I was embarrassed because this was too much like double-dating, which I had never liked. And yet, secretly, I rejoiced because if Eamonn and I were ever to go away together, he would need, if not the approbation of people like Joan Browne, at least the understanding of colleagues and priest friends.

We dropped off Pat and Father O'Keeffe in Killarney and on the drive back to Inch, I asked Eamonn why he had been so open in front of them. He shrugged it off. "They didn't think anything of it."

"You gave us away."

He told me not even to think about it. At that moment, I felt that kissing in the back of an official car was more significant in terms of the future than sleeping in the Bishop's bed in Killarney. If he was brave or foolish enough to advertise our relationship, he might be brave or foolish enough to come away with me.

As soon as we reached home, I went straight to my room, changed, and got into bed.

"Please," I begged him, "get me one of Mary's Valium."

With it, he brought back something even better, a glass of milk. I smelled it suspiciously but he made me drink it. We talked and I laughed foolishly for about ten minutes until the mix of Valium, cough medicine, and the unknown liquor in the milk knocked me out.

I awoke fourteen hours later. It was evening. He heard me moving around and came to my room. "How's your cough?"

I tested my throat and said, "Seems to have gone."

He laughed. "I should have been a doctor." He had laced the milk with poteen.

"You could have killed me," I said.

"Killed you, Annie? But I am a healer, remember?"

Chapter
Twenty-Two

SUDDENLY, INCH was full of Eamonn's relatives and their friends from Dublin and Limerick. One afternoon, eight of them, all in their twenties, came hurtling up the drive, making it plain by their shrieks of laughter that they were out for a good time. The weather was warm and the setting idyllic.

Bob Clooney, Eamonn's nephew, had brought along Sinead, his girlfriend. One of his nieces, Shelagh, a quiet pretty girl, was with her husband. Charlie had no job. Well dressed, with blond hair and fine pink skin, he ate and drank everything in sight. Eamonn's generosity toward his visitors was astonishing. The kitchen was piled high with thick T-bone steaks, chickens, hams, gâteaux, and liquor of all kinds.

Things began quietly. Eamonn was extremely careful. Highly sexed young people would find him out soonest of all. He came to my bedroom only once, locking the door behind him and staying at most for three hours.

When he left on a four-day business trip to London, the house turned wild. We had bathing jaunts on the beach, parties on the lawn, and loud, boozy sing-alongs every night.

Mary resented the visitors, Charlie in particular. He smoked the Bishop's cigars and drank his best liquors. I was no paragon. One evening, I invited the crowd down to the local pub. I was in the car with Bob Clooney and Sinead. We had our heads through the roof and the strong wind affected us like wine. We screamed like crazy going down the hill and a few hours drinking with the locals did not improve us. All I remember of that night was a loud argument about birth control. Charlie said, "You were married and had no kids, who are you to talk?" and I said, "Who's talking?" as I threw my beer in his face.

Next morning, he said I had disgraced them. "How can I atone?" I said. "Cook you another three thick steaks? Put three more of Eamonn's cigars in your fat lips?"

The crowd gathered around us.

"Take a look at yourself, you shitty American."

I said, "I don't smoke Eamonn's five-dollar cigars from the time my eyes open in the afternoon."

Bob Clooney took me aside. "Not for his sake, Annie, but for yours, let's have peace, eh?"

"Sure," I said, "peace to all present," and I walked out, slamming the door after me.

I had had to vacate my room. At night, as I lay on a mattress next to Mary's bed, I could feel her antagonism building up. She was having to clean up their messes. On the third morning, I woke to find her packing. "Someone's ill in my family," she lied.

What most stuck in her throat was that Bob spent hours behind closed doors with Sinead.

"I found them together in . . ." Her voice trailed off.

"For God's sake, complete your—"

"The Bishop's bed."

Within an hour of her departure, the couple were back in the Bishop's room.

When Eamonn returned from London, he called Inch from Killarney asking us all to drive over to meet him.

I went first into his study. "I heard you were in the pub completely blotto."

"What is this," I said, "the third degree?"

"Mary found Bob and Sinead sleeping in *my* bed."

"What's the big deal? They're getting married soon."

He said, huffily, "I want no advice from you about right and wrong."

I was astonished. It was as if it had never occurred to him before that such things happened in his house. Also, I didn't like his attitude of "Don't do as I do, do as I say." He walked one way, his shadow walked another.

"But, Eamonn, think what *you* do under your own roof."

"Guests should know better than to sin in my bed."

He spoke to Bob privately and the lad apologized. We were all going that night to Tralee but, Bob assured him, they would leave next day.

When Eamonn met up with us in a bar in the center of Tralee, he was subdued. I felt he was seeing the world through different glasses. If he was horrified at an engaged couple sleeping together, what would people think if they knew that he, a bishop, slept nightly with me?

Charlie said something particularly nasty to me. Maybe it was the strain of the last few days, but I ran out crying. Bob came bounding after me but I turned on him unkindly and yelled, "Stay away from me."

Eamonn came after me in his car. He found me on my way to the beach. Whenever I panicked, I went like a fish in search of water and he knew that.

"Annie," he pleaded through the car window, "you cannot scream like that when you belong to the Bishop's party." As always, for Eamonn appearances were reality; things were what they seemed.

"I'm sick and tired of belonging to the Bishop's party," I told him. "I don't want to be inhibited like you Irish."

"*Annie*, I had an awful meeting in England and my stomach is killing me."

"Blackmail."

"Not true. Now my house is a mess. And I thought so highly of Sinead."

"Are you telling me she's trash?"

"I was going to marry them."

"And now?"

"With her in white, it'd embarrass them, knowing that I know."

"Know *what*, that they love each other? What's the matter with you, where's the spirit of Christian forgiveness?" Religious people hate having religion thrown at *them*.

"You sure," he said, "you didn't whip this up?"

"That is despicable," I shouted. "Whatever they did in your house they've been doing for a while."

"Maybe."

I left him abruptly, heading for the beach, and he drove alongside me:

"Annie, please."

I walked on without turning my head.

"Pet, I am in a very strange place in my life."

"Explain."

"Look at me on the way back from Dublin. If I didn't know you better, I'd have said you pretended to be ill so I—"

"Pre*tended*?"

When I faced him, my anger suddenly dissolved. He was suffering so badly from his colitis. He halted and I jumped in the rear seat.

He looked at me through his rearview mirror with distrust. It was as if I were incorrigible, and the bad in me was getting worse, corrupting people dear to him.

The shift in his attitude sent a shiver through me. We had reached the summit of our relationship and from now there was nowhere to go but down.

In a subdued mood, the young people left Inch early the next morning. Within the hour, Eamonn came home.

I led him into the dining room and flipped open his cigar box. Empty. I held up my arms. "I didn't smoke them, honest."

I threw open his gutted cocktail cabinet.

Faced with desolation. "But—"

"I spent hours cleaning this house. On my own."

I followed him into his bedroom. "I'm certainly not sleeping on these sheets," he said, whipping them off his bed.

Mary returned an hour after Eamonn, and a coldness seemed to grip all three of us.

It came as no surprise to me that he came into my bedroom that night with the plain intention of not sleeping with me. When he tried to kiss me good night, I said: "No thanks." I did not want him off-loading his guilt on me. "You live your own life."

Next morning, after breakfast, he came into my room. "Annie," he sighed, "I'm lost. Many EEC grants have fallen through. Maybe I was wrapped up in you and got careless."

"Thanks," I said, sharply.

"I'm blaming *me*, Annie."

I said I knew his work came first, which was why I was going home to America.

"Not yet," he begged.

That night, when Eamonn came home from Killarney, he tried to enter my room and found it locked.

This was talking-through-doors time. I said: "I'm packing."

"Let's talk."

"In the living room after dinner."

In the middle of our talk he suggested we drive down to the beach. He got into black slacks and a white shirt. On the moonlit sands, he took my hand and we walked on the edge of the waves that sent up a fragrant cooling breeze. I rolled up the legs of my jeans and took off my shoes, so I could walk by myself in the water. It was as if I were floating, leaving no more trace behind me than the wind. I loved the silky feel of water, the broad white moon-path across the sea, the deep faraway swan-lake of stars. In silvery light, under a haloed moon that presaged a sunny tomorrow, I had an elemental feeling that everything was somehow connected with everything else. If only we could see these almost unimaginable wonders, see, if need be, through pain, that there is hope and redemption through the communion of all created things.

Across the distance I had deliberately put between us to show we had choices, even the most terrible, Eamonn said: "But you're not ready to go yet."

"You mean, *you're* not ready to let me go."

We walked in silver-shadowy silence before he responded, his arms sweeping the tremulous sea, his fingers going up-up-up to the unshy moon. "You're right. If you left now I would think I had failed you." He beat his breast. "Whatever good I did you was annulled by my concern for my image. Also, my life has gone topsy-turvy."

"Tell me how."

Another painful silence before:

"I've broken all my vows. I run around in the mornings like a maniac to make my confession. Lately, I haven't even bothered to do that because my confessor keeps saying, 'You've got to let her go.' And . . . I can't."

I had understood that for a long time. Oil and water would not mix even for Eamonn.

"On the trip back from Dublin, Annie, I lost all control. I wasn't a priest—more like an alley cat."

How sad. He saw what we did as evil, whereas for me our love was liberating and lovely.

The incident in the car had opened his eyes to his own hypocrisy.

I stopped in my tracks. "Your confessor is right. It's got to end."

"But I will so miss you, Annie."

I sobbed. "It *is* heartbreaking to fall in love with someone you can never have."

He said, "If you go in anger, it will haunt me for the rest of my days."

Since he was in the middle of a crisis, this was now-or-never time. "If I stay, it's as much for you as for me. If you keep turning your love into healing, forget it."

He held out his hand to me to join him from the water. I refused until he said humbly: "We need each other."

It was like a voice out of the clouds because he never spoke of needing anybody.

I joyfully left the sea. Ours was a real, deep embrace, for, with his acknowledgment of need, I wanted his child more than ever. All I could think of was a baby boy with Eamonn's features and Eamonn's expression on his face.

After hugging each other contentedly, we walked arm in arm, with the water lapping the cream-edged sand. This was another binding, heart-baring moment.

"The pain," he said, "is ripping me apart. This sexual thing is so much more powerful than I had imagined. And"— he touched my breasts—"you are so beautiful and intelligent and spicy and funny."

Never had I felt so much his equal. The healer had himself been hurt but, though he could not see this, the wound was healing him of his inhumanity.

I was touched by his humility at revealing to me for the first time the terrible cost to him.

Solid differences remained. His faith was in faith, whereas mine was in love.

We went on walking for another half hour, saying little, leaving two sets of tracks in the sand.

When he came to my room later, his brandy glass was full to the brim and he had tied a double-knot in the cord of his robe.

"Sorry," I said, "but just turn around and head for home."

He looked at me in his puzzled fashion.

"Only men with single knots are allowed in my bedroom. That's an insult."

"Insult?"

"You expecting me to rape you?"

"No, Annie." He giggled, and took a huge swig of brandy.

"Why didn't you come in here wearing one of those old chastity belts out of a museum?"

He approached and let me undo the first knot. "I'm not staying, Annie."

He bent down to kiss me and I smelled sea-salt and infinity on his cheek. That first gentle kiss led to a second, less gentle, until he was searching my mouth with his tongue. When he allowed me some air, I suggested he might find life easier on the horizontal.

"Why not?"

He lay down beside me and I untied the second knot. "That'll *do*, Annie."

"Fine but stop kissing me."

"I'll just hold you till you go to sleep." Then the kissing began again and his hand came up under my nightdress. There followed a forty-five-minute strip, after which he put me on top of him and stayed in me a long time.

We had a whole week of making love like this. At the end of it, I, usually so bad at verbalizing, said, "I really love you."

Taking my hands, he pressed them to the sides of his head.

"'Tis very hard for me to say—"

"I know the point you're at, Eamonn; don't say any more."

He put his fingers over my lips. "'Tis just that we never take precautions. I try to get out of you but—"

"Listen," I said. "If I had your child, it wouldn't bother me if you married me or not."

"Where would be the healing in that for you, Annie?"

"In having made the man I love immortal."

"Don't tempt me with that," he said.

"But I don't want death to rub you out entirely."

He found the idea of immortality in the flesh both damnable and alluring. His attempt to withdraw from my body at climax was now part of his fear that our love could not work. For someone like him, who thought withdrawal doubly wrong, it must have boded our final separation.

He made me promise to tell him if my period was overdue. Once more, the chasm yawned between us. His disaster would be my triumph. What he most feared I most desired, for I had no wish to be sent away empty.

An interlude was over. And, strangely, though we loved each other more than ever, we knew the end was near.

Chapter
Twenty-Three

I N THE last week of July, my father called to say he was coming to Ireland for three months and would Eamonn find him and Hannah a place to stay in Dublin. He admitted he was nervous about me because lately I had not been in contact.

Eamonn handed me the phone. I assured Daddy I was having a good time and making progress in inner healing.

The plan had been for me to stay in Ireland for six weeks and I had been there over twice that long. Daddy sensed something was happening to me that he ought to know about. His meddling made me furious. His life was tough, I knew. He couldn't talk with Mommy, whose mind was wandering. Since Mary, too, was being difficult prior to her divorce, he felt the need to be near me.

Eamonn called the visit a godsend. The length of my stay at Inch was becoming an embarrassment to him. If I got a job in Dublin, only three hours away, I would have a place of my own and could stay in Ireland as long as I liked.

Being an active person, I looked forward to moving to Dublin and getting a job. He wrote me letters of recommendation to four hotels.

Eamonn drove Pat and me to Dublin, where we arranged with a real estate agency, Lisneys, to lease in Eamonn's name a two-bedroom apartment in a leafy suburb for $250 a month. It was in a one-story building on Leeson Park Avenue. It had high ceilings, thick-pile carpets, central heating, and it backed on the grounds of a hospital. We were less than a half mile south of Stephen's Green and a five-minute walk from the Burlington Hotel.

A few days before my parents' arrival, Eamonn was due to leave for Australia, where his brother, Michael, worked as a priest. He needed a three-week break from Ireland, he said.

I helped him pack. His wardrobe was from Harrods of London. He had brightly colored cotton shirts and linen pants, several pairs of hand-crafted shoes, and a tan safari suit.

What, I wondered, would absence do to the fondness of his heart?

He told me that when next we met he would be driving a new car. The Mercedes was a gas-guzzler. He needed something smaller, especially as he would have to make so many trips to Dublin.

This desire for economy was out of character. Was he trying to see whether, if he left the priesthood, he could live a simpler life?

The last few nights before he left he was especially passionate. We had had marvelous times in Inch. We both sensed they were coming to an end and would never return. We kissed good-bye next to the big-leafed summer-long geraniums. Around us the only sound was the soft fluting of the wind.

The house seemed lonely when he left. When he returned, I hoped, he would come back tanned, refreshed, healthy-looking and find Inch filled with the emptiness of my departure.

I went to Killarney to say farewell. Pat said, "Larry will miss you. Me, too. You brought a special openness into our lives." And Father O'Keeffe: "You are more Irish, Annie, than the Irish."

I hugged them both with tears in my eyes.

At Inch, I took a last long look-around. I walked the beach and wrote "I Love Inch" in the grainy sand before the tide washed it away. I climbed the hill behind the house and waved to mountains that shivered in the heat: Farewell, Brandon and Stradbally, and, you, most westerly, Mount Eagle. I stroked the lawn on which we had lain side by side on the night of my panic attack. I said goodbye to my room, and to his, so full of memories, I knelt to kiss the rug in front of the hearth on which we had made love.

I might return, of course, spend days or weeks as his guest, but Inch would never be our home again.

I never knew how much my parents meant to me until they came through Customs at Dublin airport.

I was first struck by the familiar—I mean, the contrast in size between my parents. My father, at six feet six inches, was always imposing but, with only one leg, he walked with the stiff dignified gait of a giraffe. Next to him, my mother, looking like the Duchess of Windsor, was, even in her high heels, twelve inches shorter.

My mind flew back to the day Daddy came home complaining of a pain in his left foot. Spring at Inafield, least threatening of seasons. Forsythia blowing yellow clouds in the wind, lilacs budding, dogwood in bloom, fallen apple blossoms lying like pink shadows under the trees on the driveway. Daddy propped his foot up on the old black kitchen chair for Mommy to remove his shoe and sock. After a five-minute examination: "For Christ's sake, Hannah, tell me." "A crack in that old corn of yours," she said, "and a mean-looking inflammation around it."

Daddy's short, thickset Irish partner, Dr. Dolorhey, was summoned and, looking through his tortoiseshell spectacles: "Nasty, Jack. The dye from your sock may have infected it. Could go haywire with that diabetes of yours."

Nightly soakings, salvings, and bandagings did no good. Daddy went back to work; his sugar count rose and pus appeared on the foot. The Doctors' Hospital advised rest, medication, and Jacuzzi baths. Then Mommy spotted a red streak moving toward the toes, two of which were bloated and blackened, and the doctor said the dreaded word: "Gangrene."

First the toes went, but the foot still swelled and gave off an odor. Finally, he was rushed to the New York Hospital, where his left leg was amputated four inches above the knee.

When Mommy visited him, she could hear his screams from the end of the corridor. She heard them in her dreams and it worked better than AA; she stopped drinking for a while.

Now my parents were visiting me in my new homeland. Daddy was in an executive hat, beige trench coat, navy blue pinstriped suit, and paisley tie. He carried his usual glossy black cane. Mom, my pale, blue-eyed Mom, was in a six-hundred-dollar Sybil Connolly hunter green suit, and she had a turban on her head. They brought with them from America my home at Inafield and my childhood, my brothers and my sister, the sad times and the happy times. I felt proud of them. And I needed them.

I reached up to my father and he reached down and we kissed and hugged somewhere in between. He saw—instant relief—I was not chewed up but tanned and relaxed.

When I embraced my mother, I picked up the smell of liquor, taken because of her fear of flying.

My father adored the apartment. While Mommy was unpacking he looked out the window to the back and sighed, "Everything I dreamed of. Thanks, sweetheart."

His simple gratitude touched my heart.

"You'll never know," he whispered, "how trying your mother can be. It's not her fault but—"

"She's still drinking?"

He nodded. "You seem contented, Annie."

"I'm fine," I said noncommittally.

"And Eamonn, he took good care of you?"

"Couldn't have been nicer."

Four days later, Mary flew in with her four-year-old son, Bobby, for a two-week visit.

It was quite a family reunion.

I had written Mary asking her to bring me over a few condoms. Maybe this was my way of confiding in one member of my family.

The first quiet moment we had together, Mary came out firing from the hip. "What d'you want with those rubbers?"

"You brought them with you?"

"I forgot."

"Then I won't be doing anything with them."

"If you get pregnant you'll blame me, is that it?"

She ran her fingers through her beautiful long blond hair. And breathlessly: "You don't write Daddy but you write me long letters about this white-hat Bishop you're staying with. What's between you? Don't lie to me.''

I laughed. "Can't I even make one call to my lawyer?''

Out of her exquisite cat-like mouth came a tirade. "I'm not the cops, Annie, I'm your goddamn sister. I can tell you are screwing that Bishop, who just happens to be Mommy's second cousin. And you have no pills, no rubbers, how the hell do you think this is going to end?'' She rubbed the pouches under her eyes. "Christ, am I jet-lagged. You said rubbers are illegal in this country, even doctors get locked up for giving samples. So you wanted me to risk importing them. Jesus God, are only bishops allowed to use condoms here? So, I forgot. Have you thought of a diaphragm like Mommy used to wear? You surely can't *want* to have a bishop's brat. I mean, I must be having a heart attack, you surely aren't such a fucking idiot you want God to make lightning specially for little Annie Murphy of Connecticut?'' She groaned. "Oh, shit, why're we whispering, let's get out of this dump.''

We found a bar in King Street, not far from Stephen's Green. In an empty booth at the back, she ordered, "Give me a cold beer and one for my crazy sister.''

When the bartender was out of earshot: "This is *Ireland*, Annie. Land of saints and scholars, and they crucify sinners like you to prove it.''

"Guilty till proved innocent, that it?''

"You are having an affair with the most famous bishop in the Emerald Isle. You could be shot.''

"Shot?''

"Pious Catholics would do that just for the Indulgence. Don't you realize, Annie, that 'most every Catholic in Ireland has a gun? I read about it. You want to leave this country in a coffin?''

"Let's talk about your marriage.''

"Don't talk about the dead.'' Sharp change of mood, conspiratorial wink. "C'mon, Annie, what's the guy like?''

I winked back, told her the way Eamonn made fun of everything and everyone, especially himself, and how he suffered from colitis, even milking that for laughs, and how he drove so fast that if St. Christopher were aboard, he'd die of fright.

The more we talked the more we laughed. But eventually she said, "This thing with the Bishop inside that love nest is a catastrophe and you don't even recognize it."

"Recognize what?"

"The sin, stupid. I can feel the wickedness."

Her reaction horrified and astonished me. She was getting a divorce, which the Church says is a sin, but she, like Eamonn, was far more concerned with *my* wrongdoing.

After two weeks, Mary left me in tears at the airport to return home. "Be good, Annie," she said; "don't let that Bishop give you anything but his blessing."

Chapter
Twenty-Four

WITH MY fond memories of the Burlington Hotel I phoned its personnel manager for a job. He offered me an interview.

I entered the big glitzy lobby and gave my name at the porter's desk. A minute later, a thirty-year-old woman in a white blouse and military-blue uniform came toward me with a very arrogant walk. She had pitch-black hair pulled back in a neat bun and the biggest green eyes I ever saw. Even those eyes did not soften her chiseled handsome features.

"Murphy?" Her smiled was made all the more treacherous by a mouthful of capped white teeth. "Are you Murphy?"

Irish-looking, she spoke with a pucker English accent.

"I am, Miss—?"

Before I could read "Randall" on her identity brooch: "You're hired."

"To do what?"

"We need someone who understands the whims of Americans who make up most of our clientele." Her toothy smile seemed altogether less threatening.

"Aren't you going to interview me?"

"I just did."

"I admire your judgment," I said.

"That's two of us."

She shook my hand and said, "Call me Randall. Bridget to my enemies."

She took me to see the personnel manager. Mr. Rice was

low-key and he looked like Woody Allen. "You'll be use-ful," he said, "in information, as a telephonist, and as a guide."

I hadn't realized I was so highly qualified.

Afterward, Bridget said, "The pay's a princely twenty-five pounds a week."

It had all been so easy I wondered if Eamonn had had a word with the manager. If so, I wasn't complaining.

Randall supervised the telephonists. She showed me around the harsh-lighted exchange. When she introduced me to the four girls, their hands going like pistons, I turned an instant yellow.

"Never mind, Murphy." Randall slapped a girl on the back. "Show her how it's done, O'Toole."

O'Toole, with a mouthpiece strapped to her face and five cord plugs over her shoulder, gave me a swift garbled com-mentary while she pulled cords in and out with lightning speed. One of them hit me in the eye. "See," she said, "nothing to it. You do it."

With my eye watering, I tried and got into an awful mess.

My turn to have Bridget noisily slap my back. "Murphy, you are slicker than I thought. Any questions?"

"One."

"Ask."

"Why'd you hire me?"

"Because I can't stomach any more fucking Irish. They should all go home to England or America."

I now understood my primary qualification for the job. I also knew that Randall, in addition to a basically kind nature, had a tongue on her that could cut to the bone.

Within a few days I was slinging the connecting cords in and out as fast as the best of them.

In my free time, Bridget introduced me to raw Dublin life while my parents took me out at nights for dinner in hotels like the Hibernian and the classy Shelbourne on the north side of Stephen's Green. One evening, Daddy called up a doctor friend, Harry Burke. He lived in Howth, a suburb on the northern arm of Dublin Bay. He came over and took us to his beautiful house for a meal.

Bridget kept trying to find out what I was doing in Dublin.

We met up after work in Sonny's, a bar in Ranelagh, not far from our hotel. In that relaxed atmosphere, she freely gave information about herself. "I really wanted to be a Shakespearean actress, Murphy," she told me in the manner of Lady Macbeth. "And now look at me. Thirty-one years old. I rent a one-bed flat with running water, mostly down the walls. My job is supervising idiot telephonists in a Dublin hotel. How did I sink so low?"

Sipping my ginger ale, I said: "Shakespeare would have appreciated the tragedy."

"Tra-ge-dy," she said, theatrically. "More a Whitehall farce. And you?"

I spoke guardedly about my broken marriage and my desire to find peace in Ireland.

"That'll do," she said, coolly. "To start with."

One night, she broke down in tears as she told me of an affair that resulted in an ectopic pregnancy. "I lost one tube, Murphy, so I guess I'm sterile, and my gall bladder was in such a state it rotted my teeth."

"That's why you've had them capped."

"Murphy, you are an *awful* sod. You were not supposed to notice."

"They're really very beautiful," I said.

"Sure, so beautiful everyone notices them as soon as I open my mouth." They had not lessened her attractiveness. At least, Jim Wentworth, the hotel chief of security, found her irresistible.

I introduced Bridget to my parents and they instantly took to each other. They were all larger than life.

In the first week of September, Eamonn, back from Australia, telephoned. Daddy took the call. Eamonn invited all three of us to dinner the following Saturday night.

"You free, Annie?"

"Probably not, Daddy."

I wanted to be as relaxed about Eamonn as I could.

"Talk to him yourself."

"Hi, Eamonn," I said. "Have a good trip Down Under?"

"Can we talk?"

"Sure. And your brother?"

"There's no extension to that phone?"

"Not at all. I have a job at the Burlington which keeps me pretty busy."

"Listen carefully. I will drop your parents back at the apartment about ten and meet you straight after."

"Sounds good, but it must have been really hot there."

"Leave the Burlington by the side exit, walk left along Burlington Road. After a hundred yards cross over to the junction with Wellington Road. See you at five past ten."

"I'm sorry, too, Eamonn, perhaps another time."

"And, Annie, I've got a surprise for you."

"My parents are really keen to see you again."

My father nodded agreement from the couch.

"Pet, I love you."

"God bless, Eamonn."

I put the phone down. "He sends his love."

On Saturday night, I turned down Bridget's offer of a drink in Sonny's, saying I had a splitting headache. I was very excited at the prospect of seeing Eamonn again. What was the surprise in store? A present from Australia?

I left the hotel soon after ten. I was standing in the rain at the road junction when a medium-blue two-seater sports car drew up alongside me. All I saw was the capped head of the driver.

Just my luck, I thought, *a curb crawler.* I walked on a bit. But the driver was not giving up on me. I was young and shapely and this was Saturday night in Dublin.

I heard the window on the passenger side open electronically and a familiar voice said: "Why are you cold-shouldering me, Annie?"

"Jesus," I squawked, "you really scared me."

He had a glossy black cap on his head and he was wearing a long trench coat though the weather was mild. I glanced at the car. A brand-new expensive-looking Lancia. Was I the loose woman to go with the fast car?

"Where'd you get *this?*"

As I settled in to the lush bucket seat, he leaned over and gave me a kiss that smelled of the big cigar he was smoking. "Good to see you again. Oh, the car, I had it imported direct from Italy."

Not keen to hang around in the vicinity of the hotel, he drove off in his usual tearing hurry.

"It's got a gear stick," I said.

"Sorry about that. Restricts my hand movements somewhat. But you should see the way it corners."

"I believe you." I was anxious for him not to prove it.

The smell of new leather was almost as strong as his cigar. I had never smelled that kind of cigar aroma before. We were heading north into the rain-arrowed lights of the city, past tall run-down Georgian houses in Leeson Street toward the green.

"I shall miss the Mercedes," I said, remembering.

"No need."

"You didn't sell it or trade it in for this?"

He shook his head. "The Mercedes will be for official visits; this for, shall we say, pleasure?"

I was so pleased to see him again I did not bother to ask where he was taking me. He clearly had a precise location in mind. Any dry warm room out of the rain would do.

We headed for O'Connell Street, but just before the Liffey we turned west. The whole place was lit up and crowded at this hour. Green smoky double-decker buses kept obstructing us, so Eamonn had to shift gears like a racing driver. We continued past the huge Guinness complex toward Heuston Station with the Phoenix Park on our right. The giant Wellington obelisk in the park was my last landmark. He was telling me about his priest brother and the places he had visited, Sydney and Melbourne, and the people he had met, including many aboriginals in the outback.

I took in little, so enraptured was I by his presence. He filled areas of my being that were desolate without him.

By the time I was ready to peer through the windshield, we were in an ill-lit suburb blackened by rain. "Where're we going?" I asked anxiously.

He threw his cigar stub out the window. "Trust me."

I did, of course, but some things did not add up. We had already driven for about thirty minutes. This was not exactly motel country and, in any case, he was in his clericals. Without warning, he turned off the main road into a dark side street. As he slowed down, I sensed danger. Maybe he intended that. But this was a new kind of danger, one that did not emanate from my own inbuilt fears but from

him. He was my security; I did not like to feel nervous in
his company.

On the left, was a large paint-peeled unhinged metal gate
that looked as if it had not been closed in years. I saw what
looked like a huge cavern ahead and a small sign, "Sand and
Gravel."

Bridget had recently taken me to see Sean O'Casey's play
Shadow of a Gunman. Its eerie atmosphere had got to me.

For a few seconds, my racing brain told me: What if the
surprise is not the car but a brutal death? A bishop who
fornicates is not dependable; break one commandment, break
them all. And where better to dispose of my body than in this
out-of-the-way place? Eamonn has always covered his traces.
He has never given me a present or written me one letter to
which he signed his name.

What finally shook me was that he drove into the gravel
pit so fast and halted so sharply between piles of sand and
crushed stones that it was plain he had been there before.
How else would he have known that there was no night
watchman, that he would not run into heavy machinery? The
place was demonic. What made it worse was the excitement
of a reunion with the man I loved and who obviously could
not wait to have sex with me.

Eamonn whipped off his cap and tossed it behind him.

"Wait," I said, "I want some answers. First, how'd you
know where this place was?"

"Saw it on my way to and from Dublin."

"But you pulled up in this exact spot, as if you've been
here many times before."

"Only this afternoon, in preparation."

"For *what?*" Picking up on Mary's phrase, I said, "You
mean this is our new love nest?"

He was already tugging off his top clothes. I was reminded
of my Texas days. This was teenager stuff. Painful memories
of nights behind steamed-up car windows crowded in on me.

"Isn't this a perfect spot, Annie?"

Compared with the luxuries of Inch and its views of the
sea, it was like a doss house. Worse, lust was taking over. It
is hard to love tenderly while you are tumbling and groping
in the bucket seats of a sports car.

What was the alternative? he argued. We could not go back

to Inch on a permanent basis. He was too well known to book us into a hotel in Dublin. Once my parents returned to America, I would take over the apartment and we would be free.

I quieted down and we enjoyed a fun evening in the fogged-up dark. The front seats folded back but we soon emigrated to the back. I have never known a man so agile in such a restricted space.

We took off any clothes that got in our way and the rest were undone. He expended on me the pent-up feelings of three weeks of abstinence. His long drawn-out sigh was something to treasure.

For a couple of hours we stayed there, our chat broken up with a second session of lovemaking.

I told him about my new job. I gave him a graphic account of Mary's visit to Dublin and he hooted with laughter. He told me my parents were very pleased with the way I looked and that the ten pounds I had put on suited me. "But be careful," he warned, "your mother has noticed the spring in your step."

"Does she suspect you are responsible?"

"All I can say, Annie, is she kept looking at me out of the corner of her eye and once she said, 'Annie seems like a woman in love.' "

We agreed to meet in two weeks, when Eamonn would be free. The night ended with his dropping me off near the apartment.

My parents were in bed but next morning, my mother said: "We had a wonderful evening with the Bishop in the Hibernian Hotel. Harry Burke joined us for dinner."

"That's nice," I said.

"Yes," Daddy said. "Harry disagreed with Eamonn about the changes he made to his Cathedral. I don't think they get on."

Mommy said, eyeing me, "He sends you his special love."

"That's nice of Harry," I said.

"Eamonn did."

"Oh," I said, nonchalantly, "it's nice of him, too."

Chapter
Twenty-Five

BY DAY, I worked at the hotel with Bridget. I spent most evenings with her, too, but a few with my parents. Whenever Eamonn came to town, he had priority.

I was never really reconciled to love in a gravel pit. There was little talk and a lot of action. Nor did I like the furtive way, as soon as we drove homeward into the city lights, he asked me to hand him his collar, chain, and jacket from the backseat.

By early October, Bridget had guessed there was a man in my life. Once she got me tipsy and wheedled out of me where I had been staying before I came to Dublin.

"A very interesting man, the flying Bishop," she mused. "I've read so much about him. Quite young, too."

One Friday night, she invited Wentworth and me for drinks at her small ground-floor apartment. All she had on was a robe with blue ruffles; and she played tapes and we drank.

I walked past the apartment at eight the next morning and banged on her bedroom window.

"Get up, you sluts," I said loudly, in my best Irish accent. "I want you both out of my bed-sit this very hour."

Whispers inside before Bridget pulled back the drape. "Murphy," she screamed, "you absolute bloody shit."

I saw Wentworth's pinkie with its emerald ring appear above the sheet.

"You realize, Randall," I said, "you and that lump in bed with you will roast in hell."

Wentworth slowly surfaced from beneath the covers with a venomous, "You fecking bitch, Murphy."

Bridget came to work at midday. "Murphy, come and have a spot of tea with me in the cafeteria, if you'd be so kind."

"C'mon," I said, "don't fire me. We had such fun."

"You and I did." She sipped her tea in a melancholy way. "But a tragedy happened last night."

"What?" I asked naively.

"I was robbed of my innocence by the security officer of the Burlington Hotel."

"But he was a gentleman last night, Randall."

"I do feel a bit better today," she admitted. "But, you bastard, you encouraged him. I'm going to get you."

And she did. That very night.

I was about to climb into Eamonn's Lancia when I saw someone very like Bridget hiding behind a tree.

I had been edgy all night. The rain was pelting down and the gravel pit looked like something out of hell. The first lovemaking session was more strenuous than usual because over his boxer shorts Eamonn wore designer long johns to ease his colitis. The long johns were from Germany; they were of nylon and a remarkable cherry red. I ragged him, saying his cardinalate tights, like his socks, betrayed his ambitions.

I could see him getting worried. Was my nervousness rubbing off on him? "I am wondering, pet, if the tires are stuck in the mud."

He got into the driver's seat and switched on. When he engaged the engine, the rear tires whizzed around. This went on for several minutes. The high-pitched revving sound in that cavernous place attracted attention. A car marked GARDA slowly cruised past the gate.

"Police," I shrieked. We waited with bated breath until the car passed by a second time.

I said, "They're assuming we're lovers and they're giving us a chance to get out."

"The fecking car won't budge."

"Try again," I said, with my usual squealy laugh.

Tugging his red tights half up, he looked in his mirror and saw me naked from the top up. "For cripesakes, Annie, get your clothes on and come sit in the front with me."

I was so jittery I could not button up my blouse.

"Can't you do anything right?" he said.

"Maybe you should sit in the back and let me drive."

"You don't have an Irish license, eejit."

"Don't you call me that."

"Shut up, and get dressed, I've got to think."

"I can show the police your license."

Now he got really mad at me. "How would you get by with my license?"

"I could tell them I was a transvestite. That's what you look like in those tights."

"Oh, I could die right now." He sighed. "God, take me, I do not want to live."

"Okay, sit in the back," I repeated, scared because his pulse rate was far too fast at times. "I'll cover you with a blanket like they do in the movies."

"Grand, except I don't have a blanket and, besides, 'tis not fitting for a bishop to do so."

Eamonn had acted like a naughty boy and was getting a taste of his own medicine. This man who made Catholics tremble before him was himself trembling because of the cops. He was a member of the hierarchy who intruded mercilessly into the sex lives of others. Maybe a police inquiry into what a bishop did at night in a gravel pit might do them all good.

"Eamonn," I said sharply, "they're coming again."

"Oh God, dear God, oh my God."

I started to laugh because the situation was so earthy and so true. I contrasted Eamonn in his episcopal finery with the half-naked man next to me struggling to zip up his fly and button his shirt after making fumbling love in a gravel pit.

The puncturing of pretensions, not only his but of all humankind, made me laugh some more. And laughter healed me. And, in spite of his fears, he joined in and it healed us both because we were always able to laugh together. Nothing was too solemn or too sacred but that laughter would not make it holier and more dear. My God was a God who laughed everything into existence; and no single thing would cease existing while it still had in it the slightest capacity to make us laugh.

The Garda car passed us again. "Eamonn," I said, shakily,

"you don't think they're waiting for a backup team and a paddy wagon?"

His hands went futilely up-up-up in the air. "The driving license," he moaned, "the registration number of the car, everything is in my name. We might as well both sit here bald naked and let the Guards come take us to the Four Courts for trial."

"Get out," I said; and pointing, "Put those notebooks under the back wheel to give us leverage."

"I cannot," he said, climbing out of the car barefoot and immediately groaning because of the splashing from cold mud. "They are official papers from my last EEC meeting."

I scrambled into the driving seat. "Then"—I grabbed his coat—"it'll have to be this."

"No, Annie, that's from Harrods and it's got my name stitched into it. You don't need your clothes, do you?"

I hugged myself tight. "Never," I said. "Either your trench coat or jail."

He grudgingly stuffed his precious coat behind the back wheels and I started the engine. At the first attempt, I lurched forward out of the mud. After grabbing his coat, he ran after me, screaming, "For God's sake, Annie, come back."

I slowed down to let him catch up to me but stayed behind the wheel. "I'm thinking of leaving you here," I said. "It's about time you faced the world without your clerical camouflage."

"But, Annie," he whimpered, "you wouldn't do that. You *love* me. Here I am in a gravel pit with the cops waiting to pounce and my poor long johns are soaked to the knees."

I looked him up and down. Finally: "Okay, hop in."

Fortunately, we did not meet the cops.

"That," he sighed, "was the worst experience of my life."

"Blame it on me, Eamonn."

I could tell he already had.

Next morning, Bridget called me.

"Well, well, Murphy, fancy that. I was wondering how that Bishop treated you in Inch."

"Quiet," I hissed. "My father's next door."

"After all, the clergy are all sex-mad, as anyone in the hotel trade knows. How'd you make out with your chauffeur?"

"We had a quiet dinner to discuss my mother's drinking problem."

"Dinner, my eye. I was only poked by a poor old security guard, but you, Murphy, have been—"

I crashed the phone down.

In addition to my sister Mary, now Bridget knew, and Bridget lived in Ireland, had an Irish boyfriend, and drank heavily. But it was when I myself got drunk that I spilled the beans. This was two weeks later. Bridget blackmailed me into it by telling me, truly or not, that I was to blame for the morning sickness she was experiencing.

The night after that, the most momentous thing in my whole life occurred.

In spite of our skirmish with the police, Eamonn still took his chances in the gravel pit. He was simply more careful to park his car on firmer ground. He also brought a piece of wood in the trunk in case he needed it to get out of the mud.

Why wood? Maybe it reminded him of salvation by the wood of the cross. I told him an old sack or a piece of carpet was better.

We had no sooner reached our destination than I saw another car parked in the shadows. "Do you think the cops are waiting for us?" I whispered.

"That car is not marked."

"Undercover agents?"

The couple in the other car must have had their suspicions about us because they drove away on squealing tires.

It was the very end of October, a near-full moon was in the sky. My parents were about to leave Ireland, which meant this was probably our good-bye to the gravel pit.

I felt in my abdomen a kind of pain that was for me the sign of ovulation. I told him frankly, "Tonight is the *night*."

"Don't spoil it, Annie, please."

I smothered his warnings with kisses. That time, I insisted on being on top in the reclining front seat of the car. Had he struggled, my weight, in that confined space, would have made it impossible for him to throw me off. I wanted no spark of lust. This was to be love and only love.

Almost the grimmest place in Ireland was transformed for me that night. It was as when a perfect rose rises out of a dung heap. There was no romance in the setting, only and entirely love. This was romantic because love was reduced to its essence: two people who cared for each other and wanted only to express their love.

It struck me what we did had been done in far uglier places, in hovels, prisons, and refugee camps, among Jews in cattle trucks taking them to Auschwitz. It is an expression of richness in poverty, proof that love can conquer everything.

The car in which my child was conceived was our little church. Whether people make love on grass in the open air, in the bed of a bishop's palace, or on the floor of a hovel, whether to a background of surf, sea, and wind, or of noisy automobiles, *there* for them is their holy place. Inside me, whatever Eamonn might say, was his true place of worship, more splendid, more worthy than any cathedral built by hands.

Yet we were so ordinary. Not anarchists, not immensely wicked. Only because of circumstances were we subjects of what many would consider a sordid little drama that might easily end in tragedy. All this subterfuge and pain because society makes complicated rules and insists that God's reputation depends on us keeping them. Because society will not allow ordinary people like us to behave in the most ordinary of ways.

That night, unusually for me, I was very verbal, rapturously so. I wove a spell of words around him. I told him all that he meant to me, all that he had done for me. "My time here has been magical," I said, "and I'll never again meet anyone like you."

I wanted him to know that I would never have the slightest regret for whatever happened to me. I told him I loved him now and forever.

And when he said he loved me and came inside me I felt utter gladness and serenity, as if life itself were flowing inside me. In that mutual profession of love, I knew that in my body we were two, my child and I.

This was one of those strange psychic moments when you know with certainty what cannot possibly be known. And from this point on, from a deed done in love in the harsh surroundings of a gravel pit, my entire life was about to change forever.

Chapter Twenty-Six

MY PARENTS prepared to fly home. Daddy found Dublin an extended village with little to distract him from the raw, insinuating presence of Wishie. Then there was the yellow smear of autumn, too many days when the sun did no sightseeing, the intense cold and early dark reminding him of death. He had forgotten how soon winter comes to Ireland and how bone-rotting the damp, once September days had passed. Above all, he missed the glitz and frenzy of New York.

The morning my parents left, Daddy said, "It's good to see you so settled. I told you Eamonn would heal you."

"How'd he do it?" Mom said. "That's what I want to know."

"You can't stay here forever," Daddy said at the airport. "But whenever you come home, Annie, I'll be there."

Eamonn called to check that my parents had left. Our talk turned to money. I told him that Bridget wanted to share the apartment with me and neither of us earned a lot.

"I have quite a small income myself, Annie, and everything else is on credit card."

"Money," I said, "could be the least of your worries."

"You mean I might become a different type of father?"

"Don't let's celebrate too soon," I said.

I sensed that this man who so often prided himself on being

lucky—never so far an accident in driving or in having sex with me—was becoming resigned to the inevitable.

No matter. He was a cork on the ocean, afloat and upright even in a storm. He lived only for the moment, regardless of consequences. Which is why he made a good lover. But if and when it was confirmed that I was carrying his child, would he come away with me or discard me for good?

In my heart, I knew the answer already.

I had worked overtime at the Burlington. On the Friday after my parents' departure, I was free to stay with Eamonn at Inch until Sunday night.

On the train that afternoon, I saw little of the countryside because in early November it soon gets dark. But I began the habit of talking to my baby. "I love you," I kept saying. "I love your father and I love you and I swear to God I'll never be separated from you."

At Killarney, Eamonn was waiting for me in his Mercedes. He was very pleased to see me, but I noticed an almost forlorn look in his wide-open eyes. "I missed you," he whispered. "So good to have you back."

"And away from the gravel pit."

A wild dark night, and his driving had not changed. Inside the front door he started kissing me. Good, Mary was absent.

His hands were in my hair, on my breasts, up my dress. Locked together, we lurched down the hallway with him undressing me with trembling fingers and removing his jacket and muttering, "This thing, this thing," as though something alien had him in its grip.

I was sad for him, for his lack of control, and at the same time overwhelmed by his sweetness and innocence.

"I can't make it to the bed," he gasped, pulling me down on my hands and knees.

"Please," I said, "not here." I spoke out of pity for him.

He stretched me backward on the floor at the entrance to his room. Above me was the first Station of the Cross: Jesus Is Condemned to Death. That upset me because the chief thing I loved about the Catholic religion was Jesus, a good Man, going to an undeserved death. I imagined the look of bewilderment on His face as it dawned on Him that people were bad enough to want Him dead when He only came to help.

On Eamonn's face was the same look, of vulnerability, of someone condemned for something he did not understand; but this was allied to such deep want in him that I felt I had never loved him more. Self-sacrifice had made him deny his real self. What I saw, as I lay under the first Station of the Cross, was the real Eamonn hidden too long under all the sham desire to live like an angel.

"Let's go to bed," I said. "This floor's too much like the gravel pit."

For him, the bed was a mile away. I held him and stroked him as he quivered and quaked against me. Afterward, we lay completely still, warmed by each other, mindlessly one.

In a kind of pained dream-like soliloquy, he said, "Wild, wild, wild, hungry, to give and receive so much, to be aware of loneliness, to be so needy, to feel such warmth, to be so . . . afraid."

I stood up and held out my hand. He took it and I led him to the bed, helped him get in, and climbed in next to him.

"I really love you, Annie, but I'm scared." I touched his lips to show I did not like that last word.

"I feel as if I have been taken over by a force I can't master."

"Talk about it," I said.

He told me how he was recently at an important meeting—millions of pounds of European Community grants at stake: "And, boom, Annie, you come into my mind. Suddenly, someone coughs—'Bishop'—and I come to, unaware of anything said for perhaps five minutes. And, Annie—"

I felt honored. "Yes?"

"Even at Mass, I think of you." He was lost, muttering something about even Judas had the decency not to turn up on Calvary.

I was the last to make up his mind for him. As soon ask a sheep the way to the slaughterhouse. But my reluctance to speak was due only to my profound respect. I loved him but I could not tell him whether he should love me or not. I could not take responsibility for him giving up a lifelong calling however unsuited to it he was. I could not tell him that he had only to change his thoughts, and his love for me would seem a sign not of weakness but of strength.

My role was to support him in whatever he decided to do.

Even to say "Send me away, Eamonn, and I'll go" would be to apply the wrong sort of pressure. My silence devastated him. He blamed me for not providing an answer that only he could give. Did he want me to change water into wine by giving him back his innocence?

In years to come, I might regret my silence. I could have said that what we had done had made his life as a cleric impossible, especially if I was carrying his child. I could have begged him to swallow his pride and choose one of several alternatives. I could have come right out with "Eamonn, you might be celibate but you cannot be chaste; not because you are weak but because you were abused as a child by the imposition of a mistaken piety."

I had still to ask myself the most difficult questions.

Suppose he came away with me—would we be happy, as happy, I mean, as we had been at Inch?

Could I bear to see him stripped of his titles and banished from his Cathedral, see him exchange his bishop's robes for a collar and tie and executive suit?

Could I bear to see him lose the respect due him as a priest from his father, friends, the public at large?

Above all, could I bear to see him abandon his special role as provider for the hungry in distant lands?

Our life together had so far taken place in a world of ambiguity and make-believe. That had made it dangerous and almost mystical. Could we bear the humdrum nine-to-five job, the commuting, the heavily mortgaged house in suburbia, the quiet nights in front of the television—after we had lived inside a magic bubble?

What if our love was beautiful precisely because it was destined *not* to last? Oh, God, what if he left the priesthood and came away with me and, when the dream within a dream dissolved, we awoke to unreality and found ourselves strangers? "Who am I? Who are you?"

Having refused his offer to speak, from then on I was at Eamonn's mercy. But if I could not rely on that, what point was there in living anyway? For an hour or more we lay side by side, holding hands, not speaking a word, in dread.

While he fixed us a meal, I went into my bedroom to unpack my few things. I opened the curtains to let in the pure rays of the cloud-peeled moon. I saw in silhouette the mountains, their peaks like motionless horsemen; I heard waves pound the shore. How good to look at and listen to timeless things. How many sorrows felt to be unendurable had happened here at Inch under the watchful eyes of those mountains, against the soothing sounds of that sea, and all their pain had passed?

I played Eamonn the Chieftains' tape, "Playboy of the Western World," after which we slept in his bed and woke up about two. He fetched himself a brandy and a cup of tea for me. Eamonn the vulnerable turned into Eamonn the suspicious.

I had not told him I had used Bridget as my confessor but he was afraid that if she became my flatmate, she might wonder what he was doing on his visits. "She's as tough as old boots, Annie. An old thirty. And you could not fart, excuse me, without her knowing. Even if you did it silently she would see your skirt move that fraction of an inch."

He told me not to drink too much with her around, and I assured him I had given that up.

"Has she a boyfriend?"

I told him the name and the fact that he was a hurling player and also the security officer at the Burlington.

"An ex-cop," I said. "A detective. He drinks."

"God Al*mighty*, Annie, I'll check him out. That flat's been leased in my name. It could become a gin hall."

He rubbed his head and his stomach.

"You don't seem to realize, Annie, your beauty would shame a rose and you are very, very sexy. You could be raped."

"Thanks for the kind word."

He also feared Bridget might persuade me to date. "If you did meet somebody else," he said, in a mournful tone, "you mustn't consider me."

"Of course not, Eamonn."

He instantly demanded, "Of course not, *what?*"

His jealousy irritated me. I was even faithful to my favorite pair of jeans. I wore them practically till disgrace did us part. Could I discard my perfect love in favor of another? I said, "You fear for me in wicked Dublin? That's rich coming from the Playboy of the Western World."

"Who? Me?" he gasped. "What do you mean?"

"I mean your new Lancia and you wearing devilish red tights and misbehaving in a Dublin gravel pit so even the cops have to flush you out."

"Don't joke me, Annie. Bridget living in the flat could be far more dangerous than what happened in the gravel pit." He calmed his fears with a second helping of lovemaking.

Next morning, he left at nine, saying he would not be back till midnight.

I spent the day in a restless mood. I went out onto the lawn. Season of frugal beauty. A day of whitewashed skies and heavy-lidded sunshine, the light brassy where the sun should have been. A needlepointed wind pricked my cheeks. Somewhere, a dog barked. From a far-off gully, rain headed my way like a swarm of flies.

Nothing, not even the sere grass, the trees antlered by the fall, the last shabby rose, looked real. Low over the white blossom of the sea, a guillemot and her young chick were flying happily together when a great black-backed gull appeared and attacked the chick. The mother made frantic efforts to act as a decoy, and when that failed, she tried to beat him off with her wings. The gull swooped and swooped, forcing the chick to dip ever lower toward the sea. It was an unfair contest, but I did not see its resolution because all three birds disappeared around the headland.

That day and for many days after, I kept seeing the mother bird instinctively trying to protect her babe, her joy, her future, from the vicious black-backed gull.

Once more, the certainty came to me that I had a second life to guard. I had noticed in my first pregnancy the change of smell in my urine, this acceleration of all my bodily processes, this salmon-leap of my pulse.

I went indoors for one of Mary's Valium. At the same time, I went through her small library for a book to help me pass the time. I settled on *The Betsy* by Harold Robbins. I laughed at the impossible sexy passages.

Becoming bored, I walked the lawn in the grape-bloom light of dusk. A wind rose suddenly, fallen leaves turned into butterflies.

Back indoors, I watched TV while drinking endless cups of tea. I was all edges. Through the window I saw the rise of a sunburned moon and from the west clouds were on the march. A wind rose with the force of a sea, first going puh-puh-puh like gas igniting before banging brassy knuckles on every inch of the house. I ran to meet Eamonn when his car came up the drive. The front door fairly hurtled against me as I opened it.

He was tired and distant. So was I, for I sensed the impending conflict between us over our child. The child, the proof of our oneness, was threatening to prise us apart. The storm mirrored this. Its scattering effect only jerked us like stretched elastic suddenly released into one another's arms. At the moment we were losing each other we were closest of all.

"I wasn't sure," he said, holding me tight, "if I would make it. Trees down on the road."

He felt, in my trembling, my bad day. Not knowing it was caused by bodily changes, he assumed it was due to my spending the day alone. Bridget would help me in that, he said, and in another way.

"You see, Annie"—he was keeping apart, trying to, in the living room in front of a fire smoky from the wind—"I cannot give you a life. Bridget, without her knowing about us, may help you see that between us there is no chance of lasting happiness."

I held my peace while he wrestled with his problem.

"Our ages, our worlds are so far apart, Annie."

For the first time in his company I felt alone.

At two in the morning, I had a panic attack. The child was taking me over in ways no man ever could.

This was the most intolerant, vengeful night of storm I ever experienced at Inch. Ebony clouds charioted past the moon's scared face. A howling express wind nearly wrenched the roof off. The electricity was interrupted for a few minutes and came on, then flickered on and off for some time. When lightning woke me up, sulfur was in my throat and I was hyperventilating.

Eamonn was swallowing pills for his colitis and trying to get close enough to me to help me knock back a couple of Valium. He spoke to me for five minutes, he told me later, but I was in a black hole and did not hear a word.

"Switch off the light," I begged, and when he did not do

it fast enough I slid out of the bed and scrambled across the floor into his free-standing wardrobe.

"No, Annie," he pleaded, "this huge thing will collapse on top of you."

It was his turn to sit a long time outside the door with me inside watching the fireworks display in my head. He finally realized there was nothing for it but to leave me in peace. If I told him the reason for my being in the wardrobe, he would have run out the house in a panic and I needed him to look after me.

Twenty minutes later, I had recovered enough to leave the wardrobe. He tapped the bed, inviting me to get in beside him. When I crawled back in, he slowly, kindly, unwound my clenched hands like ferns in the morning sun until my palms were fully upturned as though signaling the total gift of myself to him. Fortune-teller, fortune-teller, do you read happiness for me—for us—etched there?

"Annie," he said, humbly, cuffing my hands and kissing them, "my colitis is bad enough. But this is worse."

I stroked his cheek—it was filmed with sweat, a sign that his colitis had broken—and said, "Thanks."

"On the john I can sit comfortably and smoke my pipe."

I was starting to laugh and he joined in. "What if someone had colitis *and* a panic attack?"

He once more improvised on a theme like a jazz musician. "What if you and I had the two things at the same time? And we were in your Dublin flat at night and we ran naked hell-for-leather to Stephen's Green and the Guards . . . ?"

We woke to the Burning Bush of morning, a Sabbath-drowsy day of extravagant sunshine.

Eamonn had an eleven o'clock High Mass to say in Killarney and he needed my help to remove the broken branches from the driveway. I went with him and attended his Mass at the back of the Cathedral. He preached for fifteen minutes. He had not prepared anything; he claimed he did not need to. After reading the Gospel, he simply said what was in his heart.

His theme that Sunday was: God supplies our needs through others. That is why we have to find Him not merely in nature but first of all in ourselves and our fellows.

I left soon after the sermon because the incense made my head ache. I walked the quiet crooked sun-drenched streets of Killarney thinking that God had come to me in the person of Eamonn. "Don't ever leave me, Eamonn-God," I prayed.

Chapter
Twenty-Seven

ABOUT 2:00 P.M., Eamonn put me on the train for Dublin. The ride in that bumpy old train really made me afraid of a miscarriage. Abortion of bishop's baby, courtesy of Irish Rail.

Bridget and Wentworth had already moved into the flat. I arrived home to find guests drinking, smoking, and making a terrible din.

I was back about a week when Bridget said one morning, in her superior accent: "Thanks to you, Murphy, I have already missed a period."

She had morning sickness; curry smells and orange colors made her ill. "If your disgusting seed has done this," she said to Wentworth, "I shall rip it out of me with my own hands."

Wentworth adored her and, wounded by her sharp tongue, took refuge in alcohol.

Among the guests at one of Bridget's parties were two hoteliers from England and a rich Arab who took a fancy to me.

I called Eamonn from my bedroom.

"Annie," he inquired, "what are you doing?"

I pointed the phone toward the living room.

"Hear it? One of Bridget's many parties. *Wild.*"

"God Al*mighty,* I knew it."

I whispered, "You were so right, Dublin is wicked. Shush. Bridget's invited an . . . Arab."

"An Arab?"

"I *know* he wants to rape me."

"What? How do you—?"

"I was dancing with him and believe me . . ."

"What did he do, Annie, you must tell me."

"He bit me."

There was a silence on the line before: "Where?"

"Say, Eamonn, is this a confession or something?"

"Tell me," he said.

"On my—I hardly know how to tell you—on my . . . ear."

"Your *ear*? They're infidels. This probably has some special significance."

"It has special significance for noninfidels, too. The things he whispered in my ear *after* he bit it."

"Don't tell me."

"I wouldn't dare."

"You've got to get out of there this minute, Annie."

"This party's going on all night."

"Oh, God, dear God, how did I get mixed up in all this?"

"Hey," I said, "it's *me* who's mixed up in all this."

I slammed the phone down.

Seconds later, it rang. "Yes, Eamonn?"

He solemnly said, "Don't ever hang up on me again."

"I was paying for the call."

"All right. How many people has she invited?"

"Dozens."

"Please, don't drink any more. I don't want you having a panic attack. And don't go near that Arab."

"But you said you'd never stand in my way."

"Indeed, but he's probably got six wives already."

"I think we should all respect one another's unbeliefs."

"Listen—"

I hissed, fibbing, "He's coming."

"*Annie*, for God's sake."

To annoy Eamonn, I raised my voice, "Abdullah, so nice of you to drop in."

"*Annie, Annie*, get that man out of your *bedroom*."

"Abdullah, darling, make yourself comfortable. Not on the bed, no." Into the phone: "Daddy, I do hope your wooden leg is not bothering you. Take care now."

I was pleased with myself until the Arab really did appear and sat on my bed. After several ear-nibbles, he asked me to marry him.

"I don't even know your name."

He told me. It was guttural and as long as the alphabet.

"I still don't know your name."

"What are names?" He undid the buttons of his shirt, revealing a bronzed chest. "Feel me and you will know."

"Pardon me if I pass on this one."

"Marry me, beautiful damsel," he sighed, "and I will make a paradise for you in the long hot nights of Arabia." He had seen far too many Hollywood movies.

"Not without Bridget," I said loyally, and he promised to marry her, too.

Though exhausted, I could not sleep. After an hour, someone burst in, moaning, "The rabbit's dead, Annie."

I shot up from under my pillow to find Bridget unsteadily waving half a bottle of red wine. "Confirmed?"

She nodded miserably. "Mustn't cry over spilled milk. I'll have to coat-hanger myself," she bawled.

Next morning, I called Eamonn from the hotel. "You've got to come to Dublin. Something's happened."

"You have not been raped by that Arab?"

"Worse."

"You are not being sick in the mornings?"

"Is *that* worse?" And I slammed the phone down again.

A couple of days later, I met him near the Burlington and outlined the bad news. Bridget certainly pregnant and calling London to get the money to go home. Annie probably pregnant. "Worst of all, the flat is practically a brothel. Yes, yes, it's leased in the name of the honorable Bishop of Kerry."

He held his head in his hands for a few minutes.

"Go on," he urged, ironically. "Tell me about you being ravaged by that A-*rab*."

"He got no farther than my ear."

"All the same, 'tis the end of everything."

As we drove to the apartment, I told him to prepare himself by taking a couple of tablets for his colitis.

We arrived around 8:30 to find a few couples still tearing into one another. Eamonn was in his clericals including his most expensive ring and big gold chain.

Once again, he amazed me. This man who braved a herd of charging elephants naturally got a kick out of being in a house of ill repute.

"Drink, Bishop?" Bridget asked, rocky on her feet but anxious to suck up to a source of possible funds.

"A little brandy would do me no harm."

He was at ease, laughing and telling the odd funny story. After an hour, he signaled me to join him in my bedroom. He had no sooner given me a hurried kiss than Bridget barged in and made a grab for his pectoral cross. With drink on board, she was a formidable lady.

"I'll get a pretty penny for that in London," she said.

Instead of fighting her off, Eamonn removed his cross and chain and handed them to her. She went with them into the living room to show Jim and the others.

"My God, Eamonn, why'd you do that?"

"She will give it back."

"She's been threatening to abort herself with a coat hanger; I just hope she doesn't use a bishop's cross."

"Dear God, 'tis in hell we are." He held his hands to his chest recently bereft of his chain of office. "I want to talk seriously."

That annoyed me. I thought we *were*.

"You have to get out of here, Annie."

For the third time that night he amazed me. Instead of bunking, he rejoined the youngsters in the living room for a drink. From my room, I could hear the sound of his laughing and singing. And a few times, "Bridget, don't hit me with that chain, it'll scar my face."

Finally and coaxingly:

"You are a very lovely young woman, Bridget, are you sure you need that cross of mine?"

"Not the cross, but I've really fallen for the chain."

"Bridget," he said, "you wouldn't insult my religious beliefs. Oh, thank you. Yes, I do want it, please. I said please. You are very, very kind."

A minute later, he came to say good-bye to me.

"I'm just off to the Burlington," I lied. "I'd be grateful, Bishop, for a lift." Soon we were whizzing off to the gravel pit that I thought I had seen the last of. He was always sexually most active when he was alarmed. We had a good time, but sex was followed by a serious talk.

He told me I had to get out of the apartment in one week at most. He would tell the estate agents that the occupants were ill and had flown back to the States.

Unfortunately, the hundred pounds he promised me was not enough for a decent place. Landlords required a deposit as well as the first month's rent in advance.

Eamonn next came to Dublin toward the end of November. I was expecting him about eleven, so I answered the door. As soon as I saw him, I started to heave. He solicitously took me by the arm and led me to the edge of the pavement.

"Is this happening a lot?"

I nodded. He helped me to the car, then drove fast until I put a handkerchief over my mouth and threatened to throw up.

"Oh, God," he groaned, "first Mary in my Mercedes, and now you in my Lancia."

I had to dig into my savings to lease a new apartment we could afford a few miles south of the hotel. It was damp and really dismal.

Bridget said, "I'm not staying in this dump."

I told her I had paid the deposit and a month's rent.

"But," she roared, "it has not been cleaned in years."

Every room had something badly wrong with it and raw sewage came back at us after we flushed the toilet. We had no choice but to knuckle down and make the place habitable.

Bridget and I were both pregnant, yet each had to hold down an arduous job and return in the dark to a flat that drove us insane.

"Christ," she would yell suddenly, as we were preparing supper, and bang me on the head with a wooden spoon. "Screw that Bishop till he gives you more money. If not, I will."

Bridget found us an apartment at an affordable price. Eamonn sent me another £200 for the move so I did not have to carry heavy things. He still believed I was having a hysterical pregnancy, but he was taking no chances.

My parents called me at the hotel for Thanksgiving on November 26. I was then sick all the time, as I had been when I lost my first baby.

Bridget came with me to the drunken doctor in Ranelagh who had confirmed her pregnancy. He was madly in love with her and chased her all around his office, promising to bring up her baby as his own. It could only happen in Ireland.

When he was finally persuaded to turn his attention to me, he took a urine sample. From then on, Bridget saw to it I did not work mornings; otherwise, my head would be in the bucket in a second.

We moved into our basement apartment on December 1. It was near Herbert Park, not far from the hotel. Bridget gave me the bigger of the two bedrooms. I thought it was her generosity till I realized it was far colder than the other and winter was on the way.

Within a few days, Eamonn came to see me and was delighted with the apartment. He fixed himself a drink as if he owned it. He asked me out to Jury's for dinner.

At the table, he told me his eighty-three-year-old father was very ill. After his second drink: "Now, Annie, tell me."

I shrugged as if to say, *Isn't it obvious?*

"So, you are—?"

"The doctor thinks I'm into my second month. He has yet to confirm it."

His head sank on his chest. "This is a tragedy, Annie. A tragedy, the very worst."

"I was always honest with you," I said, angrily. "Did I get pregnant by myself?"

He shushed me in case the other diners heard. "Maybe," he said, "it was that Arab who bit your ear."

"Say one more word," I hissed, "and I'll stand up and beat you to death."

"But you told me you were meeting other men."

"I said that and I will. To cover your ass and mine. But *you* are the father."

"You don't *know* that. You could have been drunk and—"

I picked up the water jug.

"Now, Annie. Please behave."

I pointed my finger at my breast. "*Me*, behave?"

He motioned me to sit. The escape artist was at it again.

"I'm not asking you," I said, "to leave the priesthood or marry me."

After we had eaten a little, he said, still knocking back the liquor, "The gravel pit—"

"Oh, no. I'm just not up to it."

"Will you come to Inch?"

"After Christmas, maybe. And if I do, you'll have to drive me because the train could bring on a miscarriage."

After dinner, we returned to the apartment. Wentworth was on a late shift, so Bridget was on her own in her bedroom.

Eamonn stayed late in my room, gazing for long periods into the coal fire, saying little. He had a distant look in his eyes, as if things were beyond repair.

When I lay down on my bed, he climbed alongside me.

"You can't do that," I said, pointing in the direction of Bridget's room. "She's still awake, reading."

"She'll never say a word."

He removed most of his clothes and most of mine.

"You look so bad," he said. "I only want to make you feel better."

"This is almost worse than the gravel pit," I said.

"No, no, no. But 'tis a very cold climate in here, that's for sure."

Chapter
Twenty-Eight

ONE EVENING, the drunken doctor called to say, biblically, "You are with child."

Surprised at my joyful reaction to his unangelic annunciation, he warned me, "We Irish do not exactly cheer mothers minus wedding rings."

Because of my previous miscarriage, he suggested I see a top gynecologist named Charles Feeney.

I phoned Eamonn and told him the pregnancy was confirmed. I named the specialist I hoped to see.

"You don't sound happy about it," I said.

"Annie," he whispered, "I buried my father today."

"Eamonn, I'm . . . If only . . . Oh, Eamonn."

Feeling part of him and his family, I was sad not to have been told of the death or invited to the funeral. If only I had been at the graveside, sharing his grief and afterward, in a quiet moment, telling him that, though he had laid his father in the ground, he had lifed a child, bone of his bone.

This was a testing time for him. The child was the continuance of his own story, his inextinguishable fire. Would he welcome him as his victory over death or as his disgrace?

That was provided the child came to full term. I was throwing up so much I had to be hospitalized for a day or two. When I came out, I went to see Dr. Feeney in fashionable Fitzwilliam Square. He was a big shapeless man with embalmed eyes behind half-moon glasses, and with yellow hair plastered slantwise over a shiny dome.

While taking my particulars, he scarcely lifted his gaze off the page. Except when I said I had no husband. "Oh?" and he waited.

Seeing I had nothing to add, he went on in a monotone: "In cases of unwed mothers like your good self, you see, we send them to the Coombe. From where, you see, the child is, well, adopted."

I did not like the way he said, "We send them," as though we were packages in the mail. Nor did I like his Irish assumption that all unwed mothers had their children adopted.

After he had inquired about my previous problem pregnancy, without examining me, he declared himself satisfied.

"Can you tell me, Doctor, when the baby's due?"

"When do you think it was conceived?"

I told him, "The last day of October."

"Then," he said, "the end of July." He wrote in my notes, 31 July. "I won't be taking your case. No need, you see."

I was really Coombe material.

"May I settle the fee now?"

He waved the suggestion aside. "Not one farthing."

I felt bad for having judged him harshly.

As he was showing me to the door with his big fleshy hand on my shoulder: "You come to Ireland, you see, for a rest and you get pregnant. A tragedy, a very great tragedy." He shook my hand. "Take my advice—go to the Coombe and have that baby adopted."

My shame instantly dissolved. He was parroting Eamonn, who must have got to him and probably paid his fee.

Eamonn is powerful, I thought. *I'll have to keep my wits about me if I'm to keep this child*. I called him at Killarney. "You really did a good job on that consultant," I said.

"Must you see everything in terms of a conspiracy?"

"He wouldn't take me on."

He snickered. "Didn't think he would."

"Exactly," I said, "he was a snob, too. I'd be bad for his practice."

I slammed the phone down—it was getting to be a bad habit—and started throwing glasses at the wall. "You dirty son-of-a-bitch, take that and that."

Bridget came running and slapped my face. "Murphy," she yelled, "are you out of your mind?"

She backed away and narrowly escaped a plate. She came at me again and grabbed me by the arms. When we had cleaned up the mess that seemed to symbolize the breakages in both our lives, we shared the womanly communion of a pot of tea.

"Murphy, we mustn't let these male bastards get to us."

"Eamonn's talking as if this is all my fault."

"Annie, the guy's a bishop. Grow up."

Bridget and Eamonn knew each other pretty well.

"I'm tempted," I said, "to tell the world about Eamonn."

Bridget laughed aloud. "Listen, kid, even Wentworth refuses to believe Eamonn is the father of your baby."

"I didn't know Wentworth was a good Catholic."

"Bad Irishmen are the very best."

"What hope for me, then?"

"None." She peered at me. "Murphy, don't you ever cry?"

I shook my head. "And I'm not going to the Coombe."

She took my hand in a sisterly handshake. "That makes two of us. But never tell Eamonn what you're up to. Not unless you want him to be two steps ahead of you."

On a crisp golden day in mid-January, we signed on to have our babies at the Rotunda, in Parnell Street, Dublin. It was a state hospital over which the Catholic Church had no control.

We were, it's true, assigned to a social worker who chanced to be a Catholic nun. Sister Eileen was in her midthirties with a spring to her step in spite of being a bit plump. She had a round freckled face and hazel eyes with extra-long black lashes and the friendliest smile. Bridget saw her first and came out with her thumbs up.

Sister Eileen's only personal question to me was, "Do you and the child's father have any hope of a future together?"

"None," I said.

"That takes care of that, Annie. Remember, I'm here to back whatever decision you make. Now, do you have a religion?"

"A born Catholic but I fell away years ago."

"You'll get no pressures of any sort from me."

"Pardon me, Sister," I said, "but are you a Catholic nun?"

She gave me a radiant smile.

"I like to think so, but my only task is to help you walk a lonely road." She suggested that for the last couple of months of my pregnancy I might like to live with a family in exchange for light domestic work.

I liked and trusted Eileen. No crucifixes to be seen in her verdant office. Only a fine picture of Christ ascending into glory and another of her rural birthplace in County Sligo.

Bridget and I went downstairs and waited three hours in a long line of pregnant women for a medical examination.

Hearing one woman say, "This is my tenth," I nudged Bridget. "Join the club."

That visit took a load off me. My baby was doing well and I was not going to a Catholic institution. The way to keeping my baby was now open to me.

The following week, I had four days off. Eamonn picked me up in his Mercedes and drove me more slowly than usual to Inch. The same warm love nest, but on a broken bough.

It was freezing at Inch but exquisite. In the clear air, sound carried for miles. After a proud red devil of a dawn, morning was crisp with winds so wild they needed Valium. There were white cowls on silent peaks but on lower slopes a mere early-day salting of frost.

Mary had left for her farmhouse, so I felt relaxed, especially as I was over the worst of my sickness. As to Eamonn, he was now most liberated in his lovemaking. He could not wait to get me into bed, especially as, in his unromantic words, "the damage has been done." He praised my skin, my rosy cheeks, the glow of my hair. "Lovelier you are than ever, Annie," he sighed, exhilarated by my voluptuous breasts.

He sensed, too, without seeing into it, that my soul was different. I was not so easily disturbed. My tantrums were a thing of the past. Motherhood had done this to me, but I don't think he yet connected my changed manner with a baby.

Even when he was within me, as close as he could be to our child, even when I told him, "You have to be gentler now," he was still only dimly aware of the new, already quivering rival.

I was first to grasp that the baby was taking up Eamonn's space and I became protective. Every love suffers multiple deaths and resurrections. But now, in the warmth of our embraces, we were preparing to say good-bye. Each kiss was both a pleasure and an elegy; each act of intercourse a requiem.

I tried to avoid orgasms in case I lost my baby, but without success, because Eamonn's excitement over my body aroused me. Yet what thrilled me before now terrified me.

He noticed. On the third night, we were in his bed when he complained, "You're clamping me real hard, Annie. If you're scared of losing the baby, I won't enter you."

"I *am* scared," I said.

He immediately got out of bed, opened a drawer, and returned naked to bed with a thick black prayer book. "Read it. 'Twill help you discover God's will for you."

This, his first attempt to influence me in religion, came hard on the heels of my admission that full sex between us might have to stop. I disliked the way my naked evangelist assumed that less sex meant we would become more spiritual. I was wary, knowing how God's will and Eamonn's had an annoying habit of coinciding. And I had done a bad thing: I had got a bishop into trouble.

He had marked certain prayers for me. They stuck like bones in my throat. They were about sorrow for sin and atonement. I had too much joy inside me to be in tune with them.

He read a few prayers in his melodious voice, but as soon as he mentioned God, I blocked him out.

His God and mine were not on speaking terms. His was of the male sort that sensible women hate. He loved whiners and breast-beaters and enjoyed nothing more than seeing terror in the eye. Strangest of all, Eamonn's God never laughed, whereas every day mine woke up and went to bed laughing and went on laughing in His sleep.

For the rest of that visit, Eamonn, postcoitally pious, was relaxed because he assumed that I would go along with whatever plans he made for me. I would give birth in a Catholic hospital of his choice and the baby would be adopted by a Catholic couple.

He relied on me to let him start his life all over.

I knew we were on a collision course.

For the first four months of 1974, through the harsh winter and into spring, Eamonn remained very kind. He came to town every weekend whenever Wentworth was on late shift. He took me to dinner, after which we returned to my room and slept together.

His confidence in Bridget's reliability was unshakable. And he was right, even though she said to me, "He's a fox, a real cheeky bastard." She was careful never to come anywhere near my room when she saw Eamonn's trench coat in the hallway.

I was worried about her. I wondered if she had a wasting disease, because she had no belly at all.

Eamonn admired her for not having an abortion. He could not stand the thought of anyone destroying nascent life. He brought her flowers and fruit. He offered to get Wentworth help for his drinking problem to ease their path to marriage.

One weekend about this time, Eamonn took his pleasure, as was now normal, by rubbing up against me. By then, if he had tried to enter me, the child, whom in my mind I had christened Thumper, would have kicked him out of me.

Thumper made it plain he liked the sun and long walks. I told him, "My first child died because I didn't love it. But you won't die for lack of love."

People used to eye me oddly when I was in Stephen's Green or walking through the city toward the Rotunda. I kept rubbing my tummy telling Thumper what a beautiful day it was, which were the boy and girl ducks, where we were headed.

Thumper was also possessive; he did not like Eamonn near me. Eamonn felt supplanted. From the womb, I felt the enmity between the two of them.

It was time for a bit more honesty. I told Eamonn that I was being cared for at the Rotunda.

"I thought," he said, "you were going to the Coombe."

"Did *I* say that?"

"No."

"Did *you?*"

"No, but I took it for granted."

"Why?" I asked innocently.

"Have it your way," he said, in a tone that suggested it would not be for long.

He asked if Bridget had decided to marry Wentworth.

"She's keeping an open mind on that," I said.

"Maybe she should give up her baby, too."

"She may."

I ignored his assumption about what I would do with Thumper. Thus the attempt to communicate ended with the areas of deceit widening like ripples on a lake. But he was now sure of two things. I had deceived him in the most maddening way, by my silence; and he had lost time and some of the high ground.

The enmity between two people who loved each other was coming more and more into the open. The pain of knowing your dearest friend and fiercest foe are one is indescribable. We both realized that the sincerest, most passionate kiss could be followed by one of betrayal. It was like eating blindly a bowl of strawberries, one delicious, the next rotten to the core.

The contest was even now. Now, he, too, knew we were on a collision course.

One weekend in April, Eamonn came to the apartment. Seeing that sex was a problem for me, he said, heartbroken: "You don't need me anymore, Annie; maybe I should go."

"*No,*" I assured him, "it's got nothing to do with *us.*"

He felt ousted all the same and very jealous.

"Tell me honestly, do I disgust you?" Seeing he was ready for a final good-bye for all the wrong reasons, I grabbed him and shook my head miserably at his lack of understanding.

He had no cause to be hurt. People need each other at different times in different ways. If only he had men friends at work or in the pub who could explain things to him and help him cope with this new but quite normal situation. He had learned the great pleasure of giving pleasure. It was hard for him to grasp that, at this stage of my pregnancy, I needed a comforting presence as much as I once needed sexual love to prove to me my worth. But he saw no role for himself except as my religious counselor.

I said again I was scared an orgasm might dislodge my baby.

"'Tis the baby making the commandments now, is that so? No, 'tis *you* who do not want *me*."

He came to bed with me and I allowed him to enter me, but I wanted no physical arousal. I was there only for him, and he seemed content with that.

A crisis occurred one weekend. Before coming to my room, Eamonn visited Bridget, who was still unwell. He told her he was praying for her all the time. Maybe this genuine concern led Bridget to say that we were being counseled at the Rotunda by a Sister Eileen.

"Good," was his first reaction. A nun was surely a tool in his hands. "What is she telling you to do, then?"

"She doesn't tell anyone what to do," Bridget said. "She just helps us make up our own minds about whether to keep our babies or not."

"Is that so?"

He said no more, but I could see the wheels spinning in his head.

Chapter
Twenty-Nine

I PHONED Mary, newly divorced, and told her the news. She called me a moron for being banged by a bishop.

"Is the guy giving you money? . . . No? You under a specialist? . . . *What*, after you already had one disgusting miscarriage? Okay, where're you booked in for the delivery? . . . You're kidding. The stingy bastard. His baby's going to be born in a public hospital. . . . I know, Annie, where Jesus was born, but He came to have bricks thrown at Him, didn't He? But a bishop's baby, Chu-rist."

She had too many troubles of her own to want me on her doorstep. That was why she, like Eamonn, pressed for adoption. "I'll send you some of my maternity clothes, Annie."

"No need. I'm still wearing jeans and blouses."

"At over five months? You stopped eating or something?"

A few weeks later, when Eamonn came to the apartment, I had suddenly blossomed into the tree of life. I was wearing a tied skirt and pretty maternity blouse.

Seeing my roundness, his eyes lit up as of old. "Let me see," and he lifted my skirt up. "Take it off, Annie, please, and your panties."

I did so, watching his face, as I showed him wonders in return for the wonders he had shown me. With eyes twitching, he preached eloquently, breathlessly on the size, beauty, glossiness of my gold-hued tight-as-a-plumskin belly. With trembly hands, he warmed this great globe of flesh as though it were a full brandy glass before tenderly kissing it.

"Off with your blouse, Annie."

I unfastened my blouse and bra and let them fall to the ground, so I stood naked and statuesque before the Bishop like the original earth-mother in the first of all springtimes.

"So rich you are," he gasped. "So round." He marveled at the nipples' big chestnut-colored aureoles, kissed each mellowing breast, then knelt adoringly before me shaping the roundness of my belly with a sculptor's hands, feeling, wide-eyed and open-mouthed, the kicking from within.

"A dancer like his father," I said. I stood looking down on him, mesmerized by his reverence for me and for the awesome changes that had come over me.

Now that he had felt with his own hands, seen with his own eyes what he had done, witnessed this close the golden harvest of our love, would it make a difference? Would he, in spite of that clerical garb, want to share for a lifetime the child our love had brought into being?

The answer came sooner than I expected. His joy turned to puzzlement, to sadness.

I shook involuntarily as, still kneeling, he leaned a hard head against me. His pectoral cross pressed into my bare flesh. Too near my child.

"What are you thinking, Eamonn?"

He held me tighter, his alien cross digging deeper, as he answered in a voice muffled by my belly, "Since I loved you, I feel I love God more than I ever did."

"Oh, yes, yes. Why should that make you sad?"

He lifted misty eyes to me. "Because I feel He loves me less."

"But He must love you more the more you love Him, surely?"

He shook his head. "Sometimes, I feel He is ready to hurl me into hell."

The anguish with which he said it tore at me. "How could He, Eamonn, if you love Him more than ever?"

It was a conundrum to which he had no answer.

"Even if you did wrong, Eamonn, surely God will forgive you over and over?"

He rubbed his hands fondly, almost nostalgically, over my breasts but made no answer.

Catholics are always talking about God's forgiveness but they really think they are far more forgiving than He is. They never trust Him because He is the God of Law not Love; He has to punish all lawbreakers. My own view is that God, like a loving parent, has to forgive everyone everything because He is so helplessly good.

As Eamonn once more stroked my belly, I soothed his troubled head. Poor Eamonn, he had talked about sins of the flesh for year after year yet he did not know what the flesh was till I taught him. One hand fondled my breast and he, who had heard everything, knew he knew nothing. In my arms came the sudden terrible shock of recognition.

Till then, the flesh had only been an idea, which is precisely what it is not. The flesh is the means of merging and becoming one with another, with the world, beyond all thought and imaginings, beyond all sense and consequence. Lovers, entwined, lost in one another's arms, experience in flesh the dark night of thought. To love is to die in the sweetest way in order to live anew. But my tragedy was, in teaching him about the flesh, I had unwittingly, unwantingly, made him aware, too keenly, of sin. The more he loved me, the more he despised and feared for himself.

With the same quiet inevitability with which other people accept death, Catholics deny it; they are from conception made for immortality. And I, through a love that should have banished fear, had made Eamonn fear perhaps for the first time in his life that he was headed toward immortal loss.

If he felt a failure for not making me more religious, I felt equally a failure for not weaning him from his barbaric, punitive God.

"Annie," he said, at length, "you can't go on working in Dublin. You must take good care of yourself."

So it was that I reluctantly gave up my job and my freedom. He drove me under cover of darkness to Inch.

At eleven o'clock, when we were a few miles from the house, the Mercedes suddenly stopped. He had run out of gas.

He banged the steering wheel.

"This has never happened to me before, Annie."

His religion made it necessary for him to blame somebody even for accidents and his own mistakes.

"I apologize," I said. "I should have checked the oil and the tires."

"Take those big earrings off," he barked. "And why wear a skimpy pink dress that barely covers your knees?"

The dress had simply risen up my bulging belly.

"I've got to get petrol, got to."

He was going as crazy as in the gravel pit when the cops were around. He hated the idea of a breakdown while he had a pregnant young woman in his official car.

"You want me to get in the trunk?"

"Not in your condition."

The look on his face made me laugh.

"You have no idea, Annie, how very, very serious this is." Cold rain was falling, and he turned to the backseat, only to find he had forgotten to bring his mackintosh.

"Flag a car down," I said.

He pushed his head up close to mine and hissed, "No cars around. Even if there were, the Bishop of Kerry cannot thumb a lift for himself and a pregnant woman on a dark night."

"It'll be worse if you wait for the light of day."

"'Tis true. The two of us will be one dead frozen lump."

"The three of us," I reminded him.

About fifty yards ahead there was a light in the porch of a house. He jumped out and started trotting toward it.

I shouted after him, "I hope they don't have a couple of Dobermans."

In the car's headlights, I saw him raise his fists to heaven.

Seconds later, he was tapping on the window of the house and calling out, "Hello, hello, hello."

A minute later, he was back complaining that they hadn't answered because they were Protestants.

"Protestants? Just because they don't answer you?"

"I know them."

"Okay, I'll go."

"God Almighty, no," he squawked. "The curtain in an upstairs room moved. They recognized me."

He returned down the road, tapping and then banging fiercely on the door. "Please," he kept calling out, like a dog whining for a bone. "Plea-ease."

After fully ten minutes, an outside light went on.

I cordially thanked Eamonn's God. Pathos had paid off.

A minute later, the light went out. Eamonn came back to the car, chicken-shaking the rain off his shoulders and muttering hysterically, "Didn't I tell you those Protestants knew it was me, me, me? And they have the fecking nerve to call themselves Christians!"

"Please, plea-ease," I whined, mimicking him, which only offended him more.

"I am not giving up," he said, grittily. "I swear to God I'd sooner knock that door down."

With a snort, he went back and the resulting knocks were thunderous in the quiet country air.

Someone came from around the back of the house shining a torch. I heard Eamonn asking for petrol as an emergency. Whenever he wanted anything, it was an emergency.

He came back with a can of petrol.

"There," I said, "those Protestants are Christians, after all."

"That was Paddy, their only Catholic hand."

We both laughed and were still laughing when we arrived at Inch only five minutes later. He ran at once for his brandy and came to my room. He was stroking the glass and, in his mind, maybe—no, certainly—me.

April's end. I watch and wait without envy. Most calming, hopeful, delicate of days. Mountains try to levitate. The swallow arrives, not yet the rose. Life-burst of budding and beading, lambing and sparrow-cheeping. Everything trickling and softening; everywhere, out of mold and bark and fiber, the scents of spring. In air liquefied by a still apprenticed sun, forsythias have yellowed again, trees are retenanted with feathery leaves and leaf-like feathers. Old twigs into new nests, a yeasty year-round life-lasting spring since I came to Ireland. I had loved Eamonn for a whole opulent unforgettable year.

At Inch, a new cycle was about to begin, but how different from the first.

Eamonn was excited; he seemed proud of my condition. The first three weeks that we were alone were bliss. When the weather allowed, we trod the blustery beach at night. Afterward, we had sex but I, still ripening, had overcome the need to climax. I rested, relaxed and rosy-cheeked, in voracious arms, feeling to the full his vagabonding hands.

But once when we walked on the sands he alarmed me. "Annie, that Arab who bit your ear—"

"He never came near me, Eamonn. No one did."

"You are sure?" No apology, only a repeat of the question. *My God,* I thought, *he is beginning to believe his own lies, the ones he tells people like Pat and Father O'Keeffe. To salve his conscience he makes me out to be a whore.*

I swallowed the insult like dirt. Why was he asking me this? Was it because, his gelding's luck having held for six months, he thought he never would sire a colt? Or did he feel that a bishop was entitled to special treatment from his God?

His distrust of me on such a basic thing did not bode well for the future. Yet did I not have the same distrust of him? Was I not still haunted by the thought that little Johnny, whose picture he kept at Inch, was his son?

I said, "Think what you like. If the baby's black with curly hair, you'll know, won't you? But if he comes out with a bump on his lip and a gold cross on his chest—"

"*A-nnie!*" A moonbeam lit up his face at that moment and I could see a startling thought flash through his mind: *What if that baby looks exactly like me?*

I had made a fatal mistake. Johnny did look very like him. Maybe I transferred this thought to Eamonn because he instantly returned to the story of the unwed woman in London who had wanted to keep her baby but in the end had to have him adopted.

Now I realized why he wanted me at Inch. Not to stop me working, but to keep me far away from untrustworthy Sister Eileen and Bridget, who had told him she was keeping her baby.

Two deep moon shadows stretched before us like our own separate graves. "I will help you, too, Annie," he concluded, treacherously, "if only you trust me."

From that night on began my descent into hell.

Chapter
Thirty

E ACH DAY, Eamonn came home happy from Killarney. His colleagues seemed to have bought his story about my unfortunate affair with a Dublin hotelier. He was labeling me "the young American girl in trouble."

Each night when he came to my room, I put aside my book, *Nicholas and Alexandra,* to greet him.

After we had hugged each other and he was sexually satisfied, to ease his conscience he read to me with gusto from his prayer book. When, finally, I had to tell him how much I hated it, a blackness came over him. Only his success in converting me could justify his sleeping with me.

"Annie," he implored, "cannot you see that without God you will never be able to do what is good for this baby?" I believed no one should tell anyone what to do; he believed someone, himself, should tell everybody.

I said, "I know what is good for my baby."

In a dubious tone: "Do you, Annie?"

Oh, I do, I thought. *This baby has completed your work in me, given me an appreciation of myself and the beauty of my body that I never had before.*

"God," he preached at me, "wants you to give it up in sacrifice. 'Tis the only way you can atone."

Sin needed a victim: me. I touched his surprised cheek. "I'm sorry, Eamonn, but you are upsetting me."

"Be detached, suffer in order to be reborn." He had no real sense of guilt, no feeling that this child was his.

He told me Helena was coming with her children for three weeks. She would explain to me how hard it was for a single mother to cope.

"Why don't you talk to her about fatherhood, Eamonn?" and I tugged his hair.

He jumped out of bed, saying, "Stop it, Annie, stop it."

"Wait a minute," I said. "I want my child to have nice thoughts, not the nastiest."

"No, no, *no*."

"Yes, yes, *yes*. Your prayers would put the most terrible fear of abandonment in him before he's even born."

He got into his clothes and went to the door.

"I may have to give him up," I sobbed, "but I don't even want to think of it while he's still part of me."

But he was gone without a word.

I felt sorry for Eamonn. His parents had guided him along a path which he was too young to know led to loneliness. Having given him life, they encouraged him to deny life to their grandchildren. And they did this to please the Creator who said, "Increase and multiply." How was Eamonn to know he would grow into a very sexy man who could justify his loving of me only by denial? He had to deny he was a man, deny he was enjoying me for enjoyment's sake. He even had to deny when he was inside me that he was disobeying his Church and his God.

I showed him the path to freedom. My body healed him. I opened up new worlds of wonders to his sight, to his feelings. I taught him the magic of the flesh. The sad thing was, whereas I was grateful to him, he could credit me, according to his rules, with nothing but temptation.

How different we were.

His God was a God of rules, mine was the God of love.

His God was determined to bring evil out of good, whereas mine wanted to kneel in awe of the good however and wherever it happened.

Eamonn saw sin always in terms of disobedience; because we disobeyed, there was no possibility of love. I saw sin only as lovelessness; because we loved and hurt no one, there was no possibility of sin.

Eamonn was keen to make me almost the worst thing I could imagine: a good Catholic. One night, after we made love, he said: "I've seen you walking around the Stations of the Cross, you like lighting candles and listening to Church music, you are very spiritual."

"I think so," I murmured.

"Without the faith, you will always be bitter and angry."

I already was bitter and angry *because* of what Catholicism had done to my family and to me personally.

At my first confession, I couldn't breathe because I was unable to tell the drink-sodden Father McCarthy what I had done wrong. Not to tell the truth in confession was considered an unforgivable lie to the Holy Ghost and the penalty for that was hell. A seven-year-old subjected to that sort of subtlety and moral terrorism will hardly grow up normal.

One day, we were doing catechism when devout little Benji Christman of the porcupine hair stuck his sweaty hands down the back of my pants. I couldn't confess *that*.

Nor could I confess that I used to moon a lot in the choir loft. I put a stool at the front overlooking the sanctuary, stood on it backward, picked up my dress, pulled down my pants and shook my bare butt around at anyone who cared to look. I damn well nearly broke my back doing this trick. These things were fun. I didn't know they were mortal sins till the sisters said so.

Those nuns were foe posing as friend. I wondered why our parents didn't see they were teaching us the worst possible lesson: that we were wicked and that almost everything we did was a sin. By making me feel wicked, they made me want to be wicked. And once you taste wickedness and can endure the shame, it's like heroin.

Catholics must be the worst sinners in the world because they have to be so brave. Other people do wrong although they fear the police or a punch on the nose. Catholics do it believing they will be sent to hell for all eternity.

"You told me about your confirmation," Eamonn said, coaxingly. "Have you no fond memories of your first communion?"

"None."

I was in an expensive organdy bridal dress with a veil, and because I had lied to the Holy Ghost in confession, my throat was too dry to swallow the Host. I couldn't chew it either, because the nuns said that was a sin. To get rid of it, I spat it out. The white Host, Christ, Savior of the World, landed on Father McCarthy's shiny black patent-leather shoe.

I swear to God, in that explosive moment, I realized that what the nuns had taught me wasn't true. Christ could not be spat out so He ended up on a priest's shoe.

But Father McCarthy obviously believed, because he looked at me with real hate. I don't blame him. This was his big day and he now had the job of scraping God's Son off his shoe. I screamed in terror and my mother, smart in her Saks Fifth Avenue suit with alligator bag and shoes to match, pulled my ear and told me I had disgraced my family.

All the way home Mommy was asking, "What didn't you tell the priest?" and Johnny sang, "*An*nie lied in con*fess*ion."

After that I went into the confessional each Friday and told Father McCarthy, "I swore, lied, and disobeyed." That didn't exactly please him. Like Eamonn, he felt he had the right to get inside me, but I told him, "Don't be nosy, Father."

Now, when Eamonn, through his prayers, wanted to get inside me, I said in my mind, "Don't be nosy, Eamonn."

Helena came and I had lived through all this before. Except now Eamonn treated me like a stranger. He spent most of his time with Helena. I was the whore, she the Virgin Mary.

He asked me to make a pot of tea for himself and Helena; I was not invited to join them. He moved me into Mary's room and gave mine to her children. After he had finished his breviary, he was now able to talk with Helena at all hours of the night without me overhearing a word.

Helena it was who rescued me from oblivion. "I could have become pregnant," she said, with unintended irony, "if Eamonn hadn't been around to guard me."

June was passing, it was time for me to go. I called Sister Eileen at the Rotunda and begged her to find me a family to stay with. She promised to get back to me soon.

One night around 2:30, I made sure Helena was asleep in bed and Eamonn had dropped off on the chaise longue in his pajamas and bathrobe. Clad only in my prettiest robe, I opened up her door. "Eamonn darling," I whispered huskily, "I need you."

A light sleeper, he woke instantly with his fingers to his lips. "Go away," he mouthed.

"I'm not a dog, my darling."

He gritted his teeth and shook his head. To which I responded by opening up one side of my robe. Displaying an outsized breast, I beckoned him seductively.

"No," he said hoarsely.

I opened up the other side of my robe and started to walk into the room, showing my recent marvelous tan. A heavy sigh of longing escaped him.

I removed my robe just as he came at me and gathered it before it fell to the ground. I had guessed right. He enjoyed danger. As he ushered me out, he was doing his best not to laugh aloud.

In my room, after spitting dryly on my hands, I took the cord of his pajamas and whipped him with it, then ripped his pajamas off, tearing them. For a couple of hours we were very sensuous. He found my big belly irresistible in Mary's narrow, never-loved-in bed. And now well beyond the early fearful months of pregnancy, I, too, had no inhibitions, physical or verbal.

Pay attention, Salome, watch this, Jezebel. I flaunted my considerable attractions. I took every jutting piece of him into my mouth from his ears to his toes. I used words and phrases I never knew I knew.

Eamonn kept telling me unclerically how much he loved me and how impossible it was for him to live without me.

At about 4:30, when we were both exhausted, without warning, I kicked him out of bed. He raised himself off the floor. Pathetically: "You made me bang my head."

"This bed is too small for two, which is why you gave me it."

"Come into *my* bedroom, then?"

"Forget it." I deliberately spoke in an offhand, male kind of way. "I needed to act horny tonight but I've had enough to last me a lifetime." My bitter message to him was: *Remember this, Eamonn, remember my young warm soft impression-*

able flesh, remember it when you are saying Mass, remember it on your deathbed at eighty-five, remember forever and ever in hell, if you end up there as you deserve, remember what you threw away.

"But—"

"Grab your togs and switch off the light when you leave."

"Can't you see kicking me out of bed is cruel, Annie?"

"I sure can." I turned to the wall. "Now you know how I felt when you kicked me out of mine."

But while I got my revenge, I was overwhelmed with sadness because I loved him so and because good-bye is good-bye.

In the morning, Sister Eileen called to say she had found me a family to stay with in Clontarf, a suburb of Dublin.

As soon as Eamonn came home from work he rushed into my room with a familiar glint in his eye, only to find my bags were packed. He held his hands up. Seldom can he have been so shaken.

"How," I said, "can I stay here with Helena's kids when you want me to give up my own?"

"So you *are* giving it up?"

"That," I said insincerely, "is probably for the best."

"I could send Helena away early."

"You couldn't possibly do a cruel thing like that," I said. "It's so unlike you."

He shrugged. "Perhaps. You'll be staying where?"

"Sister Eileen's found me a place in Dublin till the baby's born."

"You will let me know where?" The same old Eamonn wanting to control me.

"Do you think," I said, "I would keep anything from you?" The same old me, delighting in tricking a trickster.

"Will that sister arrange the adoption?"

"She usually does."

He smiled contentedly. "I'll drive you to Dublin."

"No need. I'll take the train tomorrow."

That night I locked my door. Two or three times I heard him tapping on it, but I did not open to him. Remember, Eamonn, remember and go on remembering.

Through my open window came the scent of honeysuckle and I saw bright broken clouds float by. It broke my heart to deny him, for never had I loved him—and hated him—so much.

But it was over. And I, poor lonely Annie Murphy, would forever have to remember, and remember, too.

Chapter Thirty-One

BRIDGET MET me at the station in Dublin and we took a cab to the hospital. "You've popcorned," Bridget said, miserably. "Why not me? I'm going to give birth to a mouse or a moron."

"What does Sister Eileen say?"

"She agrees. Seven heads, six legs, and green all over." I laughed.

"If we keep our babies, Annie, we'll owe it to her."

"You said it. Why don't you talk to your baby?"

"I tried. She doesn't answer. Not one word."

I realized that Bridget's hell was worse than mine. And some girls had hells worse than either of us.

She asked me to contribute a pound to a collection for a hotel telephonist who was going to Liverpool for an abortion. "Welcome back, Annie, to Dublin, Sin City."

At the Rotunda, Sister Eileen said, "Annie, what's that Bishop been doing to you? On the phone you sounded desperate."

I mentioned the awful prayers he made me say.

From her desk, she took a prayer book and handed it to me. Nothing about sin in it. It had pictures of trees and flowers and sunsets; it was full of light and hope, gratitude and spiritual magic.

She told me about the host family. They lived in Clontarf by the sea. Denis Devlin, a Catholic, was in publishing; his wife, Barbara, a Presbyterian from the north, was a vicar's daughter. They had one baby. How clever Sister Eileen was and maybe too brave for her own good. She was lodging me with a lady who would not be overawed by the fact that Eamonn was a bishop.

Since I had registered as a Catholic, I was advised to see the chaplain in his office, a few blocks away on Marlboro Street near the Pro-Cathedral.

Young, tall, emaciated, Father Alan Coughlin had bulging, watery eyes.

"Sit. I was expecting you." He had a rough voice. "You have an address at Inch, County Kerry. You are related in some way to Bishop Casey?"

"In some way."

"I am no great admirer of his."

I said nothing, but we had summed each other up.

In Ireland, he went on to say, unmarried mothers give their babies up for adoption. Having an illegitimate baby is irresponsible, a mortal sin, and so on.

"Questions, Miss Murphy?"

"Yes. Who the hell do you think you are?"

His face crumpled. "The Bishop's representative."

"Which bishop?"

I stood up and made for the door, but he barred my way.

"If you don't get out of my way this second . . . ," I said.

This judge-and-jury of a man turned his head aside in contempt at so harmless a threat.

"I'll scream," I continued, "then tell the cops you tried to rape me."

He shifted as if the Pope had spoken. "I only wanted to help, Miss Murphy."

"Bullshit."

Outside, I called Sister Eileen. "Did you forewarn that jamjar shark I was coming?"

She laughed. "No, Annie."

"I didn't think it was you. Do I have to see him again?"

"Not if you don't want to."

"Good," I said. "And thanks for everything."

The Devlins' house was big and full of light. Nicholas, the nine-month-old baby, was beautiful.

I was feeling free for the first time in weeks when Barbara

Devlin, a tall, dark lady aged about thirty, said, "A man keeps ringing you, Annie."

The phone buzzed at that minute. She answered it and handed the receiver to me. "Hello, Bishop," I said.

The ringing had awakened the baby.

"Annie, I thought you left Inch to escape the sight and sound of babies."

"I have to earn my keep."

"I called up that sister at the Rotunda. She talked to me as if I was just anybody."

"How awful."

"How are you getting on with the prayers?"

"A great solace," I said.

Minutes after that call, Sister Eileen phoned. "Annie, the Bishop thinks you're giving up the baby."

"I tell him what he wants to hear. I gather you didn't."

She giggled. "He and I differ on a basic question."

"Which is?"

"He likes people on wheels so he can push them around."

"Sister," I said again, "are you sure you're a Catholic?"

Nicholas did not take to me and cried whenever I went near him. I told Barbara I would do anything to help in the house but I was afraid her baby might not be good for mine.

"Also," I said, "Denis dotes on him and my baby will never know his father."

She gripped my arm kindly. "Say no more, Annie."

I began to wonder if Eamonn, Father Coughlin, and my sister Mary, who still called me urging adoption, were right, after all. How could I give my son the life he was entitled to? With only £180 left of my savings, I had few choices.

When Eamonn called next, I had primed Barbara to say I was out walking the baby. This was the first time I had rejected him.

Weeks passed. On alternate Wednesdays, Bridget and I went for an examination at the Rotunda and then we saw a movie and stayed at her flat for the night. We pulled up our dresses to compare the bulges. She was convinced her baby would have head and feet and nothing in between, like a tadpole, while mine would be born over six feet tall like my father.

Eamonn was calling so persistently now I finally had to speak with him. My stomach immediately tightened and my baby resented that. I was eating a peach at the time.

He said, "Did you say something, Annie?"

"Just telling my baby this is the best peach I ever ate."

"Speak to *me*. And don't keep talking about 'my baby.' "

"My" baby made it too human, I guess, less easy to dispose of. He doubtless preferred "the" baby.

I agreed to meet him the following Wednesday at Jury's for dinner.

I donned a nice navy maternity dress. I put my hair up and wore big earrings and my face was a rosy pink. I was proud of my big belly over which I spread my hands as I walked into the hotel lobby to greet him. This was *the* magic bubble within the magic bubble of Ireland.

He was seated in the lobby, and when he saw me he leaped to his feet and, kissing my cheek, whispered, "My God, 'tis truly pregnant you are. Is it twins or more?"

His problems seemed to be multiplying before his eyes.

"Shall we sit for a minute, Annie?"

"No need."

"There is for me," and he collapsed back into his seat and called for a brandy while I settled myself in more slowly.

"I never saw a pregnant woman look so radiant."

When he heard at dinner that I was staying with a Protestant lady, he dropped his fork on his plate and broke it.

After a waitress replaced the plate: "Is it a mixed marriage?" I nodded. "'Tis a hard road, then, they have to travel."

I felt acid rise in my throat. If he found marriage between Christians unacceptable, no wonder he did not want me, a single girl, to keep my baby.

"As soon as I've had my baby I'm leaving here."

He was not sure what I meant but he had his suspicions. "No, Annie." Reenter Eamonn, the dream-maker. "As soon as you've given the baby up, we'll go somewhere nice, a Greek island, perhaps, or the Canaries."

Seeing my clumsy figure and him in his clericals, I knew dream-time was over. I really did sympathize with his point of view. He had seen my wildness. He thought that the very thing that made me a good lover would make me a bad mother.

Yet, while he expected other women married to drunks, brutes, adulterers to cope with half-a-dozen kids, he saw me as utterly helpless. Had I not even rejected his religion? He had sinned in siring a child but he could atone if the child were given to God through adoption into a Catholic family.

Back to the terrible doctrine of atonement. There was no such thing as forgiveness without strings. Always someone had to be victimized—in this case, me and Thumper.

But I did not accept the Irish idea that a single woman was unable to bring up her child. This was a Catholic code for: An unwed woman is not fit to bring one up.

A week before, I read in the paper that a young pregnant Catholic in Northern Ireland was widowed in the Troubles. I bet no priests and nuns were pressuring her to give up her baby as soon as it was born on the plea that a single parent was unable or unfit to bring up a baby.

No, it wasn't a single parent that worried the Irish but a *sinful* single parent. It was her sin, not her singleness, that disabled her from parenthood. Nor could I imagine priests saying to that widowed woman in the north, "Ah, what a pity you are pregnant." For the child was the most precious thing her husband left her.

I was like that widow. I never saw my having a child as a tragedy; I wanted Eamonn's child and often told him so. If he had not wanted to risk it, he should not have slept with me or he should have taken precautions, which he did not.

What angered me most was the arrogant assumption of men like Eamonn that they and only they knew what God wanted.

"Say a special prayer for me," I whispered.

Was this the long-awaited spark of repentance? Eagerly: "I will, pet, but for what?"

"Ask God that when I am in labor and suffering badly—"

"Yes, yes?" he said, with pity.

"I do not shout out your name."

His mouth opened like a roller blind. "You *wouldn't?*"

"Not if you pray really hard," I said.

In the parking lot he took my face in his hands and kissed

me, and in the car he kept fondling my breasts. Near to Bridget's place, he drew up and, after giving me thirty pounds for expenses, he hugged and kissed me. ''Think over what I said,'' he pleaded.

I waved him off, but instead of going at once to Bridget's I walked east along Northumberland Road, past Jury's Hotel and the American embassy. I did not know where I was going or why. But through the gasoline fumes I could smell the sea.

Within a half hour, beyond a level crossing, I saw the sign STRAND ROAD; I was on the edge of Dublin Harbor. There was no moon or stars, so that buildings, even the two tall chimneys of the power station, seemed to be breaking up in the grainy night. To the northeast, the purply outline of the long low peninsula of Howth looked like a beached whale. To my right were the illuminated streets and houses of Dun Laoghaire. Lights twinkled on boats in the bay.

I stepped off the sidewalk onto stony sand and removed my shoes. The tide was in; it swished and shuffled a few feet away. The water came up to my knees, then to my waist, its saltiness tickling my nose. In spite of my buoyancy, it was hard to keep from sliding under. Now I knew why I had followed the sea's scent. I wanted to die.

But why when I was happy? So simple the answer and so hard to explain. *Because* I was happy. Happiness here lasts as long as you can hold a smile. It is a field poppy picked in the midday heat.

The sea was no enemy, but a friend. It was where all life came from. I waded farther in. Until, from shoreward, through a summer's open window, there came to my ears the penetrating sound of a baby crying. Was it real or imaginary? I will never know. But that pitiful wail made me see that I was doing a terrible wrong. In killing myself, in perpetuating my happiness, I was aborting my baby, I was ruining the handiwork of the mothering God of love.

Something hit me that I was not aware of till then. My father often complained of a phantom pain in his severed leg. I, too, had a phantom pain inside my body. It was the absence-pain of the child I had lost, whom I never thought of as mine. Now a new child was giving me a second chance.

That baby's cry in the night brought me to my senses. My

baby—yes, whatever Eamonn said, it was *my* baby—was now filling my body and would soon, soon, fill my life.

I turned around and pushed myself through the sighing water toward the streetlights by the shore.

Bridget saw my condition but said no word. We women know. She helped me get changed. She made me a sherry trifle, which I gobbled up before sinking into a deep sleep.

Next morning, I gave Bridget half the money Eamonn had given me and we went to Grafton Street to buy shawls and baby clothes. She bought pink and I bought blue. These small purchases were for me a mighty rebellion. My child was a real person. See, his hands go through here, his feet through here.

When Mrs. Devlin saw the baby clothes, she was excited. She called Sister Eileen and Sister called to remind me that my baby was due within three weeks and did I still intend to keep it.

"Yes," I said. "I'm keeping it."

Bridget advised me to write Eamonn a letter and send it to him just before the baby was born. "For your own sake, Annie, you have to be more honest with him."

It was true. Eamonn could not believe that I would obey my conscience rather than a bishop. He did not realize that I loved him in spite of what he was. He took it for granted that I would sacrifice my honor, as well as my future, for him. What else are women for?

In my letter, I told him that I had not been wholly truthful. I had had to fight many things since I was eight years old: my mother's alcoholism, the vengeful God of Catholicism, disappointments in my love for men. Now twenty-six, I felt this baby was a gift from God.

I told Eamonn I sympathized with him in his position but I had to think of my life and make my own decisions. I thanked him for his help without which I could not have reached this degree of maturity. The fact was, I could not give up my baby for him or for anyone. My God of love had guided me so far and would surely guide me in the years ahead. I ended with: "I love you with all my heart and I probably always will. It's a shame you can't see this baby as part of your life everlasting."

Bridget had her baby on July 15. I saw it in the nursery before I went to the ward: a perfect baby girl weighing six pounds nine ounces. In spite of my terrible back pains, I ran crying to the ward.

"What are you doing, Murphy?" Bridget roared. "I have just been through the most ghastly ordeal—ripped apart I was from belly button to arse, and now you wake me up." She smiled. "Catherine's seven heads and six legs are so beautiful, eh?"

I nodded. "Nice name, Catherine."

But I was thinking, Jesus, Randall expected a monster and the baby's exquisite. I've been expecting a normal baby and now, thanks to God's joke and judgment on me, I'm the one who's going to have a baby with seven heads and six legs.

"Listen, Murphy, if that bishop tells you to give up your beautiful baby, tell him to go to fucking hell."

Did I promise.

"Be a darling," she said, "and give Wentworth a message from me. You will? Tell the beast to stay away or I'll kill him."

I phoned Eamonn from the General Post Office to tell him the good news and mailed him my letter. He came up at once to congratulate Bridget. "Tell me, Bridget," he said, "are you going to get married or not?"

Heavens, I thought, he's still trying to organize people's lives. Why can't he stick to sorting out his own mess? Then it occurred to me: maybe he was, maybe that was the real reason he was visiting the Rotunda.

Three days later, I got a desperate call from Bridget.

"Murphy, my baby's dying."

Catherine had contracted gastroenteritis. Bridget wanted my help to get the baby into a private clinic.

I went to see her and gave her most of my freedom in the form of a hundred pounds.

The baby was admitted to a clinic in the north of Dublin. It took two buses to get me and Bridget there and the sight of so many sick babies made me feel very unwell.

Catherine looked extremely sick and close to death. On

July 30, we visited her a second time. Bridget was very happy because her baby was expected to live.

Of the two of us, I was now the weaker. We had to wait for ages for a bus. When it came, I got on and immediately got off because it was full of handicapped children on an outing. It was too much like a premonition.

Nothing for it but to walk miles back to town. That day was one of the most uncomfortable of my entire life.

When I finally reached the Devlins', my mother phoned. "I was expecting you to call, Annie. Did you forget it was my birthday?"

"Of course not," I lied.

Daddy came on the line. "I just feel there's something wrong."

"No. What gave you that idea?"

What are families for if you can't lie to them when you need to?

Mommy grabbed the phone again and, in a hiccupy howl: "Are mothers so unimportant nowadays? You'll be a mother yourself someday, then you'll know what it's like not to get ___d on your birthday."

Chapter
Thirty-Two

A T ABOUT eleven that night, I was getting into bed when my waters broke. Till then, Thumper had scarcely stirred. I had been told he was big and I was too little. Now these great jerks inside me. I tried to walk to the door but on the polished pine floor the water was as slippery as oil. I was afraid I would fall and injure my baby, so I just stood there, calling, "Denis? Somebody help me please?"

I was happy and frightened, laughing and sobbing same time, but in control. Within ten minutes, I had helped to dress and Barbara drove me to the Rotunda. It must have been around midnight when I was taken on a stretcher straight to emergency.

"Get her chart. Y'hear, her chart!"

A concerned admissions nurse examined me. "Have you had a baby before, dear?"

"Yes. Stillborn at five months or so."

She nodded. "That explains the dilation." She patted my tummy. "This little mite won't take long."

A nurse came to shave me, another gave me an enema. I was put in a small overheated room with cubicles separated by curtains. Next to me, a woman was about to have twins. I had cramps, but what she had to endure only her animal screams suggested.

Some people think God is a woman. They must be joking.

I told myself: *Mustn't get frightened. Mustn't scream.*

Mustn't curse Eamonn. It's not good for my baby. To dull the pain, to block my ears to the cries of my fellow sufferer, I put myself into a kind of self-hypnosis. Having recently read *Nicholas and Alexandra,* I went in spirit to the Crimea. I saw Yalta's mountains with their feet in the water and cypresses with cones like little bells. I inhaled scents of magnolia and wisteria vines. I walked the cool corridors of the Tsars' shiny white Livadia Palace beside the Black Sea.

It worked. In this soul-time, I heard no more screams, felt no more cramps. All I remember—this was three hours later—was being wheeled to the delivery room. Not even the Crimea could anesthetize the pain of being knifed from within. I wanted the nurses to leave me. I wanted to be alone like a cow calving in a field. Thumper seemed to sympathize with me, pushing consistently. It was as if he knew when he wanted to come out, as if he already had a sense of himself.

Suddenly, at 2:30 in the morning, I was a mother and, with the pain gone, I saw my darling child. At seven pounds two ounces and twenty-two inches long, Thumper was a string bean of a boy with dark hair, black gorgeous eyes, and a big birthmark on his left knee. He was like Eamonn in every way. They put him in my arms, and in that first instant I knew millions of mothers before me had known: I would never give him up. See, touch, feel, hold, and keep forever. They would have to cut me to bits before I gave up this vulnerable little thing who was part of me.

Instantly, the hitherto anonymous Thumper had a name. "Hello, my Peter," I whispered.

There this warm bundle lay for five minutes, mewing, scarcely moving. This miracle was all mine. Since I came to Ireland, new smells, tastes, sights, colors, sounds, and now the newest keenest most overwhelming sense of all: motherhood.

A nurse showed me Peter's feet were a bit webbed. Nothing serious, she said, smiling. Due to him being cramped in the womb. She put some kind of instrument on them. "Just for a while," she assured me.

They moved me to a room I shared with five other mothers, where, later, my son was brought to me clothed in a white fleecy gown with a little collar. He was put in a crib at the foot of my bed.

A second nurse came and said, "I'll have to take him away for a while. As you can see he's a yellowy brown." I hadn't noticed. All I could see was the beauty of him.

"A touch of jaundice, Annie. Get some rest. You'll soon have him back."

I couldn't wait to be reunited with Peter for my heart was full of him. When they gave him back, the sense of miracle was still upon me. This was a wonder that would never go away.

Hey, maybe God was a woman, after all.

I hugged him so tight the nurse had to warn me, "If you go to sleep with him like that you might smother him."

I allowed him to be put back in his crib and then slept on and off for a few hours.

Around 2:30 that afternoon Eamonn appeared. I had asked the Devlins to telephone him when I went into the hospital, but I had not expected him so soon. He scared me. Could I withstand the pressure he was bound to exert?

His shock on entering my room was even greater than mine at seeing him. I don't think it had crossed his mind on his rush across Ireland that there would be a crib at the foot of my bed, or that there would be a baby in it.

His eyes exploded with anger. Because the other mothers might hear, he said in a quiet, tense voice, "Why is *that* here?"

"Didn't you get my letter?"

"Forget the letter."

"*That*," I said, "is a baby."

"It should be in the nursery."

Something in my subconscious stirred uneasily at the little word *it*. Eamonn did not even want to know if I had had a boy or a girl.

"That baby," I retorted sharply, "is not an *it* but a *he*. It is a boy, Eamonn."

His head jerked back.

"He's my son," I said, "your son, our son."

Reality was coming ever closer to him. Danger was taking an ever more definite shape. I gestured to the crib. "Say hello to Peter."

His problem even had a name. He blinked savagely as

though a vulture not a stork had brought the baby. Maybe the word *Peter*, meaning "rock," something not easily shifted or hidden away, troubled him.

He got up to draw the curtains around us and sat near me. "It—he—cannot stay here."

"He *is* staying here. And, please, don't raise your voice. He doesn't like it."

This big tough man who ordered people around had not the courage to look at his own son. Didn't he want to know if he looked like me, like him? Where was the human being in him that I had found, touched, loved? Did he believe that by not looking at Peter, his dark little secret might go away?

"Look at him, Eamonn."

He scraped his chair even closer to the bed. With a heavy emphasis: "You know . . . you cannot keep . . . this baby."

I pursed my lips and shook my head inches away from his.

Firming his jaw, he said, "It is not yours to keep. You must give this baby up. You *must*."

Mouth open to show my teeth, I shook my head again. "I am as likely to give up my son as the Virgin Mary."

"*You* are no Virgin Mary."

"And *you*," I said, "are no Saint Joseph."

With a tremulous lift of the voice, he said, "You're not thinking right. You *will* give it up."

I was saying to myself, *I lost one baby, Eamonn, don't make me lose another*. I pushed the covers aside and, not trusting my legs now that he had unnerved me by his enmity, started to crawl to the end of the bed.

"What're you *doing?*"

"Picking him up so you can see him."

"Don't *do that.*"

As though I were kneeling on a mountain in Kerry, I gazed down upon this child in his crib, the fruit of our love.

"Look at him, Eamonn, he's beautiful. He's the most beautiful little baby. Hold him just for a minute."

"No!" His horror sent a shiver through me. There was such a gulf between us. This child was everything to me and nothing to him.

"At least look at him, for God's sake."

It hurts me to say it but, at that moment, I reckon he could have run Peter over like a lamb on the road and not cared.

Had he hated me I could have understood, but he hated our son.

"No!" he repeated. I couldn't believe this. He was a priest, he called himself father, and he couldn't rest his eyes on his own son?

"You *look* at him," I insisted, in a kind of wail. "If you don't, I'll cause a scene, I really will."

Turning sideways on the bed to face him squarely, I said: "You may not hold him but, by God, *you will look at him*."

There must have been something savage in my new mother-face that made him stand up and walk to the crib. Circling it with those restless tap-dancing feet of his, he looked down while I searched his features. There must be some sentiment, some pride, some fatherly affection there.

I saw only a skull.

After at most three seconds, he said, but not from the heart, "Yes, a beautiful child."

He could not see the child for the sin.

I went back to bed and as he sat beside me I could read what he was about to say in those eyes I knew so well. "Stop it, Eamonn."

"I will not. It must be adopted."

His face brightened up insincerely. He smiled, but it looked wrong, like a green sun. "Afterward, you can come back to Inch with me. We'll go to Greece, London, wherever you like."

I banged my forehead with my fists. "What will that do for *me?* I won't have my baby anymore."

He touched his heart, next to his pectoral cross, as if to say, *You'll still have me.* I was always worried he wore a cross so close to his heart.

"After Greece, Eamonn?"

"You could stay in a convent for a year or so to recover."

"Go into a crazy house to recover my sanity? Besides, nuns worship a different God from me."

He wasn't listening. "After you have recovered your peace of mind, you might like to work in an orphanage."

"In a *what?* Give up my baby to strangers so I can look after other people's children?"

"You would know how they feel."

I felt at that moment that I was dealing with a lunatic. Or, rather, with a man who had worked that trick before. "No, no, no, Eamonn," I said. "I'd never even talk with you again. Whenever I saw you I'd be thinking, 'This is the man who took my baby from me.' And I would hate you for that, and I really don't want to hate you."

He sighed deeply to show my words had no effect on him. It was like talking to someone for ages before you realize you are alone in the room. But I tried. I had to. "If Peter's adopted, Eamonn, I don't know what'll happen, because one day, I promise you, one day I'll turn on you."

"You are threatening me?"—as if this was only a bishop's prerogative.

"I'm just talking sense. We can't have physical relations ever again."

He shrugged as if to say, *Why not?*

"Because," I went on, "we already have a child and I couldn't have another with you. What the hell, are we going to keep on having children which you keep forcing me to give up? Are we going to fill an orphanage?"

He was rubbing the sides of his face madly and scrubbing his head and scraping his chair on the floor. I pitied him, but I could not spare him. I said, "This is horrible what you want me to do."

"Not horrible—just the opposite."

"Can't you," I cut in, "call me by my name just once?"

"The whole thing is God's way of cleansing you . . . Annie."

Poor Eamonn. What had religion done to him?

I asked, "Whose God are you talking about?"

That got through his pious defenses. He really didn't believe there was any God but his, the One he had created out of nothing and had a patent on. He spat out: "We both know you are not morally fit to keep that child."

His mouth actually twisted as he said, "That child."

"Who are *you* to tell me that? That came out where you went in."

"How," he said, waving my words aside, "can you ruin the life"—he indicated the crib as if it were a mile away—"of that beautiful child?"

"I reckon he'd take his chances with me."

"But you are a nervous wreck, Annie. Think how you hide

in wardrobes and run out of the house at nights and are unable to communicate.''

"I communicated with *you*. Time after time after time."

"Then"—with a dismissive gesture of his ringed hand—"think of your poor family, Annie."

"Did *you?*"

"Your father—"

My last question sank in and it shamed him for violating my father's trust. He went back to rubbing his face, which was getting ever redder. Eventually, he raised both hands a few inches apart, fingers stretched, in front of my face. ''You knew from the start that you and I can never be together as man and wife. I'm a priest and I'm also married to my diocese.''

He held up his finger with the ring on as if to say this was the only ring he was entitled to wear.

"You mean, after what we both did you can still be a good bishop but I'm bound to be a rotten mother?"

"I mean simply and honestly, Annie, that a single mother can never give that beautiful baby all it needs."

He had a point, but was it not better for Peter to be half an orphan than a full one?

I stopped listening. I was at the sharp end of the Church Eamonn served. I was angry that he felt his vow of celibacy bound him more than the demands of his own son. I knew he had to deal with the guilty feeling that the only Apostle he was descended from was Judas Iscariot. I also knew that sin was his profession, so to speak, and he had to make his peace with his God. But did the price of peace have to be a bloody war over our son?

I was reminded of the first night he came into my room and tried to make love to me. He was ravenous then and he was, in a hateful way, ravenous now. Violent then in wanting to possess me, he wanted now, with the same violence, to dispossess me.

But this time I was not willing to be the food to sate the massive hunger of his self-will. After about forty minutes of his pleading and silently praying, I had had more than enough. I was exhausted first from having the baby and now warding off this pressure. I felt I was about to blow like a geyser. And guess who saved me?

Suddenly Peter began to cry. Not just cry but scream. He balled his baby fists like spring buds, screwed his face up, and shook. He was his father's son. He must have sensed that there was enmity in that room and that his whole future was under threat. He had somehow—I really believe this—tuned in to my anguish, my fears, and feeling of abandonment.

Eamonn went white as my pillow. It got through to him, I think, for the very first time that there was a third person in the room. We were not just talking about what to do with the furniture. There was a little human being here with a voice of his own—and what a voice. That baby cry shook Eamonn more than if the devil himself had come screaming at him like a banshee.

As for me, I felt strangely secure. Of course, I would guard my son for as long as he needed me, but this baby boy would also in some obscure way defend me. He would fill me with the courage to face the might of Eamonn and the powerful ages-old institution that stood right behind him. Make no mistake about it, I had seen Eamonn operate, I was really scared of what he could do to me. Wasn't he the original warlock, the sorcerer who could attack from any position at any time?

He jumped to his feet, realizing, intuitively, that a mother will always listen to her child before the man who fathered him. When a baby cries, it's like the Angelus: the whole world stops. That child, a rock indeed, was his rival, and he knew it and feared it.

Maybe he even grasped dimly that, for all the wealth and force at his command, this little fellow who couldn't even feed himself would not be a baby forever. Eamonn might trust me, but could he rely on Peter when he grew up not to open his mouth and destroy his life as I never would?

"Good-bye," he said. "I'll be back."

Knowing Eamonn, I had not the slightest doubt that in this at least he was telling the truth.

Chapter
Thirty-Three

WHEN EAMONN left, I squeezed my breasts, fearing anguish would sour my milk.

No sooner had I quieted Peter in my arms than in barged Father Coughlin, goose-necked chaplain, gargoyle extraordinary, founder member of the Church Belligerent. He started in at once. "You are morally unfit to keep that child."

If he showed me any kindness during this theological stampede, I must have blinked. I was not sure if he knew who the father was, but he was shrewd in a peasant sort of way. Besides, even some of the medical staff suspected Eamonn was the culprit.

"I am not doing it for that man," Father Coughlin said. "I'm concerned with you. And you're no good for this child."

I told him that his attack on the Bishop was part of his strategy for separating me from my son. If two clerics who did not see eye-to-eye agreed that I was unfit to mother my baby, God agreed with them, they must think.

Whether he liked Eamonn or not, they worshiped the same forbidding God. If my mother was Wishie, Father Coughlin was Don'tsie. Everything was Don't do this, Don't do that. On and on he went, scouring me with his words, and I gave as good as I got by telling him he was a bag of sour wind, a bark without a dog. Finally, I had had my bellyful of clerics for one day. I clambered out of bed.

"What're you doing, woman?"

I gently laid Peter in his crib before turning on this tower of a man with "Shove off."

"I am not—"

"Get out of here this minute or"—I pointed—"I'll punch you where it hurts."

I don't suppose he had been threatened with physical violence since he wore a clerical collar. Certainly not by a woman and one recently delivered. "You wouldn't dare," he said, backing away.

"Just try me, you hypocrite. You may not be strong"—he looked as if a light wind would knock him over—"so if you don't leave I'll punch the hell out of you."

We both called out, "Nurse!" at the same time.

One came running. Seeing my ready-to-go fist, she must have wondered if I wanted her as a referee. "Will you please," I said, "for his own safety, get this out of here?"

Father Coughlin halted at the door. "I swear to God I'll be back and I'll take that boy with me."

I raised a clenched fist at him again and he went, leaving nothing but a faint candle smell behind. But Father Coughlin did get his revenge in a most terrible way.

In the hospital, a young woman with Down's syndrome, Maura, had recently given birth. The staff feared she might accidentally kill her baby; it was, therefore, taken from her. Maura had then snatched someone else's baby and, if a porter hadn't stopped her, she would have walked out of the Rotunda with it.

On the sixth day, I returned from the shower, with my hair in curlers and wearing only an old bathrobe. My baby was gone. Thinking Maura had snatched Peter, I was frantic.

A nurse said, "Father Coughlin's got him." She pointed me down the corridor.

Hearing Peter crying, still clutching my damp bath towel, I ran with dread in my heart. The storeroom was a place full of mops, brooms, and pails, and it smelled of urine, medicines, and disinfectants. There was Father Coughlin holding my baby. With two women flanking him, he was doing his best to stop Peter's bawling and not succeeding. Babies seem to scare the shit out of priests.

"What're you doing?" I screamed.

"Baptizing it."

I was dumbfounded. I had registered as a Catholic—what else when my child's father was a bishop?—but I had not asked for him to be christened. Maybe this was another way Eamonn had of demonstrating his power. "Let him be baptized and, behold, it was so," regardless of the mother's feelings.

"Name?" Father Coughlin demanded.

I was worried lest he drop or soil my baby. I said: "You know my name."

He held the baby up. "His."

Why hadn't Eamonn baptized him himself? He was, after all, in the business. Maybe he feared that would give the game away: a bishop baptizing a bastard. Or maybe that went against the rules, like absolving me after we had made love. But it was against the rules to sire Peter in the first place, and that hadn't deterred him. And why not in the hospital chapel; why the hurry? Our son was not even ill, let alone in danger of death. Even if he were in danger of death, Eamonn was not concerned with Peter's going to heaven, only with himself going to hell—this side of the grave, I mean. I concluded that Peter was being baptized as the necessary prelude to being adopted by a Catholic couple.

"His name?" Father Coughlin repeated.

"His *names*," I said belligerently. "He's entitled to more than one."

"All right." He was putting a ribbon-like stole around his neck, purple side up. "Names."

"Peter Eamonn."

His face creased even further. If he had doubted who the leg-over man was, he surely knew now.

He had brought a small bag with him like the one my father carried when visiting patients. Out of it he took a bottle of blessed water and a prayer book. He handed the baby to one of the women and somewhere along the line he poured water over Peter Eamonn's head and made him a Christian like his father.

Peter Eamonn did not seem to approve. The cold water made him scream his defiance even louder at the priest. Another proof he was his father's son.

My God, I thought, when he grows up he'll eat the likes

of Father Coughlin. But why do clerics keep making my son cry?

In my shocked state I stood barefoot in my old bathrobe, a towel girding my waist, and silent. In our family, baptisms were big things. Mommy spent two hundred dollars on a christening robe alone, and there was always a family gathering, and home movies made as a memento. And Peter was a bishop's son; he was entitled to be baptized in a cathedral. Father Coughlin's private Barnum & Bailey was over in three or four minutes. He hovered over my son and asked him in all seriousness if he renounced Satan and all his works and pomps. I felt like saying, *Why not ask that of his daddy?*

As I walked back to my room, my baby in my arms, baptism seemed to have made no more difference to him than it did to me. Who was supposed to be cleansing whom?

What worried me most was not that silly game in the storeroom but the feeling that what that priest had done had somehow, in his mind at least, given him and the institution he represented a hold over my son.

We would see about that. If there was to be a fight, I would take them all on—Father Coughlin, Bishop Casey, the Pope himself. "Don't you worry, Peter," I said, as I settled him back in his crib. "I'll give them all a bloody nose."

As a professional counselor, Sister Eileen was horrified at the Bishop's attitude. "Most inappropriate," she said, too moderately.

I had never even hinted that Eamonn was Peter's father, but she was so wise she could have found no other explanation of his behavior at Inch and now. As to Father Coughlin, she described his action not only as "bizarre" but probably against canon law. The Bishop must have put him up to it.

Eileen advised me to go to St. Patrick's, a home for unmarried mothers run by French Sisters of Charity on the outskirts of the city. There, I could make my own decision about adoption. Now that Peter was baptized, I was eligible.

I accepted Eileen's advice and she made the arrangements. Eamonn approved of St. Patrick's, possibly because it was his idea in the first place. Nuns were part of the system that he could manipulate.

On the day before I left the Rotunda, he paid me a second

visit, which was a carbon copy of the first. Except that this time he really tried to pick the baby up but, in the end, withdrew his hands as if they were too near a raging fire. I was perplexed. Each day at Mass he took a bit of bread, changed it into the body of God, and held it up, marveling. But we, in love, had taken an invisible seed and an invisible egg and turned them into the miracle of a human being and he dared not touch it.

Once more I crawled down my bed and picked Peter up. "Look, Eamonn, he's the spitting image of you, can't you see?"

He could, and it terrified him. He gulped painfully but did not react in any other way.

"He's got your bump on his upper lip, the same ears, the same big birthmark on his left knee."

He shielded his eyes. "It's unbelievable. I don't know how I did this, I really don't." His voice sharpened. "Put it down. I can't talk to you till you do."

He did not like being outnumbered two to one; I put Peter down so we could converse in a civilized way.

"If you're not ready to come back to Inch," he said, drawing up his chair close to my bed, "Saint Pat's is the best place for you."

My milk had turned sour after his first visit. What would this visit do? "Talk for as long as you like," I said, "provided you don't mention adoption."

He was unable to stop. It was his obsession. Cuckoo-time again. He had even brought adoption papers with him. He waved them in front of me. Could I not see that I was fallen, that the child deserved a proper home and family?

For an hour he went on. When he had finished, I was convinced he had composed his own special Ave. It went: *Hail Annie, full of sin . . . cursed be the fruit of thy womb, Peter*.

Eamonn was such a decent person; he really cared for the sufferings of little ones all over the world. Yet there was no room in the inn of his heart for his own son. *Oh, Eamonn*, I thought, *you are so good; how can you do this bad thing?*

By now I no longer trusted him. If Peter were adopted, Eamonn would know where he was and the name he was adopted under—wasn't he a bishop, an all-seeing peregrine on a cathedral spire?—whereas I would never know. I would always be wondering: What is he like now? Is he well? Is he making progress at school? Is he even alive? Moreover, what would Peter think of me? Would he hate me for not loving him enough or having courage enough to keep him? Would he want to look for me as much as I would want to look for him? Would we go to our separate deaths, distant graves, with unfulfilled longings in our hearts?

With all trust waning, I felt Eamonn's one concern was to cover his traces. As far as he was concerned, it would have been better if Peter, like Judas, had never been born.

From the moment he showed me round his Cathedral and entertained me in his Palace, I saw he had much to lose. Power, prestige, trips abroad. He did not realize that he was asking me to give up my future so he could keep his.

Mary called me just as I was packing for St. Patrick's. She pleaded with me to return to the States immediately. But Peter still had jaundice and I was weary enough to die. Was my refusal to go home also an unwillingness to accept that my dream was finally dead? Did I expect the wizard to do one more trick for me, maybe the biggest of all: change a bishop, himself, into a human being?

The next morning, Barbara Devlin came to the Rotunda to drive Peter and me to St. Patrick's, a home on the west side of the city. I was not feeling well. I had a high temperature and a burning sensation in my left leg.

The first sight of St. Patrick's seared my soul, and I saw Barbara recoil, too. It was in a pleasant setting on the edge of the Dublin mountains and not far from the Phoenix Park, but the black steepled building stood behind high stone walls and you went through a big wrought-iron gate to get to it. It was a prison. Except the tops of the walls were studded with broken dreams.

With a sense of foreboding, hugging my Peter tight in his white crocheted blanket with tassels, I begged his forgiveness. First, I had seen him baptized in a broom closet and now I had brought him to this prison as his first home. I had slept with Eamonn month after month without any sense of guilt, but now I was, yes, ashamed.

Chapter
Thirty-Four

INSIDE, ST. PATRICK'S was damp and gloomy, with floors so highly polished they must have been responsible for many more fallen women.

There were smirking pictures of Mary, who had got a child without you-know-what, and, in niche after niche, life-size bleeding statues of the Sacred Heart. Cruelest of all were the crucifixes everywhere. Their purpose was to tell the girls who, after all, had brought miracles into the world, that they had done this terrible thing: put nails through the hands and feet of Jesus Christ.

One heavily pregnant girl was on her knees shining the already shiny corridor tiles. Did they want the poor kid to eject her baby there and then into the bucket?

A Dublin girl called Shelagh, chief of the inmates, led me to the mother superior's office. It was comfortable, with soft green lights and only one religious icon. The superior was a small lady with rimless glasses sitting in a big chair at a big desk. In no way judgmental, she told me my duties, the pass I would need if I wanted to go out for a few hours. "Back before dark, of course." In particular, she explained that the babies were kept in one place to facilitate care and feeding arrangements.

Shelagh showed me to my room at the top of four flights of stairs. My left hip hurt, making it hard for me to move. Even when I was pregnant I walked more easily. I was sharing with three others. One of them was Morag, the girl whom I

246

had seen polishing the floor. She was from Monaghan, only nineteen years old, with black hair, white skin, green eyes, and freckles. We were separated from each other by a curtain over the entry to our own dark wooden cubicles, each with a picture of the Sacred Heart on one wall. The bed was hard and there was a tiny attic window.

The nursery was in an annex and could be reached only by going down, along a corridor, and up more steps. It was as bright as a greenhouse. The room was decorated with plants and ferns, the walls were a pale yellow, and the cots, though of iron, were painted white. There were about thirty-five babies there at that time, all in spotless white gowns. We were only allowed to see our babies when the bell rang at mealtimes. I could not breast-feed Peter, and I pointed out that he was not taking the bottle feeds. No one listened to me. Was I not in St. Pat's because of my stupidity?

To reach the laundry, we had to go into the courtyard and up more steps. It was insufferably hot because of the huge steel sinks and scrubbing boards. An elderly nun, she must have been over seventy, slight of build and with a beautiful face, took my hand and stroked it. I wondered what the hell she wanted.

Her name was Sister Ignatius. Christ, I thought, the men have taken over the women even inside a convent. They give them men's names. Why? I guess to stress the fact that male clerics can do to them what they like. And these male-dominated women were in charge of the fallen girls of St. Pat's!

The next day, I was in the downstairs corridor, which Morag was again polishing. Sister Ignatius appeared and tapped her on the shoulder with "Get up, my dear." Having heaved her to her feet, she led Morag by the arm to a bench.

"You sit here, darlin', and have a rest."

"But, Sister," Morag said, in her northern accent, "the bursar will give out to me if I don't finish soon."

Sister Ignatius merely winked at her, walked over to Morag's bucket, knelt down next to it, and proceeded to polish the floor herself.

Within minutes, a senior though younger nun named Sister Vincent appeared, looking very agitated. "Will you get up, Sister Ignatius."

She just went on polishing the floor.

Sister Vincent, the bursar, hissed, "You are setting a very bad example. Get *up*."

The old nun did not so much as move a muscle on her face. In a fury, Sister Vincent said more loudly, "Did you hear me, Sister Ignatius?"

She looked up very sweetly and whispered, "No."

As the bursar stomped off to get help, Sister Ignatius went on calmly polishing the floor.

I was ashamed. I had done an unforgivable thing: I had lumped all the nuns together. A victim myself, I was prepared to victimize everyone else. That nun must have been under a Gestapo-like discipline for fifty years and she had kept her freedom. Her inner voice drowned out all the commands of petty tyrants around her. Under her kittenish exterior, she was an almighty rebel, a rebel for her God. Through that little word *no*, I was able to see in miniature the whole history of her life, its struggles, its persecutions, its tiny but terrific triumphs.

Maybe this was why the Catholic Church produces so many saints: it makes life so damned hard for everybody. Maybe the place was stacked with saints, I don't know.

Sister Ignatius helped me when the girls stole four of my best blouses. In the laundry, she took me by the arm into a quiet place and, stroking my hand, said: "They mean you no harm."

"What would they do to me if they did?" I said angrily.

"Annie, Annie, they're nice girls in trouble."

"Those nice girls stole from me."

"Stole?" Sister Ignatius looked really puzzled. "Borrowed. They have nothing, you see. They think this rich American girl can get replacements any time she wants."

"Is that borrowing, Sister?"

"Sure, I'll get them back for you."

She did get three blouses back. That wonderful lady could have persuaded Satan to part with damned souls.

I began to sweat badly at night; Peter had a rash, would not drink milk, and lost weight. It seemed as if we both were doomed. I could not have walked without Morag and Shelagh, also heavily pregnant, supporting me. Sister Ignatius was right. These were marvelous girls victimized by life.

* * *

On my fourth day, I received the summons. Bishop Casey had appeared.

When I made it downstairs, I found him in the corridor, the center of attention. The sisters were practically gobbling him up as they knelt to kiss his ring and "My Lord" him. They kissed that ring as if they really loved it.

When I was at my sourest, I remembered Sister Ignatius and thumped my breast. She would make ten of me. I was in my dowdy dress while Eamonn was in clerical harness, with a choirboy innocence of face, talking charmingly to the sisters as if they were mental defectives. I could see them thinking, "Isn't his Lordship a marvel taking the trouble to come all this way to see a fallen woman?" How were they to know he had come from Kerry to force his mistress to give up his son? I could have told them I had kissed more than his ring; I had kissed him and he had kissed me all over. I had breastfed their bishop.

These things needed to be said, but who would have believed me?

As he dismissed his admirers with a final glossy cock-a-doodle-doo of a benediction, I almost expected him to say to me, "Follow me, my dear." He led me into a dark room furnished with cheap crucifixes and holy pictures. No economy spared.

Had I not known what he did for a living I would have wondered how Eamonn was always available when he was not needed. I wanted to go down on my knees and kiss his ring for fun, but the fun days were over. I didn't feel well and he looked awful. Peering into his hollowed eyes, I softened and asked myself, *Eamonn, what have we done to each other?*

How could he let me, who had shared his bed, stay with our son in a place like this? A home for Unmarried Mothers! Where were the Unmarried Fathers? Surely not all the babies in this place were conceived by the Holy Ghost? Unmarried Fathers must exist, but they didn't have to have their noses rubbed in it. They were invisible, like Eamonn. Not a line on his belly, a bead of milk on his breasts, not a mark of paternity on him. Was this why men were such hypocrites?

Sure, I was bitter but I didn't want to be. I had no regrets. I had my jewel, my son. I only wanted to be left alone. Which is one thing Eamonn could not allow. He had too much riding on this. Peter was his Sword of Damocles, and Eamonn was shrewd enough to know that kids grow up asking dangerous questions like "Who is my father?"

Feeling as menaced as was Herod by a baby, Eamonn began again with his demands that I give Peter up. Oh, what had happened to my jazzman who had created worlds for me on mountaintops that he was reduced to playing a single mournful note.

I was a chancer, he was saying, I was selfish, unstable, concerned only with myself. I almost laughed—it was so like a cracked record, his demand and my refusal. This could go on till we were both senior citizens. Unless he forged my signature on the adoption papers he waved in front of me— and, in my present mood, I would not have put forgery past him—Peter was mine forever.

In my room I had Peter's birth certificate. Its aim was to prove he was a person in his own right, with a country and parents he could be proud of. But under the heading "Name and surname of Father," there was a blank. This nameless unmarried Father, without any acknowledged rank or profession, who even had the same big birthmark as his son, waived his paternal rights. All but one. The right to take the boy away from plain Anne Murphy and give him to strangers who, he presumed—such insolence!—would be more capable and more worthy than she. How he despised this woman who was once good enough to grace his bed.

The irony was: he could claim his right to dispose of Peter only if he put his name on that certificate. The last thing he would do. I had read that St. Augustine had a son in sin, yet he called him *Adeodatus,* Gift of God, and was proud of him. Who did Eamonn think had given him Peter that he wanted him adopted? Oh, why couldn't he see that through his Gift of God he would live on after his death not in some distant heaven but here on earth, forever? The more he talked, the more I thought, *When will you get it into your head that I love you but I love Peter more?*

"You don't look well, Annie." Spoken with genuine sympathy. "Come back with me to Inch. I always gave you what you wanted there."

God, his kindness could be cruel. Inch. What a funny little name for such a stupendous place. I remembered how, on our first time-stopped day, the car climbed the hill and we drove through the tunnel of hedges into a secret garden. Just to hear the word *Inch* and I was, for a moment, back inside my magic bubble.

Inch! Inch! Where the winds were kind and the sun shone like a friend and, at nights, there was always, always, always, a ring around the moon. If I were to return to you now, Inch, I would climb your cliffs with Eamonn and he would throw me or I would throw myself over the edge onto pointed rocks swept by the black Atlantic. Good-bye, Inch, good-bye forever.

This final farewell to my love burst the very bubble of my being. All I wanted to do at that moment was put my arms around Eamonn and simply sob. Which is what I did. "Eamonn, please *stop*."

"Annie," he said, stiff and agitated, "if one of the sisters came in and found us like this—"

I released him. "Sorry." I wiped my eyes on my sleeve. "I just feel so bad."

"Me, too, Annie. If only you knew."

"We're such enemies now. It's as if you hate our baby."

"Enemies? Hate? No, no, no."

"Eamonn," I said, "this is Calvary. One day, unless you change, somebody's going to get crucified here. And it's not going to be my baby and me because"—my voice caved in—"we don't deserve it."

Dear Eamonn took out his handkerchief and rubbed his eyes.

"I'm not asking you for much," I said. "Just enough money to get us home."

He nearly shook his head off. In America, his problem would be beyond his control.

I stroked his troubled more than handsome face. "I adore you, Eamonn. I loved you from the moment I saw you at Shannon. I will love you to the day I die, no matter what you do. But *stop*. *Just stop it!*"

But he wouldn't.

Later that day, I started to see sparks as when a blunt blade is pressed to the grinder, and I kept falling over. I went to the doctor's office to ask for a cane. He told me I was a faker and a "whoor" and refused me. I called Barbara Devlin and she came in the guise of a concerned relative to take me home to Clontarf for lunch. "Gracious, Annie," she said, "you've got a terrible infection in your groin."

She took my temperature and it was 102. She drove me to the Rotunda and they admitted me immediately. They suspected I had an infection due to some stitches being left in. I asked to see Sister Eileen. They said she had been sent to Wales. She was not supposed to be leaving for another month. Had she, like me, been spirited away?

Next day, who should come to see me but Eamonn. Did he have a private eye tailing me? This time he really was a mess: jaundiced worse than Peter, two blood-spotted eggs for eyes, the fizz all gone.

He drew the curtain around the bed and took me in his arms. His fingers twitched as if he had Parkinson's and he was crying and begging, "Forgive me, Annie, forgive me. How could I have done this to you?"

Tears dribbled down his cheeks and met under a wobbly chin. I dried them for him. "My fault," he murmured, "all my fault."

"As soon as I take Peter home and—"

He instantly reverted to his demand for adoption. What a quick-change artist he was. Eamonn, the great survivor of every shipwreck, still keeping afloat by treading blood. In one head-chopping instant he switched from loving to hating me. Always love and hate, the two faces of the moon.

"When are you going to get it into your head," I said hoarsely, "that I will not give him up?"

"You will," he ground out, "oh, you *will*." He left without one consoling word.

Sister Moore, the head nurse, came in. She said: "You want to go into hiding, don't you, you selfish bitch? Then no one will be able to adopt your baby and he'll have to stay in Saint Patrick's for good." I was dumbfounded. The sorcerer had so many people speaking on his behalf, starting with God.

My temperature had fallen to 101 but there was a big red streak down my left leg that burned like hell and I nearly couldn't walk. These were the very symptoms Daddy had before he lost his left leg. I had visions of gangrene setting in and surgeons cutting my leg off above the knee.

Minutes after Sister Moore left, a doctor came in. He had a big red face and drink on his breath. As plain an alcoholic as I ever saw, and I had seen some. I had to take the thermometer from him to get it into my mouth and stop him from breaking my tooth. Afterward he couldn't read the damn thing. No matter. He slapped me heartily on my bad leg. "Ready for discharge," and a nurse brought me my outdoor clothes.

I was hobbling along the corridor to call Barbara Devlin when I remembered the family was now on vacation abroad. It hit me hard that I was no Pop Murphy, born and bred in Kerry. I was a foreigner. I had forgotten how deceptive this land was. When I first drove to Inch I had noticed that it seemed so alive when only shadows moved. Nothing now was coming through the soles of my feet but malice and distrust. I was alone. I did not belong.

I called St. Patrick's and a dear little old man came and drove me in a small black car back to the home.

There, all hell broke loose. Annie Murphy target practice! I was verbally assaulted for staying out overnight without a pass, for getting myself admitted to a hospital when I was perfectly all right. Not only would I not let a devoted couple have my baby, I refused even to stay around and feed him.

To cap it all, Eamonn appeared once more. Had he nothing worse to do? Was I his whole flock, his entire diocese? Once more, he waved the adoption papers in my face.

I told him, "Go shove them. I'm taking my baby with me back to America."

"Oh, no," he said, shaking his head. "Oh, no. *You* can go if you like, but that boy has to be put on your passport."

"I'll go to the American embassy as soon as I'm well."

"You will not succeed," he said, meaningfully.

He spoke to me for a long time after that but I heard scarcely a word. However, I do remember saying to him:

''We're like two dogs in a ring, you know that? And let me tell you, I'm a Murphy and a damned good fighter. You're the one who's got everything to lose.''

I looked him in the eyes, but there was no one there.

Eamonn's attempts to wrest Peter from me were a worse violation of me than any I had suffered at the hands of men. Worse than the attempted rape when I was sixteen. Worse than Jeff, my boyfriend, twice sodomizing me. Worse than my husband's prodding me with pointed objects because he did not wish to soil his hands. What made Eamonn's violation of me so much more terrible was that I still loved him and I felt that, deep down, he loved me. The force making him do such a wicked thing was alien to his naturally kind self.

Afterward, it took me a long time to climb the stairs to my room. Once there, I looked out the window and, behold, my demon-angel was in the courtyard about to climb—ah, this was an official visit—into his Mercedes. He looked up and crossed his arms twice with his hands turned toward me as if to say, ''You will *not* keep your baby.''

That did it. He would never change. Summoning all my energy, I went downstairs again, where I fed coins into the telephone box in the hallway. I got through to Mary to tell her I was coming home after all. She was crying. I realized that if I returned in my present state, it would break my father's heart and send my mother straight back on the bottle.

I was unable to get to dinner. The pain in my leg was like a huge toothache with all the nerves exposed. And now the foot was beginning to swell as, I remembered, my father's had swelled before he underwent surgery. I could see myself being fitted out like Daddy with a wooden leg and a special shoe on the end. Apart from anything else, if things did not improve, Peter and I would starve.

That night, Gina, the fair-haired nurse on duty, took me into her confidence. She gave me a few more codeine tablets to dull the pain in my leg and shared a cigarette with me. I didn't smoke, but I liked the sacred communion of that cigarette. Exhaling, she said, ''The holy guy''—the inmates' name for the Bishop—''blessed the nursery today.''

I found that funny. While I was staggering upstairs, he had blessed a room with a batch of babies in it, one of them his own son. How long was this sham going to last? Weeks, months, years? When would he leave me be or say—with pride, regret, whatever—"He is my son?"

"Annie," Gina whispered, "the nuns, especially with that oily Bishop around, don't care a shit about you, only about the baby."

She was right. In a religion that spreads pictures of the Virgin around like confetti, women do not count. My misfortune was that I, Annie Murphy, was a mere woman.

The next day, at feeding time, I managed to get to the nursery, but the head nurse took me firmly but kindly by the arm.

"Peter's not there," she said.

"Oh my God," I screamed, "where is he?"

"Calm yourself, Annie. He's in a room by himself."

"Why's he so special? Why is he so *special?*"

"His navel has an infection, and you might give him whatever you've picked up."

After Peter was fed, a nun brought him, clad only in a diaper, to see me. I was not allowed to hold and fondle him. I had to be satisfied with trying to communicate with him through a plate-glass window.

But instead of cradling him, this wooden-faced nun in a black habit, not the usual white, held him up to me from behind by his shoulders. Maybe even she did not realize that she was holding him up in the attitude of one crucified. One more brutal crucifix in St. Patrick's, a living one. My boy, a miniature Christ.

Seeing his wide-open Calvaried mouth and silent tears, the fight went out of me. I was nothing but a scattering of dead leaves. It took all my courage to return to the window. I pressed the palms of my hands against it and misted it up as I whispered to Peter: "You don't know me from Eve, my darling. Which, come to think of it, is who I am. Yes, Mother Eve, blamed for everything. But you were our bite of the apple, oh my darling, and you tasted very sweet."

Then I thought of Adam, the third terrified, guilt-ridden member of our trio, wearer of red socks, blesser of nurseries.

"Oh, Eamonn, you and I are now separated forever by sound-proof worlds. We did love each other once, didn't we? I promised I would love you forever and forever. Please don't make me break my word. Please, don't make me end up hating you. Please, *please* don't crucify our son."

Chapter
Thirty-Five

S EEING PETER cry hurt me so much I simply had to leave. After every few paces I had to hop to give my bad leg a rest. For the first time in my life, I was completely hopeless. I was about to lose my son.

I went down to the lounge and Shelagh met me there. The chief of the girls was tall, tough, but good-hearted. She fetched me tea and cookies. "Call home, Annie," she said. "What're you waiting for, death?"

After I had finished my tea, Shelagh and Morag helped me up the stairs. I was shaking all over with fever, my leg was starting to swell, and the walls were closing in on me. I was tempted to call Mary and say, "Get Daddy over here fast," but I couldn't do that to him.

Then Mary called me. I managed to get down to the lobby with the help of two girls but I was shaking all over. "You sound terrible, Annie."

"Yeah. You're wasting a fortune just waiting for me to get downstairs."

"Peter's paying and now Johnny knows about you, too. So tell us your plans."

"I'm hoping to get back to the Rotunda but I'm scared I'll pass out and they'll have Peter adopted over my head."

"I wish we could help."

One day, Bridget paid me a visit. "Holy shit, Murphy," she said. "You look awful. You've got to get out of this hellhole and into a hospital." She had no suggestions how to do it and she had her baby to tend to.

That night, on the way to the restroom, I fell and injured my elbow. I crawled to the toilet down one long hallway and halfway down another. Morag and the rest were scared that if they picked me up it would bring on their own labor.

I got back into bed and gave up. My whole body hurt and I was twice as heavy as usual. Lying in bed was the only relief from pain and the sense of the mountainous weight of my own self. For five hours I lay there, soaked in urine, unable to open my eyes. When I did look around, everything seemed cobwebby. All I could do was pray to the God of my childhood. "Please help me."

That night, around eleven o'clock, Shelagh came in, very excited. "A doctor's come to see you."

A doctor? I shot up in bed. I could still do something for my baby. My body became lighter, power reentered my legs. Somehow I made it downstairs to the Superior's study. There was Dr. Harry Burke, the family friend whom I had last seen when Daddy was in Dublin.

"Annie," he said, "why didn't you call me? I was always here for you."

Harry was short and stocky, with a shock of gray hair, blue eyes, red face, and a nose definitely made in Ireland. He sat me down on a couch with a stool for my foot. "Now what seems to be the trouble?"

"She's the trouble," I said. "Mother Superior here and Bishop Casey."

"I do assure you, Doctor," the Superior said, "she has received the best possible treatment."

"Mother," I said, "you have done a lot of things, but you have given me no medical treatment whatsoever."

Dr. Burke turned severe. "Listen, Annie, I can't have two women cackling around me." He looked up. There was only a small table lamp on. "I need to examine this young lady. I want some more light here. Thank you, Mother. Now, if you'd care to leave us."

While he took my blood pressure, he explained how he came to be there. Mary had told her ex-husband about me. Bobby, being a lawyer who specialized in medical cases, realized how ill I was. Since Daddy knew nothing about the baby, Bobby made Mary creep into Daddy's study and get Harry's number from his address book.

"Good job she did, Annie; your blood pressure is up."

Then he pulled down my jeans. "Oh my God. Bend your foot."

"I can't."

He tried to find the pulse in my leg and failed. "Your right leg's fine, but there must be blood clots in the left."

"What?" I cried. I wanted to call Daddy instantly and tell him not to let them cut my leg off.

"Don't get excited. It's curable, but your leg's very inflamed. If it had gone on much longer"—he waved his hand—"I don't know."

He called in the Superior. "I've got to use your phone." Dialing: "We've got to get Annie to a hospital immediately. This is an absolute disgrace. I intend to write a report about this."

He called the Rotunda and asked them to send an ambulance, emergency.

"We did—"

"Shut up, Mother," I said. "You should be put in jail."

"Annie—"

"Okay, Harry, okay."

He asked the Superior to leave us again.

"Now," I said, "please, what is a blood clot?"

"Your deep veins are blocked. It doesn't mean you're going to die, but it has to be treated right away."

Gina came in and whispered something. "Yes, yes," he said. "Thank you, nurse."

With a wink in my direction, she left. She had confirmed my story of being abused.

I remember nothing of what happened next until I came to in the Rotunda with half-a-dozen white-coated doctors around me. My temperature was 103.5. They took several blood samples, made me swallow tablets to thin my blood out, and put me on a drip. This went on for a couple of days. Harry Burke came in a few times to assure me I was doing well. He said: "You probably think you are shooting blood clots all over. But it's only in your leg."

"Have you told my parents?"

"I rang Mary. She thinks it's better not to tell them."

"Good."

"But, Harry, while I'm in here, what'll happen to Peter?"

"I'll make sure he's well cared for," he said.

I felt more assured, especially as I was put in charge of a Sister Steele who, Harry told me, was the best nurse in the place. Short, with black hair and a lovely figure, she seemed utterly trustworthy. What I enjoyed most about her was the way she touched the tip of my nose and laughed as if to say, "You're in my hands now, Annie Murphy, don't you worry about a thing." And I didn't.

One day, Harry came in.

"How's Peter?" I asked.

He smiled consolingly. "Fine, take my word for it."

I smiled back. "Sure."

"I just met Eamonn in the hallway. You know what I think, Annie. Children born out of wedlock are better off adopted."

"Harry—"

"Will you hear me out?"

"Okay, okay, but—"

"There you go again."

I bowed repentantly. "Sorry."

"At last! Children without fathers are better adopted. That is the Irish view and, in general, mine. Shut up, Annie. But you are twenty-six years old and I have to warn you—"

"Yes?"

He said more solemnly than usual, "You should never have another child. That's why you've got to think this through."

I was astounded. "My last chance to have a child?"

He took my hand. "I couldn't tell you before, but the leg was far gone. We couldn't suck the stuff out or do surgery. It took longer than usual to stabilize your blood."

"Eamonn?"

"He's been a bully. That's why I'm forewarning you."

"You told him?"

"Everything. I'll leave you now. Good luck."

Minutes later, I was still feeling my abdomen and thinking that if I gave up Peter my body would forever be a silent beehive, an emptied nest, when Eamonn entered. It was because of his negligence that I would never have another child.

He sat by my bed. He looked repentant again, shaking his

head and initially watching his eloquent fingers speak for him. "I can't believe this has happened to you, Annie."

"You want to see?"

"No, no. I came to tell you Peter has a special nurse caring for just him."

"Thank you. Thank you."

"They've cured the rash on his belly button." I choked back my tears of relief.

He hunched his shoulders. "I never wanted you to go to that dreadful place, Annie." He gestured to my leg. "Look what you've done to yourself."

"What I've done to *myself?*"

"Shush, shush, shush."

"Did I hear right? It was either Saint Pat's or Inch without my baby."

"You just got off the critical list. Isn't it obvious you should give up the baby?"

"My last?"

"Doctors always use scare tactics like that. I know Burke. An ignoramus. In three, four years, the scar tissue will heal. You're young, you'll be able to have another baby."

Truth for Eamonn was always what was most convenient for him. He was still mixing his own truth like a cocktail.

I said, "I'm so glad you went through all those years of medical school."

"Believe in God, He can heal anything."

I laughed aloud at his great sense of humor. "Do me one favor, Eamonn. Stop talking about adoption."

"Isn't God telling you what to do by punishing you like this?"

"*Punishing* me?"

"He gave you a blood clot."

"God didn't give me a blood clot! Are you crazy? That was due to an infection of the groin, which because of you no one bothered to help me with."

He took time out to tell me about a relative of his. "I would have come earlier, but Jenny almost died. Two blood clots in her lung. I went to give her the last rites and stayed almost three days. I told her, 'Jenny, this is what comes of disobeying God and using birth control pills.' "

"Jesus," I screeched, "what kind of a Job's comforter are

you?'' His maniac God was spreading blood clots all over the place to prove he was right about adoption and birth control. How did his God find the time?

He said, ''I told her that God was punishing her for her sins. She promised me she would never take those pills again.''

''Eamonn, I used to think you were really smart. Now I see you're nothing but a thick Mick.''

He clutched both sides of his head, and groaned. Getting up, he drew the curtains around us as if this were a confessional. ''I did not come here to be abused.''

''Can't you see, *you* are abusing *me*? Go away.''

My headache was worsening, I could feel my fever rising. ''If you stay, tell me something nice. Let's part on a happy note.''

He told me that Bridget had called to say she was getting married.

''Is that supposed to make me happy?'' I said.

He smiled wryly as if to say, *I suppose not*. ''The thing is, Annie, Wentworth is free to marry her.''

And you, I thought, *are free to marry me, if only you had the guts for it. But you don't know you are free and no one can prove you are except yourself.*

Sister Steele came in and said, ''My Lord, this patient is not allowed to have visitors for more than ten minutes.''

''I understand,'' he said, without making a move.

Sister continued, ''She seems to be raising her voice a lot, so if you would care to . . .''

Looking very irritated, he left.

I was on a drip for a week, during which Peter absorbed all my thoughts. There were times when I felt there was a river running through my body and I was getting pains all over. Finally, I started hemorrhaging.

I called the nurse, who said, ''You're getting your period, that's all.''

''It's *not* all.''

Three hours later, when I got up from my bed, blood poured out of me. I needed about fifteen Kotexes. When my nose started bleeding, the nurse got really scared. Every bit of my skin I touched or scratched started to bleed. I was scared, too, in case my son was left without a mother.

A doctor came running and nurses were all around me. They had so thinned out my blood that it had practically turned to water.

I must have slept for five or six hours. When I woke up, whispering, "Where's Peter?," there was a whole convention of medics around me. I saw I was on a monitor.

To make matters worse, in came Father Coughlin. He was picking up the sheet over the cradle to look at my leg.

"Get away from my feet, you."

He jumped so high in the air I hoped he'd bang his head on the ceiling. "I'm not doing anything."

"Tell him to get out," I told the doctors.

They turned on him and cried in chorus, "Get out, get *out*," and he went. Being near to death has some consolations.

The doctors had to get a balance between giving me too much and too little of the blood thinner. It meant I was in the Rotunda for three weeks, during which Sister Steele became my minder. I told her that relieved as I was to be out of St. Patrick's, I was worried about Peter. I was grateful to Dr. Burke and the Bishop for seeing to it that the sisters gave Peter the best of the best.

Eamonn came again to see me, of course, wearing his see-through smile. Instantly, Sister Steele was plumping my pillows, saying how vital it was for me not to get excited.

"Her family's been calling, Bishop. That's marvelous, isn't it?"

Eamonn looked daggers at her. He didn't like being preached at. As soon as she left, he flicked the adoption papers under my nose.

"Draw the curtains," I said. "Good. Listen, give me those papers and I'll rip them up."

The fight had really started. "You know I can never have another child. Anyway, apart from my parents, my whole family knows about my son. My brother Peter has promised to help me financially and you will have to chip in, too."

"Well," Eamonn said, "I'm not giving anything until—"

"Shut . . . up," I said.

He moved closer to the bed and whispered, "Hear me out."

I picked up the heavy metal jug beside my bed. "No,

because I'm gonna knock you stone fucking cold.'' I adopted my mother's drink-sodden voice.

He put his head in his hands. "Bang it, then, I don't care. Go right ahead, but I'll have my say."

I screamed, "You will not!"

I lifted the jug when Sister Steele appeared. "Annie, put that down. Fine. Now, Bishop, come with me," and she grabbed him by the shoulder.

"I am not coming, woman."

"*Bishop,* come . . . with . . . *me.*"

She signaled to another nurse to attend to me because I was shaking so. As Eamonn left with Sister Steele, the nurse said, "Take it easy, Annie," but I screamed after Eamonn, "I don't want him anywhere near me."

The nurse said, quietly, "He's a bishop, Annie."

"Haven't *I* got any rights?" I raised my voice again: "Bishop, stay away."

After I had calmed down, who should burst in but Bridget. "You're not going to believe this, Murphy, but the Bishop just got kicked out on his backside." She paused to look at me. "My God, what happened to you?"

She ran out and returned with a couple of damp towels. While she cooled me down she explained that she had arrived just as Sister Steele led Eamonn into her office. She had overheard everything. Sister invited him to sit down. He said, "I will not," and Sister said, "Then I will, Bishop, because I'm tired and, to be frank, I'm tired of you." She told him he was not to visit her ward again until I was ready to be discharged.

"Guess what else, Murphy? She told the bastard that if he came in once more he would be escorted out by security guards."

"Never!"

Bridget roared with laughter. "True, Murphy. She said His Lordship would be literally thrown out of the building on his sacred arse and the press would find out."

"What else?"

"She told him your brother's an advertising executive with a six-figure salary and your parents have a huge two-bedroom flat. So, she told him, it's silly to insist that the one and only baby she can have has to be adopted if she's against it."

"Marvelous."

"Then she said, 'Bishop, leave because I have no more time for you.' She started to read her reports as if he'd vanished off the face of the earth. And Eamonn said, 'I'll be damned. Never in my—' and, without looking up, she said, 'Well, Bishop, there's always a first time for everything.' "

Later, Sister Steele came in to say, "You don't have to worry about him anymore, Annie. He's lost the game."

It was true. Too many people knew about my baby now. I was even more cheered when the night nurse who was looking after Peter at St. Pat's called me to say the nuns loved him and Shelagh and Morag and everyone who cared about me were taking turns hugging him.

"Those girls are terrific," I said.

"They certainly are, Annie. And remember, by their own choice they're not keeping their babies."

I could not speak for some while, I was so overwhelmed at the goodness of people who were despised.

"When you get back, Annie," the night nurse said, "I'll tell you just how unusual your kid is. One thing, milk doesn't seem to agree with him. I wanted to change it, but the doctor says no. Apart from that, he's a perfect gem."

I put down the telephone with tears running down my cheeks, but I sensed victory.

Chapter
Thirty-Six

I KEPT calling the U.S. embassy to get Peter on my passport. It was early September, after the tourist season. A woman in the passport section said, "I'll call you back," but she didn't. I spoke to a man named Geraghty. He said, "Back with you soon," followed by silence. Every time I phoned and said I was Annie Murphy, they hung up on me.

"It's obviously the Bishop," Sister Steele said. "Standing at that phone box is not doing your leg any good." She provided me with a chair. Sometimes, she let me use the phone in her office. I telephoned Harry Burke and he tried. He called me back to say, "No use. It's Eamonn. Who else? Maybe he wants you to stand at that coin box till you have another blood clot and die."

Bridget went to the embassy and came back dejected. "I waited around for two bloody hours, Murphy. As soon as I mentioned your name, they shunted me into a little parlor and forgot all about me. Eamonn's done another bad thing."

After four fruitless days, I called him. "I don't need you," I said, "but I'm giving you a choice. Either you help me or I call my father."

"What are you talking about?"

"Remove the red tape so I can get Peter on my passport."

"You really think I have anything to do with that?"

"I'm in Sister's office." I gave him the number. "If I don't hear from you in two hours, I'm calling Daddy."

He called me back within the hour. "I've arranged to have the baby's picture taken at the home. I'll bring it to the Rotunda when I pick you up to take you to the embassy."

"When?"

"Today's Wednesday. I'll call for you on Friday."

"Don't forget to make an appointment."

"I already have."

"Thank you," and I hung up.

On Friday, Eamonn drove me the couple of miles to the embassy, where a snooty Irish lady handed me my passport with Peter's name on it. It made him so much more mine. When I went back to the car, I practically fell into Eamonn's arms out of gratitude.

"Keep your distance," he said, in a cold, heart-russetting tone. "Haven't I risked enough driving you here?"

"Right," I said, climbing out.

"What on earth are you doing?"

"I'm taking a cab."

"Annie, please appreciate my position. I called the embassy for you, I braved that dragon of a sister in the Rotunda. I reckon she knows and Bridget knows. This whole damn thing could blow up in my face."

"Sorry," I said, getting back in the car. "Why should you risk guilt by association?"

He was still going on about Sister Steele. "Never in my life have I been treated like that."

I reacted angrily again. "With you, it's always me, me, me. Think how you treated *me*."

"You are innocent, are you?"

"No, but I've been paying for what I did."

"Look at the cost to me."

"You mean," I said gratefully, "you are going to provide money for your son?"

"Money?" He had never heard the word before.

"Eamonn," I said, "you are the boy's father. You want me to take him home penniless?"

"I'll think about it."

He dropped me off at the Rotunda and arranged to pick me up the next day.

* * *

On Saturday, he arrived with Pat. She kissed me and whispered, "I'm so glad you decided to keep your baby. He's a beauty."

"You've seen him?"

"When we went out to the home to take his picture."

She explained that Eamonn's idea was for me to spend a couple of days with Helena to get used to my baby again. How I loved the sound of that. I had missed him so.

When I was dressed, Sister Steele handed me a small yellow plastic container and lifted the lid. "There, Annie. Codeine, aspirin, and these pills, the most important, called warfarin, a blood thinner."

"How long do I take them for?"

"Six months. Four times a day without fail at regular intervals. Take them with plenty of water and keep your leg up for some time afterward. Your life may depend on these."

She gave me a rich warm hug and, as we separated, she touched my nose. "We fought a good fight, didn't we?"

"We sure did. May I say—?" Since I couldn't say it, my tears spoke for me.

Pat took my bags and I carried nothing but the yellow container and my pocketbook. We went to a little downstairs office where Eamonn was waiting for a quiet word with me. "I'm going to give you two thousand dollars," he said. "It's every bit of savings I have."

"Thank you."

"When you get home, I'll be in touch and we'll work out some kind of payment schedule."

"For that you'll have to deal with my father."

He nodded miserably. "You don't mind going to Helena's?"

"For a couple of days."

"Or three or four."

We drove to St. Patrick's. It was a golden September day, not more than two or three sheep shearings in the vast blue sky. Even the home, bathed in warm sunshine, had lost its threatening look. Hope was painted on the world.

Morag and Shelagh came out to greet me as fast as their condition allowed and kissed me good-bye. With our arms around each other in a circle we, the maligned, seemed part of a sacred sisterhood that the rest of the world would never comprehend.

In the nurse's arms was my Peter in a white shawl. Had he changed? Not a bit, thank God: he still had Eamonn's wispy brows and bumpy mouth, and he was screaming.

"He's a yeller." Eamonn winced. "A real yeller."

I looked and saw an angel.

"Can't you see, Annie, he doesn't want to leave?"

"You'd like to drive me away and leave him, wouldn't you?"

"Indeed I would."

The silver-haired nurse was saying, "This is a very unusual and highly intelligent little boy."

"Sure," I said proudly.

"I've been nursing for twenty-five years and no child has ever been so expressive. If he's hungry, he lets you know. If he wants his nappy changed, he tells you instantly."

I nudged Eamonn. "He reminds me—"

"Shush," and he pointed to Pat sitting in the car.

"So, Annie," the nurse said, "listen to your son and you won't go far wrong."

As soon as Peter was placed in my arms, he nestled up to me and smelled me. He instantly stopped yelling and gave a huge sigh of satisfaction.

Seeing Sister Ignatius in the background, I went over to her. Her hands were twitching as if she wanted to hold him but hadn't the courage to ask. I held Peter out to her and this childless old woman took him tenderly, kissed his forehead, and said, "I pray for him every day."

"Whatever the bursar says?"

She smiled. "I pray for her, too."

Taking my son back, I said, "I hope your prayers for Peter have a better effect."

Pat jumped out of the car. "Let me hold him."

"Don't touch that baby," Eamonn warned. "It'll scream and drive us mad all the way to Helena's. Like the nurse says, that *baby* knows what he wants."

"What *does* he want, Eamonn?" I said.

"His mother."

During the drive to Helena's, I was in heaven. This was

his father's car and his father was driving us and I was in the back with Pat whom I liked and with my Peter.

When we arrived at Helena's place in North Dublin not far from the airport, she received me warmly. "Oh, my," she said, "that baby's beautiful."

While she led me up to my room, Eamonn brought in my belongings. Having unpacked the baby's things, I went down to the living room, where Helena served tea.

Seeing me feed Peter, Helena said, "He's not taking his bottle. That's why he's thin and still jaundiced."

She added sugar to the milk to see if he would like that. Out of the corner of my eye, I could see Eamonn on edge, saying to himself, "Is he going to drink it?"

He got up and stood over me. "Some babies don't like milk."

"Is there no end to your expertise?" I said.

"The minute you get back home to the States—"

I said, "Will you please repeat that?"

"Maybe you can change his feed."

I remember thinking, *Home, yes, I'm going home*. Then: *But where is home? You can't go home again*.

Eamonn did not stay long, and after Helena had shown me a few things about baby care, she took her children for a walk while I lay on my bed with Peter.

When they returned, I stretched out my hand to take my pills. Everything was there except the vital blood thinners. They should have jumped out at me because they were in a special container. Maybe I had put them in my pocketbook for safety. I went through all my belongings. It took me a couple of hours and I kept saying to myself: *Eamonn took them. Who else?*

I went downstairs to tell Helena. She couldn't help because her husband was away on business in the family car. "Call the Rotunda," she said.

"The pharmacy's closed at this hour of the day."

"Tomorrow, then."

"Helena, if I don't take two more of those pills today I could suffer a relapse."

I called the Rotunda and they told me I could have some more pills but they had no way of getting them to me.

After the meal, Helena went to visit a neighbor and I called Inch. No reply. I called Killarney and he answered. I began calmly with "Have a nice trip home?"

"I literally flew. Made it in two and a half hours."

"And how are you?"

"Grand, and yourself?" I imagined him sitting comfortably at his desk, tossing my vial of pills in the air and catching them.

Changing the mood suddenly, I said, "Why'd you take my pills?"

"Your pills?" he spluttered. "Why would I do that?"

"Because it's bad, that's why."

"You're mad. Get off the line and look for them."

"I've looked for hours. If I don't get them soon I'll get sick again. If that's what you're wanting—"

"I want no such thing."

"I don't care how you do it, Eamonn—through a courier, an ambulance, or a specially chartered archangel—but if you don't, I swear I'm going to do something dreadful to you."

"Will you stop it, Annie, stop it."

"You lousy son-of-a-bitch," I said, real Tenth Avenue, "you're the worst liar on God's earth. So help me Christ, I'm going to get a gun."

"A gun?"

"And I'll steal a car—I know how to wire cars—and I'm going to come to Killarney and shoot your yellow liver all over the Palace walls."

"Great God Almighty."

"I hate your guts."

"The devil's got you by the throat. You are possessed, you are."

"I'm not hearing you too well," I said. "Where are you?" He managed to get out, "On the floor."

"What, for Christ's sake, are you doing there?"

"I think I am dying."

"You have been dying for as long as I've known you."

"'Tis true, that is when it started."

"Get up, you hear me, man, get to your feet."

"I cannot. You are going to kill me, isn't that so?"

"Too true."

"That is why I am trying to cope with the devil who has crawled down your throat."

"Speak up."

"I have my head in my hands and the phone is on my heaving chest. Wait till I grab it. . . . There, I have it now."

I stifled the laughter that was beginning to well up inside me. That man would be laughing after he was dead. They would have difficulty coffining him up because his corpse would be shaking with mirth.

"I never thought, Annie, you would murder me."

"I never thought you would murder *me*. But you've made several attempts already."

"Oh, Annie, is this some Wild West show? You're going to get some hot rod and a gun and come and shoot the Bishop of Kerry in his own house and spread his yellow liver all over the walls. What would become of my reputation?"

I started to laugh and he joined in. It was some time before I could tell him how serious my situation was. "Are you going to get me my pills or not?"

"You crazy fool, if the alternative is to get shot up by you, I will."

"I'll await your call. In addition, I want to be out of here by tomorrow afternoon. Helena didn't want to know when I said my pills were missing. She's probably part of the plot."

"Oh, dear. She takes you into her house and you speak of her like that."

"If I don't get out of here soon, I'll bash her."

"First," he roared, laughing, "you want to kill me, now you threaten to beat up Helena."

"Call me back about the pills and have them here by eight tonight. I want you here tomorrow with my two thousand dollars and I want a plane out of here."

"Terms agreed. I'll call you back on one condition."

I half expected him to talk about adoption again but he said, "You must not beat Helena. As God is my judge, neither she nor I had anything to do with your pills."

"I reckon she knows it's your baby."

"Don't be ridiculous."

"Peter's face looks as if yours has been painted on his.

He's even got the same birthmark Helena's seen on you when you're in swimming togs.''

"God," he screeched, "don't let her change his nappy."

"Another thing. I reckon you planned to have her adopt Peter."

He put the phone down, and rightly. I had stepped over the mark. It was my anger speaking.

All the same, I let Helena bathe the baby. "Look at that birthmark," I said. "So unusual." I wanted someone to know who the father was, and who better than she?

Within the hour, Eamonn called me back. "I've paid a hospital courier. The pills should be there by about eight. Promise me one thing."

"Nothing."

"Don't lose them this time."

"What about the flight out?"

"Impossible tomorrow, but I can book you a seat the day after. But I warn you, it's Friday the thirteenth."

"How could my luck be worse than it is?"

"It leaves at eleven A.M. from Dublin. You'll get your two thousand dollars and I'll be driving you to the airport."

With my heart in my mouth, I said, "Do me a favor, Eamonn, don't bother. I don't ever want to see you again."

It was the biggest lie in my entire life.

"I know how you feel, Annie."

I was about to yell, "Come, you bastard, don't let me leave without good-bye," when he said, "How else will I get you your money?"

Now that I knew he had made up his mind to come, I said, "What's wrong with a courier?"

"I am coming in person and you and your devil combined will not stop me. I received you into this country and I'm sending you home."

"That's so touching."

"Say what you like, Annie, but I aim to see Peter off and I want to bless him."

"Bless our son? *You?* This is too hypocritical."

He said with that insinuating softness that so often crept into his voice, "This was never against him, nor, come to that, against you, Annie."

"You could have fooled me."

"Know something else? You might make a damn good mother, after all. Any woman who fights that hard for her baby . . ."

"Are you telling me, Eamonn, you made a mistake?"

In my mind's eye I saw him doing that famous sprinkling movement with his upheld fingers. "What gave you that idea?" he said.

Chapter Thirty-Seven

ON FRIDAY morning, I dressed in Levi's, white lace blouse, green sweater, and moccasins.

Eamonn appeared about nine. He had a wide-eyed look about him, like a puzzled schoolboy. He came up to my room, closed the door, and bent over Peter. He prayed over him, blessed him, and kissed him.

I knelt behind him while he did this, put my hands around him, and hugged him. "I'm so sorry," I said, "that things went the way they did. But I wouldn't have fought so hard for the baby if I didn't love you."

"You think I don't know that, Annie?"

"I knew you knew."

"I guess we knew most things about each other."

"That's why we fought so hard and hurt each other so much. Neither of us had any defense against the other."

"That's what love does, Annie."

Yes, I thought, *you can only be really hurt by those who love you.*

I got up from the floor.

"One thing, Annie, and be honest with me just this once." The fingers of my friend-foe were jumping about in all directions. "Were you really going to shoot me?"

"I was so mad with you I might have done anything." After a moment's thought: "No."

"I'm glad."

"I probably would have stabbed you."

"Stabbed me?" he screeched, falling back as if the knife had just got him right in the belly. "You say such terrible things and in front of that *baby*. You'll ruin his thoughts."

"Aren't you the best father, thinking only of his good?"

He turned to me and I kissed him before he could speak. On his forehead and on each moist eye. Trying to remember the impress of him on me, of his being on my being. Trying to eternalize the fragile beauty of the passing moment like a fossilized leaf. "I really love you," I said. "I almost feel like falling at your feet begging you to come with me or hoping you'll tell me not to go." I pressed my fingers to his lips. "It's okay—I know it can't happen."

He had his hands on my head and he kept repeating, "Thank you, thank you."

"Eamonn," I said sharply.

With big round eyes: "What in God's name is the matter?"

"I know what you're doing. Don't deny it."

"What am I doing, know-all?"

"Blessing me."

"So?"

"I don't want now or ever a bishop's blessing."

"Not even to help you overcome your fear of flying?"

"The least of my fears."

He pressed his sensitive hands even harder on my head as if he, too, was trying to do something that would outlast the ravages of time.

"Then accept the blessing of a foolish man who loved—"

"*Loves.*"

"Yes, Annie, *loves* you. Dear God"—he laughed—"the terrible things you make me say."

"I didn't make you do a damn thing, *ever*."

"I know that. I sinned all on my own."

"*Your* word." For Eamonn—oh, sad—I was always an occasion of sin, whereas he made my head swim with the glory of love.

He said, "I knew better than Moses, didn't I? Wrote myself an exclusion clause to a Thou Shalt Not." He took his hands away, saying, in his gentlest tone: "This is an emotionally hard time for you. Your parents don't know what to expect. Did you know Mary called me?"

I shook my head.

"When she said, 'Eamonn, you son-of-a-bitch, I've been looking for you all over,' I almost died."

"Almost? Shame."

"I hung up on her as if she had got the wrong number."

"The local operator was listening in like God?"

He nodded. "She called me back and I said, 'Mary, Mary, Mary,' so she knew she had done something very wrong. She told me your parents won't know about the baby—"

"About your son."

"Until you return. What will you tell them?"

"That's my problem. Daddy will probably be glad you're the father."

He stroked his chin. "I suppose he does admire me."

"Did. Get your tenses right."

"I repent of what I did with you—"

"Thanks."

"But at least I'm bright."

"Except when you're a thick Mick."

He took an envelope out of his pocket. "The two thousand dollars. I don't have a penny more. It'll take me at least six or seven months to get any more."

"Try the truth just for a change."

"So for God's sake, use it sparingly. You'll probably soon be getting a job." I was grateful to have the money and I knew my brother Peter had sent Mary a check for five hundred dollars to give me.

We went down and joined Pat and Helena and had a bite to eat before we drove to the airport. Helena was very excited. She kept picking Peter up and hugging him. Just before I left, she said, with tears in her eyes, "You take care of that *baby*."

She knew who the father was.

Eamonn looked very upset as we climbed into the car, whereas I was enthralled by Peter, who was looking up at me as if I were his whole world.

We arrived at the airport around 10:00 A.M. I checked in and was pleased to see how reluctant Eamonn was to see us go. I was provided with a wheelchair, and this gave him the opportunity to pull rank and take me alone to the departure lounge. Maybe he had planned even that. As we traveled the long green-carpeted corridor, bypassing the duty-free store,

I was aware of his gaze drilling the back of my head but I was busy with Peter, my lips brushing his oats-soft cheek and fontanel, so I was unable to pay him much attention. Until, suddenly: "Eamonn."

He stopped wheeling me and stood in front of me, expecting some final message. The ice had melted in his eyes.

"Yes, Annie?"

"You didn't steal my pills again?"

He balled both fists—just like Peter!—and held them up shudderingly to heaven where all vengeance was. "Dear God, she is not changed one bit, not one tiny bit." He lowered his eyes. "D'you think I want you telling the other passengers that you are going to shoot the yellow liver of the Bishop of Kerry all over his Palace walls?"

Now he kept going over everything I needed for the journey. Had I my pills, boarding card, passport, money?

When the flight was called, I handed him a present, which I had kept hidden. It was the only book I had brought with me to Ireland, Thomas Wolfe's novel *You Can't Go Home Again*.

He broke out in a smile, which instantly left him when a stewardess took charge of my wheelchair. Our eyes locked in a final deathless glance, an unending good-bye.

The stewardess pulled me back onto a moving ramp. It was strange and somehow symbolic, moving backward and downward as I took my leave of Eamonn, as though time itself were going slowly, pitilessly into reverse. Such a sunset moment.

Over my son's downy head I saw only him, as I had seen only him when I flew in to Shannon. What a difference of mood between an arrival and departure lounge, what a difference of tears!

He did not dance now nor did he sing. His white-knuckled hands clutched the metal rail. So sad were his eyes it hit me that this was how I first saw him in Manhattan when I was seven years old. That long-ago meeting was a premonition of a heartbreak. This time I could not say, "It's going to be all right, Eamonn. It's going to be all right."

I heard him calling out after me, ten times at least, "Good-bye, Annie. Good-bye, Annie."

Each time it got fainter, farther away, until it was no more than a whimper: "Good-bye, Annie."

That parting forsaking cry, I knew, would follow me all the days and the nights. There was so much pain everywhere, no God could have designed a world like this. "I don't believe in You," I said to Him, to get my small revenge, "but take care of Eamonn for me, please."

We were three, we would always be three; why was one of us being left behind? It was because I had asked too much of him. He had this loyalty, call it patriotism, toward his Church and I could not breach it for all his talk and deeds of sin. I might as well for my sake have asked a painter never to touch another canvas, an author or poet never to write another line, a musician never to finger another tune. For I had wanted Eamonn, for my sake, to give up not just the adulation due him as a bishop. I was asking this more-than-painter-poet-composer to stop doing the daily miracle of the Mass, stop changing bread into Christ's Body and putting God into people's mouths, stop forgiving unforgivable sins, stop smoothing the paths of the dying to paradise, stop turning the dead into seeds that would spring up into eternal life.

I had naïvely thought that love was limitless whereas now I knew to my cost there are some things that love, real love, should never ask.

But this was almost like childbirth, when a baby comes out of you and there's a brutal tearing. There was in this moment a brutal tearing from Eamonn, made so much worse because I felt I would never see him again. Such a tremendous stillbirth feeling of uncreative loss.

I looked down at Peter. I was taking something precious from Ireland, immortality, and Eamonn had the vocation that he cherished so much. By thinking of these things, I managed to pull myself together.

But not for long. Even before I boarded the plane I started to shake, and tears fell. Tears should be red, the reddest red there is. I resent the transparent blood of tears. It's incredible, but only in that desolate moment was I fully aware of all that Eamonn had given me: his courage, his strength, his vitality. And I was afraid I might not, without him, survive the long husbandless years ahead.

Summoning up all my courage, I took a final look at this gorgeous land. It was less green and leafy than when I saw it first, but indelibly green in memory and no less dear. Was it really only eighteen months since I flew in on my magic carpet and fell in love with Eamonn almost as soon as I set eyes on him and teased him about his red socks?

I was crying now because Ireland was for me a special place, my little bit of heaven. I didn't want to leave, I wanted to stay for a lifetime, I wanted my body eventually to dissolve—dust to dust—in its soil.

But none of this was possible.

I thumbed through all the memories I had stored. Inch and Killarney, Castleisland and Dublin; all the people I had met and befriended and who had befriended me; and over everything—the hypnotic presence of Eamonn, my only love.

I remembered his dancing feet and his hands that moved up-up-up in bed when his feet were still. I remembered my jazzman bringing the world—rocks, hills, distant islands, birdsong—to life on the top of a mountain and, most miraculously of all, bringing to life in me a love that other men had extinguished, I had once thought, forever.

He had healed me, after all, and risked hell itself to do it; and I knew that in time to come, if ever this story should be told, people, including those who love him, would not understand anything of that and they would say, because their rules and his rules obliged them to say it, that he did wrong.

Oh, yes, my Eamonn risked losing their respect and even that of his outraged God because he loved me.

Then I called to mind his laughter, the whole range of it from a shuddering bass snort to a high infectious giggle, and how he had made me laugh as I never laughed before, when we fell out of bed at Inch or struggled into our clothes in a gravel pit, even when I threatened to kill him. Locked in my seat, my baby, his baby, our baby who looked so like him, in my arms, I started to laugh and laugh, so that the stewardess came running.

"Is there something wrong, ma'am?"

And I couldn't answer her because, through floods of tears, I was laughing too much.

Chapter Thirty-Eight

WHEN WE flew under a cloudless sky into New York, it was dusk. The lights, bustle, noise of the airport came as a shock after the peace and quiet of Ireland.

Apart from feeling the absence of Eamonn like an open wound, being in a wheelchair confused me. I felt I no longer had control over my life. With Peter wrapped in a shawl in my arms, refusing to take sugared milk, screaming uncontrollably, I began to fear that Eamonn was right: I would not make a good single parent.

My two brothers saved me. Johnny, six-foot-two, and Peter, blond and blue-eyed, were waiting for me, positive and smiling broadly.

"You some sort of Orphan Annie?" Peter said. "Get out of that chair." And he hauled me to my feet.

Johnny, a father of three, took one look at my son and said, "He's half starved. I'm getting him something to drink."

He grabbed the baby's bottle and disappeared.

Peter told me meanwhile that he had only just called our parents. Daddy had been surprised to hear I was coming home. "Oh, I miss her so," he had said. And Peter had said, "She's had a pretty rough time." "Tell me more." "Well, Dad . . . she's had a baby." "For Christ's sake," Daddy had said, before exploding with "Who's the father?" When Peter told him, he had sighed. "Could have been worse. At least, the guy's got drive and brains."

When Johnny returned with formula milk, Peter drank it greedily. That, too, gave me fresh hope.

At about ten, I walked apprehensively into my parents' spacious sixth-floor apartment overlooking the sea at Old Greenwich.

Mommy threw her arms around me in warm greeting, but as I hobbled into the living room, there was Daddy.

Blank-eyed, arms folded, his huge cane in one hand, he was seated on his favorite black chair. Dressed in an open-necked shirt and khaki shorts, he showed a pinkish artificial leg with its big hinge, his black shoe with a white sock on the end. With his huge smooth head, he looked like a sinister giant idol carved from stone. While the lips smiled, his eyes had a pained and angry look. I would have to tread very warily.

He softened only when he looked at Peter and saw his inflamed cheeks, reddish hair, and Eamonn's beautiful lips.

"That," he said, maybe remembering his own abused childhood, "is a cry of pain. Hannah, a cushion."

Mommy put one on the long table. Another imposing gesture from Daddy, and I placed the baby on the cushion. Peter's hands immediately went up-up-up, in a nervy way.

"Eamonn, all right," Daddy said. "It's in the genes."

He proceeded with an examination. "Number one, Annie, he's too swaddled up." After I had removed Peter's clothes, with his long fingers he gently probed his limbs. "Number two, the kid's undernourished. Feed him on demand."

I nodded.

"Also, Annie, see that—a skin infection and thrush."

While Mommy dressed Peter, Daddy said, "You've been ill."

I lifted the bottom of my jeans so he could see my ankle. He shook his head. "Trouble ahead with that leg, Annie." He beckoned me to him and kissed me. "Glad you're home."

"Me, too."

I was not sure if I was or not. I was tired, emotionally drained, and suffering from a bad cold.

"Did Eamonn give you any money?"

I handed Daddy an envelope and he counted out eighteen

hundred dollars. "I'll bank it for you. You'll have to economize for the rest of your life. From now on, you answer to me, young lady."

I didn't disagree. I was his hostage.

To take care of Peter, I was going to need my parents' help. Mommy, delighted to have a purpose in life, came off the booze, and Daddy, too, was marvelous.

I applied to go back to school to train as a nurse, but I was told that my bad leg made nursing impossible. Instead, I got a job as a receptionist in the hospital across the street. To my father, that was another sign of my failure. It proved to him he had to dominate my life; and God help me if I crossed him or did anything wayward.

As the weeks went by, he interrogated me with Teutonic thoroughness. I was only permitted to answer his precise question. Slowly, meticulously, he dragged out of me the whole story, including our lovemaking in a gravel pit and how Eamonn had left me to rot in St. Patrick's. He angrily accused Eamonn of gross negligence.

For months, I refused every invitation from men to dine out or go to a movie. Daddy had hurt me too much and made me feel too guilty. Besides, the memory of Eamonn was too vivid in spite of the ocean between us. I used to calculate the five-hour time difference between Kerry and New York. What was he doing now? Was he happy? Did he ever think of me?

Love of this intensity, I sometimes felt, should not be allowed. Why this sharp pain and this equally sharp ecstasy? The pain was not in any part of me. It was everywhere and nowhere, so it seemed to be even in the things and people around me. To ease it, I tried desperately not to think of him. I walked, as it were, miles around any idea that might bring back the memory of him. I always failed.

When I was young, I dreamed of falling in love forever; now I despaired of ceasing to love. If only I could stop loving him, I told myself, my troubles would cease. But then I would cease to be me.

Eamonn was different from every other person I had ever known, but I could not explain the differences except to say that his original tenderness and thoughtfulness touched the core of my being.

What did I miss most about him? His laughter, his fantastic sense of humor. A memory of his mischievousness came back to me. I was living in Dublin before I was pregnant. It was when we had nowhere to meet except the gravel pit. Pat Gilbride's sister, Girlie, who was studying in Dublin, invited me to her apartment for a meal with Pat and Eamonn. I hadn't seen him for a couple of weeks and he kept rubbing my leg sensuously under the table. After we had eaten, he said to the Gilbrides he had to speak to me privately.

"Use my bedroom," Girlie said.

To my surprise, he lay down on her bed and, inviting me alongside him, started to fondle me. He became so enthusiastic the bed collapsed under us. One of the small wooden legs had snapped. "Put it in your handbag," he said, "and take it with you."

I started laughing and he silenced me with a pillow. Feeling suffocated, I kicked out until he let me up for air. "What're you going to do?" I gasped.

"Trust me," and, like a magician, he got up and stuck a pile of Girlie's books where the leg should have been.

I said, "Girlie will wonder all night where her study books have gone."

"She'll find them when she makes the bed."

"But how will she think they got there?"

"Girlie's not like you, pet, she hasn't a dirty mind."

With that, he climbed back on the bed. He got as much as he could from five cuddly minutes.

What would I not have given now for another five such minutes?

His presence inside my head was like a melody whose beauty never fades. In fact, though he was so far away, Eamonn was more real to me than anything around me. He had a different kind of being, a more solid density.

Even my sleep at this time was full of him. My alarm clock would wake me out of a romantic dream of Inch in which he was planting a kiss on my cheek. It would take me several seconds to realize where I was, not in Ireland but in America, and still more seconds to accept it. I would make an effort to go back to sleep, to slip back into the dream before it vanished. I would press my hand to my cheek, trying to prolong the familiar but now fading feel of his warm lips.

Then, as in many of the years to come, I had nothing to console me but my tiny bundle of joy. I took Peter with me on my visits to churches, hoping maybe to chance upon his father on an unheralded trip to New York. Every priest, young or old, in a black suit and white collar, reminded me of him. I lit candles—I always liked candles. I prayed through the light, to my dead grandparents to help me, especially Pop Murphy.

Back home, I would wrap Peter and myself in warm clothes and sit on our bedroom balcony within sight of the sea. I talked to him, as I had talked to him in the womb. I told him how happy I was that I had kept him. I pressed my face into his honey-blond hair, smelled the sweetness of his skin, and promised him we would face the world together, unafraid.

At Christmas, Daddy gave me the best of all gifts: forgiveness. He came to my bedroom. "Annie, it's time to make a new start, right?"

He hugged me and we kissed.

"Right." I was enthusiastic. The worst was behind us. He wanted to move us back to New York City, where we would all have more to do. It would help me put Eamonn behind me, which was vital if I was to get on with my life.

I made Daddy a meal of all the things he loved. While we were eating, he said: "As a diversion, Annie, I'm planning to take you and your mother with me on a trip."

I was excited. "For how long?"

"Four or five months."

"Daddy!" and I ran and kissed him. "Where to?"

"Back to Ireland. You've paid for your sin and you'll go on paying," Daddy explained. "But Eamonn's a priest and he, too, should be made to face up to what he did."

Eamonn had called Daddy, asking after me and the baby. Daddy was determined to find out his future intentions. Eamonn had to learn that from now on he was dealing not with a foolish girl but with an experienced professional man.

I still loved Eamonn; I always would. But I could not bear the thought of his rejecting Peter and me a second time. I felt sick at the thought.

When Mary came around to invite us to her place for Christmas dinner and I told her Daddy's plans, she exploded. "Go see a psychiatrist, you're all crazy."

But Daddy insisted that the trip was important. He had been hoodwinked before, but this time he would be in charge. "It's like a tune, Annie. We'll just let it play out."

Daddy called Eamonn at Inch. He spoke calmly, telling him how gorgeous little Peter was. Then, out of the blue: "We're coming over so you can get to know your little boy, Eamonn."

I heard Eamonn say, "Good, good, very good," while he must have been ready to slit Daddy's throat.

As a result of that call, Eamonn sent me nine hundred dollars to help with my expenses, and, within three days, through Harry Burke, Daddy had rented an apartment in Ballsbridge, the fashionable part of Dublin.

Chapter Thirty-Nine

ON THE trip to Ireland in February, I kept wondering
how Eamonn felt about me and how he would react
when we met. One thing was certain: with Daddy
as chaperon, our affair was at an end.

No sooner were we in our apartment than Daddy said:
"Sorry, Annie, but I just don't trust you and him."

"What *are* you talking about? You think I'm crazy?"

"Are you fitted with a diaphragm?"

I shook my head. Part of my strategy to avoid pain was
never to think of Eamonn loving me in a sexual way. That
was why I had refused to prepare for it.

"If you get pregnant, Annie, I'll beat you." He wagged
his cane at me. "As God is my judge, I'll take you to England
for an abortion and make that Bishop Casey watch."

Mommy was rubbing her hands and laughing. "You do
that, Jack. Tell the press all about that clerical goat."

"When I meet him," Daddy said, "I'll shake his hand and
leave a dozen condoms in it."

He called Eamonn to tell him we had arrived and invited
him out to dinner so they could chat. However much I rea-
soned with myself that you cannot recapture the wonder of
the past, I couldn't wait to see Eamonn again.

Daddy had prepared for this meeting by putting on his best
white shirt and striped suit. How would he deal with this?

Would he, I wondered, be chilly toward Eamonn or sarcastic or angry?

When the bell rang that evening, sending an electric shock through my body, Daddy sat down with six-month-old Peter between his legs facing outward, with Peter's big birthmark showing. He kept him quiet by rubbing the top of his head. I tidied my hair for the tenth time and, even before I opened the front door, I smelled the fragrance of Old Spice. I was home again.

Eamonn's dear happy face crinkled with delight. Oh God, no, impossible, I once more saw myself in his eyes.

He grabbed my hand and whispered, "So pleased to see you." My heart was in my throat. Our love had survived betrayal, disgust, even a kind of hatred. Would it never end?

His glance warned me not to be too expressive. Blinking and shaking my head to clear my vision and break the spell, I noticed a priest in the background. It was his thin and nervous secretary, Father Dermot Clifford.

Eamonn must have felt that a stranger would defuse the situation. More, he would not be expected to act like a father to his son. However pleased I was at this reunion, this struck me as one more act of denial.

"Come along, Dermot, come along," Eamonn said, talking to Father Clifford as if he were a pet dog.

I signaled to the living room, where Daddy was waiting. Taking a deep breath, Eamonn moved to greet the man whom he had betrayed. He bent down, almost genuflecting in front of him, casting a shadow over his own son. Grabbing Daddy's right hand in both of his, he pumped it, saying, "Thank you, Jack, thank you. God bless you, Jack."

Daddy's patriarchal eyes were guarded but, seeing the stranger, he restrained his wrath.

"It's okay, Eamonn," he said quietly. "It's okay."

Mommy went to get Father Clifford a drink. He seemed from his attitude to her to be a kind man, though I think he was trying to work out what was going on.

Daddy pointed. "Eamonn, meet my little feller here." Picking Peter up, he placed him on his good right knee.

I watched with fascination this first encounter of three generations. Eamonn came around the side to examine his infant son. Peter was shy, and though Eamonn was awkward,

I could tell he could scarcely believe he had produced so beautiful a child.

I was proud of Peter's happy blue eyes, rosy cheeks, a cowlick in which I put a brown bow, and his plump thighs. Gurgling, he buried his head in his grandfather's chest, so Daddy kept rubbing his head and saying, "C'mon, Peter, Eamonn's here to see you. Shake his hand."

This was for me a sad moment. Eamonn had engineered a false beginning because if Father Clifford had not been there, Daddy could have said, "C'mon, Peter, your daddy's here. Give him a kiss."

My father stretched out Peter's hand and Eamonn took it, giving it a gentle shake, but Peter immediately withdrew it and leaned into his grandfather once more. As if wanting to put on a show for Daddy's benefit, Eamonn grabbed Peter and, with dancing feet, held him at arm's length in the air over his head. "Hey, Petey-boy, how are you?"

When Peter started to whimper, he shook him, which only made the boy burst out crying. Eamonn said to me, "Are you letting him grow up to be a sissy?" To Peter: "Cut that out, now," and he threw him in the air and caught him, making Peter scream.

"Please don't do that," I said; but, of course, Eamonn did, making Peter catch his breath before spitting up.

Daddy pointedly said, "That's funny, Eamonn, he never screams at anybody else."

Peter was so upset he scratched my neck. To clean him up, I took him to the bathroom, where Daddy followed.

"Would you believe it?" he guffawed. "The yellow-belly had to bring a bumbling wreck as a bodyguard. That priest's so nervous he can hardly talk. Get your mother to slip a Valium in his drink."

When I returned with Peter to the living room, Eamonn said, "God Almighty, are you treating him like the infant Jesus?"

The same old Eamonn. An absentee father, he knew all about parenting. Daddy explained that he should have held Peter close to start with so he could get used to him.

My parents then took Eamonn and Father Clifford out to dinner.

At about ten, Eamonn escorted Mommy and Daddy home,

leaving his secretary in the car. Father Clifford had served his purpose. While my parents were getting out of their coats, Eamonn came to the kitchen where I was preparing the baby's bottle. Without a word, he grabbed and kissed me.

I wanted to pinch myself. Was this really happening? He could no longer pretend he was "healing" me, so how did he square this behavior with his conscience?

I backed off, but as soon as he touched me again and looked directly at me, all resistance melted. It was as if I had never left his side. For what I saw in his eyes was not mere desire but an undying love.

"Thanks for coming back, pet," he whispered breathlessly. "You never looked more beautiful."

We all put on different faces for different people and different occasions. The face Eamonn showed to me then, as always, was shorn of any mask or disguise or the best-intentioned lie. This was his real face.

"But we can't start all over again," I said, tingling under his touch.

He winked broadly as if to say he was still in charge. "I will be up to see you next week."

I told him what Daddy had said about an abortion if I got pregnant again. "An abortion," he said, laughing softly.

"But you know I can't have another child."

He laughed again. "Of course not," he said, just managing to compose himself before my parents appeared.

By the time Eamonn came to Dublin ten days later, to keep myself occupied, I had a job at the switchboard in Jury's Hotel.

I had told Daddy I was working till nine that night, after which I was going for a drink with friends. I promised to be back by midnight. Eamonn picked me up at eight near the hotel, in the Lancia and, to my utter consternation, drove toward the gravel pit where Peter had been conceived.

On the way, he stressed we had to be good. "I must not betray your father's trust again, Annie."

"Certainly not," I agreed.

Words. He was as hungry for me as I had ever known him. And I? How good, how overwhelmingly good to feel his love for me made stronger by separation.

Our doomed affair was not ended. Caught in a whirlwind of desire, we tempted fate, unable to help ourselves. If Eamonn had only wanted sex with me he could, I know, have shown restraint, but this was love, the love of two people who knew they were made for each other, now and forever.

On the way back to the apartment, he asked me to hand him his items of clerical dress. The stern, almost sadistic way he did it—"Now my clerical collar, Annie. Now my cross"—conveyed the idea that he was first and foremost a bishop. He was intimating that any hopes I had of him leaving the ministry were groundless. Maybe there was even kindness in what seemed to be cruelty.

After the third visit to the gravel pit with the same somber aftermath, I refused to go again.

From then on, he sometimes came to our apartment for a meal.

On one occasion, Mommy picked Peter up and told Eamonn how much she loved her little grandson.

"This child," she said, "has made us a family again. He has made this a house of love."

Eamonn dutifully nodded.

"Sometimes," Mommy went on, "the unwanted child, if you can make a place for him, brings the greatest joy. So, Eamonn, on my own behalf, I thank you." Eamonn took her hand and kissed it, but I doubted if these sentiments, however moving, really reached him.

When my parents retired around nine, Eamonn whispered, removing his jacket, "Ready?" and we made furtive love on the couch in the living room like a couple of college students. As always, danger made sex so much more exciting. He had told me to wear zip-up clothes for easier access.

By now, Eamonn had enough control to withdraw from me before climaxing but he distrusted the deep cushions of the couch in case he could not get out of me in time. My father was not exactly an orthodox Catholic, and Eamonn took seriously the threat of an abortion.

In case my parents thought he was overdoing the late-night visits, Eamonn sometimes called me after nine when they had retired and I pretended it was a girlfriend from Jury's. I let him in and we made love on the carpet, though he complained it hurt his knees. Afterward, when we held each other tight and in silence, we fused even more into one. Embracing when all physical desire had passed, leaving only the intense spiritual desire to be together, was the most convincing proof of love.

Not that everything was smooth between us. Once I saw him on television talking about the problems of Northern Ireland and pleading for reunion. When next we met I told him that in my view the troubles were not all political, as he had maintained, but religious. Catholicism blighted the natural buoyancy of the Irish and made them moody. Protestants of the North, I said, sincerely believed that Home Rule was Rome Rule. They had legislated for divorce and contraception and they didn't want the Pope and his bishops telling them what to do. Eamonn responded like a snapping turtle. Wasn't I an utter ignoramus? Wasn't I a terrible bossy woman?

Harry Burke was not fond of Eamonn. One night, after they had joined my parents for dinner, Daddy told me how Harry had attacked Eamonn for spending vast sums on his Cathedral when there were so many poor in his diocese. One reason for Harry's antipathy to Eamonn was that Harry was sympathetic to gays, and Catholicism was hard on homosexuals. Harry also thought that Eamonn was a hypocrite. He had tried to make me give up Peter at the time when he had spoken publicly in favor of Cherish, a group pledged to help single mothers who kept their babies. Eamonn had since become a patron of the society.

Daddy, a sophisticated man, was never in favor of clerical celibacy, which he thought unnatural. In view of what had already happened between Eamonn and me, he must have suspected we were seeing each other. Maybe he considered it a necessary risk. At least it provided us with a chance to make up our minds whether we could make a life together.

There were moments when guilt got to me. It was not my love for Eamonn that caused this but the fact that for a second time we were betraying Daddy's trust. Worse, we were doing it in his own home, a few yards from where he was sleeping. Eamonn still did not use condoms, and I had no diaphragm.

We already had one child; if I became pregnant and needed an abortion to save my life, that would crucify us both.

Around May, a minor miracle happened. Eamonn began to fall in love with his son. When my parents joined Harry Burke at Howth for the day, Eamonn paid us a visit. With joy in my heart I watched him play hide-and-go-seek with Peter among the Danish furniture. Peter, competitive even then, crawled like the wind to keep in front. Eamonn crept on the floor after him and pretended to bang his head on the refrigerator to make him laugh.

On another visit, he chased Peter on all fours out the door and along the corridor toward the elevator. An elderly couple got out and I heard the woman say, "Isn't that Bishop Casey? How sweet."

Till then, Eamonn had not bonded with him, but that changed now. It thrilled him that when he spoke the boy tried to imitate his words and facial expressions and, most wonderfully, smiled at him. Once, I found him holding Peter by the shoulders with his feet touching the ground. "C'mon, Petey-boy, dance for me."

When I smiled, he said: "When I was a kid, I wanted to go to Hollywood and study tap-dancing under Fred Astaire. I would have made it to the top, too. I can do anything I set my heart on."

On these happy family occasions, Eamonn helped me bathe Peter and put him to bed. Before we left the room, Eamonn blessed him. I prayed—futilely, I knew—that Eamonn would see that Peter had a right to a father and that his future lay with us.

To be fair to Eamonn: just as I had never hid from him my desire to bear his child, he had never once hinted that he would give up his ministry to marry me. I think he would like to have married me if it were possible, but he was like a grown man with a mother fixation. His mother was the Church; he let Mother Church do all his important thinking for him and he never acted without her approval. If only he had been able to make his own decisions, our love would have succeeded, but he was not capable of that kind of freedom.

Meanwhile, he grew so fond of Peter that his first instinct when he came into the apartment was to run and kiss him. The kiss was a real kiss. The boy was delighted to see him, and they laughed and played together.

This made the final blow that much harder when it fell.

On a warm day in May, Daddy said, "It's not going to work out, Annie. He'll never marry you. Time for us to go."

Lately, I had told myself over and over the self-same thing, but I argued with him that there was still a chance. "No, sweetheart," he said. "I've watched him on TV and read his articles in the papers. He's as narrow as you are liberal."

Daddy was also convinced that Eamonn's ambition was to be Pope of the Third World. He was chairman of the society called Trócaire, Irish for "compassion," which collects money for the poor in disadvantaged lands. This post gave him power and prestige. "He's not likely to give that up in a hurry, Annie. And you wouldn't want him to, would you?"

I sadly shook my head. I felt the two men must have talked at some length. The conversation had convinced Daddy that Eamonn wanted the best of both worlds.

"Peter," I said brokenly, "is used to him now and maybe—"

"No. You'll be nothing but a kept woman. For year after year. Until he tires of you."

"He *won't*."

He stroked my hand. "As a doctor, I've seen it time after time. He'll ignore you, love the kid, and shatter your soul." He looked out the window as if surveying the long hard years ahead. "The day will come when you'll want to leave and be unable to because it'll break Peter's heart."

However true, it was a terrible wrench to leave Ireland again, especially as Eamonn would this time lose two people whom he loved.

Daddy said, "Your divorce is through, Annie; you have to get away from here if you're ever to marry again."

"Marry again," I said heatedly, "when I can never give a man children?"

"Okay," he conceded. "I'm going back to the States to find us a place to live. Eamonn likes the boy, he's bound to look after him financially. After all, he's a big spender."

* * *

One day in June, soon after Daddy left for New York, Eamonn had Peter on his knees after a game of peekaboo, when I told him of Daddy's decision. He was shocked. "It *is* cruel," I admitted, "but it's not my fault."

"Indeed 'tis," he retorted. "You want to take Peter away and have him entirely to yourself."

"What can I do?" I said. "Daddy knows you're never going to leave the Church."

"No, no, no," he said, emotionally, "this is your idea."

"If it were up to me, Eamonn, I'd buy a small place here, somewhere, so you could keep visiting Peter, but Daddy can't bear lies. And he wants a better life for me."

I made to wipe his tears away.

He knocked my hand aside. "Just leave me be."

He was still angry when, as Daddy had suggested, I brought up the question of providing for Peter. Eamonn seemed to think that since I alone had chosen to keep him, his own liabilities had ceased.

"I will send you fifty dollars a month," he said grudgingly. America, I told him, was far more expensive than Ireland and fifty dollars would not even provide Peter with food and clothes. But he would not relent.

On our last few nights together, even our lovemaking changed. So aggressive was it that maybe, subconsciously, we wanted to manufacture another crisis to prolong our love affair.

We talked money again and Eamonn said, pinch-lipped, "All right, I will give you seventy-five dollars a month." At our final session, Eamonn said one hundred dollars and not a penny more. My lover had turned pawnbroker.

I said, "That won't provide your son with a roof over—"

He almost shouted, "*He is not my son.*" As Peter started to whimper: "He's entirely yours now, isn't that what you want?"

How could I tell him in this bitter mood that I wanted nothing less? Here we were reenacting our confrontation in St. Patrick's. I picked Peter up, calmed him, and tried to put him in Eamonn's arms with "Go to Daddy."

He turned his head away. There was something terribly final about that refusal.

"Shall I put him to bed, Eamonn?"

"Let him stay," he said. "Maybe he'll remember this."

I responded in kind with "And remember his father's generosity."

"I will send you three hundred dollars every quarter."

I had been reading Morris West's book *The Shoes of the Fisherman*, which told of a case like mine. "Listen, Eamonn," I said, no less angry and frustrated. "I'll give you forty-eight hours to think again. If you don't raise your offer by then, I'll take Peter to Rome."

"God Al*mighty*, what for?"

"I'll bang on the door of the Vatican and demand that your son is made a ward of the Church."

"You would like nothing more than to betray me, isn't that so?"

At that, I started to cry. Peter looked up at me wonderingly before crying with me. Though Eamonn stomped out without saying good-bye to Peter or to me, I must have convinced him of my resolve because, next day, he called. "It'll bankrupt me, but one hundred and seventy-five dollars a month," and before I could answer, he slammed down the receiver.

I listened incredulously for several minutes to the silence on the line. Such a long deep silence. And such a sad sad end to the happiest phase of my life.

Chapter
Forty

THIS TIME when we flew into New York, Peter was beginning to talk and was interested in everything going on around him. He was pleased to see his grandpa again and liked the noise of honking taxis. He was an American.

Daddy had found us a lovely apartment in Peter Cooper Village. It was a fine spot to bring up a child, with tree-filled parks and children's swings and slides. The only trouble was, the apartment was on the fourteenth floor, which brought back my panic attacks. I kept having visions of Peter falling out the window while I was at work. I spent $500 for bars and safety catches to the windows, a sign, I guess, that for me the whole world was unsafe. My only source of security was Peter. I used to sing to him over and over, "You are my sun in the morning and my moon at night."

I began the habit of working at nights, until Peter was four. After giving him his dinner, I left at 5:30 and my parents looked after him while he slept. I arrived home at about 1:45 in the morning, slept until 8:00 and was then able to spend the day with him.

My first job, for $150 a week, was as a switchboard operator at the Algonquin. I met many famous writers there, including Leon Uris who had written *Trinity*, a fine novel about Ireland.

Ireland, so many reminders. A phase of my life in lavender. In this downstream period of my life, I saw a poster advertising vacations in Ireland. A fat cow in a green field, broken clouds, a ruined abbey. It made me feel terribly homesick. In spite of the sourness of our good-bye, I missed Eamonn. I leaned against a building and burst into tears.

When I soaped my body under the shower, his long sensitive hands glided over me. I put on an earring and it was the one that I had left behind once in his bed. I saw a fire in a hearth and we were sitting in the living room of a low Georgian house overlooking the sea, talking, storytelling. I never got into a car but he was driving me along narrow winding Kerry lanes or to the gravel pit where we made love.

Oh God, a geranium, a poplar tree, a sunset had the power to remind me of him, and the least tangible things—smells, tastes, sounds—reminded me of him most. What hope for me when the smell of mown grass or the taste of my morning cup of tea wiped out weeks and months and the thousands of miles separating Eamonn and me?

That was when I realized that, in spite of my efforts to forget, I would always miss him, and Peter, with Eamonn's looks and temperament, was my fond daily reminder.

Peter, my Columbus, who introduced me daily to new worlds, was two years old when, in 1976, Bridget invited me to stay with her for three weeks in London, England. She wanted to repay me for helping to save her little girl's life.

Bridget now had two children, the second, Justin, a year old. She had recently separated from Wentworth and was living with her mother in the noisy suburb of Edgware. With her contacts in the trade, she found me a job in the magnificent Grosvenor House Hotel where I had to look after Arabs and rich Americans.

I called Eamonn to tell him where we were. I hoped that on his travels through London, he might find time to meet us. He called a few times but never visited us, though I deliberately extended my visit.

Once he phoned to say he was going away on a six-week retreat to put his life in order. "If we ever meet again, Annie," he confessed humbly, "we both know 'twill start all over again. And this time it could get really scary."

He feared meeting Peter and having his heart broken again.

By then, Peter was adorable and speaking really well, so Eamonn's fears were justified.

I used to go to newsstands and thumb through the Irish press for word of him. In the late summer, I opened up a paper and there was his lovely face. How, I thought, can he look so young and happy? He had been appointed Bishop of Galway. A long article spoke of him as the most dynamic and charismatic bishop in Ireland. It was strange reading an outsider's view of the man I knew so intimately. The writer told how the Kerry people admired his warmth and good humor and were sorry to see him go. It detailed his fundraising ventures and arduous trips to the Third World. He was fulfilling his ambition to be the Pope of the Poor.

The article included extracts from Eamonn's latest pastoral letter to the faithful in which he encouraged a more Christian attitude toward unmarried mothers. He appealed to parents to help any daughter who wished to keep her child. He said:

> *We once allowed our justifiable attitude of disappointment and disapproval towards the circumstances in which new life was conceived to affect our attitude towards the mother and child, sometimes to the point of rejection. . . . Because of our natural concern for the right moral standards, we often have not cherished these children, and in so far as we did not we were wrong.*

One day, Peter was playing with a little girl who accidentally pushed him against a wall. He suffered a bad cut between his eyes. He had never been injured before and, seeing all the blood, I thought at first he had lost an eye. The hospital put in four stitches. There was no permanent damage, they said. A couple of weeks later, however, he lost his sense of balance and started falling. A neurologist tested him for a blood clot, and before the results came through, I called Eamonn at Inch.

"The facilities in London," he assured me, "are the best in the world."

I thought he might offer to come and see his son, but he didn't. Was he serious about cherishing children born out of wedlock?

Two weeks passed and he still did not call to ask about his son's health. With Eamonn, words were still only words.

I knew from the newspaper article that he was busy with preparations for his Enthronement on September 19, 1976, as Bishop of Galway. His acceptance of a new diocese and his disinterest in Peter were final proof that he had cut himself off from us forever.

I was tempted to take Peter with his bandaged head to Galway and introduce him to the crowds who had come to witness their bishop's investiture. I was in a black mood when, at about eight, the night before his Enthronement, from the house of Bridget's mother, Mrs. Randall, I telephoned the *Irish Times* in Dublin.

My call was taken by the night desk.

"Can I help you, ma'am?"

"No, but you might be able to help the people of Galway."

"In what way, please?" He sounded young and earnest.

"I would like to wish Bishop Casey all the best for his Enthronement in Galway. His two-year-old son also sends his best wishes."

"Thank you," the reporter said, in a tired voice.

"And here is Peter himself."

I put the mouthpiece to his lips. "Hi, hi," Peter said.

For some reason, the child's voice shocked the reporter into the realization that he might have chanced upon the story of a lifetime. Maybe the paper had heard rumors about Eamonn and me, or he simply thought that if there was one bishop in Ireland capable of fathering a child, it was Eamonn.

I heard what sounded like a chair being shoved backward and bouncing off the wall. "Wait there," he said. "Please, ma'am."

"Hi, hi," Peter said again.

"Where are you? I'll come. If need be, I'll send a car."

"I'm not in Ireland."

"I'll book you a seat on a plane. All you have to do is convince me you're telling the truth."

"You don't believe me?"

"I need some sort of proof."

"Oh, I can provide it."

At this point, Mrs. Randall was laughing loudly on the bed and saying, "You can't do that, Annie, it's not right."

Bridget ripped the phone out of my hand. The last thing I heard before she cut me off was the reporter pleading, "If you could just give me your number. Your—"

Bridget shrieked, "Murphy, you could get us all killed." For her, the Catholic Church was like the Mafia. It would protect its own, especially its bosses, at any price, and she feared for her children's safety. Not for the first time, Bridget saved Eamonn's skin.

If Bridget had not cut me off, what would I have said? I do not know. But from then on I made a firm resolve to be silent. The height of compassion is to conceal another's shame. I had made my decision to keep Peter; I would have to bear my own disgrace and was prepared to do so willingly. But that was no reason to shame Eamonn. It was time for me to leave London.

Three days later, after reading of the magnificent ceremony in Galway Cathedral, I returned to America.

With my dreams dead, I settled down to the life of a single mother. It was tougher than I had anticipated. As before, I relied on my parents to look after Peter at night and put him by day in a play group so he could have companions of his own age.

My job at this time was quite demanding. I was working as a receptionist in a New York hospital near where we lived, still for $150 a week. But I felt that my son had the right to a mother with a lively brain. That was one reason why I took writing courses and deepened my appreciation of literature by reading the classics, including Chaucer and Shakespeare.

My life at this time was so centered on my buoyant, beautiful son that my social life was practically nonexistent. But, to tell the truth, I was not interested in men. Whenever I was asked out to dinner or a show, I saw again Eamonn's shining eyes and friendly face, felt the touch of his hand on my cheek. "No, thank you," I would say, as graciously as I could.

Sometimes I was bitter and resentful. Hearing a friend speak of her husband or seeing a couple embracing in the subway, I wondered if Eamonn was initiating another young woman in the intricate discipline of loving a bishop. Was he healing another wounded soul? Was he knocking on another's door in the early hours of the morning?

To ease my heart, I used to take Peter for walks under the big maples in the park, and listened to him chatting away. His chief interest at the time was in superheroes—Batman, Spiderman, the Incredible Hulk. In his games, he was always one of these. I thought it might be his way of compensating for the lack of a father.

He was having a routine checkup at New York Hospital when the doctor noticed the large coffee-stain birthmark on his knee and feared it might be cancerous tissue. He called Daddy, who confirmed Peter was born with it. He also told him that Peter's father was an important man who had deserted me.

The doctor, a qualified psychologist, offered to counsel me. When I told him who the father was, he advised us never to contact Eamonn, only respond if the Bishop made the first move. He also suggested that if I wanted Peter to have a religion, it should not be Catholicism but one more compassionate and understanding.

"In my experience, Annie," he said, "the boy won't be much interested in his father until puberty. Then he'll probably want to know everything."

By the time Peter was three, he used to ride his little blue tricycle up to the park benches in Peter Cooper. He told the old people about his grandfather taking his leg off every night and how his grandma gave him candy in the store and forgot to pay for it so they were known as the candy thieves. The boy was so gregarious and so folksy that he was even known by some of the retired inhabitants as the Mayor of Peter Cooper.

One day, I overheard him tell a friend that his daddy had nearly killed me and put my blood all over the wall. That was why my leg turned black every night. Mommy must have been talking, and Peter had heard and misunderstood. I wondered how many other strange ideas he was picking up from her. It came, therefore, as something of a relief when my parents decided to move to another apartment. It enabled me to rent a place of my own.

One evening, a friend, Robert Vanstant, invited me to a party. He introduced me to Coln O'Neill, a witty, handsome man. I only had a couple of drinks, but so low was my resistance to alcohol, I got tipsy. Coln took charge of me. No question about it, I was his girl.

After three years of marriage, Coln had been divorced three years before. He admitted that he was still in love with his ex-wife, and I told him about Eamonn. He was fascinated by the different facets of Eamonn's personality: Eamonn who was kind and cruel, loving and cold, outgoing and self-centered, incredibly careful and, as Peter's existence proved, equally careless.

In the summer of 1978, I started to leave Peter in the care of my parents on weekends so I could stay at Coln's place. I was experimenting with the idea of a permanent union. Coln took to Peter instantly and included him in all our midweek dates. It is not true to say I liked Coln just because he was fatherly toward my son, but it was no small consideration.

After our third weekend together, Coln said, "I'd like to spend the rest of my days with you."

He was my first boyfriend since Eamonn. A new phase of my life opened up. Having loved Eamonn, still loving him in spite of the pain we had caused each other, I wondered if I, with what I called my hundred-year-old leg, would be able to sustain a relationship with any other man.

How would Coln compare with Eamonn? Would he be my soulmate? Would he be able to erase the vivid imprint Eamonn had made on me so I could love him for himself and not as a substitute for the real thing?

After hesitating for a long time, in the fall of 1978 Coln and I began living together.

Chapter Forty-One

THOUGH COLN was quiet, funny, and generous, it did not take me long to realize that the strongest link between us was our past loves. We were both living on what might have been.

Nonetheless, to begin with, we had a lot of fun together. He had a big circle of friends, many of them brilliant if a trifle crazy. We went to plays and galleries, dined out at the best restaurants, danced, and, on weekends, when Peter was with my parents, drank a lot.

Daddy was suspicious of Coln's drinking, but he thought it better for me to work things out for myself. In fact, Coln could hold his drink very well, while I had no capacity for it. Coln even said I must be allergic to it. A couple of drinks sent my heart racing. I would jump up on a bar, kick off my shoes, and dance.

Coln wanted to settle down, but every time he asked me to marry him, I was haunted by the thought that I could never give him children. He kept up the pressure by taking me to doctors, hoping they would say, "Go ahead, have another child," but all of them advised against it. I insisted we take precautions. I used a diaphragm and sponges or I asked him to use a condom.

In Needle Park where the junkies hung out, Coln used to buy different drugs and mix them. The dealers had guns and knives but, like Eamonn, Coln was fearless. I had never taken drugs myself, but knowing the perils he faced when he went to the Park, I wanted to share the excitement.

Once, I followed him, taking swigs out of a vodka bottle. A drunk tore the bottle out of my hand. I slapped him; he slapped me back. Fortunately, Coln was on hand to rescue me. But drink made me careless in another way.

One weekend, I forgot to put in my diaphragm. I knew within a couple of weeks I was pregnant because I threw up violently, couldn't get up in the morning, couldn't walk or breathe, and my panic attacks returned. When I missed a period, Coln took me to see Dr. Reynolds, a middle-aged man with a nervous tic.

"Annie, you are—"

"Don't say it," I said.

"If you like, I'll perform the abortion."

Coln became hysterical. "Are you *sure* she can't have this baby?"

"Absolutely not," the doctor said. "There is no way she could bring it to full term."

"For God's sake," Coln said, "she's young and healthy."

Dr. Reynolds said solemnly: "They both would die in the fifth or sixth month."

That night, Coln and I had a long talk. We both sensed that an abortion would wrench us apart. He had grown to love me and was keen for us to stay together.

I feared to lose a dear companion. More than that, Peter, now in his fourth year, would be deprived of a father figure. Coln adored him, and strangers assumed that Peter was his son. Coln carried him to preschool every day on his shoulders. He spoiled him with expensive gifts. He insisted on taking him with us to Chinese restaurants and parties. Peter even came with us to galleries, where he played quietly in the background or painted pictures in his big artist's book.

Coln loved children, and I knew that the destruction of his first child would be too hard for him to bear. "Come on, Coln," I said, holding his hand. "Tell me what to do."

He nodded slowly. We had no choice. What was the point of two people dying?

By this time, I did not set a great value on myself, but I had Peter to think of.

"That bishop," Coln said, sadly, "lives in our life."

Honesty compelled me to say, "Yes."

He went on. "You talk to him sometimes when you drink."

This really shook me. "I do?"

"I've often found you staring out the window, saying, 'Eamonn, Eamonn,' and you sing to him. Sometimes you speak his name in your sleep."

Tears sprang to my eyes. In spite of my best efforts to forget, how deep inside me was the man I left behind in Ireland. We were still connected. He was as real to me as the walls of the room, as the couch I was sitting on. "I am so sorry, Coln."

He brushed my apology aside as if to say that no one can help things like that. Though we had been together less than six months, I knew this was the end for us as surely as I knew my marriage was over when I miscarried. Strange that Peter should be surrounded before and after by the loss of another child. It made him so much more precious.

Later that same night, while Coln was out on business, by an unhappy chance I switched on the TV, only to see an abortion. I watched with horror as a thirteen-week-old fetus was vacuumed out of the womb. It must have been a partisan program because the commentator spoke of the silent scream of the fetus.

Sitting bolt upright in my chair, I could hear a scream of pain rise out of my own womb and echo in my head. I rushed into Peter's room and went on my knees beside him. Thank God, he was still safe and sound. With his closed eyes and quiet breathing, he was the one oasis of peace in my life. To protect him, I had to sacrifice everything.

When I retired and finally managed to get to sleep, it was that silent scream that woke me in the night.

One afternoon in December 1978, I left Peter with Mommy and took a bus to Cornell Hospital, New York. The Swedish doctor asked, "You want to be awake or asleep?"

"Awake? Are you kidding?"

How could I watch the destruction of Coln's child?

A nurse gave me an initial jab and, soon after, I was wheeled into an operating theater. I felt a blast of hot air and blinked at the harsh lights. On the table, my legs were put in stirrups. I felt like an animal. Once again, Catholic guilt swept over me. Would I ever be free of it? If I died on this operating table I'd go straight to hell.

After another injection, I started counting backward from a hundred. After ninety-five, I remembered nothing until I woke up in a curtained cubicle.

The doctor hovered over me in the half-light.

"You all right?"

"Yep," I said, though I felt sore inside and utterly exhausted.

Immediately, I clambered out of bed.

"Someone coming to meet you?" the doctor asked.

"No need." I wanted to punish myself even then.

He gave me some big pads to wear and a supply of pills. "Any cramping or excess bleeding, Annie, and you get back to me at once, right?"

I took a cab home.

Coln, really upset, came in half an hour later with a big bunch of flowers. He had arrived at the hospital to find I had left. "Are you trying to prove something, Annie?"

"What?"

He tossed the flowers aside, seeing I did not want them. "That you're so goddamn tough you can do without me? That we don't belong together anymore?"

I walked into the kitchen and he followed me, saying, "What do you think *you're* doing?"

Without a word I started to prepare dinner, though I could not have kept down a mouthful of broth.

"Are you telling me you're on your own from now on?"

"What do you want with your steak?" I said.

He grabbed me by the shoulders and looked into my eyes. "Was it my fault? Why punish me?"

I removed his hands and went on preparing a meal.

"If that's the way you want it," he said, "that's fine. But at least let me go to your mom's and pick Peter up."

"He's *my* son," I said pointedly. "I'm going."

As soon as Daddy set eyes on my white face, he knew.

I became anorexic. It was another way of punishing myself.
In the public library, I read medical books on blood clots. I
got it into my head that I could somehow dissolve my clot
and thin out my blood. That way I could have another child.
With this in mind, I swallowed pints of vinegar. Though I
still held down my job in the New York University Medical
Center, I wasn't eating or sleeping and was hyperactive.
Weekends, when I left Peter with my parents, I was drinking
so that Coln had to stay dry and drug-free to watch me full-
time as once I had watched my mother.

In desperation, he went to Daddy and told him that I was
a different person. Maybe I had a death wish.

Daddy gave me a prescription for twenty-five Valium.

One night, I went alone to a bar and came back with a bad
bruise on my head. I had been mugged, but I remembered
nothing. A transit cop had picked me up on the subway with
coffee grounds all over me. I was far away in Brooklyn, with
no idea how I had made it to there.

Christmas approached. I was walking hand-in-hand with
Peter down Fifth Avenue. We passed a Santa Claus ringing
a bell; we looked in the windows of Lord & Taylor with
displays depicting Christmases of long ago. It made me feel
sad and lonely. Eamonn and I had never spent a Christmas
together and I began to fantasize about what it would be
like. Eamonn planning with me for the Christmas festivity,
deciding what to buy for our son, insisting on a Yule log fire
in the hearth, playing carols on his mother's piano with Peter
and me singing the words.

Living with Coln had made me even more aware of Eamonn's absence. It was unfair of me to compare Coln's cool-
ness now with the intense warmth and concern of Eamonn. I
tried desperately to forget him, but he was too deeply an-
chored in my heart.

Feeling my tensions rising and fearing the effects of drink,
I took instead to smoking pot, which Coln kept in the apartment. I felt I could control it. I kidded myself that a few puffs
had a calming effect on me whereas liquor made me black
out. Soon, with my guilt increasing and my soul eroded by a
sense of desolation, I was taking both.

It was only a matter of time before disaster struck.

Chapter
Forty-Two

JANUARY 3. THE windows were blanked out with snow driven northwest through the canyons of New York.

I had read Peter a story when, thinking his room was too cold for him, I moved him into Coln's and mine. The hollow wind filled the hollows in my body and my heart.

I had got my haircut for the new year and bought myself an expensive outfit of velvet pants and a white silk top. But I still could not hide from myself that I was a barren woman.

Coln was preparing supper. I popped my head into the kitchen, saying, "We need a bottle of wine."

"*We* do or *you* do?"

Without answering, I put on my mauve Irish cape and slipped out of the apartment. Snow fell white-black like newsprint, silencing the sound of traffic and making all the streets alike. Somehow—was this deliberate?—I lost my way. I had been drinking, something I normally did only on weekends when Peter was staying with my parents. Drink brought on panic and I ran and ran. What was I running away from?

Everything. Past, present, and future.

I slid to a dead halt inches away from a giant snowman. Looking up at it breathlessly, I found myself inches away from an ebony face with jutting cheekbones and big shiny teeth.

Smiling crudely, he dangled in front of my snow-flaked eyes what in college we called a nickel bag. "The sweetest Colombian red this side of the Rio Grande."

His stiff sleety presence so startled me, I whimpered, "How much?"

"For you, lovely *la-dy*," he drawled, "how 'bout *fifteen* dollars."

I handed him a twenty, grabbed the bag and—"*Thank* you, lovely *la-dy*"—flew down what I now recognized as 77th Street and into the corner liquor store.

Freddie, the owner, a thin pop-eyed man with a gleaming bald head, knew me. In his reedy voice: "You seen a ghost, Annie?"

It took me a few minutes to get my breath back and tell him I had forgotten to bring my purse.

"Choose," Freddie said, gesturing; "pay me tomorrow." I picked up a bottle of Beaujolais.

Outside, in the darkness of West End Avenue, I opened the nickel bag and inhaled. Delicious. On a wintry night like that, I looked forward to a pleasant evening of pot and booze.

At home, I threw off my cape.

Coln immediately picked up on my mood. "What's with you?"

I touched the side of my nose. "Surprise, surprise."

"Come *on*."

Laughing, I dangled the nickel bag in front of him.

He frowned. "Where'd you get it? You won't say? Make sure you let me try it first."

"Okay, I'll cook spaghetti, you roll the joints." Running smoky-breathed into the fogged-up kitchen, I poured a glass of vodka and tonic out of the cupboard where I had hidden the supplies and swallowed swift and hard. Ah, velvet. Replacing the glass, I picked a paper from the drawer and rolled myself a fat joint in readiness.

Coln ambled in and examined the bottle of Beaujolais. "My favorite. Thanks," and he uncorked it.

"Open the living room windows a bit," I said. "It'll help clear them."

"Sometimes I think fog suits you."

"What d'ya mean?" The giggles were already on me.

"You're a witch, that's what."

I put my arms around his neck and looked for miles into his eyes. Not a tree, bush, blade of grass. Emptiness.

"Okay, so I'm a witch."

He wrenched himself free. "Can't you ever be serious?"

"Hey," I complained, "it was you who said I was a witch."

"So you damn well are."

"And I just risked my life getting you the best Colombian red."

"I'd be happier, Annie, if you told me the truth for a change, starting with why you're starving yourself to death."

I gritted my teeth before saying, "So I can forget."

"Forget what?"

Jesus, he wanted me to spell it out? Tell him I was still in love with someone in Ireland who filled my nights and days but who would as soon marry me as fly to the moon? Tell him we were through?

He went to the living room and put on a disc by the Rolling Stones. I heard caterwauling about a girl with faraway eyes. To steady my nerves, I drained my secret glass of vodka before pouring myself a glass of wine. I could feel my cheeks turn red and the knots in my neck and stomach untying.

Before I knew he was there, Coln was touching my face. "What caused that, Annie, winter's wind or wine?"

"Both."

I stretched up to plant a kiss on his lips, but his mouth was closed to love.

He rummaged around in the cupboard till he found my glass, empty save for a few melting cubes of ice. "Getting a head start?"

"Is that a crime?" I said, unable to stifle a laugh.

"You tell me."

I suddenly exploded in wrath. "Sure it's a crime, like everything I do. I killed your child, didn't I?"

"You did nothing of—"

"You asked me a question so you *listen*."

I poked him in the chest, hard. "I ripped your kid out of my womb. I wouldn't take a risk with my son's life for yours and mine. Yeah, say it, Coln."

"Say what?"

"That you'll always take second place with me. I have other commitments. It's that bishop bastard in Ireland, isn't it?"

"Bishop bastard," he repeated vacantly.

"Go on, *say* it, *mean* it."

He looked at me, through me.

"Say *something*," I yelled. "What am I good for? For making you lousy spaghetti dinners, for giving you a few puffs of pot? I'm just a few cubic feet of fog."

In a frenzy I grabbed him by both hands. "Go on, Coln, take a big breath and blow me away."

He stood quite still, not breathing, refusing to look into my eyes for fear of what he might see there.

Then, defeated, a murmur: "Oh, Annie."

"You tell me the truth, Coln: haven't I just said what you wanted to hear?"

His refusal to answer was answer enough.

"Okay," I said with forced gaiety, "let's enjoy the night."

He waved his hand in front of me as though wanting to erase me like writing on a blackboard and went back to the living room. Wind rattled the kitchen window as I poured myself another vodka. There was no hope for me, so why not just get wasted? Vodka, wine, a few tokes of pot, and I'd be able to laugh in the face of Satan himself.

Coln was pretending to read the *New York Times* when I approached him with a glass of wine in one hand and a joint in the other. "Wanna share?"

He gazed fixedly at his paper. "Get away; you're drunk."

"Oh, *really*, Coln? You *never* are? You wake up with the shakes, you dilute your breakfast orange juice with the remains of last night's vodka, but Coln O'Neill, gentleman, is always perfectly sober." I sloshed the remains of my wine in his face and ran into the bathroom, locking the door behind me.

He came after me with unaccustomed haste.

Banging on the door: "Listen, you goddamn bitch. I've had enough. That fucking bishop made you barren. Fly to him, I'll pay. Vent your fury on him."

I waited a long moment before asking, with my face pressed to the inside of the door, "You feel he murdered our child?"

As he walked away, I heard him say, "I guess I do."

I turned and sank to the floor. Minutes later, when I opened up, he was sitting distantly on the couch.

I lit the joint, took one deep inhalation, and a cyclone hit my head. I took another puff and the whole room changed, concertinaed in and out. I panicked. I stumbled across to Coln and grabbed his arm.

"Help me. For God's—"

He shrugged me off with "Shit, haven't I had enough for one night?"

"No, no, please, *please*."

His eyes and ears changed places before his head split apart. Blood gushed out of him and ran down the walls and I couldn't remember if I was to blame. Jagged multicolored light flew at me like pieces of glass, stabbing my eyes and mind. I had just enough sense to know the pot was laced with a hallucinogen, God knows what.

"Call the cops, fucking cops."

With pot on the premises, Coln wouldn't hear of it.

Had he not been so furious with me, he would have known this was an emergency. I staggered into the kitchen, fearing I would fall into some drug-induced coma. I fumbled in my purse for the Valium. Swigging from the vodka bottle, I swallowed tablet after tablet until all two dozen were gone. I clasped my hand over my mouth to make sure none popped out.

I didn't want to die, I just wanted to be knocked out.

Then I remembered Peter was in my bed. Jesus, what would become of him if anything happened to me?

My eyesight was failing. I went into the living room, knocking over a chair. It was dark everywhere. I opened the front door.

"Annie, where're you—?"

Without any time or space intervening, I was in the hallway. Vernon, the doorman, called out to me, but I was already in the street. It had stopped snowing. The moon was a string of pearls.

Thud! Could that be me who was hit? I was no longer running except in my mind. Someone, with Vernon's voice, picked me up. "My God, Annie, you coulda got yourself killed."

Once on my feet, I sped back through the hallway into my apartment. The door was still open. A two-headed Coln was still reading a couple of papers.

"I took the pills. All of them."

"So?" said a couple of mouths. "Sit down and you'll be okay."

I was feeling not okay. Light was bursting my head. I made it to the bathroom through the airport landing lights, groped for the cabinet, and emptied half a bottle of aspirins into my hand and started chewing. Anything to drown out the painful light inside my head. Oblivion—I wanted it at any price.

I reeled into the kitchen and drank from the only bottle I could find. It tasted vile. I spat most of it out. Before I lost my power of speech altogether, I got through to the operator.

"Please help me."

"Sure, baby."

"Get me a number in Ireland. I want to speak to Eamonn Casey, Bishop of Kerry."

"Listen, kid, you don't want no bishop across the ocean, you need nine-one-one. When I hang up, I'll plug you into emergency. Speak to them. Okay?"

Hearing me mention the Bishop, Coln gave up on me. He was convinced I was playing games at his expense.

"That you, Eamonn? Why don't you answer?"

As I put the receiver down, my vocal cords started seizing up. Unable to talk, I mounted a chair and screamed. It was an Alpine scream that went bouncing off mountains, echoing in every valley.

Coln came near me, his eyes big red angry suns. I was screaming for life, for time to repair myself, to have the strength to look after my and Eamonn's son.

My vision turned from swirling brown to giddying red-black and, after that, all I remember was falling into a void.

I came to lying on my side. I was dead and had made it to hell in the shape of a cockroach. One of my new family was munching on my left eyebrow. Beside me was a pool of green discharge afloat with the undigested remains of Valium and aspirin tablets. I swished away a dozen fat Upper West Side cockroaches, rolled over onto my stomach, and squinted at the light. The windows were no longer steamed up.

I laughed, pained but happy. I had survived my death.

The green vomit was the remains of the Janitor-in-a-Drum cleaning fluid I had swallowed. It had saved my life, though it had scorched my throat and, by the feel of it, burned holes in my stomach.

I got up with difficulty. My head throbbed and my ribs hurt. I checked that Peter and Coln were sound asleep. "Thanks, God."

I called the cops and, holding my throat and stammering, gave my address. "Just tried, I think, to kill myself. Overdose."

Minutes later, a police car drew up with flashing lights. I opened the door myself.

One of the cops, young, with blond hair and sharp features, looked over my shoulder. "Where is she?"

I pointed to myself.

He shoved me back inside, sniffing the air as he followed me in. "Sit," he ordered, like a dog trainer.

I dropped onto the couch.

His partner, middle-aged, relaxed, said, "Easy, Mike."

He took no notice. "What's this all about, lady?"

I explained, in between coughs, about the pills and the liquor.

"I was reared by alcoholics," Mike sneeringly said, for his own benefit. "You alone?"

I pointed to the bedroom.

"My son . . . my friend Coln."

Mike exploded with self-righteous wrath. "You try an' kill yourself with your kid in the next room? We're gonna have to take him away. Go get him, Charlie."

Mike dragged me to my feet and handcuffed me. "Suicide's a crime, don't ya know that?"

Coln appeared with Peter asleep in his arms. He did not like the look of this roughneck cop.

"What the hell," he asked coldly, "is going on?"

"So," Mike said, "you and the bitch have a fight, she tries to kill herself because of you and—"

"Now, wait a minute," Charlie butted in, "take it easy, let's just start over."

"At the station," said Mike, prodding me toward the door with his stick.

"Mike, will you take that fucking stick out of her back?"

"He'd better," Coln said. "She calls for help and they send a moron like that."

"Shut it," Mike said. "She's just admitted to attempting suicide."

"Whatever happens," Coln insisted, "I'm taking her boy to his grandparents."

I went across to him. "Thanks," I said, and stretched my cuffed hands so they went around Peter's warm red cheeks and kissed him. "Good-bye, my darling."

Mike pointed me toward the door. By the time I reached the sidewalk, an ambulance drew up. I was about to get in when Coln came out with Peter, fully awake, on his shoulders.

"It's cold," I said to Coln. "Take him back in."

"Mommy, Mommy," Peter cried. "I want to come."

I held up to him my cuffed hands in prayer, silently pleading forgiveness. I felt ashamed. In my head now, Eamonn was saying, "Did I not tell you, Annie, you would never make a good mother?"

How could I have done this? I had fought hard to keep Peter from being adopted, and now, in one night of madness, I had risked giving him into the hands of strangers.

As Charlie uncuffed me and two paramedics took me by the arms, I whispered to Mike, "You're right, I deserve all I get."

In the ambulance, time stopped. Nothing of importance happened. All I wanted to do was kiss my son, stroke his soft hair. On the journey, a paramedic took my blood pressure. "It's low. Pulse slow, too. Warn them we may need a pump." To me: "What kind of pills did you take?"

I told him.

"These bruises, some guy beat you up?" I explained about running into the street and being hit.

In minutes, I was wheeled into the emergency room of St. Luke's Hospital. Hands, voices. "Strip her. She's pretty beat up. Fingernail missing. Looks like a break in small finger on left hand, book her for X ray. Contusions on face, arms, ribs"—I was turned over—"My God, on her back, too, like she's been dragged over stones. Blood pressure low, but rising. Prepare alkaline solution for her stomach. She'll be drinking that for weeks."

After my wounds were dressed, I was sent upstairs to see a psychiatrist. Minds don't get fixed as easily as ribs.

He was young, relaxed, with big blue eyes. I told him everything. It took a couple of hours, with the cops waiting impatiently outside and him taking notes. After which:

"Ever done anything like this before?"

I shook my head. "Never. And never again."

He pondered for a few moments, went out of the room, came back in again, yawning. "I want you to go to AA. Heard of Alcoholics Anonymous? Good. If I let you go, promise you'll come back and see me in forty-eight hours?"

"Let me go? Sure, you can count on me."

He scribbled on a pad. "Bring me a note from AA that you've been to see them."

I nodded, speechless.

"You say you have a son. Will you do this for him?"

"Oh, yes."

He looked at his notes. "Coln, yes? Your companion, he drinks, too. Break it off with him, in five days at most? Fine. Otherwise, I'll be obliged to pass your citation on to the family court."

I went home and called my father. He told me not to worry, that he would look after Peter for as long as I needed. However bad I looked, I went to work at the hospital. I would need the money.

I realized finally that my affair with Coln would never work, not after I had discovered the real meaning of love on the dunes of Inch beach. Never would I be able to say to any man, "I love you," with the same truth and intensity as I had said it to Eamonn. In a moment of unbearable honesty, I admitted to myself that I would rather have died than abort Eamonn's child.

That night, when I met with Coln, no words, no explanations, no kisses. Just: "Good-bye, Annie."

One more time in my life: "Good-bye."

That hurt, but I was overjoyed to have been given one more chance.

Chapter
Forty-Three

WHEN I went to a downtown AA group on 23rd and Seventh, I was introduced by Ethel. She reminded me of Sister Ignatius—anyone could tell she was a saint, in her case a reformed one. Five years before, she had lost custody of her child. Under the influence of drink, she had blacked out and beat him, breaking both his arms and legs.

I attended AA weekly for three years. The meetings usually lasted an hour. Sometimes I went in the middle of the night when I had a break at work, sometimes I rose at 7:00 A.M. I never touched liquor during that time.

I took a small apartment at Stuyvesant Town and my parents rented a place a couple of blocks from me. Daddy asked if he could come with me to the open AA meetings and I often picked him up by cab. "For my benefit, sweetheart," he said, but it was really so he could stay close to me.

We went through the various steps together, making amends for the hurts we had caused. We made coffee and helped clean the place up. Never had we been so close. It was one of the great blessings resulting from my fall.

My new AA friends reminded me of the girls at St. Patrick's. Only when you hit bottom do you appreciate the greatness of other people.

At one meeting, I admitted to having had an abortion. Afterward, Daddy drew a diagram and explained to me how the embryo develops. "At this stage, sweetheart," he said, gripping my arm fondly, "it's not a life. Abortion is wrong as a form of contraception, sure. It's bad for the body and the psyche. But you were *saving* a life, your own." He tapped my arm. "In future, be more careful."

Another time, he said, "Apart from one six-week spell, you've been a damn good mother. Everybody's entitled to one mistake, eh?"

"If you say so."

"I do say so. However awful you feel, you never miss a day's work, you always put your son first." He smiled on me kindly. "You certainly proved Eamonn wrong, didn't you?"

I said yes, but without conviction.

"To be a successful pagan like you," he added, "you need to be a good Christian and then some."

I rejoiced in his new mildness until—oh God, oh, no—it hit me that this was his way of preparing for his death.

I saw other signs. His favorite phrase, repeated over and over, became "I don't give a damn about this or that," as if he had left planet earth already. He also helped me find a job in a law firm, which sent me to a word-processing school. This gave me a valuable skill and meant a raise in salary.

One memorable incident occurred at the end of September 1979, eight months or so after Coln and I parted. Eamonn appeared on television in company with the Pope, who was on a visit to Ireland. He was in a biretta and cassock with a purple-lined cape, which fluttered in the wind. I saw the same animated face, the same fluttering movements of the hands. He had filled out a little but seemed not to have aged at all.

The item was so brief, I scarcely had time to grab Peter and fix his gaze on the screen. Afterward, with a lump in my throat, I said, "That man was your daddy."

"Which one?" he asked.

A few days later, I was able to show him some pictures of Eamonn in an Irish-American newspaper. His five-year-old son was not too impressed.

"What's that funny hat he's wearing?" he wanted to know.

I bought several copies of the paper and cut out Eamonn's pictures and the account of Pope John Paul II addressing a crowd of two hundred thousand people, mostly youngsters, at the Ballybrit Racetrack in Galway. The Pope descended by helicopter and celebrated Mass in green vestments. At the Mass, assisted by Eamonn, he had said: "Do not close your eyes to the moral sickness that stalks your society today. . . . How many young people have already warped their consciences through sex and drugs?"

Hardly an uplifting message, but the crowd enjoyed it.

I was reminded of my halcyon days in Ireland and the wonderful people I had met there. I was genuinely pleased for Eamonn, who was doing what he loved. Maybe he would make it to cardinal, after all.

When Peter was in kindergarten, I was doing two jobs. I made $175 a week as a secretary in a lawyer's office and another $90 working nights as a switchboard operator in a hotel. It was at this time that Daddy started to say frantically, "You've got to get Peter out of New York."

Peter certainly hated kindergarten. A few times he had been beaten up for his lunch money. Another reason Daddy wanted us to move was that he thought a change of air would improve his own health.

Signs of cancerous growth in his right nostril had given him a premonition of his end. He kept insisting, "If anything happens to me, sweetheart, take your mother and Peter to one of those nice Connecticut towns like Westport or Ridgefield."

One April day in 1980, I visited him after work to find him pale, weak, and vomiting. Subsequent investigations showed he had cancer of the pancreas. It spread to his kidneys, lungs, stomach, bowels. Mommy couldn't cope, so I had to lift and diaper him. As he got worse, I spent the nights with him and, in the end, I took to living permanently at his place to be near him.

Once, he awoke and, seeing me beside him, said, "Didn't you promise me once when I cursed you that when I neared the end you'd get back at me?" I nodded. "Shoot, sweetheart."

"You're not dying yet."

He winced. "You'd better believe it."

In spite of all the damage we had done to each other over the years, the bitterness was long gone.

"Okay, Daddy, ready? Well, you may not be able to take this because you are a dry old stick. But . . . I really love you. I only loved one man more and that was because he reminded me of you. Even when you called me a—you know what you called me—I knew you loved me and this was your way of expressing it."

He waited for a couple of minutes before saying, with a grateful smile, "Sweetheart, you really know how to turn the knife in the wound."

The time came for him to be hospitalized. Very quietly, he said to the nursing staff, "Let me die." He turned to me for support. "Please, Annie."

It is hard to hear the man who gave you life say that.

In the twenty-one days that followed, I saw his body blow up and change color. His brain became affected; his speech became difficult. When I put my ears to his lips, all I could hear was "Peter. Peter. Peter."

I whispered back, "It wouldn't be fair to him."

"I want to see my grandson."

It struck me that my dying father understood what Eamonn did not: that Peter was our hope, our life after death.

I was crying now. When I shook my head, I showered him with tears. But he was obsessed with the idea.

On my next visit, I sat Peter down on a bench in the corridor and told him that Grandpa had changed. I showed him a picturebook with colors of purples and blues, and said that some kinds of illness made the body look like that. I felt really guilty. Peter was not yet six. To ease my father's pain, I was risking putting my son through an experience that might haunt him for life. If only I could have asked Eamonn for his opinion and had his support.

"Peter," I said, "can you bear to see Grandpa?"

"I'll try, Mommy."

"Good boy. He'll only be with us for a couple more days."

"A coupla days. Where'll he live then?"

"Just take him by the hand and you'll make him happy forever. Just think of that. Making your lovely grandpa happy forever."

As we were about to go into the room, my brother Johnny joined us. It was he who suddenly lifted Peter up and put him on Daddy's breast. Daddy was so pleased he hugged the boy tight with his long bony fingers.

Peter screamed and I had to wrench him out of Daddy's

grasp. When I quieted him, Peter took Daddy's hand, saying softly, "Sorry, Grandpa, you understand, don't you, Grandpa?"

I took him by the shoulder and led him out of the room. "You're so brave," I said. "Now Grandpa can go away happy."

We all went downstairs to the chapel, where Mommy was praying. I knelt in front of the statue of St. Jude, patron of hopeless causes. I prayed for Daddy's early release. A light streamed through a stained-glass window behind the statue and I knew something had happened. Leaving Peter in charge of my brother, I ran upstairs and burst into Daddy's room. He had just died.

I went downstairs and took Peter out of the chapel.

"Grandpa's left already," I said, feeling suddenly lonely.

"I'll miss him," Peter said, "but I'm glad I saw him in all that pain."

I clasped him tight for comfort. "Why?"

"Now I know death was good for him," he said.

Mommy was relieved that Daddy's suffering was over. But then she kept me awake all night not by grieving but by compulsively counting her money. She feared that Daddy was going to steal it. I had been so absorbed in Daddy's illness, I had not noticed that Mommy was showing signs of senility.

We buried Daddy on a hot July day in Redding, Connecticut, where he was born. My two grandmothers were buried there, too, as was old Grandfather (Pop) Murphy. I remember little apart from the wealth of flowers, but word-fragments of the ceremony were to haunt me for days. "I am the Resurrection and the Life." Feeling more desolate than I had felt in years, I was chiefly thinking: *If only Eamonn were here conducting the funeral or at least present to lay his hands on our shoulders to comfort us.*

We should have shared everything, he and I, but I had missed the funeral of his father and now he was missing Daddy's.

Chapter
Forty-Four

OUT OF respect for Daddy's wishes, three days after the funeral I left New York City. I found a job in an accounting firm in Westport, Connecticut, one of the most affluent towns on the East Coast. There, Mommy and I were able to rent a small Dutch colonial-type house on a tree-lined street. Life seemed good to us at this time.

I earned $225 a week. We were close to an excellent school. Peter enjoyed the sea, and took an interest in flowers and birds. He was able to go on hikes, spend days on the beach with friends, and take school trips to Boston. At this time, he was easygoing, very friendly, and he also proved to be a good student, showing a talent for art and poetry.

Mommy was on antidepressants, and in the calm atmosphere of Westport, her memory came back. She was especially sweet to Peter, who loved her dearly. He often sat next to her, talking with her, stroking her hands, and telling her how much he loved her.

In March 1981, I chanced to see an item in the *New York Times* about Eamonn. He had become a celebrity. He had denounced U.S. military aid to the El Salvador junta, which he called "a regime of naked terror." He spoke of the Reagan administration as being unprincipled. Most staggering of all, he called on the Irish government to break off diplomatic relations with the United States.

Heavens, I thought, Peter's father wants to create an international incident!

I bought a copy of an Irish-American paper for details. Archbishop Oscar Romero of El Salvador had been supported by Trócaire, the Irish society that Eamonn chaired. It financed Romero's newspaper and radio station; these had brought to light the Duarte government's appalling record of torture.

When Romero was murdered in March of 1980, Eamonn represented the Irish Church at his funeral. Grenades thrown by government supporters exploded among the crowd. In the stampede, sixty people, mostly women, were killed.

Eamonn had described Romero as "the true, present-day martyr of the Church, a champion of the powerless, the poor, a courageous defender of human dignity." Now, one year later, Eamonn was trying to raise two million pounds—a staggering amount for a small country like Ireland—for projects in developing countries. He had accused his own government of being "callous" and of making Ireland's name "mud" in the eyes of the world by its minute contributions to Third World aid.

In view of Eamonn's tiny payments to us, I was amused by his stout defense of the poor. Yet, I admit it, I was proud, too, knowing he was fulfilling his ambition to be Pope of the Third World.

To secure Peter's future, in September 1981, with the help of Daddy's insurance, I bought a place in Simsbury, Connecticut. In Westport, I had always paid rent on time, kept the house in good condition, and even done some landscaping. Still, when I was about to move out, my landlady wanted to hold on to two hundred dollars out of my seven-hundred-dollar security deposit; some of the paintwork, she claimed, was not to her satisfaction.

When I mentioned this at a local AA meeting, I noticed a short, sturdy, mature man studying me. He resembled the playwright Arthur Miller. His name was Arthur, too, and he had Miller's high brow and fine chiseled nose. Arthur Pennell took me aside after the meeting and in a melodious Scots accent said, "I'll pop over and advise you."

The next day, he kept his promise. Seeing the paintwork in question, he told me that it did not justify a two-hundred-dollar penalty. He fixed it in ten minutes.

To the landlady, he said, "Your banister needs mending."

"Please do it," she said. "After that, I have two or three cupboards for you to fix."

In less than an hour, Arthur had completed all the jobs.

Afterward, he said to me, "I'll be back tomorrow at six."

He turned on his heel and left. I said to Peter, "That Scot is a formidable guy."

The next day, he proved he was not just physically strong. He was very courteous to the landlady but he showed he had studied every law relating to building and renting. Quietly and efficiently, he silenced all her objections. Without a word, she went to fetch my two hundred dollars.

He gave me his number. "If you need me, call."

Simsbury is a picturesque town. Even the banks are located in grand early-nineteenth-century dwellings. I chose it because it had every amenity for children, including pools, skating rinks, tennis courts, and slopes for tobogganing.

Peter was proud of our new home. It had four bedrooms and a family room and he declared it to be the best house around. Within days of our arrival, half-a-dozen kids from the neighborhood made it noisy with their play.

We had hardly settled in when Arthur Pennell casually walked through the door and surveyed the house from top to bottom. "Not much of a place," he declared with what seemed to be his customary arrogance. "But knock down this wall and you'll have a different floor plan. You'll be able to breathe."

"I'll think about it," I said, having no money left for renovations.

"What kind of paint are you using?"

Of course, I had chosen the worst possible. He drove me to the store and bought me the best on the market for five dollars a can more. In his none-too-subtle way, Arthur took over my life. After three years of trying to cope on my own with my ever more ailing mother, I was ready for it.

He said, "Give your mother repetitive jobs like folding things, or she'll drive you mad. She likes to clean the sink? Then give her plenty of Ajax. Be sure she uses gloves or she'll burn her hands off." Arthur was already organizing everybody like a Scottish nanny. He stayed for the weekend, sleeping on the couch and fixing things and painting everything in sight. When I protested that I was broke, he said he didn't need payment. He was in between jobs and about to move on to California. But once he was in with us, there was never a question of his moving out.

He had been married to a German woman but divorced for ten years. Father of three grown boys, he had lived in the States for over two decades. In the two months it took for us to be intimate, I had a renovated house and, at age thirty-three, a new way of life.

While I went to work in a real estate office, with extra typing of legal documents at night to make ends meet, he kept his eye on my mother. He and Peter seemed to hit it off, too.

I felt relaxed with Arthur because, with kids of his own, he didn't need me to make him a father.

Maybe we would be a family at last.

Arthur never inquired about my past until I received news of money waiting for me at the offices of a New York law firm. As Arthur drove me there, he asked for an explanation.

How Eamonn's quarterly contribution was paid is a story in itself. It showed how tricky he could be when his interests were at stake.

Mark Krieg was a young Jewish lawyer. For five years, someone who never identified himself came regularly to Krieg's home and handed him cash in an envelope. A junior partner in a Catholic firm, he rode the subway to his office, where I collected the envelope.

I had spent the last four months writing to Eamonn in code. With a huge rise in the cost of living over the last five years, it was vital to get him to contribute more to his son's upbringing. When he had several times refused, I called Galway.

"Listen carefully, Eamonn, because I am not repeating this. My lawyer is hungry. He'd love to take you to court over maintenance. So it's either two hundred and seventy-five dollars a month or your neck."

He chose his neck.

When on the way home from collecting my money in New York I told Arthur who Peter's father was, he laughed so hard I had to drive. "Eamonn Casey, Bishop of Galway? You're kidding. Sell your house, Annie, get a ghostwriter, and do a movie about this.''

Arthur was relieved. Peter's father, a Catholic bishop living three thousand miles away, was no rival to him. Nor was he a rival in the usual sense but something more. To Eamonn and to him alone had I given the best of me. Only to Eamonn had I ever been able to say, ''I love you forever.'' He had taken the more than willing gift of my young self and made with me a miracle, my son.

Arthur judged correctly that Peter, now turned seven, was a persistent little fellow. If he wanted his many friends over and Arthur said no, Peter told them to wait outside while he argued the case. By sheer logic and persistence, he usually won. Maybe this was why Arthur said, ''Someday, Annie, your kid'll need to know who his old man is. Then things might get messy.'' He grasped something that Eamonn had known from the time he wanted to have him adopted: the danger to Eamonn's position came not from me but from his son.

Since I had shown Peter Eamonn's picture in the paper, he had never once referred to him. At school, when he was asked about his father, he simply replied, ''He lives a long way away and he works for the poor. He can't stay with me but he sends me money.''

Arthur wanted to know if Eamonn ever wrote to his son, sent him a birthday card, Christmas card, called him. When I said, ''No, no, no,'' he was astonished. His Presbyterian hackles rose. He could not account for the coldness of a man who preached God's fatherly love.

Neither, of course, could I. Eamonn had more love in him than any man I would ever meet. Why did it stop short at his own son?

Mommy's condition deteriorated so rapidly that one day she tried to burn the house down. Arthur offered to give up his job as a house painter and stay home on a permanent basis to look after her. Without him, I would have had to go back to the city and put her in a home. In the next year and a half, Arthur made the best use of his time at home by totally renovating the house.

Our time at Simsbury was busy but happy, too. By now I was earning up to $250 a week with a month's summer vacation so that I could be with Peter. He was getting high grades at school and his teachers told me he was bright and hardworking with a feel for language as his poems showed.

One was called "Love's Blur":

> *It tastes like chocolate*
> *It looks like a billowy cloud*
> *It feels like cotton*
> *It sounds like the waves*
> *It smells like roses on a summer's day.*

Another was called "Hate":

> *It looks like the devil*
> *It smells like a foul stench*
> *It feels very rough*
> *It tastes like bile*
> *It sounds like an angry dragon*
> *It makes me feel mad.*

I only wished his father was on hand to praise his nine-year-old son for his many achievements.

One day, Arthur said we ought to take advantage of the current property boom. Why not sell the Simsbury house for a profit and go where the money was, namely, back to Westport? If we bought a rundown house there, he could fix it up and we would sell it at an even higher profit.

In days of ever-rising property prices, it seemed a sound way to make a living. With money from the sale of the Simsbury house, augmented by extra savings from Daddy's insurance, I bought an old wreck of a house with just under an acre of land and a small two-bedroom cottage. The cost was $95,000.

Mommy liked the idea of living in Westport because she would be closer to Mary. Also, Johnny promised to take her out to dinner each month. I got a new job as secretary in a real estate office. It paid me $17,000 a year and we had extra income from renting out the cottage. When I was offered a three- or four-nights-a-week job in the local hospital from 11:00 P.M. to 7:00 in the morning, I took that, too. I used to come home from working in the real estate office, wash and feed Mommy, shower, and go straight on to my second job.

For eighteen months, we fixed the house up and enjoyed the spaciousness of its rooms. Then Arthur decided it was so structurally unsound that it was useless to touch it up. If we wanted to sell, we would have to rebuild from the floor up. "I can do most of it myself," he said, "but we're in for a year and a half of hell."

Eamonn came into our life once more, unexpectedly through television. In the summer of 1984, President Reagan was visiting Ireland, to trace his roots. Eamonn, who detested U.S. interventionist policies in Central America, persuaded the other Irish bishops to boycott the visit. Reagan's cavalcade was shown on TV rushing past Galway Cathedral on his way to the National University to receive an honorary doctorate of law.

For the first time, Peter, nearly ten years old, grasped that his father was important enough to cause problems to the President of the United States. Unlike his friends' fathers, his was real *because* he was on television.

I saw the boy watching his father wide-eyed. He was thrilled to hear that Eamonn was on the side of the underdog. He battled oppression, from apartheid in South Africa to right-wing dictatorships in South America. This was a man Peter was keen to get to know. Why, then, was he always kept at arm's length?

As I put him to bed, he said, "He looked like a nice guy."

Elated myself at having seen Eamonn's dear face again, I smiled. "You like him?"

"I think so. Can I tell my friends my dad's been on TV?"

I shook my head. Peter, too, was now part of the conspiracy of silence.

"It's okay," he said wistfully. "They wouldn't believe me anyway."

Arthur had not underestimated the scope of the problems of the house. The misery would be worth it if at the end we made a good profit. Then I could get a caretaker for Mommy as well as buy our next house. Such were the costs of extra labor and materials, though, that I had to borrow a big sum at a high rate of interest to make our monthly repayment of $835.

By this time, Mommy's senility was so bad she had to be tied to the bed to keep her from wandering. She got thin and refused to eat anything but chocolate cake. In caring for her, Arthur proved to be something of a saint. Once, when I tried to sponge-bathe Mommy, she nearly tore my eyes out. Arthur came to the rescue. Every other day, he put on his swimming trunks and carried her screaming under the shower with him. For six months, when the house was a virtual shell, he made Peter and me sleep in the now-vacant cottage while he slept in the living room of the house so he could hear Mommy if she cried in the night.

The strain eventually told on all of us. Arthur was temperamentally like a thistle, pretty to look at, sharp to touch. One minute he would be relaxed, the next he would strike like a cobra. Peter started to distrust him, then to rile him. He bargained with Arthur before he would help out. Part of the bargain was that Arthur had to be nice to him and curb his tongue. I had been overprotective of Peter, so I approved the idea of Arthur putting a bit of steel in him.

One day in August 1986, my life brightened when my seventy-six-year-old mother had a sudden burst of lucidity. She had not spoken for almost a year and now, in a four-hour spell, she was able to talk with me about the past and the good times we had spent together. I pulled back the drapes to let in the light and stroked her silver hair. Peter joined us for a while and sat on her bed, and all three of us prayed for Grandpa.

After Peter left, she said, "Do you know, I was never able to think badly of Eamonn. Whenever I was tempted, I looked at Peter and said to myself, 'God brings so much good out of evil.' "

In those few precious hours, Mommy and I ranged over all the people we had known and loved, all the crazy things we had done; we asked pardon of each other for mutual hurts. This was the most unexpected boon of my life.

"I'm hungry, Annie. Could I bother you for a hamburger?"

Never had I received a request with such joy. "With onions and relish?"

"You bet. And a chocolate milk shake."

"You got it," I said.

I went down to prepare them. When I returned minutes later, she did not even know who I was. I looked helplessly at her, at the tray of food in my hands. I sadly closed the drapes, but in my heart I knew my God had been kind to both of us.

Two weeks later, on a golden September day, Arthur called me at work. "Annie, I'm going to give your mother a cup of tea with a drop of whiskey in it to warm her up."

Give a glass of whiskey to an old alcoholic?

Then I grasped what he was telling me. "She's dying, isn't she?"

"I'm going to carry her out to the garden, Annie. I want her to sit in the sun."

"I'm coming home," I said.

When I got there, she was, with Arthur standing over her in mourning, like a part of the fall, a leafy lost-looking fragment of a lady sitting hunched in a garden chair, holding an empty cup. I went down next to her and cried. I felt overwhelmingly all the pain and the innocence of her damaged life. She had deserved better.

But she was with Daddy now. Paradise, the renewal of all that is best at its best. We buried her next to him.

Our house was nearly finished. It was beautiful. We even had a goldfish pond and an arbor with wisteria. I was sorry Mommy could not see it.

To cut out the middlemen, I advertised the house myself and sold it to a young couple, both investment bankers, for $430,000. That was $40,000 more than a real estate agent had said was possible. After paying back our loans, we were left with $280,000. I grabbed Peter and hugged him fiercely. We had made a start in the world. We had choices.

Chapter
Forty-Five

IN THE neighboring town of Weston, I paid $260,000 for 5 Fanton Hill, a small ranch-style corner house with a small plot of land. Weston is a picture-postcard town in the heart of Fairfield County. It is full of oaks, poplars, silver birches, and Scotch pines. In those days, most houses, usually with several acres, were selling for half a million to two million dollars. We did not know it at the time, but we bought at the height of the real estate boom.

I was fortunate to find a $400-a-week job in insurance but within a month, I got basal cell carcinoma on my right nostril. With Peter to care for, I was terrified. The doctor said the cancer had progressed inside and out. He was afraid that it would reach the nerve, causing the right side of my face to collapse.

I kept the news from Peter. He was making great progress with his studies and I did not want to upset him. As to Arthur, he had endured a lot since he came into my life. He had proved to be good and generous yet, always honest, he admitted: "If your face sinks, Annie, I'll probably say good-bye."

The time came for the doctor to operate on the side of my nose. After I came around, he started to remove the dressing. His message to me was: "However bad you may look in the future, it could have been much worse." When he handed me a mirror, I took one look at myself and passed out.

When, seconds later, I came to, he told me I would have to do my own dressings for a couple of weeks and swallow

some awful-tasting medicines until he was able to do recon-
structive surgery. Meanwhile, fearing to lose my job, I continued working in the insurance office.

I was relieved to return to the hospital, where the doctor
took material from behind my left ear and rebuilt the nostril.

When, a couple of weeks later, he handed me a mirror
for a second time, I had to agree I didn't look too bad.
Even so, I lost confidence. Apprehension, the trauma of
the operation, worries about what people thought of me
brought on a deep depression. The music went out of my
life. Often I stretched out my hand as though wanting someone whom I trusted to take it and sing to me and lead me
on. But only one person was capable of doing that and he
belonged to my past.

Arthur wanted to build our house upward in a big way.
He was already talking of selling this mythical monster for
over a million dollars. His previous renovations were only
an apprenticeship. This new project was a trial of strength
from which he hoped to emerge triumphant as never before.
The only trouble was, I was too tired to support him. For
the first time in years, it was an effort for me to go to work.

"All right," Arthur conceded grumpily, "we can't afford
to live in this area. We'll fix this place up, sell it, and buy
cheaper somewhere else."

We put it on the market but there were no offers. This was
1987, when the stock market crashed.

There was one reminder of Eamonn at this time. A friend
from Ireland sent me a newspaper clipping, a couple of
months after the event to which it referred. Eamonn was
found guilty of having excess alcohol in his blood while
driving in the heart of London. He was fined two hundred
pounds. The police had no idea that they had hooked a bishop.
In Ireland, of course, he would most likely have got off with
a caution, but this was in Protestant England where he was
not well known.

This warning had come none too soon. When the news
leaked to the media, he claimed that his friends were to blame
for forcing drink on him. His instinct was always to deny.
Later, he wrote a public letter of apology to the faithful,
which was read out at all Masses in Galway.

* * *

One small incident dictated the future course of our life.

Peter, a thirteen-year-old six-footer with a burly frame, was playing with Arthur in the garden when he threw a ball that knocked Arthur's glasses off, smashing them. "Glass in my eyes," Arthur yelled. "What're you trying to do, kid, kill me?"

Peter stood his ground. "It was an accident. I only wanted someone to play catch with. That's why I miss my dad."

Quite out of character, he ran to me, threw his arms around me, and burst into tears.

I don't know which of the three of us was most shaken.

Peter, who was doing well at his studies and seemed so content with his many friends, was revealing for the first time how profoundly lonely he was. He had no father to speak to; no point of reference for his life.

Arthur was sobbing, "Oh my God, Peter, I'm sorry. I don't care if I go blind, anything to make you happy."

"It's not your fault," Peter said. "*You're* not my father."

The boy's cry of dereliction, my operation and lack of energy, the strain of rebuilding the house and not being able to sell it, precipitated a crisis.

In early May 1988, Arthur simply took off. I looked for him, made several phone calls, but he had vanished.

It was a whole week before I got a call from Arthur, and from the unlikeliest place.

"This is—"

"I know *who* you are. *Where* are you?"

"Shannon Airport." Sounding like a whipped dog, he said, "I'm just back from seeing Eamonn in Galway."

"What did he say?"

"He called you a whore and your son a bastard."

"He did *what?*" I said.

Within twenty-four hours, he was back home, repentant, frightened, trying hard to explain. He had figured that I could sell the house, pay back the mortgage, and still come out with $120,000. It would be better for both of us if he went home alone to Scotland. Once in Edinburgh, he had the brilliant idea of doing Peter a last favor. He would go to Galway to confront his father.

I could not have chosen a more unsuitable envoy.

In Galway, he feared that if he drove unannounced to the Bishop's Palace, he might not be allowed in. He went to the bus depot. There, he told a cabdriver that he was a close friend of the Bishop's cousin and he had come on her behalf to discuss with him a family matter. For twenty pounds, the cabdriver agreed to drive ahead of him up Taylor's Hill to the Bishop's door. He made a call to check that Eamonn was at home and to say that he was bringing a foreigner on a family matter.

Eamonn himself came to the door of the Palace and the cabdriver made a quick introduction. "This is Arthur Pennell from Connecticut."

"Come in, come in, come in," Eamonn said, anxious not to make a scene in front of a witness.

In the Bishop's study, the conversation did not last long.

Arthur said, "I'm with Annie, Bishop. I have been taking care of your son for nearly seven years."

"*My* son?"

"Peter's a teenager now and getting rebellious. He needs the attention that only a father can give."

"He is *not* my son." Eamonn insisted the child could be anyone's. Annie was a wild young woman without religion, living in Dublin at the time.

"I've lived with her for years, she's just not like that."

To which Eamonn responded, "People change."

"But," Arthur said, "you made payments over the years."

"Prove it," Eamonn said.

Arthur knew the routine. He could prove nothing. In despair at the brilliance of the Bishop's defenses, he said, "A court could order a blood test."

Eamonn laughed at so preposterous a suggestion. "Let's face it," he said. "You have her word against mine and I'm an Irish bishop. If you make a public fuss, I will deny all connection between me and her. Moreover, tell her I would resign rather than have anything to do with that boy of hers. Now, would you like a cup of tea and a sandwich?"

Fearing he might hit him or hold him hostage and call the press, Arthur left and drove straight back to Shannon where he reported to me.

I have only Arthur's account of this meeting. I believe it is basically correct. But it sounded to me like a confrontation between two jealous men. The mere fact that I was living with Arthur must have persuaded Eamonn that I really was a whore. Had I been decent, would I not have remained faithful to him till death?

Peter, of course, wanted to know where Arthur had been. How excited he was when he heard. "Did Eamonn admit he was my father or did he say I was the son of a milkman? Tell me."

I said, "He admitted nothing."

"I can just see him." Peter was deeply hurt. "He's a real rat."

"Please don't say that," I pleaded, though he expressed my sentiments precisely.

To my utter surprise, Peter said, "He is totally corrupt."

I lifted my hand to slap his face but he did not flinch. "Didn't you ever hear, Mom, that all power tends to corrupt and absolute power corrupts absolutely? Well, that's him."

He went outside, mumbling, "He won't even talk to me." Seconds later, through the open window, I saw him raise his hands to the sky like Eamonn and let out a long unearthly scream. It was animal, primeval, and it scraped my heart.

When I went to kiss him good night, he enfolded me in his strong arms and said, ominously: "I'm warning you, Mom, that guy is not safe from me, not anymore. I've a score to settle with him."

Peter's bitterness, his sense of being abandoned, affected me. I had seldom called Eamonn and never asked for much. I had never betrayed him because I loved him. Yet he had told Arthur that he would have no hesitation in betraying me—and, worse, Peter, too—if he had to.

I was madder than I had ever been in my life.

As far as I was concerned, Eamonn was no longer protected. It was open season.

Chapter
Forty-Six

HAD I reprimanded Arthur, he would have gone straight back to Edinburgh. I was lonely and Peter, too, needed him.

Arthur decided that if we were to sell the house we would have to rebuild it. The new planning permission was for one of 7,000 square feet, which, in my view, would cost us an extra $100,000. Pointing to the garden, I said to Arthur, "That hole out there, we might just as well jump into it," and Peter suggested we turn it into a swimming pool.

I had made the mistake of buying into Arthur's dream. The debts started to rise; our resources dwindled. My panic attacks returned. It is probably impossible to convey to people who do not suffer from them just how distressing they are. Fear has specific causes and distinct objects. You might be afraid of mice or fast cars or being trapped in a blazing house. But panic has no object, and its causes are difficult to fathom. I have checked medical encyclopedias in which panic attacks are not even mentioned. Those that do mention it tend to refer to it as a mystery illness with no one cause and no one remedy.

Nights terrified me most. I woke up regularly at 2:00 A.M. and instantly took flight. My soul wanted to escape from whatever treacherous thing was troubling it. Once I jumped out of bed and ran out of the house into the road, where I narrowly missed being hit by a truck. Sometimes, I ran into the woods, where it took Arthur and the cops hours to find me. At times like these, only Eamonn could possibly have calmed me.

When Arthur woke in the night and found me missing, he called 911 and told the friendly neighborhood cops, "She's gone again." They knew who he was and what he meant. The cops picked me up and either let me stay at the station to calm down or took me to the hospital. One Irish patrolman named Collins was really scared to see me shaking as if I had DTs with my pulse up to 160–180.

"If you were a dog, lady," he said, "I'd shoot you."

"Why," I responded, "should dogs get all the breaks?"

Sometimes I called Collins on his own line and he would help me just by talking to me for ten minutes. Most attacks went on for up to three hours. Each time the ambulance brought me back, Arthur turned the TV up so Peter would not know what was happening.

Only once, when he was thirteen, did Peter see me in the middle of an attack. I had been given strong drugs after surgery on my nose. The phones were not working because of a storm. I woke at 2:30 with my diaphragm paralyzed; no air could get in or out of my lungs. I could hardly talk. While Arthur went to wake Peter, I summoned up all my strength and ran out and banged on a neighbor's door, calling, "Help," before I passed out.

The ambulance came. My blood pressure was 60 over 40. I was taken to St. Vincent's Hospital in Bridgeport where the doctors struggled to get my blood pressure up before they could do something for my panic attack.

Arthur brought Peter to see me. The boy was in the lobby watching the miniature Doctor Ruth, the sex specialist, on TV. When he was allowed in to see me, he started imitating her. He sank on his knees to make himself tiny. "I am goin' to talk to you, voman, about six. You see, you haf thees leetle spot, a button, oh, so sensiteev, I can't tell you."

He so cheered me up, my breath began to come back and one of the nurses said to me, "You don't need medication, that kid of yours will make you better."

With Eamonn's contributions months in arrears and the house taking up all our funds, we gave up luxuries, then even a necessity, the car. In spite of our efforts, we were soon facing foreclosure.

We refused to give in. Arthur worked as a house painter. Without a car and holding down two jobs far from home, I often had to bed down where I could. We both went without to supply Peter's needs. In spite of our best efforts, by the spring of 1990, our financial situation had worsened.

I had no option but to give Peter absolute priority. I was haunted by that scream of his when he realized that his father had denied him. Surely it was time for Eamonn to act as a father should when his son's entire future is at stake. Peter was a teenager with talent, but if I were bankrupt, how could I provide him with a roof over his head and the education he needed?

After years of struggle, I felt it was right to ask Eamonn to contribute more. If he refused to pay for Peter directly, I would have to make a claim on my own behalf for damage done to my life.

On the recommendation of a friend, I went to see a New York attorney. Peter McKay was a burly, bushy-haired, handsome man in his early forties.

He sat me down and let me speak without interruption for an hour about my relationship with Eamonn. McKay, gazing out the window over Central Park, was, I could tell, skeptical of my claims at first. But after I finished my long monologue, he said in his gravelly voice: "Your story is absolutely incredible. It must be true."

"You mean I would need to be a genius to invent it?"

"Right. But tell me, Annie, how in the post-Watergate era has this story been kept under wraps for so long?"

"It happened in Ireland."

That fitted, he said. He visited his mother in Ireland most years. It was probably the one country in the western world where a scandal of this size could be covered up.

The lawyer in him demanded proofs. I gave him one: the biological. Father and son had exactly the same big birthmark in the same place. The odds against that, apparently, are one in many millions.

"Tell me, Annie, what do you want me to do?"

I said I wanted to avoid at all costs the accusation of

blackmailing Eamonn. I wanted no behind-the-scenes settle-ment, no quick fix. "Go straight to the courts," I said, "so we get a settlement that sticks."

"Pardon me," McKay said, "but if you go public right away, you will be immediately accused of trying to blackmail the Bishop."

I really had not seen that. I thought that bringing the matter into the open would demonstrate my good faith.

"Has the Bishop a lawyer, Annie?"

I could answer that. When Mark Krieg left his law firm, the old system of payments broke down. Maybe Eamonn felt that, with the passage of the years, he was safe. Lately, I had been paid by drafts of the Allied Irish Bank. These were sent at Eamonn's request by Robert Pierse, a Kerry lawyer from Listowel, who, doubtless, had no idea what the payment was for.

McKay advised, "Talk to Eamonn privately, Annie; tell him if he doesn't help out, his son will end up in public housing, possibly on welfare, with all the problems that go with it."

"I've talked with him privately for years."

McKay pointed out that legal costs can be prohibitive, especially if you lose. He encouraged me to write a long deposition and give Eamonn a chance to answer it.

I agreed to do that.

"Do you have a figure in mind, Annie?"

I told him that a friendly attorney, Anthony Piazza, had said the claim was worth $100,000.

"Maybe too modest," McKay said.

I stood by my calculation. It was against all my instincts as an independent person to ask for more than I needed to provide for Peter.

In the end, I let McKay approach Eamonn privately. "But," I concluded, "if Eamonn offers less than one hundred thousand dollars, I'll go public. He won't leave me any choice."

McKay wrote to Listowel on April 12, asking Robert Pierse for a response from his client, Dr. Casey, about "a sensitive matter" between Ms. Anne Murphy and the Bishop. If Pierse had ceased representing the Bishop, he might like to forward his request to Dr. Casey's new counsel. He requested a reply by April 26.

Robert Pierse's fax came on April 23: "I have been unable to contact the named person so far. I will endeavor to do so. He appears to be away."

Was Eamonn in hiding? McKay extended his deadline to Pierse to May 10. "I trust that we will be able to resolve this among ourselves."

Though Eamonn refused to communicate with McKay, he kept calling me. Astonishingly, when I heard his voice, the old feelings returned. I had to steel myself against him. Our son's future was at stake.

"You're talking to the wrong person," I said. "From now on you'll be dealing with a lawyer named McKay."

I advised him to act fast before disaster struck. "You have choices, Eamonn, I don't. Please don't call me again."

Trembling, I hung up.

Time was running out for all of us, because in late April I had lost my best-paid job in a word-processing department. A lawyer from Legal Aid managed to get our light and oil bills paid. This was the only time in my life I have had to suffer this humiliation. With foreclosure looming, it looked as if we would have to go into public housing in South Norwalk. It had a reputation for barred windows, handguns, and frequent murders. If that happened, I would have no compunction in publicly shaming Eamonn for not helping his son. I prayed it would never come to that.

Sheriff's notices were nailed to the doors of our home; court orders, injunctions, and demands for repayment of loans were piled on our dining room table. The framing of the house, the french doors, over a hundred windows, the flooring, insulation, and wiring were completed but funds had run out. Ten more days and we would lose everything.

On April 28, a firefighter who was building his own home came by. We had $22,000 worth of lumber stacked on the lawn amid the fallen petals of apple, cherry, and dogwood blossom. It was meant for the large decks and the three-car garage with a studio above it. He offered us $6,000 for the lot, which, since it was not nailed down, we were entitled to

sell. It was the best price we could get in the time available.
Next day, he came with three trucks and, within hours, the
lumber was gone.

Peter came home from Weston High School where he was
so happy. He was astonished to learn that we were moving.
How was he to tell his friends Sean and Charlie? "Hey,
Mom," he said angrily, pushing his favorite Yankee cap to
the back of his head, "I've only a couple of months of this
school year left. Didn't Eamonn offer to help?"

I explained that if we did not leave soon, whatever money
we might get from Eamonn would go to pay our outstanding
debts. Peter McKay had advised us to move out for another
reason. Eamonn would not know our whereabouts, so he
would be forced to deal with my lawyer.

"Where will you be, Annie," McKay asked, "when I
want to contact you?"

I told him we were headed west. We hoped to find a less
expensive place where Arthur and I could both get jobs and
provide Peter with good schooling. I promised to call him
when we were settled.

We arranged to store our furniture for $100 a month and
hired a truck from Ryder Rental for one day to help us move
it. With only twenty-four hours to wrap up our lives, Mary
and her friend, Stan, came to help us pile everything into
boxes and suitcases. We crated the TV and radios, Peter's
toys, memorabilia from *Star Wars,* baseball cards, his boom
box. Early on May 3, my forty-second birthday, we left the
house that we had hoped would make us a fortune. With only
$6,000, Arthur and I had one final ambition: to give Peter a
sense of the wider world outside our narrow circle. We wanted
him to see with his own eyes that the round earth is beautiful
and to inspire him with new ambitions. He had to learn to
believe that things do change. My hope was that though we
were powerless now, Peter might still acquire a sense of the
magic and challenge of life.

To evade prying eyes, we left Fanton Hill at the ungodly hour
of one in the morning. Arthur and Stan were in the truck,
Mary was driving Stan's car, while Peter and I headed the
convoy in ours. I had the cash in my shoes. Driving on money

helped me feel secure. Also, hearing the river run over the rocks after spring rains gave me the first hint of hope.

As I made the turn out of Weston into Westport and onto the throughway, I handed Peter a book of maps. "How'd you like to see the whales in Seattle, Washington?"

"Great, Mom."

"I'd like to live in Seattle. On the way there we'll see some wonderful sights." We took Exit 14 through South Norwalk, past the housing projects. Slanting buildings with bars on every window, men in rags asleep on park benches with newspapers for bedding, litter scuttling like mice in the night breeze—poverty is the cruelest of all prisons. I would fight to the death to keep my son from that sort of jail.

Saying good-bye to Mary and Stan, we drove through the night. Beyond Philadelphia, we started our quest for stability but never found it. We chose cheap motels, which depressed us. We passed ghettos, like the one on the south side of Chicago, that made their counterpart in Norwalk seem like paradise. And in between the dirt and devastation, we saw scenes of awesome beauty.

Arthur wanted us to settle in Vancouver. Unfortunately, such was the price of property, even to rent was beyond our slender means and job opportunities for people with our skills did not exist.

I called McKay and he brought me up to date. Hearing nothing from Listowel by his deadline, on May 11 he had faxed Pierse again, saying, "I shall assume that your client, Bishop Casey, has no interest in resolving this matter in a private forum and shall so instruct my client. I am sorry that Bishop Casey saw fit not to take advantage of this opportunity."

Pierse had replied that Eamonn was dealing with the matter himself. "Wait for the good news," McKay told me cheerily. "The Bishop finally phoned to say he's coming to New York on June fifteenth or twenty-first. He wants to see you."

To see me? After all those years? I was so flustered I did not know how to respond.

I disliked the delay in settling but since we had come so far and had time to spare until that meeting, we drove down the West Coast to California and then eastward through the blazing South. Arthur even took Peter to Disneyland as a diversion.

The worst moment of all was near the end at Newark, New Jersey. We pulled into a truck stop with a McDonald's on site. The parking area was full of ancient cars crammed with adults and children sleeping. They were transients, one step away from the sidewalks of some street without a name. Filled with terror at a fate that could so easily be ours, I jumped back into the car, causing Peter to wake up.

Yawning, he got out and walked along the line of cars. Moments later: "Mom, people live in those things. They've got pillows, blankets, paper plates. They homeless, Mom?"

"Yes," I said.

"Are we?"

I made a big display of showing him the money we had left. "Homeless? Us? Never. Look"—I pointed—"the New York skyline."

"Forget that," Peter said, with the sudden leap of a near-sixteen-year-old into manhood. "I'll make Eamonn pay up."

"Sure," I said, "but let's do it peacefully, eh?"

"I don't know about that," he said, with a fierce look in his eyes.

Chapter Forty-Seven

AFTER EAMONN delayed his trip to the United States, James J. Kelly, a friend of Eamonn's from his hometown of Adare in Ireland, finally fixed a meeting with Eamonn for July 15. Kelly, a Brooklyn priest, was also an attorney at law.

Peter insisted on coming with me to McKay's office. "I want to sit across the room from him, Mom. He doesn't have to talk to me, but I tell you he's gonna have to look me straight in the eye."

"Are you sure you—?"

"I need to know who this guy is and who I am. He denied me to Arthur, if he denies me to my face, well—"

I admired him. He was fearless, like his father. But since he had not been brought up a Catholic, I tried to explain to him the problems from Eamonn's point of view. As a priest, he was not supposed to have relationships with women or father children. It was hard for him to admit that he had been untrue to his vows.

From Connecticut where we were staying with Mary, we drove into the city early on a sunny afternoon. At the Paramount Building, I left Peter in charge of McKay's young assistant, Richard. In the lobby was a white-haired priest, probably Eamonn's chaperon. I had guessed, correctly, that Eamonn had arrived early. I told Richard I refused to see Eamonn. This was strictly business. Besides, with Eamonn

unwilling to acknowledge his son and accusing me before
Arthur of sleeping with any number of men, I might say
something I would regret.

The truth was I was scared of what I might see or not see
if I looked into his eyes.

Before long, Peter came down to the lobby, pale and dazed.

"To think I waited sixteen years for *that*."

I was sad for Eamonn that he found it impossible to speak
with his own son, a boy who should have evoked pride in
him. I was sadder still for Peter. He had pinned his hopes on
this long-delayed encounter. As we went out for a bite to eat,
he babbled on.

"I really wanted to get to know him, Mom, but he wouldn't
let me in. It was like talking with a stranger. A butcher or
a mailman meeting me for the first time would have been
friendlier."

"How long did he give you?"

"Four minutes."

It was the length of an average confession.

"I was a mistake, Mom, wasn't I?"

McKay, he said, had hidden him in his library until he had
finished his business with Eamonn, then he introduced him
as "Peter Murphy." Eamonn was too surprised to decline to
meet him. As McKay prepared to leave, Eamonn shook Peter's hand. There was no embrace, though he had not seen
his son since he was a baby.

I said to Peter, "Didn't he say *anything?*"

"He asked me what I wanted to do with my life. He told
me he prayed for me twice a day. Then good-bye."

"That was it?"

Peter nodded. His hurt was slowly turning to hostility.
"What did you ever see in him, Mom? He lacks the basic
decencies." He screwed his face up. "I intend to nail that
bastard to the wall."

It was with redoubled fury that I went back to McKay's
office after lunch.

McKay came from a theatrical family. His meeting with
Eamonn, he told me, was the most intriguing in his career
since he represented George Wallace, the governor of Ala-
bama, in a libel suit.

Eamonn came alone into his office, dressed in full clericals.

Maybe he thought that a "McKay"—good Irish name— would be intimidated by the trappings of power. After all, Richard, a practicing Catholic, had stooped to kiss his ring.

"Eamonn really does have an aura about him," McKay said. "In seeing him, you sense the power of the Church he represents."

McKay had thanked him for coming. Then: "Bishop, we have a problem, sir."

"Yes, Peter, we do. What will it cost?"

When McKay told him $125,000 in total, he seemed to sigh inwardly with relief and they shook hands on it.

"It was all over in one minute, Annie. I could have got you up to half a million!"

I said, "I only wanted enough to provide for my son."

He sympathized with me for the curt way Peter had been treated. "When Peter left the room," McKay said, "I went back in. The Bishop seemed quite indifferent to the boy. All he wanted was for Peter to sign a paper to the effect that now all his paternal responsibilities ceased."

"Never!" I gasped.

McKay nodded. "I pointed out that this was *your* settlement, Annie. For damages caused over the years to you, your health, your life. I told him why you felt you could never marry again. If you sign, I promised Eamonn, you will no longer be able to sue."

"And Peter?"

"I said, he can't sign because he's under age. There's no question of him giving up his rights to paternal maintenance. For that we'd need a guardian in the court system. We'd have to disclose the reason for the guardian to the court."

"What did he say to that?"

"Keep it private."

"As always," I said.

"For me," McKay mused, "the most perplexing thing is the Bishop's blind spot. He still doesn't see that his only danger comes from Peter."

On July 25, 1990, the promised money was paid to me by McKay after receipt of a check from Father Kelly. I signed a paper releasing Eamonn from all responsibility toward me.

But, as McKay had seen so clearly, some stubborn streak in Eamonn prevented him from taking the boy seriously.

* * *

Keen to try and make a new life in the old world, on July 29, 1990, just before the Gulf War, we flew on a Kuwaiti 747 to London, England. From there, we took the train to Arthur's old city of Edinburgh. I had only one month to try to settle Peter in a school for the next academic year.

Unfortunately, it soon became clear that the minimum cost of a decent house was £50,000, which was beyond our means. Moreover, in that part of Scotland, neither Arthur nor I had any job prospects.

McKay had warned me that in my desire not to ask Eamonn for too much I had asked for too little.

We swiftly toured Scotland, a kind of consolation prize to Peter. Then, not wanting to squander our money, we took the train to Holyhead in Wales, whence we caught the ferry to Ireland. Since Ireland was a poor country, the housing situation was bound to be better there.

On the boat, Peter came down with food poisoning. He was so ill, I went up on deck and facing west cursed this bitch called Ireland that was once more blighting my hopes. Someone must have heard. Peter recovered after a couple of days in St. Michael's Hospital, four blocks from the ferry. The nuns and doctors were the most caring people I had ever met.

After trying several places on the east coast, we settled on the southern town of Kinsale, County Cork. It has a fine harbor on the Atlantic. But properties here were expensive, too. In the end, we paid £32,000 for a rather plain two-bedroom cottage a couple of miles out of town. It came with a nice piece of tree-lined land overlooking rolling hills and the wide Bandon River. There was plenty of scope for development.

On the Friday morning, we enrolled Peter in the local Catholic school of Our Lady of the Rosary. We chose it because of its high academic standards. Peter was horrified at the thought of nuns, uniforms, church, but I told him he would have to put up with that if he wanted to go to the university. There was also something shrewd and honest about Sister Mary, the head of the school, that made me trust her instantly.

That same afternoon, we rented a car, threw some luggage in the back, and headed for Kerry. How good it was to go back to Killarney. It had kept the flavor of a market town. As we approached the Great Southern Hotel, Arthur opted to stay there overnight. "No," I said, "we're driving to Inch," and Peter backed me.

Arthur suspected I was reliving my times with Eamonn. He did not want me retreating again into what he called a fantasy world. Yet he knew I had to return to Inch for the boy's sake, to help him find out who he was and the strange circumstances that had brought him into being.

On the way, I noticed many new whitewashed bungalows with red-tiled roofs. Intruders. Opening the car window, I smelled the sea of fifteen summers past. The hills rose to mountain heights and there—at last, at last—was the Inch strand jutting out into the gray Atlantic with its grass-covered dunes and ocean roar.

I turned into the parking lot and braked. Without a word, without thinking, I leaped out of the car and ran.

"Hey, Mom, where're you—?"

I did not stop running till I kicked my shoes off and ran, sparrow-splashing, into the surf and gazed toward the glistering west. I was hungry to be by myself. I wanted all to myself the waves, the blue-white sky, the purple-streaked sun setting in oranges and pinks.

Peter was a stranger beside me, clutching my arm, saying, with wonder, "I never saw you move like that before, Mom. You looked on fire."

Arthur, the stranger's friend, said, only half mockingly, "She thought Eamonn was calling her from the sea."

"Be quiet," I said, "and look at the sea and the sky." But I was really looking at yesterday.

In a meltdown of the years, it all came back to me. How hand-in-hand, under a clean white moon, we walked these sands and listened to the precise slow rhyming of this sea. Nights I remembered, oh, such long sweet nights when we made love. Time had passed slowly since then, but my love had not waned; it had throbbed however painfully in the long dull hours between the seconds of my life.

Arthur, trying gallantly to understand, said, "I'm really

pleased you're sharing with Peter the part of his life denied him till now."

"Thank you," I murmured, still gazing out toward the sun-lipped sea in which Eamonn and I had bathed together.

"I think," he went on, "you were running to meet *him*."

I nodded.

Slowly, achingly, he said: "I swear to God, Annie, if I had it in my power to make him appear this minute so all three of you could go down this beautiful beach together, I'd walk away without a sound."

I gripped his arm in gratitude.

"But he's not here, Annie. He hasn't been around you for years. And I have." Heart-cut, he released my arm as if to let me go.

Poor Arthur. He did not seem to know that true love never dies, is never replaced by any other.

With the noble grief of his words, the year turned to 1990. I looked landward. Above the path was the hotel, vacant, boarded up, its yellow-white paint peeling, half covered by time and drifting sand. There was a beach shop, deserted, on whose gabled end was a fading inscription: "Dear Inch, must I leave you? / I have promises to keep / Perhaps miles to go to my last sleep."

I waved to Eamonn's retreating ghost, crying out, "Good-bye, good-bye," and he, dancing, tripping over the sand, looked back at me over his broad shoulder, singing repeatedly and ever more faintly, "Good-bye, Annie."

"Let's go," I said heavily to my two men.

My hands were so shaky, Arthur was behind the wheel as we drove up the road toward the house. At the exit to the drive-way was green lettering on a brass plate: "Red Cliff House B&B."

"Stop," I yelled, "you've got to stop. They do bed and breakfast. Peter has to see this."

Arthur carefully navigated the concealed graveled drive lined with rhododendrons, azaleas, and hydrangeas and drove under the twelve-foot-high hedge, a tunnel entry into a magic kingdom.

There it was, preserved in sunset amber. The same Geor-gian one-story house in red sandstone with slate roof and french doors, the sea on one side, the mountain on the other. The same shimmering poplars. A thrush busy cracking a snail on a stone was probably descended from the thrush that once sang for me.

Peter knocked on the front door. "They have two spare rooms."

It was little changed inside. The Stations of the Cross had been removed but on the ceiling I saw the ornate moldings and on the hallway floor the same gray-and-white tiles on which Eamonn walked when reciting his breviary. I peeped out of the small windows onto the changeless, ever-changing sea.

In the living room, Eamonn's piano was gone as were his candelabra and Waterford crystal. The rest was as it had always been. The same rugs and drapes and wallpaper, same tables, chairs, and sideboard. Was Eamonn's ghost here, mocking me?

Come out, Eamonn, I urged, come out from behind the drapes and show me the star-spangled view across Dingle Bay. Come, Eamonn, light the fire, warm two frozen selves, make me sit at your feet; and let us tell each other the stories of two lonely lives that might have merged—had I but had the wisdom and you the courage—into a single story wherein there was no loneliness.

Arthur and I were given the bedroom that was once the sacristy. Again, the same furnishings, even to the broad dresser with low drawers in which Eamonn had kept his vestments. In the bottom drawer, I had once hidden his episcopal ring. That was when, yes, I remembered, I came back pregnant to Inch and Bridget had jokingly said, "Make sure you return to Dublin, Murphy, with a contribution from the Bishop." So I grabbed his precious ring and put it on my finger, calling myself the fiancée of the Bishop of Kerry and, after a couple of drinks, I forgot where I had hidden it, and we searched the house for it for hours. We looked in the toilet bowls, down the sinks, in the flower beds with a flashlight. And all the time Eamonn was moaning, "If it doesn't turn up we shall spend the rest of our lives paying for it." And I remembered where it was only when he was inside me, but he told me puffily that I could not go after it at that inconvenient moment.

Peter had installed himself in my old room, not knowing it was mine. It was uncanny. Nothing had changed, not the wallpaper, rugs, dresser, all were embalmed by memory. The bathroom where Eamonn hid in terror from his niece had the same old shower-stall and yellow curtain, the same tarnished light. Most heart-tugging of all, the bed was my bed. We had first kissed and made love there. I, who was nothing, was made important there.

I pulled back the bottom sheet and there was the same dark brown mattress of horsehair.

"This place is spooky," Peter said. "Like it was waiting for us to come back."

"Come back?" I repeated. "Oh, yes," for Peter, too, had been there before, inside me.

I went outside in the great hallowing of night and stood amid the bristling wind-stroked grass admiring majesty. I recalled so many things as I watched all that crystalline beauty under the climbing moon.

It was altogether like a fairy tale in which sleepers awake in, or travelers return to, a treasured place after a thousand years and nothing has changed. Memory is a kind of private heaven in which things and people you love are kept safe beyond the touch of pain, grief, death. Change them? You would as soon alter the shape and incandescence of a star.

That night, with the scent of Old Spice in his nostrils, Arthur said, "I can't sleep here. He's in the room, in the bed with us."

Unable to sleep, we went for a walk up the winding dirt track at one in the morning but he soon gave up, saying, "You used to walk here with him, didn't you?"

Back in our bedroom, he looked out the window at the white, toppled moon-tower on the sea and forgave me. We snuggled up into one of two single beds to keep warm—oh, Ireland, in September—and finally drifted off to sleep.

We did our best to make a life that winter in Kinsale. In his thorough way, Arthur knocked down a wall to give more light to the living room and beamed it in pine, painted the place white, and put down beige carpeting.

Yet, try as we would, we could not settle. Peter was missing his friends; the children around him did not speak the same language or enjoy the same games of baseball and American football. He was too relaxed and seemed unmotivated. Even the education suited neither his tastes nor his needs. He had already set his heart on studying law and how could he do that outside his homeland?

More important still, though Eamonn lived only a few hours away, never once did he offer to meet Peter. Whenever I tried to contact him, I was told he was in El Salvador or Guatemala or Nicaragua or too busy making preparations for a tour or writing reports up afterward.

He seemed to be keeping to his original intention. He would never acknowledge his son.

Peter, often seeing on TV the great man that his father had become, was shaken and hurt anew to find he could not spare him a few minutes of his time.

Knowing that the pressures on Peter were building up, we decided to move back to America.

Chapter Forty-Eight

LEAVING KINSALE on January 13, 1991, we returned to Connecticut, where we found a small one-bedroom apartment in Ridgefield. Peter had to sleep on a divan bed in the living room. The rent was $800 a month. Eamonn's contribution of $275 did not go far.

In May, with our Irish cottage still unsold, I wrote to Eamonn. I sent him the Kinsale solicitor's name and address, hoping he would know some retired Irish priests or nuns who might like to buy our place at the price we paid for it. I promised to use the money entirely for Peter's education.

I also said in my letter that the refusal of Peter's father to speak with him was seriously undermining his confidence. "Can you imagine," I asked, "such a two-footed cad walking your lovely Emerald Isle?"

In a postscript, I spoke enviously of the Bishop living in Ireland during its most beautiful season, spring.

His reply came within a couple of weeks. He said he would have called me but my number was not listed. Maybe he reckoned there was in my letter some underlying threat to him, but there was not. He said he was coming to the States on August 21. If I sent him my telephone number, he would call me and arrange for us to meet in New York. Meanwhile, he promised to inquire about the sale of the house.

Once back in the States, Peter recovered all his drive and his ambition. Aged sixteen and a half and towering over Arthur and me, he had tremendous stamina. He worked weekends at Stop-and-Shop to earn money. After school, he was taking night classes in law with a view to making it his profession. Having a passion for helping people unjustly treated, he had set his heart on a job with Amnesty International.

When he heard of Eamonn's impending visit, he said, as if Eamonn himself were speaking: "This time, I'm going to get from him some proof that he's my old man."

I smiled. "He's pretty slithery, Peter."

"Then we'll have to be slithery, too."

He was looking to his own future. He was not far from graduation, to be followed by college. He was farsighted enough to realize that one day he might want to enter public life, even politics. "Maybe when I'm thirty-five, Mom, I'm going to have to tell the world who my father is and he may be dead by then."

But how was he to get the proof he needed?

Arthur, having watched too much TV, said, "When your mother meets him, she should be wearing an electronic device."

He investigated and found the best bug cost six hundred dollars. "You expect me to pay *that*," I said, "when my car is practically falling apart?"

Arthur bought a hundred-dollar bug and taped it to me. He tested it out in my car, in the street, in restaurants.

"Too mushy, Annie," he said. "For the kid's sake we've got to invest in the expensive model."

Just then Peter rushed in. He had come from the home of my friend Jim Powers. Jim, a big heavy guy with red hair, had bought a camcorder.

"A great machine," Peter said, breathlessly. "Eamonn's never met Jim, so he can video you when you meet Eamonn."

The sound system on the camcorder plus the hundred-dollar recording device taped to me during the forthcoming meeting should provide Peter with the proof he wanted.

"I want no part of it," I said, horrified.

Undeterred, Peter brought Jim over to our place. Peter pretended to be Eamonn while Jim practiced on the two of us in conversation.

"It'll never work," Arthur said, glumly.

Peter turned on him and, speaking ironically: "These are

my parents. I can get them on tape. Mom and Dad. First time ever. For my family album.''

I shook my head. "As I said, count me out."

Eamonn came, as planned, to New York in late August. Peter took his call at our home in Ridgefield and once more all Eamonn said to him was that he wanted to talk to Annie.

This really stunned me and made me feel Peter's pain more keenly than ever. Eamonn's dogged refusal to speak with him finally persuaded me to go through with the crazy plot to entrap him. How could I go on defending Eamonn at his son's expense?

I had two jobs at this time to save for Peter's college education. I worked as a Stamford secretary for a salary of over $20,000 a year but I was also employed nights from 5:30 to 9:00 at the Grand Hyatt Hotel on 42nd Street in New York, getting home around 10:00. That is why I arranged to meet Eamonn at the Hyatt. It had a huge lobby, which was vital if Jim was to elude security as he taped us.

Early in the evening, Mary took me to her place and dressed me up in a smart suit. "This is for your son, Annie. You can't meet your old flame looking like a bum."

From Greenwich, I went to Jim's place to have the bugging device fitted under my blouse. Peter taped it inexpertly; it pinched my belly and kept slipping down.

"If he puts his arm around me," I said, "he'll feel it."

Peter said, "If he lays one finger on you—"

That evening, I walked hand-in-hand with Peter to the hotel entrance.

Basically, I admit, I get a lot of fun out of trickery, but not this time. My emotions were mixed as never before in a life of considerable emotional turmoil.

Everywhere I looked, there was treachery. I was setting out deliberately to betray the only man I ever wholly loved.

I felt like Judas going into Gethsemane to plant a kiss on Jesus' cheek. Why was I doing this appalling thing? Because for over seventeen years Eamonn had betrayed his and my son; he had steadfastly refused to give Peter the recognition he needed to be a whole person. He had refused even to speak with him.

I kept telling myself, *There must be some other way, some way less cruel. There must be.*

But there wasn't.

I had to choose between Peter and Eamonn, my child and his father, the two great and enduring loves of my life. This burden was intolerable. Had not Peter's hand been firm in mine, I would have turned and run.

"Where's Jim?" I asked.

"In position. I gave him Eamonn's picture so he'll recognize him." Eamonn would be in the lobby already. With his suspicious nature, I never doubted he would arrive early and reconnoiter.

It was, oh, no, not *sixteen* years since we had last met in Dublin when, after we made love, he had uttered words so terrible they had echoed in my mind ever since: "He is not my son."

Sixteen years. I was a young woman, full of hope and vitality, when last he set eyes on me. And now I was—oh God, I didn't want to think of it. What did I look like? Would he think I'd aged? Would he notice I'd had surgery to the side of my nose? Had I applied my makeup well enough to hide it? If I perspired, would the scar appear? Was it already noticeable?

I was so damned nervous.

Peter let go of my hand, with "Good luck, Mom," and suddenly I was alone, like a warrior going to do battle with . . . my dearest friend.

The lobby light was dim. My breathing was heavy, almost out of control. My legs were ready to give way.

Oh God, was that him? Could that be him? In New York? In 1991? This was surely a dream, you just don't roll back the years like this.

Then suddenly I *knew*, knew that between him and me there was no passage of the years. Time would rub out mountains but not us, not Eamonn and me. Time would leave us intact for each other; our story would live on as bright and new as when it was first told. Nothing in ourselves, we would always be everything in one another's eyes.

He was smart in a navy blue blazer, open-neck sports shirt, gray flannel pants, and polished shoes. He had slimmed down and could have been taken for an American businessman. Positioned with a view of the entrance, his eyes were wary.

When he saw me, those hawk's eyes instantly softened and he jumped up excitedly. "Annie, good God, 'tis you, Annie."

I had resolved to dislike him. No, I had practiced for hours in my heart to despise him. Then one look, one word from him, and I knew it was impossible. Tender feelings, exquisite memories flooded back. I was so happy that in a complete seesaw of the emotions, I was ashamed of the snare we had laid. He seemed suddenly, yes, so innocent.

He grabbed both my hands and kissed me. "Sit down, please. So good, so good—"

How effortlessly we made the long leap over the years. Sitting opposite one another, smiling broadly all the while, we just looked at each other for a long time, shaking our heads, biting our lips, trying to clear our eyes.

Then, as if jerking out of a dream, he began to talk about my home in Kinsale and what it was worth. Afterward, we moved on to Peter's education. I was so engrossed in Eamonn that I had forgotten about Jim and the camcorder until he appeared over Eamonn's shoulder in my line of vision. He was buzzing around us like a bumblebee.

I tried scratching my face as a signal to make him back off.

Eamonn said, "What's the matter?"

"Just tired. I work really hard at two jobs."

Jim came still nearer to pick up the sound and I started coughing to stop myself from laughing aloud.

Eamonn said, "You sure you're not allergic to something?"

I shook my head.

He finally confessed that any attempt on his part to sell my Kinsale house would leave a dynamite trail back to him. What he did offer out of the blue was three thousand dollars a year toward Peter's university education.

"It'll cost almost ten thousand dollars," I said, "but I can manage."

"It'll be tough on me, Annie, but I think that for one year—"

"Please," I interrupted him. "You drive a BMW that cost

seventy thousand pounds and you live on Taylor's Hill, in the richest part of Galway, with a beautiful view of Galway Bay. But thanks.''

His cousin, Jacky O'Brien, a retired priest in New Jersey, kept Mary well informed.

With Jim still dive-bombing us, I could not concentrate. Fortunately, at this point he withdrew to get a long shot.

Only now did I realize that as far as Eamonn was concerned, this was not just a social meeting. He had turned warm toward me. It made me feel wanted, really wanted for the first time in years. I dreaded the thought of our just shaking hands or kissing on the cheek and saying good-bye.

I suggested we go to the bar.

"Fine by me, Annie. I fancy a beer, what'll you have?"

"Seven Up."

"Come on," he urged, "this is a special occasion."

"I've been in AA for years, Eamonn. You know what booze does to me."

"One glass of wine for old time's sake. You're with me, you'll be fine."

With that, he ordered for both of us.

One sip of that wine and it hit me like a brick on the temple. I downed the glass and called for another just as Jim came into the bar in search of us. Already a little high, I lifted my hair up and with my fingers gave him the sign to go away. At the entrance to the bar I could hear Peter's quivery laugh, so like his father's. He was behind a plant, having a Coke.

"'Tis awful queer what you are doing with your hair," Eamonn said, getting edgy.

As Jim went away to get a shot from above, Peter came out from behind the plant and waved to me. I could have thrashed him.

"I've been wanting to ask you, Annie," Eamonn said. "One night, some while back, an operator was trying to get me from the States on your behalf."

"That," I said, "was the time I had an abortion."

"An a*bor*tion?"

"Now don't you get on your moral high-horse."

"Did I say a word?" he said.

"It was wrong of me to get careless, but once I got pregnant I had no choice—we both would have died."

He murmured something about medical necessity.

"Read me the riot act and . . . I don't know what I'll do."

He laughed. "Pet, you will cause a scene here. You have not changed one bit."

"Are you sorry?"

He shook his head.

"See how important birth control is?"

He laughed again. "No change, none."

He took my hand and held it while he asked about my mother. When, after a while, I turned the conversation to Peter and his plans for the future, Eamonn was not interested.

"Did you ever think, Eamonn, that by avoiding Peter you might be digging your own grave?"

"He would not be vindictive."

"Don't count on it. If it comes to a showdown, remember, I go with my son. He is always first and last with me."

When he offered me another glass of wine, I accepted because I did not want him to leave me.

"Not too fast, Annie, you must not get drunk on me."

"I'm okay," I said, feeling instantly unwell.

"Over the years, I really missed you."

With that, he grabbed me and kissed me passionately. He wanted me to know he had come for me, not for Peter.

I was as surprised at that as at our very first kiss and told him so.

"Why, Annie? You think my feelings have changed?"

I nodded slowly. "I thought they were dead long ago."

"No, no, no."

I drained my glass. "Maybe they've revived for tonight."

His face creased in a smile. "No doubt about it."

I took his smile away by asking, "Why'd you tell Arthur I was a whore?"

His head jerked back. "I never did."

"Didn't you deny you were the father and say it could be one of many men?"

He nodded. "I suppose."

"And you refused to see Peter."

"I saw him last year."

"Because it was sprung on you. Even so, you only gave him four minutes of your precious time." I drew back at this point. I did not want to antagonize him, because in his presence long-repressed feelings in me surfaced all over again.

"Annie," he said, echoing my thoughts, "I don't want to leave you."

"Why don't we spend the night together talking? One night in sixteen years."

Shrugging: "I don't know."

"You'll be safe, my estrogen count is way down."

"'Tis not *you* I'm thinking of," he retorted.

Chapter
Forty-Nine

W ITH THE night advancing, Eamonn grabbed me
and held me tight and rubbed my face fondly. I
was half gone with a mixture of drink and love;
his gentle hands, his tender voice, made me feel sad and
lonely. I said, "I may never see you again. Next time we
meet we'll both be dead." Tearfully, I repeated, "We should
talk the night away."

"But where could we stay, Annie?"

I went and inquired at the front desk before running to tell
him they could give us a room for $180. I delightedly took
his wallet out of his pocket and plucked out his Visa card.

He was horrified. "I'm already booked into somewhere
else. The diocese pays for me. How could I explain I was in
two expensive hotels on the same night?"

"Fine," I said, giving him back his card, "I'll stay with
you at your hotel."

"But security is very strict there and they know I'm Bishop
Casey. I'd be destroyed."

"Think about it," I said, "while I go to the ladies'." I
descended the stairs just as Jim was coming up. He accompa-
nied me down and when I went into the ladies' room, he and
Peter followed me in.

Jim said, "You're not staying with *him* tonight?"

"I don't care a damn what you think of me," I said. "If
I make passionate love to him all night that's *my* business."

Peter grabbed me by the shoulders. "Mission accom-

plished, Mom. You're coming with us.'' Then he softened.
''I've never seen you have so much fun with anyone.''

''I never have.''

Relaxing his grip on me, he said softly, ''So you really did
love each other. It was worth all our efforts just for me to see
that.''

Jim exploded. ''Are *you* crazy, too?''

Peter said sadly, ''Why couldn't we have shared our life
together?''

Jim chipped in with ''Is that a Klonopin pill you just stuck
in your mouth, Annie? If you go with that bishop, anything
could happen.''

''What difference does it make?'' Peter said with a shrug.

Heading for the bar, I told myself, *My darling son understands me better than I thought*.

Eamonn was jumping up and down. ''Who was that big
red-haired man I saw you speaking to?''

''Peter's godfather,'' I lied. ''He brought Peter here so you
could see him if you wanted to. But you didn't.''

''Peter's here? Good.''

I was delighted. ''Thank God. You mean you'll see him?''

''No, he can take you home.''

''Too late—he's just gone home with Jim. Besides,'' I
said archly, ''I told Peter I was spending the night with you.
Don't . . . disappoint . . . him.''

''God Al*mighty*, you told your son—''

''Our son.''

''That you are spending the night with a bishop?''

''He does realize I did it before.''

''You shouldn't put such ideas in young people's heads.''

''For heaven's sake,'' I spluttered, ''he knows more than
you ever will.''

''I really would like to speak with him.''

''For another four minutes? No, you only want to use him
to get rid of me. You'd break his heart.''

''I am sincere.''

''Prove it. Buy him a hot dog and walk with him round
Central Park for a half hour.''

He did not say yes or no.

''Now, Eamonn, kindly walk me to the train station.''

As soon as I said it, I was aware of how passionately he

still felt toward me. I knew the signs from long ago: the rapid eye movements, the shaky chin, the way he jingled the change in his pocket. "No, Annie," he said tenderly, "you'd be a wreck. You will have to stay the night with me."

I wanted that more than I could say.

He took out his cash and counted up sixty dollars. I had fifty. Outside the hotel, I said to a police sergeant, "We're stranded in New York. We missed the last train and we only have one hundred and ten dollars."

Eamonn kept his distance in the shadows. He stuck his hands in his pockets, half pretending he wasn't with me, determined not to betray his origin by opening his mouth. He was wise, because the cop was Irish. He was starting to direct us when two black men told us where the cheapest place around was, only fifty-five dollars.

I could see Eamonn thinking, *Is she trying to get herself stabbed to death?* With him there, I really didn't care what happened to me. The cop said six blocks away was the Travel Inn. Looking at his watch: "It's after one. You should get a room for ninety."

As we began to walk, I felt very strange. My heart was bumping at around 150. Eamonn was the only person in the world with whom I could have made it to the motel.

After two blocks I pointed to a seedy-looking hotel. "A whorehouse," he said, in disgust. "Bedbugs, muggers. We would both end up lying there in bed with"—a vivid gesture—"our throats *slit*."

We passed a theater showing X-rated movies. "We could stay in there all night," I said.

"You are cracked, Annie. You have led me into a hell and no mistake."

Poor Eve, still getting the blame.

We finally reached the Travel Inn. They had a room in our price range.

I registered with Eamonn in the background shuffling his feet uncomfortably without even a suitcase to hold on to. "Now," I told Eamonn, "I have to call Arthur."

He cringed. The mere mention of the name made him keep his distance from the booth. I called Mary, instead.

"Where are you, Annie?" she shrieked. "Arthur's been calling me, asking questions."

"Tell him," I whispered, "I'm staying with Peter at Jim's place."

"Already did. I said he couldn't check it out because Jim just got an unlisted number. Before you thank me, hear me out."

"Go ahead."

"Arthur called the Ridgefield cops."

"To tell them I'm missing?"

"More. That you're sleeping with an Irish bishop. Who's Peter's father. He said if the Bishop finds out you're wearing a bugging device, he'll have you dumped in the East River."

"For heaven's sake, Mary, as if Eamonn would do a thing like that."

"Where *are* you?"

"Never mind. What did the cops say to Arthur?"

" 'Annie Murphy,' they said, 'the lady who has panic attacks, *she* is having it off with an Irish bishop in a New York hotel?' "

"Jesus."

"Yeah, now who's crazy? they said."

After the call, Eamonn said, "What did Arthur say?"

"He trusts me," I said.

As we went up to our sixth-floor room, he saw there was a swimming pool in the middle of the complex. Scratching his head: "Oh, no. You are not wanting to throw yourself in? Not tonight, Annie, plea-*ease*."

"It's tempting."

"After booze and Klonopin, you'll drown."

My heart was racing so much I swallowed another Klonopin. Only when I went to the bathroom of our suite did I remember I still had a recorder taped to me. I whipped it off and put it in my pocketbook.

When I returned to the room, I was staggered to see Eamonn had removed all his clothes except for his showy underpants.

"Hey," I said. "You used to wear boxers, now you're in jockey shorts. What does this tell me about your lifestyle?"

"Don't you trust *anyone,* Annie?"

"What," I whispered, "if there's someone on the balcony taking pictures of us?"

He became agitated. "Is that what you were phoning about below?"

"Aren't I entitled to one family shot, Eamonn?"

"Have you set me up, Annie? Get down on the floor." Pushing me down, he crawled to the window and, kneeling, peered through the curtain to the balcony.

"Eamonn," I said, "don't you trust anyone?"

He had not changed since we slept together in the Bishop's Palace in Killarney.

Nor had I.

"No one there, Annie. I knew you wouldn't do that to me."

"Don't bank on it," I said, as I went to lie down wearily on the second double bed.

"You can't sleep in your clothes, Annie, not if you are going to work in them tomorrow."

"True," I said, stripping to my bra and panties.

"Congratulations, Annie." His eyes glowed as he climbed into bed. "You still have your figure. Take off the rest?"

"No, if I have a panic attack and make for that water—"

From the horizontal, he opened up the covers of his bed to let me in. Tears sprang into my eyes as I remembered the first time he had invited me to share his bed with a movement like that. Oh, Inch, Inch. How happy we might have been.

That single gesture brought home to me all the days and nights we had missed, the waking up each morning beside each other, the sharing of our son, family vacations, family snapshots, family reunions, the sharing of heartaches and joys. Peter had often complained that he had not a single photograph of himself with his father.

As I slipped in beside Eamonn, he drew the covers over me and, uttering a great sigh, began kissing me. That was the last I knew till I awoke later that morning with him hovering over me with wide-eyed concern.

"How are you?"

I smiled. "Fine."

"You look awful. Don't go to work today."

"I must, Eamonn, but believe me, this is far harder for me than for you."

"How often do you take the day off?"

"Never."

"Today's the exception. I have over three hours till my meeting on Fifth Avenue at eleven and I can see you after that."

I shook my head. If Arthur called me at work and found me missing, he would alert the media.

"Who're you seeing on Fifth Avenue, Eamonn?"

"A few bishops and . . ."

I remembered he now moved in the highest circles.

"Who else? Cardinal O'Connor?"

"Indeed."

The sheer honesty of his reply made me gasp. We looked steadily into one another's eyes and both sadly smiled. We respected each other too much to go back to deceiving ourselves and others. Above all, in my eyes, to misbehave would be to betray our son.

I began to get dressed.

We had no money for a cab and he refused to call me a car on his Visa card. So he walked me slowly to Grand Central Station. At the platform entrance, I said, "The next time we see each other, we'll probably be in heaven."

He rolled his eyes, full of mischief and sadness. "If we make it."

"*I* will," I said, expressing a confidence I did not feel. "If I did wrong, I paid for it a thousand times. But your refusal to see your son—"

He hugged me tight. "Good-bye, Annie."

"'Bye."

I disengaged and walked on, with commuters whizzing in all directions around me, hoping he would call me back, hoping he would hug me and say to me, "Come away with me at last, Annie, I'll leave the Church, we can still make a life together."

Had he done that, no matter how much he had hurt me and betrayed me and my son over the years, I would have left everything and everyone and gone with him.

Not wanting to burst into tears, I did not dare look back. That was when I knew finally after eighteen lonely years that Eamonn and I would walk our separate ways forever.

Chapter Fifty

N O SOONER was I at my workplace in Stamford at 9:30 than Arthur called. His tone was hostile.

"Where'd you stay last night?"

"Didn't Mary tell you?"

"How could you stay with a raving bachelor like Jim Powers?"

"Peter and I slept on the couch."

"I didn't sleep a wink."

I just managed to get in "Don't you trust anyone, Arthur?" before he slammed the phone down.

When I got home that evening, Arthur fell on me like a tiger. His eyes were wild, his sparse hair was on end. Grabbing me by the throat, he pressed me against the wall. In slow, ominous tones: "I . . . want . . . answers."

Fearing I would choke to death, I kneed him in the crotch.

His eyes were watering even before he fell on his knees, clutching at himself. When he was nearly recovered: "Why . . . do . . . that?"

"Because I can't stand violence," I said.

As we shared a cup of tea, he said: "I imagined you sleeping with Eamonn. Then I thought slimeball Jim slipped you a mickey and *he* had it off with you."

"You are worse than Eamonn," I screeched. "In one night, you have me in bed with two different men?"

"I can't forgive you, Annie." He went to bed and stayed there for two days.

When Peter came back from Jim's, he was pleased Arthur was out of the way.

"The video," he said. "Jim only got about half of the back of Eamonn's head. We did, though, get a shot of him kissing you."

"Great, Peter," I said without enthusiasm.

"Where's the tape you made?"

I fished it out of my pocketbook. I had made up my mind never to listen to it. I never did.

"The craziest night of my life," Peter said excitedly before a sudden switch of mood. "Do you reckon Eamonn'll call me?"

I said he might because he still had a few days before he went to Toronto to baptize the daughter of his first cousin Tim. Day after day I prayed that Eamonn would call Peter. He never did. Why was he so stupid?

Eventually, Peter said, "Isn't this just peachy? He goes hundreds of miles to baptize a distant relative and he can't give me a half hour. I really like my dear old dad."

There were tears in his eyes as he said it. The tears were of grief; the eyes were of one hurt more than any jilted lover.

Next day, he told Mary that this grand family man, Eamonn, was in future going to have to deal with him. Without consulting me, he went to a lawyer I knew, Anthony Piazza.

Piazza got from Peter an assurance that this was on his own initiative, not mine. He pointed out that it would take six months to get the case to an American court. By then, Peter would be over eighteen and it would be too late. He suggested Peter get an Irish lawyer to represent him. He recommended an acquaintance of his, Justin McCarthy, a solicitor with the firm of Kenny, Stephenson & Chapman in Upper Mount Street, Dublin.

I called McCarthy on Thanksgiving Day 1991. I explained that I was representing Peter in his claim for child support and recoverability of arrears against his father.

"Who is?"

"A bishop in Ireland."

I did not name the bishop, but from my description McCarthy seemed to have no difficulty identifying him.

Such cases, McCarthy said, were held *in camera* in Ireland

but since it was such a small place, the Bishop, fearing the news might spread, should come to a speedy settlement.

In his follow-up letter to me on December 4, 1991, McCarthy stressed he believed in "basic rules of fairness." He wanted no part in a vindictive campaign. If I gave him these assurances, he would go ahead in quest of arrears of maintenance, a financial contribution to Peter's further education, and succession rights under Irish law.

Having received documentation from Piazza that included a copy of Eamonn's check paid to settle his suit with me, he wrote me again on January 14, 1992. In his view, Peter might get a legal Declaration of Paternity, but an Irish court would probably hold that $100,000 was sufficient settlement of all outstanding claims against the Bishop. Anything more, he felt, would smack of blackmail.

He was also concerned that the father's identity should be protected even from the court staff. "I am making arrangements," he wrote, "to discuss this with our senior judge."

Peter was furious. Eamonn had already agreed that my settlement was distinct from his. Moreover, Peter did not want any more coverups; he had been kept hidden as the Bishop's secret sin for far too many years already.

McCarthy's suggestion that the demands of justice were somehow a form of blackmail of poor Eamonn was bad enough. Worse was the thought that the Irish legal system, from a senior judge down, was prepared to shield Eamonn from the public gaze. Peter, a budding lawyer, exclaimed, "Justice must be *seen* to be done."

He was more than ever determined to fight. Had Eamonn not been in the dead center of this hurricane, he might have approved of his son's courage and resolve.

In mid-January 1992, Peter asked Peter McKay to take on his case. McKay was as keen as McCarthy to keep it in the private forum. Within days, he had renewed his contact with Father James Kelly from Brooklyn.

When, at McKay's suggestion, I called Father Kelly, I found him anxious to work with us on a private solution to the problem of Peter's education. I told him the boy was no longer interested in that approach. Kelly replied that no lawyer, certainly none in Ireland, would advise differently.

There was no movement for a few weeks. Until Peter said he simply had to prove that he was neither a blackmailer nor an extortioner. Money was not important, but justice was. He was fed up with his father always being seen as the innocent party in need of protection. "I'm the bastard, my mother is the bad woman. This has got to stop. I intend to clear my name whatever happens."

There spoke Eamonn's son.

He was fed up with taking what he called "dirt money." Either his father talked with him and admitted everything or he would have to suffer the consequences. Peter told Arthur he now knew no lawyer was going to help us and that he wanted to air the whole matter publicly.

One night, Arthur whispered to me: "Peter can't keep going through this torture, Annie. He's going to do something wild, something he can't control. He has no idea of the power of the Church of Rome. If he holds a press conference, he has no proof. He'll be crucified."

Right. Who would believe him? Publicity of that sort would only show me up as a thieving whore who was trying to blackmail a bishop who had proved himself the Pope of the Third World.

After getting my agreement, Arthur rose at four the next morning and called the *Irish Times* in Dublin. He asked for the editor because it was a highly charged political and religious matter. He was finally put through to the news editor. John Armstrong told him if he had documents to confirm his story, he would send his Washington correspondent to meet us within three days. He warned us it could be a long drawn-out affair, not least because the libel laws in Ireland are very stringent. Also, once the story was in the open, there would be no going back.

One cold early February night, Conor O'Clery of the *Irish Times* telephoned and came to see us at 10:30, soon after I got back from work. A tall, handsome man with friendly eyes, he struck us instantly as not only very professional but someone we could trust. We gave him lawyers' letters, copies of checks received in recent years including the big one from Father Kelly, and my official letter of release to the Bishop.

After interviewing each of us, O'Clery's conclusion was

that we had a strong case. But not strong enough. His paper needed more proof. Father Kelly offered a "large sum" for Peter's education.

"Too vague," Arthur said. "Name a figure, please."

Kelly said that to get Peter through college would cost about $35,000. Law school would cost $30,000 a year for three years. "We're probably talking one hundred and fifty thousand dollars to do it right. If he needs more, we can go higher."

Arthur, never less than honest, said, "You have to understand, sir, I have already spoken to the *Irish Times*. We are not going to stop this. Eamonn may pay up and still be exposed."

Father Kelly, who was tough but very fair, said it was a matter of basic justice. "I think you should take the money, anyway."

Arthur said, "If we go public, I reckon Peter would think that wrong."

In March, in addition to sending two checks totaling $10,000 on Eamonn's behalf for Peter's first year in college, Father Kelly wrote, "I have assurances from Eamonn that the total tuition costs will be paid."

Eamonn had finally seen the raised paw of the tiger. If only he had tried shaking it, instead of thrusting money into it.

Feeling worried about Eamonn's fate, I tried even at this late hour to make peace between son and father. "Peter," I said, "money is your passport to an education. Please think about Father Kelly's offer."

He had thought about it and made up his mind not to take any more hush money even if it meant only one year at college. He wanted nothing less than a public acknowledgment that Eamonn Casey was his father.

At this time, strange things started to happen to our car. Tires were slashed, the brakes were tampered with. Arthur was a good mechanic. He tightened the lug bolts and, next morning, they had come loose. Arthur felt a noose was tightening around us. Each morning, he was the one to start the car in case it had been tampered with or booby-trapped.

Bridget, remarried, had moved back to Ireland and was living in Galway. I called her to tell her that a journalist from the *Irish Times* might want to interview her. Also, if it came to a court case, Peter might ask her to be a witness.

"If you don't want to be involved, just say so."

"I'll have to think about this," Bridget said. "Remember, I'm now living in Eamonn's diocese."

We joked a little about our Dublin days and how Eamonn and I had carried on our affair at Inch and in a Dublin gravel pit.

"Dear old Eamonn," she said, "also spent many a juicy night in our flat, Murphy."

For me, the most heartbreaking night was when Eamonn called Arthur. Peter and I were sitting close enough to Arthur to hear both sides of the conversation.

Eamonn was whimpering, "I'm begging you not to betray me, Arthur."

I put my hand in my mouth to stop myself crying out in pain.

"How can you betray me?" Eamonn was saying.

"To hell with *you*," Arthur said. "You betrayed your son year after year. You still are."

Eamonn said that he had already sent $10,000. "Didn't Monsignor Kelly tell you I'm prepared to pay the entire cost of the boy's education?"

"The money isn't important, never was," Arthur snapped. "The kid wants recognition."

"Sure I'll give him that, too."

"Too late, Eamonn. You may be a bishop and I'm only a carpenter. But I know a shithead when I see one. You've been given a hundred chances to make it up with Peter. That's why I'm going to take from you your seat, your miter, your ring, your palace, your car. Every goddamn thing."

"Plea-*ease*."

I couldn't take any more. I tried to grab the phone. When Arthur prevented me, I ran into the bathroom, jumped into the empty tub, and put my hands over my ears.

Afterward, Arthur told me he had given Eamonn one more chance. If he called Peter and talked with him man to man, he would stop the story and deny whatever the papers printed. He also said Eamonn was going to the Philippines for his usual two-week post-Easter break.

I waited and waited. Still Eamonn never called Peter. He intended spending a couple of weeks in the Philippines and he hadn't one half hour to spare on his son?

In an angry mood, I phoned Galway. To the woman who answered, I said: "Bishop Casey, please. I want to talk to the father of my seventeen-year-old son."

She dropped the phone, screaming, with laughter or tears, I don't know, "Oh God, oh God, oh God."

Eamonn came on the line with "What did you just say?"

"Only what I'm going to say to the whole damn world."

"You know I'm going on my usual two-week holiday."

"You son-of-a-bitch," I exploded, "you can run but you can't hide."

"Annie, please, what do you want?"

"I want you to know I have you taped. Literally. Remember Peter's godfather, Jim? You were right—I did set you up. He was filming you with his camcorder when you kissed me in the Grand Hyatt."

"Stop it, Annie, stop it."

"Maybe Jim even recorded us in that motel room."

"The devil's got you by the throat."

God, even his phraseology hadn't changed over the years. "You keep ringing here and you don't talk to your son? How *dare* you? So have a nice vacation in the Philippines and dream on. If I turn up in Manila—"

"You would not betray me."

"I have already been to the press."

"I am *still* going on holiday, so good-*bye*."

And, on Tuesday, April 21, he went. I had the strange feeling that he had already made up his mind to resign.

I called O'Clery to tell him Eamonn was going to the Philippines. The *Irish Times* tried to trace him but failed. Eamonn had, in fact, gone to Malta.

He did call us once, again offering money for Peter's education but still refusing to speak to Peter. That was when I knew beyond a doubt that he had some kind of death wish and not even I could save him.

I had the impression that the traditionally Protestant *Irish Times* was being overcautious. Reluctant to seem anti-Catholic or to intrude into a man's private life, it was only interested in the public matter of where the Bishop got the money to pay us.

I decided to give the paper a bit of a push. On April 27, I called O'Clery in Washington, D.C. His wife, Zhanna, said he had gone to the *Times* office in Dublin. "That's odd," I said, "I'm speaking from across the street from the *Times*. I'll wave to him."

Conor's wife telephoned him and he started a search for me. I wasn't at work. Arthur said I wasn't at home. They got frantic, thinking that I might be about to give their scoop to another paper. Finally, when Conor called our house again, I admitted I was there. He was not amused.

"Nor am I," I said. "I swear if you don't break this story, Arthur will. We're scared. Last night, the lug bolts of our car came unscrewed again and a wheel flew off."

Conor, who obviously thought we were paranoid about the car, said the news was about to break. It would be one of the biggest stories ever to hit Ireland. They had finally tracked Eamonn down. He had promised to speak with them as soon as he returned to Ireland.

On Saturday, May 2, Eamonn left Malta on the normal afternoon flight from Valletta to Rome. He was met at the Rome airport by a clerical colleague and taken to the Irish College.

On May 3, the *Irish Times* sent a photographer to take our pictures around Ridgefield and in front of our house.

In Rome, on Tuesday, May 5, Eamonn had two Vatican appointments. The first was to discuss Trócaire matters with Cardinal Etchegaray, head of the Pontifical Commission on Justice and Peace. The second was to hand in his resignation to the Congregation of Bishops. It was formally accepted by Pope John Paul II on Wednesday, May 6. Eamonn flew back to Dublin that same afternoon.

He broke his promise to talk at the Dublin airport with the *Irish Times,* presumably on orders from the Vatican.

Having driven to Galway, he told his colleagues in the Diocesan Chapter that he was resigning for personal reasons. He issued his public statement of resignation shortly before midnight, Irish time. We heard it on TV that same Wednesday evening, May 6.

On Thursday after lunch, he was chauffeured to Shannon and whisked aboard an Aer Lingus 747, flight EI 105, arriving in the early evening at New York. There he was given VIP treatment. A blacked-out limousine picked him up at Kennedy, whence he disappeared.

It hurt me to see him run like a frightened rabbit without one word of explanation or regret. Is this the way, I wondered, that Catholics, especially Irish Catholics, deal with their problems? What lesson is this for young Irish people? Even more worrying to me was this final proof of what the Catholic Church had done to daunt this once brave man whom I loved.

Chapter
Fifty-One

ON THURSDAY, May 7, the *Irish Times* added to its report of Eamonn's resignation a cryptic note about payments to a woman in Connecticut. It was hardly the presentation we had hoped for. Without intending it, the paper may have suggested to some readers that I had blackmailed Eamonn.

At one in the morning New York time, the madness started. We were besieged by journalists and photographers. It went on without a break for eight days. I was still working two jobs and getting three hours' sleep a night. I was even followed as I drove to my office in Stamford.

I had naïvely thought the story would cause a stir in Ireland. I had no idea it would go around the world. I found myself entertaining the press from many countries, offering donuts and coffee in our small one-bedroom apartment.

The Irish media in particular treated me with courtesy but while some supportive letters did come in, I was deluged by hate mail. "Hell hath no fury like a slut scorned," summed it up.

It was assumed that I had pilloried the Bishop or had not prevented it when I could. I was blamed entirely for the Bishop's disgrace. Irish Catholics in America and Ireland took it for granted that I had wickedly tempted and betrayed a good man for revenge and/or money. Irish priests are always seduced, never seducers; they are frail and innocent even after

their fall. Women are sinners always. I was told I should have
kept my mouth shut.

One person wrote: "Everyone knows you seduced poor
innocent Eamonn, in fact, people say you came to this country
with that intention. . . . If you want to stay *alive* with your
bastard son keep out of Ireland."

Even the bastard son is mine, not Eamonn's.

"A Disgusted Catholic" from New York, after calling me
a "lowlife slime" prophesied: "God will punish you if not
here then hopefully in the hereafter. . . . Your son is also
lowlife to keep trying to know his father."

Yet another letter read:

> *You are a very mean, lowdown, sidewinding, two-*
> *timing broad the way you treated Eamonn Casey.*
> *He was a man held in high esteem by his people until*
> *you dragged him into the gutter.*
>
> *He stole $70,000 [sic] from his parishioners to*
> *shut you up and still you had to squeal. I will be in*
> *Ridgefield very soon and will put oatmeal in the*
> *radiator of your car and cut the brake pipes, so*
> *watch your ass.*
>
> *Cordially yours.*

I am glad he did not write in an uncordial mood.

Peter was upset that Eamonn had given no reason for his
resignation when his one aim was to make him admit paternity. I was less surprised, knowing how stubborn Eamonn
was. My chief worry was that he might suffer to no purpose.

I was at work on Monday evening, May 11, when Conor
phoned my home to tell Peter that Eamonn had issued a
dramatic statement at midnight Irish time saying that Peter
was his son.

When an excited Peter passed the news on to me, I was
astonished. It must have cost Eamonn a great deal to make a
public confession after all those years, years which all his
many admirers were bound to reassess in the light of it.

Next day, I read Peter the full statement in the paper. When
he heard the words *he is my son,* he stood up, raised his fist
in the air and let out a loud shout of victory. In my mind, it

erased the bitter memory of Eamonn's saying to me all those years ago, "He is not my son," and Peter's earlier cry of dereliction.

By his courage and persistence, Peter had at last achieved the minimum to which everyone is entitled: his birthright.

The full text was:

> *I acknowledge that Peter Murphy is my son and that I have grievously wronged Peter and his mother Annie Murphy.*
>
> *I have sinned against God, His Church and the clergy and people of the dioceses of Galway and Kerry.*
>
> *Since Peter's birth I have made contributions such as they were, towards my son's maintenance and support. All payments came from my personal resources except for the one sum of IR£70,669.20, paid to Annie Murphy in July 1990 through her American lawyer.*
>
> *That sum was paid by me from the diocesan reserve account on my personal instructions to a third party. I confided in nobody the nature and purpose of the transaction. It was always my intention to repay that money.*
>
> *The sum of IR£70,669.20 and interest has, since my resignation, been paid into diocesan funds of the diocese of Galway on my behalf by several donors so that the funds of the diocese are no longer at any loss.*
>
> *I have confessed my sins to God and I have asked His forgiveness as I ask yours.*
>
> *Prayer, guidance and dialogue are clearly necessary before final decisions are reached about how I can set about trying to heal the hurt I have caused, particularly to Annie and Peter. I have already set out on that road and I am determined to persevere.*
>
> *I trust that you will respect my need for some time and space to reflect and pray so that, with God's help, I can again hope to serve Him and His people, especially Peter and Annie, in my new situation. Pray for me.*

The most surprising part of the statement was Eamonn's admission about how he had acquired the $125,000 he gave us.

He had written out a check from a diocesan reserve fund to a Galway businessman, presumably countersigned it, and paid it into his own account. He said he intended to pay the money back but two years went by and he never did. Had an American banker or politician acted like that, he would have been accused of forgery and embezzlement.

The seventeen-year cover-up was ended. Eamonn had used those years to help many people. He had played masterly poker with a very weak hand. Sadly, as I had predicted, the Bishop got crucified. Calvary followed him to Galway.

What people think of me I no longer care. I am only sorry that Eamonn has been made to look a rascal in the eyes of many. They would have sympathized had he left to marry me in 1974, but he had furtively taken forbidden fruit; he had privately indulged what for years he had publicly and vehemently decried.

Once, though, when I said to him jokingly, "I do have a lot of power over you, don't I?" he replied, "I'll fight you to the death so the truth doesn't come out, but if it does, I won't give a damn."

He was always positive. He believed that whatever happened, God had a plan for him. He was not afraid.

On May 12, I gave a press conference, chaired by Peter McKay, in the midtown Peninsula Hotel. The room was crowded with TV cameras and over a hundred journalists from many nations. After years of secrecy I could now speak openly; I was a whole person again. I felt proud of having helped to vindicate my son.

"I'm sorry," I said, "the Bishop has gone through pain. We have all gone through pain. . . . I am looking for Eamonn to do the right thing, that is, take the time and effort and some soul-searching to come forward and meet Peter. The time is past for him to be a father figure. Maybe they can be friends."

Once the story was in the open, I felt obliged to tell it in its entirety, or others would tell it in a faulty or malicious way. I do not have Eamonn's luxury of confessing my sins in secret. But I, too, needed to be a penitent and to find healing in making public my own shortcomings, my wildness, my own hypocrisy.

I also wanted my son to know that he was born of a genuine and long-lasting love. This book, in a sense, is his family album.

My hope is that it will provoke change, especially in the Catholic discipline of clerical celibacy. I know from bitter experience the harm it causes. How many priests and bishops are behaving like Eamonn, how many women and children, like me and Peter, are suffering as a result?

My story is shocking, I know. The long secrecy and deceit have been shocking, too.

Many things in the story will be new to Eamonn and to Peter. They will both suffer because of it. But I have come to believe that ultimately truth can heal if we are brave enough to face it.

What have we to share, we the little ones of the earth, except our small grain of truth?

Epilogue

How strange love is, how unpredictable. Lovers move in the same fantastic orbit, they dream the same dream.

How could our love, Eamonn's and mine, survive the bitter goodbyes and long, long absences? It was a mystery, like a seedling that sleeps year after year in the desert. One shower and it spikes the earth, blossoming instantly in beauty.

Our love was like that. We had only to hear the other's voice or see the other's face and, whatever our resolutions, our sleeping love thrust upward through the desert sands and bloomed again. When we were together we filled every place we were in; never was there time enough to say all we needed to say.

But why did this divine love not flow from Eamonn to Peter? Why could Eamonn not stop loving me and not begin to love the fruit of our love? Why could I, who loved them both, not help them love one another? This, too, is a mystery.

My father warned me that if I stayed in Ireland, Eamonn would tire of me and only love Peter. When I left for America, the opposite occurred. He continued loving me and was indifferent to Peter. Yet Eamonn is really concerned for young people. Hence my hurt and bewilderment.

I wish I could blame myself entirely; guilt can be so satisfying. But looking back, I see it was neither my obduracy nor Peter's vindictiveness that finally brought Eamonn down. It was chiefly an inexplicable lack of love in a very loving human being. I felt like saying to Eamonn: "Stop praying for

Peter twice a day, for it does you and him no good. Use the time saved to meet him. Look at him and say yes to him, say amen to him, for he is your own flesh and blood and for that alone he is lovely and twice-blessed and in him you are graced with immortality.''

Peter says that Eamonn has probably been a child too long to grow up at this stage. Mother Church is still telling him what to do and not to do. Peter was less a child at sixteen than Eamonn is in his sixties. Maybe Eamonn did Peter a favor by staying away. Peter, too, might have led a life of endless denials.

Eamonn had one last surprise in store for me. After all the reported sightings of him from Peru to Florida to parts of Ireland itself, I learned in November 1992 that he had spent the first few months of his self-imposed exile a few miles from me. He was counseled by a Jesuit priest who was also a physician and psychiatrist in the Institute of Living in Hartford, Connecticut. Though we were only an hour's drive apart, he was still unable to fulfill the promise made in his public statement to try to heal the hurt caused to Peter and me. My heart goes out to him; his inability to communicate shows his hurt must be far deeper than ours.

A last word on the three main players in this drama.

First, Peter.

My companion, my beloved and my constant joy, how glad I am I never gave him up. I fought that fight almost to death and would fight it again a hundred and a thousand times. I never realized that the hardest part of bringing up my son would be his father's indifference to him. Why did I fail for so long to appreciate Peter's Siberian solitude, his sense of being a half person in a half world?

Peter is now studying political science at the University of Connecticut. I pray that Eamonn will be present at his wedding, even at the christening of his first child. How or when it will be I do not know, but I remain convinced that one day my son and his father will meet again and, at last, be friends.

Next, Eamonn.

There have been nights since his exposure when I have not slept because of him. I felt he was conveying his anguish to me.

My wish for him is that by telling this story I may help him to become his own person at last, not to hurt or humiliate him. He has been a victim since his father pressured him when he was small to dedicate himself to the Church.

Though many critics will say that I encouraged Eamonn to betray himself, I believe that the only time he was anywhere near to being his true self was when he was with me. Who but I saw his big green wondering sea-haunting eyes, and all the hopes and desires that shone in them? If I did not make him feel valued, why did he always love me? Could it be that one reason why he did so much good in his ministry was because I had given him the always-remembered, never-retracted comfort of love?

Eamonn was not only weak, he was also unbelievably strong. I, who have been in his arms, know it was not easy for him to give me up. Even later, he acted as he did not only to save his skin but to save his soul and, being a bishop, to save others' souls.

How many people he made happy, how many he housed, clothed, and fed. Arthur has written of him words so generous I can only repeat them here: "May the people of Ireland extend to Eamonn their hope and acceptance of his plight. And recognition of all that is great within him so that he may come home and share with them once again in the greatness that is his."

Finally, myself.

What a relief to no longer have to live a lie. I live in today with the hope of a better tomorrow. Having faced the abyss, I am finally free of myself, free *for* myself. What the future holds for me I do not know.

Do I still care for Eamonn when we have caused each other so much pain? Do I still miss him? Yes and yes. He will always be my beloved jazzman, the daring dancing laughing music-making ghost who wanders in and out of the byways of my heart.

I miss walking hand-in-hand with him up winding mountain roads and on blown white sands beside a milk-white sea.

I miss, while strong winds rattle the gray slate roof, the fireside storytelling.

I miss the whispered intimacies, kisses, love-clasps, and silent thunders of the flesh.

I miss waking by his side to fresh new dawns and the delicate singing of a thrush.

I miss what was and, this hurts so much more, what might have been.

Sometimes, but more rarely now, a chance word, a sound, a smell, a chord of music makes me close my eyes and I return, oh yes, to Inch to revel in the green-leaf times and feast my mind on memories of paradise.

By the year 2000, 2 out of 3 Americans could be illiterate.

It's true.

Today, 75 million adults… about one American in three, can't read adequately. And by the year 2000, U.S. News & World Report envisions an America with a literacy rate of only 30%.

Before that America comes to be, you can stop it… by joining the fight against illiteracy today.

Call the Coalition for Literacy at toll-free **1-800-228-8813** and volunteer.

Volunteer Against Illiteracy. The only degree you need is a degree of caring.

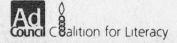

Ad Council   Coalition for Literacy

Warner Books is proud to be an active supporter of the Coalition for Literacy.